INFORMATION LAW SERIES – 8

COPYRIGHT AND ELECTRONIC COMMERCE

The titles in this series are listed at the back of this volume.

INFORMATION LAW SERIES – 8

COPYRIGHT AND ELECTRONIC COMMERCE

Legal Aspects of Electronic Copyright Management

Editor

P. Bernt Hugenholtz

Contributors

Kamiel J. Koelman
Lee A. Bygrave
Lucie Guibault
Natali Helberger
Annemique M.E. de Kroon
Bernardine W.M. Trompenaars
P. Bernt Hugenholtz

2000
KLUWER LAW INTERNATIONAL
The Hague • London • Boston

Published by
Kluwer Law International Ltd
Sterling House
66 Wilton Road
London SW1V 1DE
United Kingdom

Sold and distributed in
the USA and Canada by
Kluwer Law International
675 Massachusetts Avenue
Cambridge MA 02139
USA

Kluwer Law International incorporates
the publishing programmes of
Graham & Trotman Ltd
Kluwer Law & Taxation Publishers
and Martinus Nijhoff Publishers

In all other countries sold and distributed by
Kluwer Law International
PO Box 322
3300 AH Dordrecht
The Netherlands

ISBN 90-411-9785-0

First published 2000

British Library Cataloguing in Publication Data
A catalogue record for this book is available from the British Library

Typeset in 10/11pt Times by RTR Information Design, London.
Printed and bound in Great Britain by Antony Rowe Limited, Chippenham

Contents

Copyright and Electronic Commerce: An Introduction

P. Bernt Hugenholtz

Electronic commerce is taking the world by storm. The spectacular success of online retailing, electronic banking, Internet auctioning and other forms of network-based trading has taken even the techno-optimists by surprise. It is generally expected a major portion of the trillions of ECUs, dollars and yen that will be earned on the Internet in the years to come will derive from selling 'content'. More and more information and entertainment products that are currently distributed as tangible goods (music CDs, videos, books, newspapers, magazines, CD-ROMs, etc.) will be sold and delivered over the Internet. This is where electronic commerce and copyright, the main theme of this book, come together.

Already, the complicated copyright problems of the Internet have generated ample literature[1] and legislative initiatives. In December 1996, two treaties aimed at adapting international copyright law to the digital networked environment were concluded in the framework of the World Intellectual Property Organisation (WIPO). The WIPO Treaties were soon followed by the enactment of the Digital Millennium Copyright Act in the United States (DMCA) and a proposal for a European Copyright Directive. Even so, many important copyright issues still remain unsolved: problems of private international law, the scope of copyright protection and exemptions, etc. Moreover, even if equipped with all the rights that they so persistently demand, rights-holders will remain vulnerable to digital piracy and other forms of unauthorised use that content providers are exposed to when entering the online marketplace. Indeed, to content owners the Internet may sometimes appear as a 'global copying machine' with millions of irresponsible and anonymous pirates pushing the buttons, making the problems of copyright enforcement mind-boggling.

Growing concerns over the effectiveness of the copyright system in a digital environment have inspired content providers to look for alternative protection regimes or strategies: contract law and information technology. *Prima facie*,

1 See, e.g., P. Bernt Hugenholtz (ed.), *The Future of Copyright in a Digital Environment*, Information Law Series, Vol. 4, The Hague/London/Boston: Kluwer Law International 1996.

Copyright and Electronic Commerce (ed. P. Bernt Hugenholtz; ISBN 90-411-9785-0; © Kluwer Law International, 2000; printed in Great Britain).

contract law has all the makings of a perfect alternative to copyright. The structure of the Internet facilitates the establishment of a multitude of contractual relationships between information producers and end-users, either directly or through intermediaries. The World Wide Web is uniquely suited for this purpose. Both its 'textual' environment and its interactive nature are ideal conditions for a contractual culture to grow and flourish. Contract law, thus, may become the ideal instrument to fill the legal vacuum of the Internet. Information producers, intermediaries and end-users are free to create their own rules, without government intervention, and to experiment at will with novel legal approaches. Ideally, new legal norms may emerge from this self-regulatory laboratory; norms far better tailored to the new environment of the Net.

However, contract law has a darker side as well. Cyberspace is no egalitarian society with equal chances for every 'netizen'. In a world totally ruled by contract, weaker parties risk being subjugated and fundamental freedoms may be jeopardised. Freedom of contract may become contractual coercion, especially when dominant undertakings abuse their marker power to impose contractual rules on powerless consumers, as if they were public authorities.

Besides contract, content providers may employ a wide range of technological protection measures to protect their valuable 'goods' against piracy and leakage: encryption, the use of passwords or special log-in procedures, anti-copying devices, electronic 'watermarks', etc. Contract and technological protection together constitute important features of the *Electronic Copyright Management System* (ECMS), a fully automated system of secure distribution, rights management, monitoring and payment of copyright protected content.

Various experiments with ECMS are currently underway or have already been completed. Possibly the largest multidisciplinary study conducted on ECMS until this day is the IMPRIMATUR project,[2] which was subsidised by the European Commission's Esprit Programme until its termination in 1999. The project involved several large European content providers, collecting societies, intermediaries, telecommunications operators and universities. The Institute for Information Law of the University of Amsterdam (IViR) joined the IMPRIMATUR project as its legal partner in February 1997. In its Legal Work Plan, the Institute identified a number of legal issues crucial to the development of electronic copyright management systems. IViR's legal work has resulted in a handful of studies written under the responsibility of the Institute in the 1997-1999 period. This volume brings together the studies considered most relevant to the main theme of this book: copyright and electronic commerce. Before becoming chapters of this book the reports were carefully updated, revised and in some cases even totally rewritten.

As the title illustrates, this book is not simply an inventory of legal issues related to electronic copyright management. The topics discussed in each chapter

---

2 See <http://www.imprimatur.net>.

have wider implications for the law of copyright in general. Moreover, several chapters directly relate to aspects of information law outside copyright, such as defamation, data protection, privacy and freedom of expression and information. Last, not least, general questions of contract law and tort law play an important role as well.

The first chapter, written by Kamiel Koelman, deals with the liability of the 'providers' acting as go-betweens between content creators and consumers. The liability of Internet providers is one of the most controversial legal issues to emerge from the digital environment. Can providers be compared to electronic publishers, and thus directly liable for all the infringing gigabytes flowing through their servers? Or are they merely the postmen of the superhighway, exempt from any liability? The study describes the state of the law, and draws comparisons between civil law and common law jurisdictions. It deals with liabilities not only stemming from copyright law, but also from 'tort' law in general (notably defamation). In this context both the DMCA and the proposal for a European Directive on Electronic Commerce, which provides for a 'horizontal' solution to the issue of online liability, are discussed. Assuming service providers will be subjected to a certain level of liability, what then should be the standard? Should a duty of care be imposed upon the provider, or should liability be assumed only in cases of actual knowledge of infringement?

The second chapter, written by Lee Bygrave and Kamiel Koelman, examines the way in which legal rules for the protection of privacy, data protection and related interests can impinge upon the design and operation of electronic copyright management systems. The study first focuses upon rules that specifically regulate various stages in the processing (collection, registration, storage and dissemination) of personal data. To what extent does the monitoring of individual usage comply with data protection law? Do so-called privacy enhancing technologies (PETs) make a difference?

The second part of the chapter focuses on the interface between copyright law and the law of privacy in general. It describes the legal and technological balances that have been struck between the privacy interests of users and the interests of copyright holders, and considers the impact that an ECMS might have on the existing equilibrium. On a more general level the study contemplates the crucial, and controversial, question of whether the fundamental right of privacy poses an intrinsic limit to the scope of copyright protection.

Chapter 3, written by Lucie Guibault, deals with another highly topical issue, the so-called interface between copyright and contract law. To what extent may the terms of a copyright licence override statutory copyright exemptions aimed at preserving user freedoms? Are copyright limitations default or mandatory rules? More fundamentally, should there be limits to the freedom of copyright contracts and, if so, on what grounds should such contracts be regulated? Should we differentiate between negotiated contracts and mass-market licences? Surprisingly, even if the European legislature were pioneers with mandatory exemptions in the

Software and Database Directives, the proposed Copyright Directive is silent on the question of 'overridability'. In contrast, the US proposal for a Draft Article 2B of the Uniform Commercial Code — a model law that was recently adopted under a new name: the Uniform Computer Information Transactions Code — has put the issue firmly on the map in the United States.

Chapter 4, written by Kamiel Koelman and Natali Helberger, deals with the legal protection of so-called technological measures (TMs). TMs may serve various functions: provide access control, usage control, protect content integrity or meter usage. This chapter first analyses present and future legislation in respect of TMs protecting copyrights, with special emphasis on the DMCA and the Copyright Directive. To what extent are copyright exemptions that protect user freedoms respected by the new regime? Next, the legal protection of technological measures is compared to other areas of the law protecting comparable interests. What is nature of this novel right, and do we really need it? The final part of the chapter concentrates on the legal protection of conditional access services, a topic intimately connected to the protection of TMs, but generally ignored in copyright doctrine.

From technological measures to copyright management information (CMI) is only a small step. Chapter 5, written by Annemique de Kroon, describes the legal protection of CMI, which is another important feature of the WIPO Treaties, the DMCA and the proposed European Copyright Directive. Perhaps more than any other provision on the 'digital agenda', the protection of CMI illustrates the importance of electronic copyright management for the law of copyright. This chapter first describes the various standards used for CMI, with special focus on the 'DOI' (Digital Object Identifier). Next, the legal protection of CMI against removal or alteration is examined. To what extent is CMI already protected under general legal principles, such as moral rights, trademark law or unfair competition law? Finally, the relevant provisions of the WIPO Treaties, the DMCA and the Copyright Directive that specifically protect CMI against removal or alteration are examined and compared.

The last chapter of this book deals with the legal questions of contract formation in an online environment. Are so-called 'mouse-click' or 'click-wrap' licences concluded in a dialogue between man and machine as valid as their equivalents in paper form? The report describes various national and international initiatives, including the UNCITRAL model law, the proposed European Directive on Electronic Commerce, and the Draft Article 2B of the Uniform Commercial Code of the United States.

Finally, a few words about the authors of this book. Although the Institute's participation in the IMPRIMATUR project was a collaborative effort involving all the authors of this book and many more, the chapters presented in this volume have individual authors; in two cases authorship is shared. Kamiel Koelman (koelman@jur.uva.nl) wrote Chapter 1, and is co-author of Chapters 2 and 4. He has been a research associate with the Institute for Information Law since 1996, and is currently writing his dissertation on the protection of technological measures. Lee

Bygrave (lee.bygrave@jus.uio.no), the co-author of Chapter 2, is a post-doctoral research fellow at the Norwegian Research Centre for Computers and Law of the University of Oslo. The author of Chapter 3, Lucie Guibault (guibault@jur.uva.nl) is a research fellow with the Institute since 1997. She expects to complete her dissertation on contracts and copyright exemptions in the year 2000. Annemique de Kroon (adekroon@jur.uva.nl), author of Chapter 5, and Natali Helberger (helberger@jur.uva.nl), who co-authored Chapter 4, both joined the Institute in 1998 as project researchers, and have been involved in a number of externally funded research projects. Bernardine Trompenaars (Bernardine.Trompenaars@-cend.minvenw.nl) wrote Chapter 6 on commission from the Institute as a freelance researcher. Her dissertation on the role of UNCITRAL in the unification of private law brought her a doctor's degree in 1989 from the University of Utrecht. She is currently employed as senior legal officer at the Ministry of Transport, Public Works and Water Management in The Hague.

The studies that were produced by the Institute for Information Law in the framework of the IMPRIMATUR project were written under the sole responsibility of the Institute and the individual authors. The same is true for the chapters of this book. Even if most of the studies that preceded this book were discussed in workshops in the presence of IMPRIMATUR partners, the opinions presented in this book do not necessarily reflect the views of the IMPRIMATUR consortium, or any of its partners, nor should this book be taken as a publication for which the consortium, any of its partners or the European Commission Esprit Programme that sponsored the project, share responsibility.

As coordinator of the legal work carried out by the Institute in the context of the IMPRIMATUR project and editor of this book, I wish to thank all the authors for the creativity and hard work they invested so enthusiastically in the project in the 1997-1999 period. Special thanks are due to Anja Dobbelsteen, who was indispensable in managing the project, and to Sari Galapo, who assisted in editing the present volume. Finally, I wish to express my gratitude to Chris Barlas, general coordinator of the IMPRIMATUR project, for placing his trust in the Institute for Information Law, and for making our IMPRIMATUR years such a memorable experience.

I. Online Intermediary Liability

Kamiel J. Koelman

1. Introduction

One of the most important legal issues presently facing providers of information services is the question of online liability. In the digital networked environment content is rarely, if ever, conveyed directly from the originator to the end-user. Usually, as in the case of the Internet, a range of 'providers' act as go-betweens between content creator and consumer: hosting service provider, communications or network provider, and access provider. What, then, is the legal position of these middlemen?

The issue has been the subject of debate, of countless articles in legal journals, of judicial decisions, and even of legislative action both in the United States and the European Union. The main focus of this chapter is on these legislative initiatives and their impact upon civil and common law tortious liability of online intermediaries. For a better understanding of the recent developments and their implications, however, it is necessary to set out how the problem has (previously) been approached by courts, commentators and legislators. This chapter will deal primarily with German, US and Dutch law, but French, Swedish and British law will also be addressed whenever relevant. Issues of intermediary liability may arise in a number of different fields of law, such as trade secret law, misrepresentation, unfair competition law, product liability law, copyright law and defamation law.[1] However, since most precedents concern defamation and copyright law, these fields of law have been singled out for the purpose of this survey.

In this chapter only the position of 'true' intermediaries will be examined i.e. those who play a role in the dissemination of content, but neither initiate nor take any part in any decision to publish particular material. Currently, different types of intermediaries are involved in delivering content online to end-users. Typically, making a work available over the World Wide Web will involve a chain of intermediate service providers. First, one will need to acquire an account with a

1 See Julià-Barceló 1998, p. 453.

Copyright and Electronic Commerce (ed. P. Bernt Hugenholtz; ISBN 90-411-9785-0; © Kluwer Law International, 2000; printed in Great Britain).

hosting service provider. This intermediary then provides space on a 'server' (best thought of as a very large hard disk that is directly accessible from the network) on which the subscriber can set up (or upload) his own website. A provider may also enable users to post messages in so-called newsgroups. In both cases the service enables the dissemination of information by allowing for material to be stored on the intermediary's facilities which are accessible from a network. An access provider, in turn, enables customers to access the network and the information that is available on the network. Additionally, this type of intermediary plays a role in transmitting messages from the host server to the end-user's computer. On the way from host to access provider to subscriber the transported material passes through the infrastructure of a network provider, who, apart from providing the physical facilities to transport a signal, will also transmit and route it to the designated recipient. It is not uncommon that one (legal) entity provides all of these services. However, since tort law deals with liability for one's acts or omissions *in a specific case*, it is important to understand that an intermediary's position will depend on its role in the dissemination of the material in the particular case that is at stake.

Before EU and US legislation are discussed some general notions of tort law will be explained in Section 2. This will be followed by a brief examination of the requirements for liability to arise under defamation law and copyright law (Sections 3 and 4). Subsequently, specific issues of online intermediary liability will be dealt with, in particular by discussing recent legislative initiatives expressly aimed at regulating this issue in Germany, Sweden, the United Kingdom and the Netherlands (Section 5).

The core of the chapter, Section 6, consists of an analysis of proposed EU and enacted US legislation on intermediary liability. Since the law regarding injunctive relief generally follows different rules to those governing liability for damages, liability to provide for injunctive relief is dealt with separately (Section 7). Finally, in Sections 8-10 the grounds and rationales for specific rules on online intermediary liability (freedom of expression and information, communications privacy, public interest) are described and analysed.

2. Tort

Liability for harm done to (the interests of) others is generally governed by tort law. For a better understanding of the issues at stake where liability for online intermediaries is concerned, some of the main concepts of tort law are described below. Unavoidably, in the course of these generalisations, the subtleties of the various national systems will be lost. For the purpose of this chapter, however, the following summary will suffice.

2.1 COMMON AND CIVIL TORT LAW

The approach to tort law differs between civil and common law countries. Most evidently, in civil law countries the national civil codes contain general provisions regulating tortious liability,[2] while such general provisions are lacking in common law jurisdictions. As a result of this distinction, in the former system all different forms of tortious liability are, in principle, based upon the same provisions and therefore follow the same general rules, whereas in the latter jurisdictions different types of tort must be distinguished, such as the torts of trespass, conversion, defamation and negligence, subject to their own specific rules. Thus, under civil law, in essence, the same general requirements must be fulfilled for a tort to be found in cases where a copyright is infringed, a personality right is violated, or any other wrongful act is committed. In common law countries, on the other hand, by the nature of tort law, different conditions must be fulfilled for liability to be found under each type of tort. These — conceptual — differences in approach, however, become less significant since courts in civil law countries have defined specific conditions that must be fulfilled for liability to be found under each form of tort. Perhaps the most accurate way of defining the distinction between the law of torts of the different legal systems is that in common law countries different *torts* exist, while in civil law countries different *forms of tort* are recognised. According to Englard, another distinction is that in civil law countries delictual liability is exclusively concerned with the allocation of losses, whereas common law relies on tort liability also for the determination and direct enforcement of rights, and, where it serves the latter purpose, applies a strict liability rule. In civil law countries, in contrast, distinct provisions regarding the rights of a property owner or possessor are often included in the civil codes.[3]

2.2 UNLAWFULNESS AND FAULT

In all investigated jurisdictions, harm caused to the interests of another person will not always result in liability for the damages. Often, the elements of fault and/or unlawfulness must be fulfilled. 'Fault' refers to a state of mind or the attitude of the tortfeasor, while the notion of 'unlawfulness' is intended to qualify the act or omission of the defendant.[4]

However, these notions are often blurred. Particularly, in the case of a tortious omission, fault and unlawfulness are difficult to distinguish. This is exemplified by the fact that under common law the term negligence refers to a state of mind (a

2 See for Germany, Art. 823 ff. of the German Civil Code (GCC, *Bürgerliches Gesetzbuch*); see for the Netherlands, Art. 6:162 ff. of the Dutch Civil Code (DCC, *Burgerlijk Wetboek*).
3 Englard 1992, p. 22; see also Markesinis 1986, pp. 19–20; Markesinis 1994, p. 2627.
4 Markesinis, 1986, p. 40.

species of fault) as well as to a specific form of tort, i.e. a type of unlawful conduct.[5] Somewhat similarly, in Germany it has been heavily debated whether lack of reasonable care is part of the concept of the unlawfulness of a person's conduct (*Rechtswidrigkeit*) or rather of the concept of fault (*Verschulden*).[6] Also, in the Netherlands breach of a duty of care may be of relevance in determining whether the defendant acted unlawfully (*onrechtmatig*) as well as for finding the existence of fault (*verwijtbaarheid*) or both.[7]

2.3 UNLAWFULNESS

In civil law countries the concept of 'unlawfulness' plays a major role in tort law. In Germany and the Netherlands it is a separate element which needs to be fulfilled for liability to arise. In both jurisdictions a violation of a subjective right — such as a copyright — will fulfil the requirement *ipso jure*. However, even if a person does not directly infringe a right, his actions may be unlawful on the basis of a breach of a duty of care demanded by society (*Sorgfaltspflicht, zorgvuldigheidsnorm*). This is somewhat comparable to the tort of negligence in common law countries.[8]

2.4 FAULT

Basically, two kinds of liability are distinguished: with-fault liability and strict (or no-fault) liability. The application of the requirement of fault may be viewed as expressing the ethical maxim that people are morally and psychologically responsible for their actions (or omissions) only when they, having the freedom of will, could and should have avoided the harm. That is, only if a person is to blame for his actions, should he be held liable.[9] In legal practice, liability based on fault may require various specific mental elements, varying from intention to mere knowledge. Under certain circumstances mere inadvertence or negligence will suffice to find fault on the part of a defendant. Negligence, in turn, may be measured according to an objective criterion: the behaviour of 'the reasonable man', which, according to some, may result in strict liability (whereas failure to satisfy this objective criterion will trigger liability, regardless of whether the defendant actually knew or could have known of the consequences of his deeds, what matters is whether he *should* have known). Strict liability, on the other hand, may be 'absolute' when no defences whatsoever are available, or it may be mitigated, *inter alia*,

5 Rogers 1989, p. 45.
6 Markesinis 1986, p. 42.
7 Van Dunné 1998, p. 39; Koelman 1998, pp. 207-208.
8 See Markesinis 1994, p. 68 ff.; *Onrechtmatige Daad (oud)* (Jansen), aant. 81.
9 Fesevur 1998, p. 4; Englard 1992, p. 9.

through the requirement of legal cause (see below). Another intermediate form of liability is the with-fault liability with a reversed burden of proof; in principle, fault is required, but because of the reversal of the onus of proof this may come very near to a strict liability. In sum, there exist many shades of grey between the extremes of strict and with-fault liability.[10]

2.5 Duty of care

As follows from the above, failure to satisfy a 'duty to take care' may constitute an unlawful act or a tort in itself, or may play a role in the requirement of fault and therefore result in liability. Either way, similar factors are used by judges in the different jurisdictions to establish whether a duty of care exists, whether it has been violated, and what the consequences of such violation should be. German, British, US and Dutch courts all typically consider such factors as the probability of harm, the costs of avoidance, and the magnitude of the danger if it is realised.[11] Additionally, one cannot be expected to perform illegal activities to avoid harm to others. In all jurisdictions examined, the social utility of the activity is taken into account in establishing the scope of a duty of care. Through the latter factor, public policy considerations and fundamental rights may play a role in determining the existence and the limits of a duty of care, and consequently, in establishing the scope of liability.[12]

2.6 Causal connection

Even where fault is not a requirement, usually a causal connection must be established for liability to be found. Generally, the criterion is whether the act or omission was a *conditio sine qua non* for the damage to occur. In common law this is known as the 'but-for' test: would the plaintiff's harm not have occurred 'but for' the defendant's conduct? If it would not, the conduct concerned is the cause of the harm, and the defendant will be held liable. This is sometimes called 'factual causation' or 'cause in fact', and is said to be based upon the physical sequence of events.[13]

---

10 Rogers 1989, p. 30; Englard 1992, p. 22.
11 See Markesinis 1986, p. 45; Van Dam 1989, pp. 109–130; Hepple and Matthews 1985, pp. 216–222.
12 Markesinis 1986, p. 41; Dias and Markesinis 1984, pp. 20–22 and 34–35; Hepple and Matthews 1985, pp. 223–224; Van Dam 1989, p. 122.
13 Markesinis 1986, p. 64; Hepple and Matthews 1985, p. 245; Jansen 1996, p. 39.

2.7 LEGAL CAUSE

If an act is found to be the factual cause of the harm, a defendant may nevertheless escape liability if his conduct is not regarded as the 'legal cause' of the harm. In common law, under the tort of negligence, the predominant test is that of 'foreseeability' or 'remoteness of the damages', i.e. a person is only liable for those consequences of his deeds that were reasonably foreseeable at the time that he acted.[14] In Germany the theory of the 'adequate causation' is mostly adhered to (*adäquater Kausalsammenhang*). An adequate causation is found if an act or omission has, in a general and appreciable way, enhanced the objective possibility of a consequence of the kind that is the subject of the case. In deciding this, account is taken of all the circumstances recognisable at the time the event occurred.[15] Evidently, the civil and common law criteria can very well be compared. The main purpose of the tests is to put a limit to the extent of liability for wrongful acts. Commentators stress that the determination of legal causation often reflects policy considerations.[16]

3. Defamation

Below we will investigate how the concepts underlying the law of tort are applied where liability for copyright infringement and publication of defamatory statements are concerned. First, defamation law will be investigated. For obvious reasons, the emphasis will be on the liability of intermediaries for third party statements, e.g. publishers who publish readers' letters or third party advertisements, mere distributors of hard copies and telecommunications carriers. Defamation law consists mostly of case law. However, both Dutch and French criminal law provide precedents of how intermediary liability has previously been dealt with when specifically addressed by the legislature.

Under common law, defamation constitutes a separate tort. Traditionally, a rule of strict liability existed under the law of defamation. According to Englard, this expressed the 'right-creating' character of common tort law. In that sense, the doctrine of defamation corresponded with torts dealing with interference with property, such as trespass, conversion and copyright. In other words, here liability had a 'vindicatory objective' — one vindicates one's good name, as opposed to seeking compensation, which is emphasised by the remedies available such as retraction.[17]

---

14 Dias and Markesinis 1984, p. 79; Rogers 1989, p. 131 ff.; Emanuel 1991, p. 106–113.

15 Markesinis 1986, pp. 67–71. For a discussion of adequate causation in relation to contributory copyright infringement under German law, see Nordemann, Vinck and Hertin 1994, pp. 567–568.

16 See Dias and Markesinis 1984, pp. 36 and 79; see also Englard 1992, p. 181.

17 Englard 1992, pp. 135–136.

Over the last decades, however, in the United States the strictness of liability for defamatory statements has eroded, mainly because of public interest considerations, notably, the freedoms of expression and information.[18] Currently, fault amounting (at least) to negligence with regard to the defamatory nature of a message must be established.[19] That is not to say that it must always be proven. For the purpose of US defamation law, all who take part in the dissemination of a defamatory statement are regarded as 'publishers' of the statement and may therefore be held liable.[20] However, so-called 'primary' publishers, such as newspaper and book publishers, and broadcasters, are presumed to have published defamatory material knowingly, on the basis that they have had the opportunity to review, edit or reject material before publishing it. 'Secondary' publishers, on the other hand, i.e. mere distributors who deliver or transmit material created by others, are assumed to be ignorant of the unlawful nature of the material published.[21] Similarly, common (telecommunications) carriers can only become liable for transmitting defamatory third party content if the plaintiff proves that they did not know nor had a reason to know of the unlawful character of the message transmitted.[22] Thus, while with regard to primary publishers a with-fault liability with a reversed burden of proof exists, express proof of fault is required where secondary publishers and common carriers are concerned.

United Kingdom defamation law is less lenient towards publishers and distributors of third party material. Editors, printers and publishers cannot escape liability on the basis of lack of fault, but are instead held strictly liable. Distributors are presumed to be liable, but can invoke the defence of 'innocent dissemination', which was developed through case law, but is now laid down in the Defamation Act 1996.[23] Pursuant to the Act, a distributor must prove that he took reasonable care in relation to the publication and did not know, nor had reason to believe that his actions caused, or contributed to, the publication of the defamatory statement.[24] Consequently, publishers are held strictly liable while, to escape liability, distributors have the burden of proving that they did not act negligently.[25]

In civil law countries, defamation is dealt with under the general rules on liability. Since for damages to be awarded, fault is usually required — or a duty of care must be violated — the same is true with regard to defamation.[26] In 1990 the German Federal Supreme Court (Bundesgerichtshof) held that, because the scope of a publisher's duty of care is determined by the freedom of expression and

---

18 See *infra* Section 8.
19 Emanuel 1991, p. 323 ff.
20 Perritt 1992, p. 98.
21 Guenther 1998, pp. 56–58.
22 See extensively Perritt 1992, pp. 101–108; *infra* n. 165.
23 Rogers 1989, pp. 317–318.
24 The Defamation Act 1996 is available at <http://www.hmso.gov.uk/acts/acts1996/96031–a.htm>.
25 See also Angel 1996, p. 112.
26 Markesinis 1986, pp. 37–39.

information, a publisher may only be said to have acted negligently, if he publishes third party material that is *evidently* unlawful. A more onerous duty would conflict with the constitutionally guaranteed freedom of expression and information, as it would make it impossible for the press to do its socially beneficial work.[27] Thus, even though it is presumed that a publisher has had the opportunity to review the contents, he will only have acted negligently if third party material of which the unlawful character is easily ascertainable is published. If, however, a publisher actually knows of the infringing nature of a statement, it cannot be a defence to hold that its unlawful nature was not obvious.[28] Similarly, according to some commentators, telecommunications operators may have a duty to block the further dissemination of unlawful content if they have knowledge of the role they play in the actual publication and did not do all that can reasonably be expected to prevent dissemination.[29]

In France the situation is largely similar. Interestingly, however, under Article 42 of the Act on the Regulation of the Press of 1881 (*Loi sur la réglementation de la presse*), liability for crimes committed by the press — such as defamation — is organised in a cascading system. In principle, publishers or editors of printed matter are liable, while the author can be held liable as an accomplice. In the absence of a known publisher, the author will be held solely liable. Only if none of the above actors is available for prosecution, the vendor and distributor are the parties that are held accountable. With the Act on Audiovisual Communications of 1982 *(Loi sur la communication audiovisuelle*) this system was extended to apply to audio-visual communications.[30] A French Court of Appeals has applied these regulations by way of analogy to a hosting service provider. If such provider allows customers to post material anonymously on his server, he willingly takes the risk of being the sole actor accountable and must therefore bear the consequences of unlawful material being disseminated over his installations.[31]

Dutch law applies similar rules. Generally, for damages to be awarded some form of fault needs to be shown. Defamation is not exempted. A publisher will therefore only be held liable if he has had some dealings with the contents.[32] Interestingly, under Dutch penal law a cascading system exists that is slightly different from that under French law. Pursuant to Articles 53 and 54 of the Dutch Penal Code (*Wetboek van Strafrecht*) a publisher or a printer 'as such' (*als zodanig*) — i.e. an actor who neither produced the statement, nor was involved in the decision to publish it but who merely invests in publishing or printing — can only be held

27 *Pressehaftung I*, German Supreme Court (BGH), 26 April 1990, [1990] GRUR 1012; see Pichler 1998, pp. 85–86; see also *infra* Section 8.

28 *Pressehaftung II*, German Supreme Court (BGH), 7 May 1992, [1992] GRUR 618.

29 Rütter 1992, p. 1812; see also *infra* Section 10.

30 See Institute for Information Law 1997 (S. Dusollier), p. 35.

31 *Estelle Hallyday v Valentin Lacambre,* Court of Appeal Paris (*Cour d'Appel de Paris*), decision of 10 February 1999, available at <http://www.legalis.net/legalnet/judiciaire/decisions/ca_100299.htm>.

32 *Onrechtmatige Daad VII* (Schuijt), aant. 167.

liable if he does not identify the author and if the author is not available for prosecution. The rationale for introducing this system was to avoid a situation whereby publishers would act as censors. Therefore, it may be viewed as serving the freedom of expression.[33] The Dutch and French cascading systems differ, in that in the Netherlands a publisher may pass on liability to the originator of the material, while in France a mere distributor may divert liability to the publisher or author by identifying them, but a publisher will always be liable even in the event that the actual author is available for prosecution.

Apparently, the reasoning behind the French and Dutch cascading systems is that, although it may be preferable to hold accountable a person who has had some responsibility with regard to the decision to publish (i.e. who acted with fault), there must always be some actor that can be prosecuted. Interestingly, a similar rationale is applied in product liability law, as is laid down in the EC Product Liability Directive. The ground rule is that the 'producer' is liable for the damages, but a mere 'seller' (an intermediary) may be held liable if the producer cannot be found. Article 3(3) of the Directive explicitly provides that a 'seller' may escape liability by providing the identity of the producer.[34] As will be shown below, newly enacted and proposed legislation on online intermediary liability may leave the aggrieved person without an identifiable defendant.

4. Copyright

Just as 're-publishers' may be held liable under defamation law, anyone who plays a part in the communication to the public of a copyright protected work (e.g. by publicly performing or displaying it, or by distributing it) may, in principle, violate the exclusive (copy)right of communicating a work to the public. Additionally, copyright law covers the act of reproducing a work. In the course of online dissemination several reproductions may occur. First, a work is copied onto the server of a hosting service provider. Then, it will be reproduced during transmission — when transmitted over the Internet, a work is repeatedly 'stored and forwarded' on so-called 'routers'. Often the access provider's facilities will play a part in that process. Furthermore, an access provider may choose to 'cache' content retrieved from the World Wide Web on his own installations. His subscribers then need not retrieve the pages at the original location, but have immediate access. Can an intermediary be held directly or indirectly liable for (his contribution to) copyright infringement, and if so, under what circumstances? As will be shown below, the

33 Schuijt 1987, pp. 163–167.

34 Council Directive 85/374/EEC of 25 July 1985 on the approximation of the laws, regulations and administrative provisions of the Member States concerning liability for defective products, OJ L 210/29.

answer to this question depends upon whether the defendant performed a restricted act for the purpose of copyright law. Therefore, it will be investigated whether an online intermediary should be viewed as performing any such act. But first, the rules governing liability for direct and indirect infringement will be examined.

4.1 DIRECT INFRINGEMENT

For the purpose of applying the general provisions on tort in civil law countries, a *direct* infringement of copyright, i.e. the unauthorised performance of a restricted act, is considered an interference with a person's subjective right and therefore constitutes an unlawful act in itself.[35] Following the general rules on liability, however, some form of fault must be shown for liability to arise.[36] For this purpose, courts generally find that direct copyright infringers are subject to a rather stringent duty of care, even to such an extent that they are almost strictly liable. In Germany, for instance, a printer cannot escape liability by relying on statements of his customers, but must investigate for himself whether the printing of a certain publication constitutes a copyright infringement in order to fulfil his duty of care.[37] Similarly, in the Netherlands a publisher has a duty to investigate whether the publication of material supplied by a third party infringes copyright. A retailer, on the other hand, cannot be expected to be on guard, or to control whether each item he deals in violates a copyright, unless he has a reason to suspect that the particular item is copyright infringing.[38]

In the United States, copyright infringement constitutes a specific tort following its own statutory rules. A direct infringer is expressly held strictly liable.[39] However, even though lack of fault cannot exonerate a direct infringer, if he is successful in proving that he was not aware nor had a reason to believe that his acts constituted an infringement, a court may mitigate the statutory (or punitive) damages under US law. But even then, the defendant will be fully liable for the actual damages.[40]

Interestingly, the United Kingdom Copyright Act distinguishes between so-called primary and secondary infringers, a differentiation which is comparable to

---

35 Markesinis 1986, pp. 33–34; *Onrechtmatige Daad (oud) I* (Jansen), aant. 81.

36 The Dutch Copyright Act does not contain any specific provisions on liability. In the Netherlands, therefore, the general rules on liability apply. In the German Copyright Act specific provisions on liability are included (Arts 97 ff.). These, however, merely repeat the requirements that are mentioned in the German Civil Code. See Institute for Information Law 1997, p. 15.

37 Nordemann, Vinck and Hertin 1994, p. 574.

38 Quaedvlieg 1998, pp. 159–160.

39 See s. 501 of the US Copyright Act. The US Copyright Act's strict liability rule probably derives from the notion of copyright as a property right. Under other proprietary torts, such as trespass and conversion, the defendant is similarly strictly liable, i.e. it is sufficient that he intended to do an act that has the effect of interfering with another person's property. Intention to cause harm is not a requirement. See Englard 1992, p. 49; Emanuel 1991, p. 30.

40 See s. 504 of the US Copyright Act.

the distinction between primary and secondary publishers in US defamation law. With regard to primary infringers, a with-fault liability with a reversal of the burden of proof exists; in principle they are strictly liable, but may escape liability if they show that, at the time of the infringement they did not know, nor had a reason to believe that copyright subsisted in the item.[41] Secondary infringers, such as mere distributors and organisers of performances, are considered copyright infringers only if they knew or had reason to believe that they contributed to an infringement. Thus, some form of fault appears to be included in the notion of (secondary) infringement.[42] Despite the conceptual difference in approach between the aforementioned civil law jurisdictions and the United Kingdom, it seems that the outcome of a dispute will not differ substantially. Under civil law a distributor may be considered an 'infringer' for the purpose of copyright law (i.e. violate a copyright), but may at the same time avoid liability through the *separate* requirement of fault, whereas in the United Kingdom, a distributor who does not (have a reason to) know that he contributed to the distribution of an infringing article is not an 'infringer' in the first place and therefore not directly liable. Moreover, due to the extensive duty of care imposed on printers and publishers under Dutch and German law, the publisher's and printer's positions are very much the same as they are in the United Kingdom.

4.2 INDIRECT INFRINGEMENT

Under the general doctrine of tort in the Netherlands and Germany, the distinction between direct and indirect infringement of rights is generally accepted. Indirect infringers are persons who do not themselves violate a right, but whose actions or omissions contribute to such a violation. They may have acted unlawfully because of a breach of a duty of care. Thus, whereas with regard to direct infringers the duty may be relevant in establishing *fault*, with regard to indirect infringers, negligence may result in the act or omission being *unlawful*.[43]

According to the German Supreme Court, anyone whose deeds are related to a copyright infringement in a way that fulfils the criterion of 'adequate causation' may be liable as a concurrent tortfeasor. Consequently, copy-shop owners and providers of recording equipment may, in principle, be held accountable for copyright infringements taking place on the machines they provide, even if they do not themselves perform a restricted act. However, since the further one is removed from the actual acts of infringement, the narrower the scope of the duty of care

41 Articles 16–21 of the CDPA deal with primary infringements and Arts 22-26 deal with secondary infringements. Articles 96 and 97 of the CDPA are on liability in general.

42 See Institute for Information Law 1997.

43 See for Germany Markesinis 1994, pp. 74–75; see for the Netherlands *Onrechtmatige Daad (oud) I* (Jansen), aant. 81.

becomes, ultimately, these actors were in fact not found to have acted unlawfully. An organiser of a performance, on the other hand, may act negligently if the performing artists that he hires violate copyright. Factors determining the extent of a duty of care are, *inter alia*, the control one can exercise over the actual acts of infringement and the indirect infringer's financial interest in those acts.[44] Dutch copyright law is somewhat similar. Commentators state that, the further a person is removed from the actual infringing activity, the less likely it is that breach of a duty of care or fault will be found.[45]

The indirect infringer's position is not expressly regulated in the US Copyright Act. In 1984, however, in its *Betamax* decision the US Supreme Court affirmed that the concept of contributory liability, which was developed in other areas of law, applies under copyright law.[46] Contributory liability consists of personal conduct that forms part of, or furthers, the infringement, or of the contribution of machinery or goods that provide the means to infringe. To be regarded contributorily liable, proof of fault, i.e. actual knowledge or a reason to know of the infringing nature of the activity of the primary actor, is required. Thus, whereas a direct infringer is held strictly liable, the liability rules are less stringent with regard to the indirect infringer.[47]

The difference between US copyright law and the law in the aforementioned civil law jurisdictions is that in the United States there is a sharp division between requirements for direct and indirect liability to be found, whereas in Germany and the Netherlands there is a gradual shift in the extent of the duty of care, which determines whether fault exists with regard to direct infringers, and whether the indirect infringers' conduct was 'unlawful' for the purpose of the general provisions on tort.

4.3 RESTRICTED ACTS

The position of the defendant differs depending on whether he is considered an indirect or a direct infringer, or in other words, whether he did or did not perform a restricted act under copyright law. Is an online intermediary a direct infringer? Much ink has been spilled over this controversial issue.[48] In the following it will be

---

44 See Decker 1998, p. 10; Nordemann, Vinck and Hertin 1994, pp. 567–568.

45 See Spoor and Verkade 1993, pp. 341–343; Koelman 1998, p. 206; Gerbrandy 1988, p. 317; Hugenholtz 1998, pp. 226-227; Brinkhof, Dupont, Grosheide et al. 1998, p. 212 ff.

46 *Sony Corp. v. Universal Studios, Inc.*, 464 US 417, 435 (1984). The Court stated that the "absence of such express language in the copyright statute does not preclude the imposition of liability for copyright infringement on certain parties who have not themselves engaged in the infringing activity. For ... the concept of contributory infringement is merely a species of the broader problem of identifying the circumstances in which it is just to hold one individual accountable for the actions of another".

47 Nimmer and Nimmer, § 12.04[A][2][b].

48 See e.g., Zscherpe 1998, pp. 404–411; Aplin 1998; Elkin-Koren 1995, pp. 352-362; Decker 1998, p. 11; Panethiere 1997.

briefly investigated how courts have dealt with this question and to what extent it has been settled by international regulations. Before that, provisions of the US and United Kingdom Copyright Acts that specifically regulate the direct liability of certain 'old-fashioned' online intermediaries will be discussed.

Pursuant to Article 111(a)(3) of the US Copyright Act, which was drafted in order to deal with cable retransmission, any 'passive carrier' who has no direct or indirect control over the content or selection of the primary transmission and whose activities with respect to the secondary transmission consist solely of providing wires, cables, or other communication channels is exempted from liability, but only with respect to the restricted acts of performing and publicly displaying a work.[49] Under United Kingdom law, a person transmitting a television programme will only be considered as performing the primary infringing act of 'broadcasting' (Article 20 CDPA), 'if he has responsibility to any extent for its contents' (Article 6(3)(a) CDPA).[50] Thus, under both regimes a retransmitter who has no control over the contents cannot be held liable for direct copyright infringement. This is a reversal of the approach under defamation law, where the fact that an intermediary has editorial control may result in the presumption (in the United States) or establishment (in the United Kingdom) of fault. Here the lack of editorial control seems to result in the presumption that an intermediary cannot be blamed and therefore is not liable. Apparently, instead of separately requiring fault for these intermediaries to be held liable, some form of fault is introduced in the definitions of the restricted acts of performing, publicly displaying or, in the United Kingdom, broadcasting a work. Thus, liability is less strict where these 'passive carriers' are concerned. However, even though Internet intermediaries may have an equally passive role, a US district court ruled that online access providers cannot apply for the exemption of Article 111 of the US Copyright Act.[51]

Must online intermediaries then be viewed as direct infringers, because copyrighted works are reproduced on their installations, or because they are to be considered as performing any other restricted act? Particularly in the United States, this issue has been addressed in several decisions. At first, the courts approached the issue rather rigidly. In 1993, for example, in *Playboy Enterprises v. Frena* a district court found a Bulletin Board Service (BBS) operator to be liable, even though the operator had not uploaded the work and was unaware of the infringement taking place. The Court found that the operator had *directly* infringed copyright and

---

49 See Panethiere 1997, p. 20.

50 See Dworkin and Taylor 1989, p. 196 ("It would not be appropriate in all circumstances ... for the person making the transmission to be regarded as the person making the broadcast and thus its author. British Telecom, for example, provides common carrier services for several broadcasters by transmitting services to satellites, without being in any way responsible for, or necessarily even aware of, the contents of the programme. Thus, the requirement that the person transmitting the broadcast is the 'broadcaster' only if he is responsible to some extent for the contents, is to ensure that common carriers such as British Telecom are excluded").

51 See note 12 of the *Netcom* decision (*infra* n. 54).

simply stated that 'intent or knowledge is not an element of [direct copyright] infringement'.[52] Other district courts have followed a similar approach.[53]

In the landmark *Netcom* decision of 1995, a US district court for the first time mitigated the strictness of the liability of online intermediaries.[54] The Court found that temporary copies made while transmitting a work over the Internet constitute reproductions for the purpose of copyright law and acknowledged that fault is not required under the US Copyright Act. However, mainly on grounds of public policy and sheer reasonableness,[55] the Court required an additional element of 'volition or causation' to hold the access provider liable for direct infringement. The reasoning in the *Netcom* case was followed in several decisions where it was found that a BBS operator cannot be a direct infringer if he does not 'directly cause' the infringement.[56] According to these decisions, where an intermediary does not initiate the infringement nor create or control the content of its service, he cannot be considered to have *caused* the infringement and therefore is not a direct infringer. Apparently, the notion of foreseeability, that plays a role in establishing legal cause, is introduced as an element of direct infringement to limit the US Copyright Act's strict liability rule. The courts in these decisions added that an intermediary may still be held indirectly liable under the doctrine of contributory infringement, in which case fault on the part of the provider must be proven (i.e. the plaintiff must show that a provider knew or should have known of the direct infringer's conduct). Some other post-Netcom decisions, however, have held an online intermediary directly liable even if the defendant was equally as passive as Netcom was.[57]

In Europe, a considerably smaller volume of case law exists concerning an online intermediary's liability for copyright infringing third party content. A Dutch lower court came to a similar result as did the Court in the *Netcom* decision. In the Dutch *Scientology* case, the Court found that a hosting service provider does not directly infringe copyrights and may only be held liable if he knows or has a reason to know of the actual wrongful act taking place over its installations.[58] Contrary to

---

52 893 F. Supp. 1552 (M.D. Fla. 1993).

53 See e.g. *Sega Entertainmant, Ltd. v. Mapphia*, 875 F. Supp. 679 (N.D. Cal. 1994). See for a critical analysis of these decisions Elkin-Koren 1995, pp. 350–375.

54 *Religious Technology Center v. Netcom Online Communication Services*, 907 F. Supp. 1361 (N.D. Cal. 1995).

55 The Court stated, *inter alia*, that the "plaintiffs' theory would create many separate acts of infringement and, carried to its natural extreme, would lead to unreasonable liability ... Where the infringing subscriber is clearly directly liable for the same act, it does not make sense to adopt a rule that could lead to the liability of countless parties whose role in the infringement is nothing more than setting up and operating a system that is necessary for the functioning of the Internet. Such a result is unnecessary as there is already a party directly liable for causing the [infringement]".

56 *Sega Enterprises v. Sabella*, LEXIS 20470 (N.D.Cal. 1996); *Sega Enterprises v. Maphia*, 948 F. Supp. 923 (N.D.Cal. 1996).

57 *Playboy Enterprises, Inc. v. Russ Hardenburgh, Inc.*, 982 F. Supp. 503 (N.D. Ohio 1997); *Central Point Software, Inc. v. Nugent*, 903 F. Supp. 1057 (E.D.Tex.1996).

58 *Scientology*, President of District Court of the Hague, 12 March 1996, [1996] Mediaforum B 59, available in English in M. Dellebeke (ed.), *Copyright in Cyberspace, ALAI Study Days Amsterdam, 4–*

this decision, a German lower court required a lower level of fault and held a BBS operator criminally liable for direct copyright infringement, because the operator did not fulfil his duty of care to ensure that third parties could not download copyrighted software from the electronic bulletin board.[59]

Clearly, the issue is far from settled. On the international level, several attempts have been made to deal with it. An 'Agreed Statement' accompanying the WIPO Copyright Treaty of 1996, which contains a broad right of communicating a work to the public that is specifically designed to cover online dissemination, clarifies that:[60]

> "It is understood that the mere provision of physical facilities for enabling or making a communication does not in itself amount to communication within the meaning of this Treaty or the Bern Convention".

Literally taken, the statement deals only with the provision of facilities, i.e. not with the provision of transmission services or, in other words, the 'pumping' of a signal through a network. Even so, the intention of the Statement seems to be to clarify that an intermediary may not be held liable for *direct* infringement, at least not where the 'right of communication to the public' is concerned.[61] Indirect infringement is not necessarily affected by the Statement, nor is direct infringement of the right of reproduction. Perhaps because the WIPO Treaty does not contain a provision on the 'right of reproduction' which is specifically tailored to apply in the digital environment, there is no similar statement regarding a provider's position in respect of the right of reproduction.

Particularly controversial is the status of the temporary copy which is made during the 'store and forward' process in the course of transmitting material over the Internet. This issue was discussed at the WIPO Conference in 1996, but because the Contracting Parties could not agree, no provision was included in the Treaty.[62]

(Cont.)
8 June 1996, Amsterdam, Cramwinckel 1997, p. 139. See Dommering 1998a; Hugenholtz 1998, p. 228.

59 Local Court (*Amtsgericht*) Nagold, 31 October 1995, [1996] Computer und Recht 240.

60 Agreed Statement with Art. 8 of the WIPO Copyright Treaty, WIPO document CRNR/DC/96 (23 December 1996), Agreed Statements Concerning the WIPO Copyright Treaty, adopted by the Diplomatic Conference on 20 December 1996. Remarkably, a similar statement is lacking in the Agreed Statements Concerning the WIPO Performances and Phonograms Treaty, even though Art. 14 of that Treaty contains a similarly broadly defined performers' right of communication to the public. WIPO Document CRNR/DC/97, 23 December 1996, adopted by the Diplomatic Conference on 20 December 1996.

61 See *WIPO National Seminar on Digital Technology and the New WIPO Treaties*, 22 August 1997, WIPO/CNR/SEL/97/1, p. 7.

62 See Foster 1997. In Art. 7(1) of the Basic Proposal for the Substantive Provisions of the Treaty on Certain Questions Concerning the Protection of Literary and Artistic Works to Be Considered by the Diplomatic Conference (WIPO document CRNR/DC/4, 30 August 1996) it was proposed to include in the Treaty the following provision: "The exclusive right accorded to authors of literary and artistic works in Article 9(1) of the Berne Convention of authorising the reproduction of their works shall

There is an Agreed Statement with the WIPO Treaty which declares that digital copies are considered reproductions for the purpose of (international) copyright law.[63] This does not, however, expressly clarify the status of the 'transmission copy'. Notably, both in Europe and the United States, the temporary storage of computer programs, as a particular class of works, is expressly considered a reproduction under copyright law as is the temporary storage of databases in Europe.[64] In the United States, transient reproductions of other classes of works should probably be viewed as reproductions under copyright law as well.[65]

The European Commission has taken it upon itself to address the issue in a Directive. Article 2 of the proposed Copyright Directive states:[66]

> "Member States shall provide for the exclusive right to authorize or prohibit direct or indirect, temporary or permanent reproduction by any means and in any form, in whole or in part".

The provision is drafted broadly enough to cover the transient reproduction occurring while transmitting a work over a network. To exclude, *inter alia*, such reproductions from the scope of copyright law, Article 5(1) of the proposed Directive provides:

> "Temporary acts of reproduction referred to in Article 2, such as transient and incidental acts of reproduction which are an integral and essential part of a technological process, including those which facilitate effective functioning of transmission systems, whose sole purpose is to enable use to be made of a work or other subject matter, and which have no independent economic significance, shall be exempted ...".

In many cases, access providers make 'proxy cache' copies of web pages recently retrieved by their subscribers. Proxy caching enhances access to these pages because

---

(Cont.)
include direct and indirect reproduction of their works, whether permanent or temporary, in any manner or form".

63 Agreed Statement with Art. 1(4) of the WIPO Copyright Treaty states that "[t]he reproduction right, as set out in Article 9 of the Berne Convention, and the exceptions permitted thereunder, fully apply in the digital environment, in particular to the use of works in digital form. It is understood that the storage of a protected work in digital form in an electronic medium constitutes a reproduction within the meaning of Article 9 of the Berne Convention" (WIPO document CRNR/DC/96). See also Agreed Statement Concerning Articles 7, 11 and 16 of the WIPO Performances and Phonograms Treaty (WIPO Document CRNR/DC/97) which contains a similar statement regarding performers' rights.

64 See Bygrave and Koelman elsewhere in this volume, p. 104.

65 The *Netcom* Court (*supra* n. 54), for example, found that under US law transient transmission-copies are relevant under copyright law.

66 Amended proposal for a European Parliament and Council Directive on the harmonisation of certain aspects of copyright and related rights in the Information Society, Brussels, 21 May 1999, COM (1999) 250 final.

they need no longer be retrieved from the originating server. One may question whether such caching in all circumstances meets the requirements of the exemption. An access provider who proxy-caches certain particularly popular pages is able to provide access to the content significantly faster than one who does not. Probably, a faster connection will be worth more. Certainly, fast access will be attractive to potential customers. Is the cache-copy therefore economically significant within the meaning of Article 5(1) of the proposed Directive? Or should the provision be understood to imply that the reproduction must constitute a separate exploitation *of the work* and that the requirement of having no economic significance thus does not apply to the value added to a mere transmission service? The inclusion of the word 'independent' could perhaps be interpreted as an indication that the latter view is correct. This conclusion is supported by a statement in the Explanatory Memorandum with the proposed E-Commerce Directive, where the Commission states that a proxy cache copy "does not as such constitute a separate exploitation of the information transmitted".[67] Moreover, even though proxy caching is strictly speaking not an essential part of transmission over the Internet, as the Internet could also function without proxy caching, it certainly does enhance the network's efficiency, by preventing network congestion.

Whatever the status of the copy that occurs while a work is cached, the transient copy that is made in the 'store and forward' process is probably intended to be exempted by the proposed Copyright Directive. Thus, actors who in the course of providing transmission services make transient copies are likely not to be considered direct infringers of the right of reproduction. A hosting service provider or BBS operator, on the other hand, may still be regarded as directly infringing that right. On the basis of the above-mentioned Agreed Statement with the WIPO Treaty, which is repeated almost verbatim in Article 3(4) of the proposed Copyright Directive, these latter will probably not be regarded as direct infringers of the right of communication to the public. Neither the Statement nor the provision of the Directive, however, exclude them from being directly liable for violating the right of reproduction.

In sum, the intermediary's position under copyright law remains unresolved by the WIPO Treaty, its accompanying Statements and the EU proposal. However, due to recent developments in the legislative field, the issue of how to qualify an intermediary's conduct under copyright law may be of less relevance where liability for the damages is concerned. Recently proposed and enacted legislation deals with online intermediary liability to provide for monetary relief directly, without addressing the question of whether the intermediaries' activities directly or indirectly violate any exclusive rights. As will be shown in Section 7 below, however, whether or not an intermediary is to be considered a direct infringer may

---

67 Explanatory Memorandum with the E-Commerce Directive (*infra* n. 68), Commentary on Individual Articles, Chapter 1, Section 4, Article 13.

still matter in relation to the question of whether an injunction may be imposed on an intermediary.

5. Specific Legislation on Intermediary Liability in EU Member States

In November 1998, the European Commission issued a proposal for a Directive regulating several issues related to e-commerce (the E-Commerce Directive), one of which is online intermediary liability.[68] By then, the US legislature had enacted the Digital Millennium Copyright Act (DMCA), which contains provisions specifically dealing with online intermediary liability under copyright law.[69] As early as 1996, the US legislature had statutorily determined the provider's position under defamation law. The EU proposal, if enacted, will supersede legislative initiatives in Germany, Sweden, the Netherlands and the United Kingdom, where the issue is addressed in enacted and proposed legislation. Before extensively scrutinising the above-mentioned EU and US regulations, the developments in these EU Member States will be briefly described.

5.1 UNITED KINGDOM

The United Kingdom was the first European country to deal with online intermediary liability by statute. The Defamation Act 1996,[70] which codifies the 'innocent dissemination' defence for distributors of hard copies, also applies to service and access providers. Like any 'ordinary' distributor, an online intermediary may escape liability for third party material, if he sustains the burden of proving that he took reasonable care in relation to the publication and did not know, nor had a reason to believe that he contributed to the publication of a defamatory statement. In determining what would constitute reasonable care or whether an intermediary should have known of his contribution, courts must expressly take into account the extent of editorial control and the nature and circumstances of the publication and the prior conduct of the author.

---

68 Proposal for a European Parliament and Council Directive on Certain Legal Aspects of Electronic Commerce in the Internal Market, Brussels 18 November 1998, COM (1998) 586 final. The Amended proposal did not alter the provisions on online intermediary liability. See Amended proposal for a European Parliament and Council Directive on certain legal aspects of electronic commerce in the Internal Market COM (1999) 427 final.

69 Public Law 105-308-OCT. 28, 1998.

70 *Supra* n. 24.

5.2 SWEDEN

In May 1998 the Swedish Parliament passed the Act on Responsibility for Electronic Bulletin Boards (*Lag om ansvar för elektroniska anslagstavlor* (1998:112)). The Act regulates criminal liability but is nevertheless of interest for the purpose of this chapter. It obliges service providers to remove obviously illegal or copyright infringing material from their servers. In order to fulfil this obligation the provider must supervise the activities of his subscribers in so far as can reasonably be expected in view of the size and the purpose of the service.[71] In fact, the Act appears not to limit the scope of intermediary liability, but to broaden it instead; it will only apply if the provider is not liable under the general provisions of the Penal Code or the Copyright Act. Network provider liability is expressly excluded from the Act. Presumably, access providers liability is not dealt with either.[72]

5.3 THE NETHERLANDS

The Dutch government intends to rewrite the provisions on the 'cascade' system in the Penal Code (discussed above in Section 2) to ensure that they apply to online intermediaries. The existing rule, that dates from the nineteenth century, by its wording only applies to a 'publisher' (*uitgever*) or a 'printer' (*drukker*). Under the proposal, not only publishers or printers, but all 'intermediaries' (*tussenpersonen*) can escape criminal liability if the author is known or his identity is provided to the authorities by the intermediary at the commencement of a preliminary inquiry.[73] Additionally, the intermediary must do all that can be reasonably expected to prevent further dissemination upon the request of the public prosecutor. The proposal does not distinguish between service and access providers. One of the reasons for which commentators have maintained that the proposal is unreasonable, is that, unlike a service provider, who will often have a direct relation with the information provider, an access provider will in most cases not be able to benefit from the exemption, because it will be impossible for him to produce the originator's identity.[74]

---

71 In the Explanatory Memorandum the Swedish Government explains: "The provider must regularly go through the content of the electronic bulletin board. How often this is done varies from case to case depending on the content of the service. Commercial services must check more regularly than private services. It is not intended that the activity of the supplier be seriously hampered by the act. If the number of messages is so large, that it is too cumbersome to check them all, it can be acceptable to provide an abuse board, to which users can complain of the existence of illegal messages". Translation by J. Palme.

72 An English translation with a commentary by J. Palme is available at http://www.dsv.su.se/~jpalme/society/swedish-bbs-act.html. See also Julià-Barceló 1998, p. 457.

73 Proposal *Wet Computercriminaliteit II* of January 1998, Tweede Kamer, 1998-1999, 26671, nrs. 1-2.

74 See Schuijt 1998, pp. 72–73; De Roos 1998, p. 56.

5.4 GERMANY

Germany was the first country to enact legislation specifically to regulate online intermediary liability in its Multimedia Act of 1997 (*Informations- und Kommunikationsdienste-Gesetz*).[75] The Act intends to regulate liability 'horizontally', i.e. its rule applies equally under all areas of the law. Three types of 'service providers' (*Diensteanbieter*) are distinguished: information providers, hosting service providers and access providers. To the first category, the rules of general law apply in full. Providers of the second class, who 'offer for use' (*zur Nutzung Bereithalten*) third party content, are only liable if they have actual knowledge of the content and if the prevention of further dissemination is technically possible and can reasonably be expected of them. Thus, unlike the Swedish and the British Acts, under the Teleservices Act a duty to monitor or investigate further can never be imposed on service providers. Moreover, the Act requires a high level of fault (actual knowledge) and specifically includes the factor of the costs of avoidance of the harm that is applied while establishing the scope of a duty of care under general tort law. The reasoning in the explanatory memorandum is that this is the just threshold for liability to arise, because the provider did not initiate the dissemination of the content, and that, in practice, it would be impossible for the provider to have knowledge of all the contents and control their lawfulness.[76] Access providers, finally, are totally excluded from liability, either resulting from the 'mere provision of access for use' of third party content (*lediglich den Zugang zur Nutzung vermitteln*) or from the act of temporarily copying in the course of the provision of access. The rule of the Multimedia Act is said to act as a filter, in particular where the hosting service provider is concerned (an access provider will never pass the 'filter'); only if the requirements of the Act are met, may a court consider whether the service provider is accountable under general law.[77]

6. The DMCA and the E-Commerce Directive

Recapping the above, in Sweden the legislature chose to impose a duty of care upon service providers, while in Germany such actors can only be held liable if they have positive knowledge of the illegal content and access providers are totally exculpated. In the United Kingdom, both types of intermediaries need to prove that they did

---

75 Article 1 of the German Multimedia Act contains the Teleservices Act (*Teledienstegesetz*) of which Art. 5 addresses intermediary liability. The Multimedia Act is available in German and English at <http://www.iid.de/iukdg/>.

76 Deutscher Bundestag- 13. Wahlperiode, Drucksache 13/7385, p. 20.

77 Engel-Flechsig, Maennel and Tettenborn 1997; Pichler 1998, pp. 86-88; Engel-Flechsig 1999, p. 46; Bulst 1997.

not act negligently to avoid being held accountable under defamation law.[78] Under the Dutch proposal, a provider may escape liability on the condition that he provides the identity of the originator of the illicit content. Thus, the (proposed) statutory liability rules differ substantially from country to country. It was these emerging differences, among other things, that brought the European Commission to issue a proposal for a directive on e-commerce regulating, *inter alia*, online intermediary liability.[79]

The E-Commerce Directive applies to so-called 'information society services' which are services 'normally provided for remuneration, at a distance, by electronic means and at the individual request of a recipient of services'.[80] The liability rules are modelled upon the German Multimedia Act, in that they regulate liability in a horizontal manner and serve as a filter; only if a provider fails to qualify for the liability limitations of the proposal, may he be held liable on the basis of the general law.[81]

In the autumn of 1998 the US Online Copyright Infringement Liability Limitation Act was enacted as part of the DMCA. The Act adds a new section 512 to Chapter 5 of the US Copyright Act, which deals with the enforcement of copyright. Because the EU proposal is heavily influenced by the latter Act and both pieces of legislation are therefore very much alike, they will be analysed and compared below. However, whatever the similarities between these regulations, it is important to keep in mind that the proposed E-Commerce Directive intends to deal with online intermediary liability 'horizontally', while the DMCA only governs liability under copyright law.

6.1 MERE CONDUITS

Both under the proposed Directive and the US Act, a provider acting as a 'mere conduit' may not be held liable to provide for monetary relief.[82] These actors are defined as providers who merely transmit third party content or provide access to communications networks. Clearly, this exoneration not only concerns the provision of the infrastructure (as it may be under section 111 of the US Copyright Act or the Agreed Statement with the WIPO Copyright Treaty), but also the activity of providing transmission services. To qualify for this exemption providers may neither initiate the transmission, select the receiver nor have any editorial control by selecting or modifying the material. The latter criterion is reminiscent of the Dutch 'cascade'

78 See *supra* Section 3.
79 *Supra* n. 68.
80 See Explanatory Memorandum with the E-Commerce Directive, Commentary on Individual Articles, Chapter 1, Art. 2.
81 See Explanatory Memorandum with the E-Commerce Directive, Commentary on Individual Articles, Chapter 1, Section 4.
82 Art. 12 of the proposed E-Commerce Directive and section 512(a) of the US Copyright Act.

system and the exemption for 'passive carriers' in the US Copyright Act, and is used to determine whether a publisher can be presumed to have acted with fault for the purpose of defamation law. However, whereas under existing defamation law a distributor (and even a common telecommunications carrier)[83] may be held liable if he was aware of his role in the publication or communication of unlawful material, a mere access provider is completely exculpated even if he had actual knowledge of a third party's unlawful activities, as long as he did not select or modify the information. In terms of general tort law, one could say that fault on the part of the 'mere conduit' is completely excluded and that a duty to block access will never arise.

Presumably for the purpose of clarifying the intermediary's position under copyright law (which may be self-evident with regard to the DMCA, but not where the E-Commerce Directive is concerned), it is stipulated that acts of transient storage, which take place for the sole purpose of carrying out a transmission and do not last longer than is necessary for that transmission, are considered as part of the provision of access or transmission services. Thus, it is clarified that a mere conduit can never be held liable for infringing the reproduction right, even if the transient copy would constitute a copyright infringement. Consequently, rather than determining whether a 'transmission-copy' is a reproduction for the purpose of copyright law, the legislature has chosen to simply rule out liability for transient copying during transmission.[84] The US legislature could have perhaps followed the 'passive carrier' precedent of section 111 of the US Copyright Act (i.e. provide that the intermediary does not directly infringe a copyright),[85] but nevertheless has elected to address the liability issue 'head-on'. A similar approach is followed with regard to storage of third party material by a hosting service provider and proxy-caching by an access provider.

6.2 PROXY CACHING

A copy in a proxy cache is comparable to a transmission-copy in that it is intermediate and temporary. To be considered a transmission copy for the purpose

---

83 See *infra* Section 10, n. 165.

84 See Explanatory Memorandum with the E-Commerce Directive, Commentary on Individual Articles, Chapter 1, Section 4: ("It should be clear, however, that the provisions of this section do not affect the underlying material law governing the different infringements that may be concerned"). See also US Senate, *The Digital Millenium Copyright Act of 1998, Report together with Additional Views to Accompany S. 2037*, submitted by Senator Hatch, from the Committee on the Judiciary (Report 105-190, 11 May 1998), pp. 19 and 55 ("Section 512 is not intended to imply that a service provider is or is not liable as an infringer either for conduct that qualifies for a limitation of liability or for conduct that fails to so qualify. Rather, the limitations of liability apply if the provider is found to be liable under existing principles of [copyright] law ... New section 512 does not define what is actionable copyright infringement in the online environment, and does not create any new exceptions to the exclusive rights under copyright law. The rest of the Copyright Act sets those rules ... New section 512 simply defines the circumstances under which a service provider, as defined in this Section, may enjoy a limitation on liability for copyright infringement").

85 See *supra* Section 4.3.

of the DMCA and the proposed Directive, however, a copy may not be accessible to any person other than the anticipated recipient and may not be maintained for a period longer than is reasonably necessary for the transmission. However, a copy in a proxy cache will usually be retained for some time and be accessible to more than just one specific recipient.[86] To escape liability for maintaining cache-copies, an intermediary must abide by more stringent rules.[87] Aside from requirements implying that he be unaware of the contents of a copy, because there was no editorial control, under the DMCA an intermediary must expeditiously block access to the information if he receives a notification of infringement, but only if the material has previously been removed from the originating site. Thus, unlike a provider who functions as a mere conduit, an intermediary who has made a cache-copy may become liable if he has actual knowledge of the potentially infringing character of the material and does nothing to prevent its further distribution. However, only if he obtains this knowledge in a specific way, namely by receiving a notification that meets certain statutory requirements (see below), will he incur liability. If a provider obtains knowledge in any other way, he will still escape liability. The EU proposal does not contain any specific notice and take down procedures. However, under the proposal too, it is not the knowledge of the unlawful character of the cached material as such, but knowledge of removal at the initial source or of the fact that a competent authority has ordered such removal that may prompt an intermediary to block access to the cached copy.

Additionally, both regimes include some requirements that appear to be intended merely to protect the originator of the material, such as the operator of the cached website, who is not necessarily the person who will incur harm from the dissemination of unlawful material, e.g. where defamatory material is disseminated, or in cases where the operator of the site is the copyright infringer. First, both the US Act and the proposed Directive provide that the material may not be modified. Note that this requirement has a double function; it both indicates that the intermediary did not have editorial control, and thus implies that there is no fault on his part, and it ensures that the interests of the originator are served. Secondly, the intermediary must comply with generally accepted standards regarding the updating and refreshing of cache-copies.[88] Thirdly, he may not interfere with technology associated with the material which sends back data to the originator (e.g. the number of 'hits'), in so far as such can reasonably be expected. And finally, if, at the original location conditions are set upon access to the material (e.g. the

86 The Act and the proposed Directive subtly speak of 'transient storage' where liability for providing transmissions is concerned and of 'temporary storage' in respect of caching.

87 Article 13 of the proposed E-Commerce Directive and section 512(b) of the US Copyright Act.

88 There is no indication that, by inclusion of the latter two requirements, the legislature intended to protect the originator's moral rights under copyright law. However, one might argue that they protect comparable interests. On the other hand, the originating website owner will often not be the 'author' for the purpose of copyright law.

insertion of a password),[89] the intermediary may only permit access to the cache-copy if these conditions are met.

6.3 HOSTING SERVICE PROVIDER

The threshold level of fault required for holding a hosting service provider liable is somewhat lower.[90] A service provider may be held liable for storing third party content, if he does not 'expeditiously' block access to the material when he has actual knowledge of its unlawful character or is aware of facts or circumstances of which that character is apparent. The EU proposal does not provide any guidance on the exact meaning of the latter criterion, but, as it probably derives from the US Act, it may refer to the same thing. The US legislature explains that the 'awareness criterion' intends to express that an intermediary has an obligation to investigate and block access if he has a special reason to suspect that infringing activities are taking place.[91]

To qualify for the exemption in the DMCA, the intermediary may not receive financial benefit directly attributable to the infringement and must remove the material upon reception of a notification of claimed infringement. Consequently, the threshold level of certainty by the intermediary regarding the infringing character of the material appears to be somewhat higher if no notification is received; a service provider must remove material that is *claimed* to be infringing upon notification, while content of which he becomes aware in any other way needs only be removed if it actually *is* infringing. Perhaps, the difference is justified by the statutory 'notice and take down and put back up' procedures that are set out below. In requiring actual knowledge, the intention of the US legislature is to take the criterion that was applied in the *Netcom* decision one step further. The level of fault

---

89 See Koelman and Helberger, elsewhere in this volume, p. 166–167.

90 Article 14 of the proposed E-Commerce Directive and section 512(c) of the US Copyright Act.

91 See Senate Report, *supra* n. 84, p. 44: ("[This] can best be described as a 'red flag' test. [A] service provider need not monitor its service or affirmatively seek facts indicating infringing activity (except to the extent consistent with a standard technical measure ...), in order to claim this limitation on liability (or, indeed any other limitation provided by the legislation). However, if the service provider becomes aware of a 'red flag' from which infringing activity is apparent, it will lose the limitation of liability if it takes no action. The 'red flag' test has both a subjective and an objective element. In determining whether the service provider was aware of a 'red flag', the subjective awareness of the service provider of the facts or circumstances in question must be determined. However, in deciding whether those facts or circumstances constitute a 'red flag' — in other words, whether infringing activity would have been apparent to a reasonable person operating under the same or similar circumstances — an objective standard should be used"). The House Committee on the Judiciary adds that "[these] circumstances include the absence of customary indicia of ownership or authorization, such as a standard and accepted digital watermark or other copyright management information": US House of Representatives, *WIPO Copyright Treaties Implementation and On-line Copyright Infringement Liability Limitation, Report To Accompany H.R. 2281*, submitted by Mr. Coble, from the Committee on the Judiciary (Report 105-551 Part 1, 22 May 1998), p. 25. See extensively on such 'indicia', De Kroon elsewhere in this volume, p. 229 ff.

required is somewhat higher than it is under the doctrine of contributory infringement, where an indirect infringer may also be held liable if he has a 'reason to know' of the direct infringer's conduct.[92] However, by inclusion of the 'awareness criterion' and the obligation to act upon notification, the 'reason to know' standard seems to be reintroduced. Furthermore, due to the reversal of the onus of proof (see below), it would seem that a service provider is more likely to be found liable under the DMCA than under the doctrine of contributory liability.

6.4 NOTICE AND TAKE DOWN

From Recital 16 of the EU proposal it can be concluded that the European Commission expects 'notice and take down' procedures to evolve in the form of self regulation.[93] The US legislature, on the other hand, felt that it was necessary to regulate such procedures by way of statute to ensure that access is not blocked without proper justification.[94] The Act specifies certain formal requirements for a notification that must be fulfilled for it to impose a duty to block access on an intermediary.[95]

Of course, if a service provider were to take down material that turns out to be non-infringing, the website owner may have grounds to hold him liable for the damages suffered as a result of the removal of the material. To deal with this problem, it is provided that an intermediary cannot be held liable if he blocks access in good faith reliance upon a notification or believing that the material is infringing,

92 See House Report, *ibid.* ("This standard differs from existing law, under which a defendant may be liable for contributory infringement if it knows *or should have known* that the material was infringing").

93 See also Explanatory Memorandum with the proposed E-Commerce Directive, Commentary on Individual Articles, Article 14 ("Service providers will not lose the exemption from liability if after obtaining actual knowledge or becoming aware of facts and circumstances indicating illegal activity, they act expeditiously to remove or to disable access to the information. This principle, established in the second indent of the paragraph, provides a basis on which different interested parties may lay down procedures for notifying the service provider about information that is the subject of illegal activity and for obtaining the removal or disablement of such information (sometimes referred to as 'notice and take down procedures'). It should nevertheless be stressed that these procedures do not and cannot replace existing judicial remedies. The Commission is actively encouraging industry self-regulatory systems, including the establishment of codes of conduct and hot line mechanisms").

94 See Senate Report, *supra* n. 84, p. 21 ("The Committee was acutely concerned that it provide all end-users — whether contracting with private or public sector online service providers — with appropriate procedural protections to ensure that material is not disabled without proper justification. The provisions in the bill balance the need for rapid response to potential infringement with the end-users legitimate interests in not having material removed without recourse").

95 The notification must be in writing, signed, sufficiently identify the allegedly infringing material, contain the address of the complaining party and a statement that that party has a good faith belief that the use of the material is not authorised by either the rights-holder or the law, and, under the penalty of perjury, include a statement that the complaining party is authorised to act on behalf of the copyright holder: section 512(c)(3) of the US Copyright Act.

regardless of whether the material is ultimately determined to be infringing.[96] Additionally, the DMCA states that, to remain immune for all claims, a hosting service provider who removes material upon notification must promptly notify the subscriber that access to his webpage has been disabled, and put the content back up, upon receipt of a 'counter notification' from the website owner claiming that the removal was unjustified.[97] Furthermore, the provider may not enable access upon counter notification, if the first claimant, upon being informed of the counter notification, has filed an action seeking a court order to restrain the alleged infringer from engaging in the infringing activity. Finally, perhaps to serve as a disincentive for issuing an unjust (counter) notification, it is determined that any person who knowingly misrepresents that material is infringing or mistakenly removed is liable for the damages incurred as a result of a provider acting upon such misrepresentation.[98]

6.5 INFORMATION LOCATION TOOLS

Contrary to the EU proposal, the US Act deals with two other kinds of intermediaries as well: universities and intermediaries who refer users to infringing content, whether by directly providing a hyperlink or through a search engine. The latter, providers of so-called 'information location tools', are basically treated as hosting service providers.[99] Thus, as is the case for a hosting service provider, this type of intermediary has a limited duty of care; to remain immune for liability he must investigate further and remove a reference if at the place it refers to obviously infringing activities are going on.[100] Also, the provider of a reference may be held liable if he does not disable access when he has actual knowledge of the infringing activities and must comply with the 'notice and take down' procedures to avoid becoming liable.

Commentators are uncertain as to whether a person's liability for providing a hyperlink is governed by the German Multimedia Act's provisions regarding access

---

96 Section 512(g)(1) and (4) of the US Copyright Act.

97 Section 512(g)(2) of the US Copyright Act. This counter notification must comply with similar formal requirements as are applicable to the notification of claimed infringement, but also must contain some sort of choice of forum provision: section 512(g)(3) of the US Copyright Act.

98 Section 512(f) of the US Copyright Act.

99 Section 512(d) of the US Copyright Act.

100 See US House of Representatives, *Digital Millenium Copyright Act of 1998, Report together with Additional Views to Accompany H.R. 2281*, submitted by Mr. Bliley, from the Committee on Commerce (Report 105-551 Part 2, 22 July 1998), p. 58 ("The knowledge or awareness standard should not be applied in a manner which would create a disincentive to the development of directories which involve human intervention. [A]ctual knowledge [or] awareness of infringement ... should typically be imputed to a directory provider only with respect to pirate sites or in similarly obvious and conspicuous circumstances, and not simply because the provider viewed an infringing site during the course of assembling the directory").

or, in particular, service provider liability. The activity may fall within the scope of the notions of 'offering for use' third party content or of providing 'access for use' to such content.[101] The E-Commerce Directive, however, speaks of 'storage' of third party material and of the provision of access 'to a communication network' (rather than to content), and therefore does not directly affect the position of a person who refers to unlawful third party content.[102]

6.6 Universities providing online services

The second category of providers whose position is specifically regulated by the DMCA and not under the EU proposal is that of non-profit institutions of higher education who act as online intermediaries.[103] These are not accountable for the infringing activities of their staff, so long as these activities are not related to the employees' teaching or research functions and where the institution has no reason to suspect that the employee is an infringer by repeatedly receiving notifications of claimed infringement. The provision is included because it was acknowledged that, due to academic freedom, the relationship between a university and its faculty members differs from an 'ordinary' employer-employee relationship. To prevent a university from being held liable for the actions of its employees under the principle of *respondeat superior*, the wrongful act of a faculty member will not be considered an act of the educational institution and the knowledge or awareness of an employee will not be attributed to the university.[104]

6.7 Duty to monitor and technology

From the above, it can be concluded that, only if an intermediary encounters particularly suspicious circumstances, he may be subject to a duty of care to investigate further whether material he hosts or refers to is unlawful and, where found to be so, to block access. Additionally, both the EU proposal and the US Act explicitly stipulate that a duty of care to the extent that a provider must actively search for unlawful activities may not be imposed.[105]

---

101 Flechsig and Gabel 1998, pp. 352-354; Waldenberger 1998, p. 374; Bulst 1997, pp. 36-37; Pichler 1998, p. 87 (arguing that it can be deduced from the structure of the Multimedia Act that it too deals with the technically defined act of 'storage', and not with the more abstract 'offering for use' of third party content).

102 The principles laid down in the E-Commerce Directive may, however, influence decisions concerning references to unlawful third party content. See also Waldenberger 1998, p. 74 (arguing that the German Multimedia Act could (and probably will) be applied to a provider of a hyperlink by way of analogy).

103 Section 512(e) of the US Copyright Act.

104 US House of Representatives, *Digital Millennium Copyright Act,* submitted by Mr. Coble from the Committee of Conference (Report 105-796, 8 October 1998), p. 74.

105 Article 15 of the proposed E-Commerce Directive and section 512(m) of the US Copyright Act.

However, in the United States, the exclusion of a duty to monitor is not as absolute as it appears to be in the E-Commerce Directive. To qualify for the liability limitations of the DMCA, a provider must accommodate and not interfere with (future) standard technical measures that are used by copyright holders to identify or protect copyrighted works, to the extent that the implementation of such technologies imposes neither substantial costs on the provider nor substantial burdens on his systems.[106] Apparently, the availability of such technical measures may result in a duty to monitor the contents of transmitted, cached or hosted material or content to which one provides a hyperlink.[107] Moreover, according to the US legislature, awareness on the part of the provider, for the purpose of the Act, may follow from the absence of technological tags that normally indicate ownership or authorisation.[108] Consequently, the availability of technologies that facilitate monitoring may widen the scope of an intermediary's duty of care, which, in turn, is limited by the burden that the inclusion of such technology may impose upon (the systems of) the intermediary. A similar result could have been reached by applying the principles of general tort law, where, in establishing the scope of a duty of care, the likelihood and magnitude of harm to the plaintiff are balanced against the cost of avoidance to the defendant and the public utility of his activities.

It seems that the availability of technology that facilitates monitoring will not affect the scope of a duty to monitor under the EU proposal. The provision that forbids Member States from imposing a general duty to monitor includes no reservations with regard to the future existence of technologies that would facilitate monitoring, as does the US Act. Moreover, even though Recital 16 of the proposed Directive states that the provisions of the proposal "should not preclude the development and effective operation ... of technical systems of protection", it is hard to see why intermediaries would cooperate with the implementation of such technologies; mere conduits and proxy-caching intermediaries would have nothing to gain and the position of hosting service providers would worsen. The application of monitoring techniques would result in these intermediaries being more likely to be held to have sufficient knowledge or awareness, and thus would probably extend their liability.[109]

---

106 Section 512(i) of the US Copyright Act.

107 See Section 512(m)(1) of the US Copyright Act ("Nothing in this section shall be construed to condition the applicability of [the liability limitations] on — (1) a service provider monitoring its service or affirmatively seeking facts indicating infringing activity, except to the extent consistent with a standard technical measure ..."). See also the Senate Report, *supra* n. 84, p. 44.

108 House Report, *supra* n. 91, p. 25.

109 See Decker 1998, p. 13; Pichler 1998, p. 87. Both authors note that the German Multimedia Act suffers from a similar problem.

6.8 DEFAMATION

It was precisely the latter dilemma that brought the US legislature to codify intermediary liability for third party defamatory contents. In the *Prodigy* case, a US lower court held that a BBS operator who exercises editorial control, *inter alia*, through the use of automatic software screening programs, must be regarded as a 'primary publisher' and therefore can be presumed to have knowledge of a defamatory third party statement.[110] Consequently, the application of monitoring technologies may lead to greater liability, and intermediaries who do take care to avoid unlawful statements being disseminated over their installations are more likely to be held liable than those who do not. Due to concern within the US Congress that the decision might therefore serve as a disincentive for online service providers to apply such technologies or to restrict access to unlawful contents, a so-called 'good Samaritan defence' was included in the Communications Decency Act 1996.[111] The provision forbids the States (defamation being a State cause of action) from treating a provider 'of an interactive computer service' as a 'publisher' of third party content.[112] Several courts have deduced from this provision that under no circumstances may an online intermediary be held liable for defamatory third party content, even if he actually knows or is notified of the presence of the material on his systems.[113]

Thus, as is mentioned above and contrary to the approach of the European Commission, which intends to apply the same rules for intermediary liability under, for example, copyright and defamation law, the US legislature does not apply a 'horizontal' solution for the problem of intermediary liability, but regulates liability specifically and distinctly in each of these areas of the law. Perhaps, a non-horizontal approach is only natural for a system of law that, unlike civil law, specifically recognises different torts.

6.9 IDENTITY OF THE ALLEGED INFRINGER

Clearly, one of the main justifications for limiting intermediary liability may be found in the fact that it is another actor (the information provider) who initiates the unlawful act and is liable.[114] As there is a person to hold accountable, the Internet

110 *Stratton Oakmont, Inc., v. Prodigy Services Co.* No. 31063/94, 1995 WL 323710 (N.Y. Sup. Ct. May 1995).

111 See Guenther 1998, pp. 82–88.

112 Section 230(c)(1) of Title 47 of the United States Code.

113 See *Zeran v. America On Line Inc.*, 985 F. Supp. 1124 (E.D. Va. 1997), aff'd 129 F.3d 327 (4th Cir. 1997), review denied 22 June 1998, U.S., No. 97-1488; see also *Blumenthal v. Drudge*, 992 F. Supp. 44 (D.D.C.1998).

114 One of the factors that led the *Netcom* Court to mitigate direct intermediary liability was that the infringing subscriber is clearly directly liable (*supra* n. 54). See also *Nota wetgeving voor de*

need not become a lawless 'pirate-zone' if intermediaries are exempted. To facilitate holding accountable the primary liable actor, under the DMCA an intermediary is obliged to reveal the primary infringer's identity upon receipt of a subpoena. However, this obligation apparently exists only if the identity is actually available to the provider.[115] Consequently, providing the identity of the original infringer is not a condition for escaping liability, as it is in the proposal intending to modernise the statutory 'cascade' system in the Netherlands and as was implied by the French Court of Appeals.[116] Whereas the E-Commerce Directive forbids the imposition of a higher standard of liability than is provided in the Directive, EU Member States may not be required to produce the identity of the primary liable person as a condition to escape liability. Thus, under both pieces of legislation there may be circumstances where there is a party that may, theoretically, be responsible, yet neither the intermediary nor the primary infringer can, in practice, be held accountable. The former may escape liability because the requirements of the liability limitations are fulfilled and the latter simply because his identity is unknown.

6.10 BURDEN OF PROOF

The E-Commerce Directive does not give any guidance on who bears the onus of proof. Must the intermediary show that he did not know of (the unlawful nature of) a subscriber's activities, or did not have any editorial control, to qualify for the liability limitations, as is the case under the UK Defamation Act 1996, or must the plaintiff instead prove fault on the part of the intermediary? Needless to say, the answer to this question will substantially affect the practical implications of the liability regulations. The US legislature, while likening the DMCA's liability limitations to the copyright exemptions (e.g. fair use), expressly states that the limitations in the DMCA are affirmative defences and that the defendant therefore bears the burden of establishing his entitlement to the relevant limitation of liability.[117] However, while a defendant must show that he *did* use a work 'fairly' to

---

(Cont.)
elektronische snelweg, The Hague 1998 (Tweede Kamer, vergaderjaar 1997-1998, 25 880, nrs 1-2), p. 118 ("[Als] uitgangspunt [dient] te worden gehanteerd dat voor onrechtmatige handelingen in een elektronische omgeving altijd een verantwoordelijke moet zijn aan te wijzen").

115 Section 512(h) of the US Copyright Act. Whereas pursuant to section 512(h)(3), that prescribes the contents of the subpoena, it may only be ordered to disclose information sufficient to identify the alleged infringer "to the extent such information is available to the service provider", there appears to be no obligation if the intermediary, for instance, does not keep subscriber records, or allows anonymous use of his services.

116 See *supra* Section 3.

117 House Report, *supra* n. 91, p. 26 ("The exemption and limitations provided in this subsection are affirmative defenses, like the exceptions and limitations established elsewhere in title 17. While the burden of proving the elements of direct or contributory infringement, or vicarious liability, rests with

apply for the fair use exemption, a service provider has the burden of proving that he *did not* know of the primary infringer's conduct, and an access provider that he *did not* have any editorial control. Keeping in mind that it is, to say the least, not particularly easy to prove that something did not happen or exist, it remains to be seen to what extent intermediary liability will, in practice, be limited by the Act.

7. Injunctions

The liability rules both in the E-Commerce Directive and the DMCA that are discussed above only set limits upon intermediary liability *to provide monetary relief.* Under both pieces of legislation, different rules apply with respect to the imposition of injunctions. This is not surprising, since under general tort law two different requirements must be fulfilled for an injunction to be granted. Most obviously, fault need not be established.[118] Whereas the E-Commerce Directive and the DMCA may be viewed as defining whether and when an intermediary may be considered to have acted with fault, and therefore may be held liable for the damages, it is in accordance with general tort law that the statutory threshold levels of fault do not apply to the granting of injunctions.

Injunctions come in various forms. The two main types are the prohibitory and the mandatory injunctions. A prohibitory injunction orders the defendant to desist from certain wrongful conduct. A mandatory injunction orders the defendant to take positive action to rectify the consequences of what has already occurred. In common law countries, more stringent criteria must be fulfilled for a mandatory injunction to be ordered. Another distinction is made between permanent and interlocutory or preliminary injunctions. The latter may be issued pending the settlement of either the legal or factual basis of the plaintiff's claim. These injunctions may be prohibitory or mandatory. Generally, an interlocutory

---

(Cont.)
the copyright owner in a suit brought for copyright infringement, a defendant asserting this exemption or limitation as an affirmative defense in such a suit bears the burden of establishing its entitlement").

118 See for Germany Markesinis 1994, pp. 413–414. The GCC does not specifically provide for injunctive relief in tort cases, but it has long been available on the analogy of Art. 1004 GCC, which does not require fault. The German Copyright Act expressly provides that an injunction may be granted in the absence of fault. See Art. 97 of the German Copyright Act; see for the Netherlands Asser-Hartkamp 4-III 1998, p. 115; Van Nispen 1978, p. 131. Commentators on common law are less outspoken in this respect. Nevertheless, Art. 97 of the UK CDPA states that the defendant may escape liability for the damage if he proves no fault on his part (see *supra* § 4.1), but adds that other remedies (such as injunctions) are not affected by such proof. See Dias 1989, p. 1569. Not surprisingly, in the United States, where strict liability exists even with regard to compensation for damages, the Copyright Act provides that the same applies in respect of injunctions: section 502 of the US Copyright Act. See Nimmer and Nimmer, § 14:06[B].

injunction will only be granted if the plaintiff shows a good arguable case on the merits.[119]

In civil law jurisdictions there is no requirement that fault be established for an injunction to be imposed. In these countries, however, the 'unlawfulness' of the defendant's activity must nevertheless be established. This is where it may matter whether an intermediary does or does not directly infringe a copyright. If he has performed a restricted act under copyright law, the requirement of unlawfulness is fulfilled *eo ipso*. If, however, he is considered an indirect infringer, a court must determine whether he acted negligently and will consider several factors while deciding whether an intermediary violated a duty of care and therefore acted unlawfully.[120] Consequently, in the latter case an injunction is less likely to be imposed. Similarly, in the United States an injunction can only be granted if the defendant's acts (would) result in liability under copyright law.[121] Thus, as liability is less likely to be found if an intermediary is regarded a contributory infringer, there too the qualification of an intermediary's conduct under copyright law may affect the possibility of imposing an injunction.

An injunction will normally be refused if compliance would involve an illegal act.[122] It cannot, for instance, be ordered that a subscriber's activities be monitored if this would violate secrecy of communications (see below). Also, the practical and economical feasibility of compliance is often taken into account.[123] Finally, the public interest in the continuation of the defendant's activities may be of relevance.[124] In conclusion, it can be said that roughly the same factors that are considered in determining whether a duty of care has been violated are of importance where (the scope of) an injunction is concerned.

Both the EU and the US legislature have taken these factors into account while determining the scope of injunctions that may be imposed on online intermediaries. The proposed E-Commerce Directive repeatedly applies the formula: "Member States shall provide in their legislation that the provider shall not be liable, otherwise than under a prohibitory injunction . . .". Interestingly, earlier drafts used the broader notion of 'injunctive relief' instead of 'prohibitory injunction'. In conjunction with the prohibition against imposing a general obligation to monitor third party activities, from the current wording one might conclude that the proposal intends to limit the forms of injunctive relief that may be granted: a provider may be ordered to block access to identified unlawful content, but a court may never demand that affirmative steps be taken to avoid future unlawful third

---

119 Rogers 1989, pp. 636–640; Dias and Markesinis 1984, pp. 429–431; Nordemann, Vinck and Hertin 1994, pp. 569–574; Dias 1989, pp. 325-338; Van Nispen 1978.

120 See *supra* Section 2.

121 Nimmer and Nimmer, § 14:06[B].

122 Dias 1989, p. 375.

123 Dias and Markesinis 1984, p. 430.

124 Rogers 1989, p. 637.

party activities, because this would necessarily involve some kind of monitoring and may be considered to amount to a mandatory injunction.[125]

The DMCA is somewhat more explicit as regards (the scope of) injunctions that may be imposed.[126] Pursuant to the Act, a provider acting as a 'mere conduit' may be ordered to terminate the account of a subscriber to its own services or to take reasonable steps to block access to a specified, identified, online 'location' outside the United States. Apparently, it may be ordered that access be blocked to an entire server if the specific infringing content or website falls outside the reach of US copyright law. The fact that hosting service providers may only be ordered to block access to a 'site', rather than to a 'location' (the latter appears to be a broader notion) may support this assumption. However, factor (C) below may serve as an impediment to the ordering of such a broad measure. As is mentioned, hosting service providers may be ordered to block access to infringing material available at a particular 'site' on their own systems or to terminate the account of an infringing subscriber to their own services. Note that a (mandatory) injunction in the form of a duty to monitor is lacking. However, it is added that courts may order any relief they consider necessary, but, at the same time, must select, of equally effective measures, the injunction that is least burdensome on the intermediary. As a guidance to the courts, the DMCA includes four factors that must be considered while contemplating the granting and the scope of injunctive relief:

> "(A) whether such an injunction, either alone or in combination with other such injunctions issued against the same service provider ..., would significantly burden either the provider or the operation of the provider's system or network;
> (B) the magnitude of the harm likely to be suffered by the copyright owner in the digital network environment if steps are not taken to prevent or restrain the infringement;
> (C) whether implementation of such an injunction would be technically feasible and effective, and would not interfere with access to non-infringing material at other online locations; and
> (D) whether other less burdensome and comparably effective means of preventing or restraining access to the infringing material are available".

---

125 The German Federal Supreme Court (*Bundesgerichtshof*) has found that an order to monitor all future issues of a weekly magazine for defamatory statements concerning a specific person on an importer of magazines could lawfully be issued (3 February 1976, [1977] *GRUR* 114). By way of analogy it could be concluded that a service provider can be ordered to monitor permanently whether a specific website contains certain infringing or defamatory material. The proposed Directive, however, appears to limit the possibility of imposing such an injunction on an online intermediary.

126 Section 512(j) of the US Copyright Act.

Again, this is reminiscent of the factors that are to be considered in the determination of breach of duty of care. Interestingly, factor (C) appears to be included to protect freedom of speech, as it implies that an access provider may not (readily) be obliged to block access to infringing content, if such blocking would affect the availability of non-infringing material.[127]

8. Freedom of Expression and Information

Apparently, while drafting the liability regulations, the legislature has taken into account the freedom to receive and impart information. The DMCA includes the elaborated 'notice and take down' procedures, which give an alleged infringer the opportunity to object, and provide a disincentive to issuing unjust notifications by allocating liability to a person who knowingly misrepresents the infringement of copyright. As mentioned above, freedom of speech plays a part also in the provisions governing injunctions. The liability regulations in the EU proposal may be less obvious in this respect, nevertheless, the Explanatory Memorandum asserts that the principle of freedom of expression and information as is laid down in Article 10 of the European Convention on Human Rights is taken into account while drafting the proposal.[128]

Indeed, limiting liability to instances where a high level of fault is established may be seen as serving the freedoms of expression and information. Particularly in the context of defamation law, courts have established that the level of fault required for liability to arise is determined by this constitutionally guaranteed freedom.[129] In 1974, the US Supreme Court held that:[130]

> "so long as [the States] do not impose liability without fault, [they] may define for themselves the appropriate standard of liability for a publisher or broadcaster of defamatory falsehood injurious to a private individual. This approach provides a more equitable boundary between the competing concerns involved here. It recognises the strength of the legitimate state interest in compensating private individuals for wrongful injury to reputation, yet shields the press and broadcast media from the rigors of strict liability for defamation ... Here we are attempting to reconcile state law with a competing interest grounded in the constitutional command of the First Amendment".

---

127 See also Sieber 1997a, p. 586 ("Bei der Beurteilung von Kontrollmaßnahmen ist daher nicht nur — wie dies in den bisherigen strafrechtlichen Ermittlungsmaßnahmen erfolgte — zu berücksichtigen, inwieweit sie zu wirtschaftlichen Aufwendungen der Provider führen. Entscheidend ist vor allem auch, inwieweit sie (z.B. bei der Sperrung von Servern) den Datenverkehr unbeteiligter Dritter beeinträchtigen").

128 See Explanatory Memorandum with the E-Commerce Directive, under IV, 5, p. 16.

129 See Perritt 1992, p. 100.

130 *Gertz v. Robert Welch, Inc.*, 418 U.S. 323, 94 S.Ct. 2997, 41 L.Ed.2d 789 (1974).

Previously, in *Smith v. California*, the Court found a law holding bookstores strictly liable for the (obscene) contents of the books they sell unconstitutional. It was said that placing such liability upon vendors would oblige them to read all material they offer for sale in order to avoid liability and since there are limits to what one can read, fewer books would be available to the public. Thus, public access to forms of the printed word would be limited.[131]

In *Cubby v. Compuserve*, where online intermediary liability for defamatory third party material was first examined, the US District Court held, in accordance with previous decisions of the Supreme Court:[132]

> "Given the First Amendment considerations, the appropriate standard of liability to be applied [to a BBS operator] is whether it knew or had reason to know of the allegedly defamatory statements".

Similarly to the US Supreme Court, the German Supreme Court found that the level of fault necessary to hold an intermediary liable for disseminating third party unlawful content is determined by freedom of speech. While distinguishing between knowledge of the existence of the contents and knowledge of its unlawful character, the Court held that, although a publisher may be presumed to have seen all the contents of a publication and, therefore, to 'know' of them, he cannot be assumed to have actual knowledge of the unlawful character of third party material and will only have acted with fault if *obviously* unlawful content is published. To apply a lower threshold of fault would lay too great a burden on the shoulders of the press and therefore hamper freedom of expression unconstitutionally.[133]

Similar considerations are seldom seen in decisions on copyright law. Interestingly, however, the Dutch lower court that decided the *Scientology* case, where the issue was whether a service provider can be held liable under copyright law, similarly found that a service provider may only be held liable if it is 'unequivocally clear' (*onmiskenbaar*) that the material is unlawful.[134] Also in the context of copyright infringement, the *Netcom* Court held that fault for the purpose of contributory liability will not be found if an intermediary has a reason to doubt that the material infringes copyright. Such doubt may arise, *inter alia*, because of a possible fair use defence, which, as the Court observed, is related to freedom of speech.[135] Similarly, the Swedish legislature, while regulating intermediary liability,

131 361 U.S. 147 (1959).

132 776 F. Supp. 135 (S.D.N.Y. 1991).

133 *Pressehaftung I*, German Supreme Court (BGH), 26 April 1990, [1990] GRUR 1012; *Pressehaftung II*, German Supreme Court (BGH), 7 May 1992, [1992] GRUR 618. These decisions concerned a publisher's liability for third party advertisements under the German Act on Unfair Competition (*Gesetz gegen dem unlauteren Wettbewerb*). The reasoning, however, will also apply where liability for third party defamatory statements is concerned. See Pichler 1998, pp. 85-86.

134 *Supra* n. 58.

135 *Supra* n. 54. The Court held: "Where a BBS operator cannot reasonably verify a claim of infringement, either because of a possible fair use defence, the lack of copyright notices on the copies,

inter alia, for copyright infringement, decided that a duty to block access should arise only when the material is obviously illegal.[136] Do the newly enacted US and proposed EU liability regulations require an equally high level of certainty regarding the unlawful nature of the material concerned? In other words, does freedom of expression and information prevail in cases of doubt as to whether an infringement took place? In any event, under the DMCA, the claimant gets the benefit of the doubt where a notification is received.

Commentators argue that the knowledge requirement under the German Multimedia Act applies only to the knowledge of the existence of the contents and not to knowledge of their unlawful nature.[137] If this view is correct, and the EU proposal was enacted in its current form, the German Act may need to be redrafted to comply with it since the proposed Directive undoubtedly refers to the second level of knowledge. The EU proposal requires that a service provider have 'actual knowledge that the activity is illegal' for liability to arise, thus requiring knowledge of the unlawful nature of the content or activity. Similarly, under the US Act a hosting service provider must have "actual knowledge ... that the material ... is infringing".

The freedom of expression and information may be of relevance not only where liability for damages is concerned, but also as concerns the question of whether and in what form injunctive relief may be granted. As was shown above, under the DMCA freedom of expression is implicitly a factor to be considered. Moreover, under the prior restraint doctrine US courts have long been wary not to place restrictions upon freedom of speech before it is conclusively determined that the material is not protected by the First Amendment. Therefore, courts are reluctant to grant preliminary injunctions in defamation cases or in respect of allegations of obscene 'speech'. Often courts find that, whereas the likelihood of success on the merits of a case usually suffices to grant a preliminary injunction, if a restraining order affects freedom of speech, it would be unconstitutional to impose such injunction, unless the defendant has a particularly strong case. It is therefore insufficient for it to be merely likely that the claim will succeed for an injunction to be granted.[138]

In this context, the question may be posed whether the 'notice and take down' procedures in the DMCA comply with the policy not to restrain speech before a final judicial decision is handed down, since, due to these procedures, an

---

(Cont.)
or the copyright holder's failure to provide the necessary documentation to show that there is a likely infringement, the operator's lack of knowledge will be found reasonable and there will be no liability for contributory infringement for allowing continued distribution of the works on its systems ... [T]he First amendment argument is merely a consideration in the fair use argument". See also *infra* n. 141.

136 See *supra* Section 5.

137 See Pichler 1998, pp. 87–88; Bulst 1997, pp. 34–35.

138 See extensively Lemley and Volokh 1998.

intermediary is bound to block access upon a mere *claim* that the material is infringing. Furthermore, the originating site's operator may have an opportunity to object, but if the rights-holder subsequently files an action in court, the information must nevertheless be taken down *pending* a judicial decision.[139] However, under copyright law, where the Act applies, the prior restraint doctrine appears to be of less importance and, unlike cases of defamation law, preliminary injunctions are routinely issued. Mostly, it is enough to show likelihood of success on the merits of the case. (Note that this is still a more stringent criterion than that of claimed infringement. Does the DMCA's procedure therefore conflict with the principles expressed in the prior restraint doctrine?).[140] This may reflect that, until now, freedom of expression concerns have generally carried less weight in copyright decisions than they have in defamation cases. This is true under US, Dutch as well as German law,[141] and is underscored by the fact that a publisher's duty to prevent third party copyright infringing activities is not limited to instances of evident, easily recognisable infringements, as it is under defamation law.[142] The difference may follow from the assumption that freedom of information and expression is served sufficiently through the limitations of copyright law.[143] Will US courts apply

139 For an alternative procedure which may foster the freedom of expression and information to a greater extent, see Julià-Barceló 1998, pp. 461–462. She proposes establishing a 'special body' that would judge whether a claim of infringement should lead to an obligation to block access. Thus, there would be a fast means of redress and, at the same time, unjustified removal would be avoided. Hugenholtz argues that, if a website operator objects and the material is not obviously unlawful, the content should be taken down only *after* a judicial decision, not *pending* one, as is the case under the DMCA: Hugenholtz 1998, pp. 230–231. De Roos has similar objections against the proposed update of the Dutch 'cascade' system (see *supra* Section 3). Even though an examining magistrate is involved when a preliminary inquiry is commenced, it would be unjust to oblige an intermediary to take down content at that stage pending a judicial decision. See De Roos 1998, p. 56; see also Schuijt 1998, p. 72.

140 Lemley and Volokh 1998; Nimmer and Nimmer, § 14:06[A].

141 See for the United States Nimmer and Nimmer, § 1.10[A]; Institute for Information Law 1997, p. 21. See also Guibault elsewhere in this volume, pp. 147–148. Until now, US courts have refused to admit a separate First Amendment defence in copyright cases, while, as is shown above, the First Amendment is expressly taken into account in establishing the required level of fault in defamation cases. See for Germany Nordemann, Vinck and Hertin 1994, pp. 380–381. In Germany there are some cases in which the Copyright Act's permission to quote was interpreted broadly in the light of Art. 5 of the Basic Law (which guarantees the freedom of speech). In 1996, the Dutch Supreme Court (*Hoge Raad*) found that there may be circumstances in which the exercise of copyright may be barred by the freedoms to receive and impart information (*Dior/Evora*, Dutch Supreme Court, 20 October 1996, [1996] Informatierecht/AMI 43). See also *Volkskrant v. Beeldrecht*, District Court Amsterdam, 19 January 1994, [1994] Mediaforum B34. Judicial decisions in both Germany and the Netherlands have long expressly balanced the freedom of expression and information against the interests (or personality rights) of the defamed person. See for Germany Markesinis 1994, pp. 65–66; for the Netherlands *Onrechtmatige Daad VII* (Schuijt), aant. 20 ff. In short, the freedom of expression may affect the (scope of) copyright exemptions, or be expressed in those, whereas it often explicitly plays a part in determining the threshold level of fault under defamation law.

142 See *supra* Section 4.1; see extensively Decker 1998, pp. 11–12; Panethiere 1997.

143 The US Supreme Court seems to imply this (*Harper & Row, Publishers, Inc. v. Nation Enters.*, 471 US 539 (1985)). See Lemley and Volokh 1998; Nimmer and Nimmer, 1.10[B]. See also the *Netcom* decision (*supra* n. 54), quoting *Capital Cities v. ABC, Inc.*, 918 F 2d 140, 144 (11th Cir. 1990): "The

a similar reasoning with regard to the statutory 'notice and take down and put back up' procedures? In any case, if a similar statutory procedure were introduced to regulate intermediary liability under defamation law, it is not at all inconceivable that it would be struck down because of a conflict with the First Amendment.

9. Communications Privacy

Under general tort law, a duty of care cannot be so broad that acts performed in observance of the duty would be illegal. Therefore, the privacy of communications, which bars certain actors from intercepting transmitted signals, may affect the scope of an online intermediary's duty of care. If an intermediary is prohibited from intercepting the material transmitted, he can hardly be said to be acting negligently by failing to monitor the transmitted signal.[144]

In 1997 the so-called ISDN Directive was adopted.[145] The Directive obliges EU Member States to ensure the confidentiality of communications by means of a public telecommunications network and publicly available telecommunications services. The interception of communications through such networks or services, without the user's consent, must be prohibited.[146] Due to the broad definitions of 'public telecommunications network' and 'telecommunications service', it appears that the Directive applies to communications services provided by Internet network and access providers.[147] Consequently, it may be illegal for such providers to monitor the contents of transmitted signals. Moreover, Recital 10 of the Directive expresses the intention for the Directive to apply to new services such as interactive television and video-on-demand services, which are obviously comparable to Internet services. Indeed, Recital 11 of the proposed Directive on E-Commerce states that the ISDN Directive is fully applicable to 'Information Society services'.

Somewhat similarly, the US Electronic Communications Privacy Act (ECPA) prohibits the intentional interception of electronic communications.[148] Both the US and EU legislation clearly apply to e-mail messages. As is mentioned above, the ISDN Directive may additionally include within its scope the signals of transmitted

---

(Cont.)
copyright concepts of the idea/expression dichotomy and the fair use defense balance the important First Amendment rights [with copyright]".

144 See for the United States, Perritt 1992, p. 108; for Germany, Rütter 1992, p. 1812; for the Netherlands, Koelman 1998, p. 211.

145 Directive 97/66/EC of the European Parliament and of the Council of 15 December 1997 concerning the Processing of Personal Data and the Protection of Privacy in the Telecommunications Sector, OJ L 24/1.

146 Article 5(1) of the ISDN Directive.

147 Article 2 (c) and (d) of the ISDN Directive.

148 Section 2511(1)(a) of Title 47 of the USC.

web pages, since it covers any communication that takes place between defined points. A transmission from a website to an end-user may well fit this description. It is less obvious that the ECPA will apply to such transmissions, since it specifically deems lawful the interception of an electronic communication "that is configured so that such ... communication is readily accessible to the general public".[149] The average website is designed to be accessible to the public at large. Nevertheless, under the heading 'Protection of Privacy' in the DMCA it is stipulated that the liability provisions do not imply that an intermediary (including a hosting service provider) is obliged to monitor its service or actively search for infringing activities. As shown above, however, in the United States a duty to screen subscriber activities may follow from the availability of technologies that facilitate monitoring. The Act implies that even then such a duty is limited by the protection of the privacy of communications.[150]

Finally, even if the above-mentioned provisions were not applicable to access providers, user privacy may still limit the scope of a provider's duty to monitor when taken into account in the balancing process involved in the determination of whether a duty of care was breached.[151] The German Supreme Court, for example, found that a copy-shop owner cannot be held liable for copyright infringement, because a general duty to monitor customer behaviour cannot be reasonably expected, *inter alia*, because such monitoring could violate the customers' general right to privacy[152]. The broad statutory limitation of access provider liability and the prohibition on imposing a general duty to monitor stipulated in the E-Commerce Directive and the DMCA may be the result of a similar balancing process.[153]

10. Public Policy Considerations

Fundamental rights reflect views on how society should be arranged and thus may be said to be expressions of public policy considerations. Apart from such interests that are crystallised in fundamental rights, more 'down-to-earth' economic policy

149 Section 2511(2)(i) of Title 47 of the USC. See also Perritt 1992, p. 108. Perritt finds that the policy behind the ECPA may result in an obligation to police content of potentially harmful e-mail messages, at least when a communications provider has special knowledge of potential harmfulness.

150 Section 512(m) of the US Copyright Act, quoted *supra* at n. 107; see House Report, *supra* n. 91, p. 26. The difference between the EU and the US approach to the communications privacy is that the former focuses on the communications channel, and the latter on the nature of the communication. See Dommering 1998b, p. 117.

151 See Sieber 1997b, p. 658.

152 *Kopierläden*, German Federal Supreme Court (BGH), 9 June 1983, [1984] GRUR 54, see Bygrave and Koelman elsewhere in this volume, p. 102.

153 See the Executive Summary with the Explanatory Memorandum with the proposed E-Commerce Directive ("A careful balance is sought between the different interests involved ...").

considerations appear to have played an important part in establishing the online intermediary liability regulations as they are laid down in the proposed E-Commerce Directive and the DMCA. Both the EU and the US legislature stress that online intermediary liability had to be regulated to 'facilitate the flow of electronic commerce' of which much is expected.[154] For this purpose it was felt that the uncertainty regarding the intermediary's position had to be resolved and, moreover, intermediary liability had to be limited. In the words of the US Senate Committee on the Judiciary:[155]

> "[B]y limiting the liability of service providers, the DMCA ensures that the efficiency of the Internet will continue to improve and that the variety and quality of services on the Internet will continue to expand".

Obviously, uncertainty on the risks involved may hamper investments in intermediary services, which play a crucial part in enabling e-commerce — arguably, they are a pre-condition for the mere existence of the online environment. Furthermore, if it were necessary to monitor third party contents, either to avoid a strict liability or to observe an extensive duty of care, due to the sheer volume of material and the complexity that may be involved in determining whether content or subscriber activities are actually unlawful, an intermediary would require a large staff to avoid liability, which might amount to a grave financial burden. Technologies may facilitate the screening of material to some extent, but will probably never be able to accommodate all complexities and subtleties of the law.[156] An intermediary may then choose to accept only material that is obviously legal, block access immediately in cases of doubt, or restrict access to the Internet to parties that are considered sufficiently trustworthy. Needless to say, this would not contribute to an 'expanding variety' of online services (not to mention the freedom to impart and receive information that would certainly not benefit from such business decisions).[157] On the other hand, representatives of the copyright industry

---

154 See the Executive Summary with the Explanatory Memorandum; see also House Report, *supra* n. 100, pp. 22–23.

155 Senate Report *supra* n. 84, p. 8.

156 Elkin-Koren 1995, pp. 404–405; Julià-Barceló 1998, pp. 460–461; Decker 1998, p. 11–12. In the context of copyright law it may be unclear whether an exemption applies, who is the copyright owner and whether an adequate licence is obtained. The complexity multiplies by the fact that the law may differ from country to country and that it will often be unclear which country's law applies. There may in the future be technologies that indicate whether a use of a work is properly licensed. See Hugenholtz 1998, p. 230, n. 86; see also House Report, *supra* n. 91, p. 25. However, as the applicability of many copyright exemptions depends upon the circumstances, it is hard to see how technologies could recognise whether a use is exempted in a particular case. See Koelman and Helberger, elsewhere in this volume, p. 197. Similarly, statements are only defamatory in the context in which they are presented and what is considered unlawfully defamatory in one jurisdiction may be completely permissible in the other.

157 Hugenholtz 1998, p. 232.

stress that a low liability standard will cause reluctance on the part of copyright holders to distribute their property online. This will not promote divergence in the online environment either.[158] Then again, as the costs resulting from a high level of liability will probably be passed on to subscribers, and therefore make more expensive the means of expressing and accessing information, the likely result would be a decreased number of (potential) users. Finally, the US Senate statement quoted above illustrates that, apart from the incentive to invest in online intermediary services, network efficiency considerations were taken into account while drafting the liability provisions. Accordingly, the provision on proxy-caching in the E-Commerce Directive expressly limits liability where the copy is made to 'make more efficient the further transmission' of material.[159]

The preferred approach to online intermediary liability is not entirely unprecedented. In the United States, for example, several courts have held that immunity granted to common carriers must be broad enough to ensure efficient public service.[160] In the Netherlands, until recently a common carrier's liability for network failure was limited, because it was felt that unlimited liability would bring about higher costs, which would, in turn, be passed on to the subscribers, and expensive electronic communications would conflict with the public interest.[161] However, even though the service of providing access to a network is comparable to the service of merely providing telecommunications services, an access provider is not (yet) a true common carrier.[162] A common carrier distinguishes itself in that it is subject to extensive regulation, which oblige him, *inter alia*, to provide 'universal access' and non-discriminatory services and charges. Some commentators argue that a special liability standard for common carriers is applied in return for the obligation to provide non-discriminatory services.[163] Since, until now, neither access

---

158 Julià-Barceló 1998, p. 462.

159 Article 13 of the proposed E-Commerce Directive.

160 Elkin-Koren 1995, n. 185; Perritt 1992, p. 103.

161 Article 12 of the Dutch Telecommunications Act (*Wet op de telecommunicatievoorzieningen*), which was replaced in 1998; see Tweede Kamer, vergaderjaar 1987-1988, 20 369, nr. 3, p. 35. Other European countries had similar provisions. The statutory limitation is abolished in the Dutch Telecommunications Act of 1998, because it was felt that market forces will keep prices down in a liberalised market and contractual limitation of liability will suffice. See Huisjes 1998, pp. 20–21; Van der Meent, 1997. However, as in the situations discussed in this chapter intermediaries will in many instances not have a contractual relationship with the aggrieved party, the latter solution cannot solve these liability problems. Of course, hosting service providers could perhaps obtain warranties and indemnifiers from their subscribers. However, whether a provider, if held liable, is able to get redress from the subscriber depends on the latter's solvency. The question is then: should intermediaries or rather (potentially) aggrieved parties bear the risk of the information provider's insolvency? Contrary to hosting service providers, access and network providers will often not have a contractual relationship with the primary tortfeasor, and therefore are unable to pass-on liability for the damages contractually.

162 See note 12 of the *Netcom* decision (*supra* n. 54), where the Court held that an access provider is not a common carrier since it does more than "provide the wire and conduits" and is not a "natural monopoly, bound to carry all the traffic that one wishes to pass through".

163 Bovenzi 1996, p. 131 n. 229; Huisjes 1998, p. 20.

nor service providers are obliged to provide their services 'universally'[164], following this reasoning, these providers would not 'deserve' preferential treatment.[165] From a public policy point of view, however, one could argue that both the obligation to provide universal access and the limitation on liability are manifestations of one and the same underlying rationale, i.e. the fostering of the public interest in widely available and accessible, and not too expensive, electronic communications channels.

Apparently, both the EU and the US legislature adhere to the latter view. The legislation explicitly limits Internet network and access provider liability for third party content even further than common carrier liability was ever limited. There is no legislation or case law clearly and conclusively indicating that common carriers are totally immune from liability arising from their role in the dissemination of third

164 Currently, it is under discussion in the EU whether the obligation to provide universal service, which traditionally only applied to voice telephony, should be extended to the provision of Internet services. See Resolution on the Communication from the Commission to the Council, the European Parliament, the Economic and Social Committee of the Regions on Universal Service for Telecommunications in the Perspective of a Fully Liberalized Environment — an Essential Element of the Information Society (OJ C 20/156, 20 January 1997).

165 The doctrine on 'common carriers' was developed in late nineteenth and early twentieth century US common law and dealt with, *inter alia*, railroads and telegraph companies. These operators, who were monopolists in the areas of the transportation of goods and messages, services that were considered to be of great public importance, were obliged to serve all who applied. Failure to comply could result in tortious liability. Clearly, there is a tension between a duty to transport all and a duty to censor unlawful content. A common carrier therefore has a good argument to escape liability which is based upon a duty to prevent the dissemination of unlawful third party content. If an entity is not under the obligation to carry all communications, this reasoning will obviously not apply. However, even with regard to a 'true' common carrier it is not clearly established that total immunity for the transport of unlawful third party contents exists. To our knowledge, only on one occasion did a US court hold that the 'reason to know' standard that applies to any 'republisher' under defamation law does not apply to telecommunications carriers (*Anderson v. New York Tel. Co.*, 320 N.E.2d 647, 647 (N.Y. 1974)). See extensively Perritt 1992; see for the Netherlands Koelman 1998, p. 211 (finding that there is no authority expressly stating that a common carrier is immune under Dutch law); for Germany Rütter 1992, pp. 1819–1820; Koch 1997, p. 201, nn 39 and 40 (basing telecommunications operator immunity upon the impossibility of intercepting messages, by virtue of the communications' secrecy, and the theory of adequate causation, rather than on the obligation to provide universal access); see also Koenig 1998, p. 6 (finding that nowhere in the German Telecommunications Act liability for third party content is expressly regulated, let alone a telecommunications carrier exempted). Moreover, the afore-mentioned reasoning applies with regard to the concept of 'common carrier' in US common law, which is not the same as it is under the US Federal Telecommunications Act or under EU telecommunications law. The obligation to provide 'universal services' in the latter legislation, is not necessarily equivalent to an obligation to 'carry all'. The emphasis in the US Act and EU law is on the provision of non-discriminatory services, access and charges, even to the most remote areas (see Arts 201 ff. of the US Telecommunications Act, Title 47 of the United States Code; Arts 3-5 of Directive 98/10/EC of the European Parliament and the Council of 26 February 1998 on the application of open network provision (ONP) to voice telephony and on universal service for telecommunications in a competitive environment, OJ L 101/24). If a provider retained the right to block unlawful contents in its standard contract terms, this could be considered a non-discriminatory legal basis to censor which would apply to all subscribers. The above-mentioned argument would then not provide for a valid defence.

party content.[166] Instead, case law and commentators suggest that these carriers may be liable for the damages if they have actual knowledge of the illicit nature of particular messages and fail to prevent publication when this can reasonably be expected. Both the DMCA and the E-Commerce Directive for the first time explicitly exempt from liability for unlawful third party material those (actors) merely transmitting such material, or providing access to unlawful content, even if they are under no obligation to provide 'universal service'.

11. Conclusions

To promote the development of e-commerce, and apparently taking into account the fundamental rights to freedom of speech and to communications privacy, the EU and US legislatures have chosen to exempt access and network providers from liability for damage.[167] A provider who proxy caches material may only be held liable if he obtains knowledge in certain specified ways of the presence of unlawful content in the cached material. A hosting service provider is liable for damage if he has actual knowledge or has a special reason to believe that unlawful third party activities are being carried out on his installations. In the United States, it is additionally provided that failure to block access to unlawful content of which a hosting service provider has been notified may result in liability. The E-Commerce

166 The German legislature, however, while stating that access providers must be exempted because they should not be treated differently from telecommunications providers, apparently presumes that telecommunications carriers are totally immune from liability resulting from the transmission of unlawful contents. Deutscher Bundestag- 13. Wahlperiode, Drucksache 13/7385, p. 20. See Koenig 1998, p. 6 (struggling with the fact that, contrary to access providers, who are exempted in the Multimedia Act, mere network providers, whose liability is not governed by the Multimedia Act, are not explicitly immune from liability by statute or any other authority, and resolving the problem by deducing immunity from the communications secrecy provisions of the Telecommunications Act).

167 The question may be posed whether the legislatures have complied with Art. 45 of the Agreement on Trade Related Aspects of Intellectual Property Rights (TRIPS) which requires that parties who 'knowingly, or with reasonable grounds to know, engaged in infringing activity' are held liable for damage. Since it is not conclusively established that an access or network provider does not directly infringe copyrights (see *supra* Section 4.3), and under the new liability regulations such intermediaries cannot be held liable even if they knew of the infringing activities, the EU and the US liability limitations may violate TRIPS if these providers happen to be regarded as direct copyright infringers by the courts. The provisions on proxy-caching encounter similar problems. Does TRIPS allow for actual knowledge to be construed as narrowly as it is with regard to the provider who makes cache-copies? The knowledge and awareness requirements that apply to hosting service provider liability probably do comply with Art. 45 TRIPS, i.e. if the awareness criterion in the proposal and the Act are similar to that of constructive knowledge under TRIPS. Perhaps, if the intention is to provide immunity to intermediaries to the extent of the DMCA and the E-Commerce Directive, TRIPS would necessitate for the status under copyright law of transmission and cache-copies to be directly addressed. See Gervais 1998, pp. 206-207; Panethiere 1997, p. 16; see also Decker 1999, p. 8 (finding that the German Multimedia Act's limitation of hosting service provider liability is in accordance with TRIPS).

Directive does not expressly state the same, but it is not at all inconceivable that courts will find that actual knowledge or sufficient awareness for the purpose of the Directive is established when a notification is received.[168] However, whereas in the United States an intermediary has a duty to act upon notification of *claimed* infringement, due to freedom of information and expression concerns, European courts may find that such a duty will arise only if it is evident that the content concerned is unlawful. Perhaps, the US rule is justified by the elaborated 'notice and take down and put back up' procedures in the DMCA, which are absent in the proposed Directive and which require a service provider to put the material back up if the website operator objects to its removal. According to the US Senate Committee on the Judiciary, these procedures "provide all the process that is due".[169]

In terms of general tort law, the above-mentioned criteria can be seen as defining whether and when an intermediary may be held liable for breach of a duty to block access. Both the EU and US provisions additionally address the issue of whether and to what extent an intermediary has a duty to actively search for unlawful activities being conducted on his facilities. In the EU proposal such a duty is ruled out completely. Under the DMCA a duty to monitor may arise, if, considering the financial burdens on the intermediary and the technical burdens on his systems, it can be reasonably expected that an intermediary applies future technologies that facilitate the detection of infringing material.

The scope of the injunctive relief that may be granted is related to the scope of the duty of care: one can only be ordered to refrain from certain conduct if that conduct is unlawful, or results in liability. Therefore, not surprisingly, the principles set out above are reflected in the rules governing injunctions. The proposed E-Commerce Directive expressly allows only for prohibitory injunctions (i.e. mandatory injunctions that would involve monitoring may not be imposed). The US Act appears to do the same, but it additionally implies that freedom of information must be taken into account when considering (the scope of) an order to block access. As is the case under general tort law, an injunction can be imposed in the absence of fault; i.e. it is not necessary that the intermediary knows, is aware or was notified of the unlawful content. Similarly, injunctive relief may, in principle, be granted against an access or mere transmission provider, even if fault on his part is completely ruled out.

The main differences between the EU and the US liability regulations are, first of all, the 'horizontal' approach adopted by the European Commission , as opposed

168 See Bulst 1997, pp. 34-35; Decker 1998, p. 9. Decker finds that a notification will be enough to trigger liability under the German Multimedia Act. However, as stated above, for the purpose of the German Act mere knowledge of the content existing on the provider's installations suffices, while the proposed Directive additionally requires knowledge of the unlawful character of the material (see *supra* Section 8).

169 Senate Report, *supra* n. 84, p. 21.

to the US legislature's regulation of online intermediary liability distinctly under defamation law and copyright law. Secondly, as mentioned above, the limitation of a provider's duty to monitor is not as absolute in the DMCA as it is in the proposed E-Commerce Directive. Thirdly, the US Act contains regulations regarding providers of an 'information location tool' and makes allowance for the peculiarities of universities that act as intermediaries, which the E-Commerce Directive does not. Finally, the DMCA places a statutory obligation to act upon the reception of a notification of claimed infringement and includes specific 'notice and take down' procedures, while the European Commission expects such procedures to evolve from self-regulation and does not expressly oblige the removal of content when a provider is notified by an aggrieved party.

It is likely that if the Directive were adopted in its current form several EU Member States would have to adjust their national legislation. The statutory duty to monitor subscriber activities under the Swedish Act on the Responsibility of Electronic Bulletin Boards would need to be abolished to comply with the proposed E-Commerce Directive. The Dutch legislature may not require supplying of the identity of the primary infringer in order for an intermediary to escape liability, as it intends to do under its proposal to update the 'cascade' system existing in criminal law. If the EU proposal places the burden of proving fault with the plaintiff, the United Kingdom Defamation Act 1996 would need to be altered. And even the German Multimedia Act, which expresses an approach similar to that of the proposed Directive, would need to be redrafted because it does not define intermediary activities in terms of transmission and storage, but uses the notions of 'offering third party content for use' and 'providing access for use' to such content, and because, according to commentators, it only requires knowledge of the contents, and not of the unlawful character thereof.

From the above it follows that the E-Commerce Directive treats intermediaries more leniently than the legislature of the various Member States. Whether a hosting service provider is better off under the DMCA than under existing US law remains to be seen. Several US courts have applied the contributory infringement test, which, contrary to the new Act, allocates the onus of proof of knowledge or a reason to know of the primary infringer's conduct with the plaintiff. Probably, access providers and other 'mere conduits' will benefit from the new regulations (presuming lack of editorial control can easily be proven). These are now completely immune from liability to compensate for monetary relief, whereas previously the exemption of even common carriers was never clearly established.

Interestingly, the DMCA introduces a novelty in US copyright law: even if an access or service provider is found to be a direct infringer, fault is a *separate* requirement for direct liability to arise. Until now, just as other proprietary torts, copyright was analysed under a strict liability rule; if a person performs a restricted act, liability follows automatically. Therefore, the *Netcom* Court could not limit liability through requiring fault, but had to mitigate the intermediary's direct liability by applying the doctrine of legal cause where it felt that liability would be unreasonable. Similarly, the requirement of control over content in section 111 of the US Copyright Act had to be made part of the direct infringement test to limit a passive carrier's liability. Interestingly, there was a similar development under US defamation law, where several decades ago a strict liability regime applied which by now has evolved into a with-fault liability regime due to freedom of expression concerns. Now, under copyright law too, as a result of similar concerns combined with economic policy considerations, even if an intermediary is a direct infringer, fault is an express and separate requirement for liability to arise.

If viewed from the perspective of general tort law, the new liability regulations may be said to determine the level of fault and/or negligence (the latter, breach of a duty of care, either as part of the concept of fault or of unlawfulness) necessary to hold an intermediary liable. The requirement of fault is often seen as a reflection of the ethical maxim that one can only be held responsible for the harm that a person, having the freedoms of will and action, could and should have avoided, i.e. only if a person can be blamed, should he be held liable.[170] From the emphasis placed by the legislature on the inability to control all contents as a factor determining the scope of liability,[171] it may follow that the legislature has taken into account such aspects of moral and psychological responsibility in establishing the scope of legal responsibility. If an intermediary simply cannot control (or know of) the third party information disseminated over his installations, he cannot avoid the harm, and thus should not be liable.[172] However, this cannot be a conclusive argument for limiting online intermediary liability since there are many examples of situations where persons are held strictly liable even if they could not possibly have avoided the resulting harm. Negligence, either as a form of fault or unlawfulness, or as a specific tort, may also be found in cases of unavoidable error.[173] In German legal doctrine, for instance, the ground rule applies that whoever establishes in everyday life a

---

170 See Dias and Markesinis 1984, p. 23; Fesevur 1998, p. 4; Van Dunné 1998; Englard 1992, p. 49.

171 Chapter III, Section 4 ('Liability of intermediaries') of the Explanatory Memorandum with the E-Commerce Directive reads: "In view of the limited degree of knowledge providers have about the information that they transmit or store via interactive communication networks, the main problem that arises is the allocation of liabilities between online service providers transmitting and storing illegal information and the persons who originally put such information on line. Questions also arise as regards the ability of providers to control the information they transmit or store". The German legislation expressly states that actual knowledge is required to hold a hosting service provider liable, because it is impossible to know of all contents and control them for their unlawful nature. See Deutscher Bundestag- 13. Wahlperiode, Drucksache 13/7385, p. 20. A similar reasoning is applied by the Dutch Lower Court in the *Scientology* case (*supra* n. 58).

172 Many commentators assert that there is no sound or conclusive conceptual basis for limiting liability to instances where the defendant acted with fault: first, because it is debatable whether such things as freedom of will and of action actually exist (see Fesevur 1998; Willekens 1998, p. 67); secondly, from an economic point of view it is argued that strict liability is superior to fault, because it achieves better accident prevention and more efficient loss distribution, while the other extreme, no-liability is more efficient, because it does not entail the transaction costs that are involved in litigation: Englard 1992, pp. 98-99; Willekens 1998; see also Dias and Markesinis 1984, pp. 15, 23.

173 Dias and Markesinis 1984, p. 23.

source of potential danger which is likely to affect the interests and rights of others, is under a duty to ensure their protection against the risks thus created by him.[174] Such duty, however, is not absolute. The issue is then how much trouble society will require the alleged tortfeasor to take in order to avoid or lessen the harm that will inevitably occur through the operation of his business.[175] In seeking an answer to this question, courts usually balance several factors, such as the probability and magnitude of the harm, the costs of avoidance and the social utility of the activity.[176] A similar balancing of interests appears to lie at the root of the E-Commerce Directive and the DMCA. Holding an intermediary liable for all unlawful third party activities, even if these, due to the vast amount of material transmitted, cached or hosted, cannot be avoided, would provide a disincentive for investment and would probably result in expensive intermediary services, and thus limit access to these services. The EU and US legislature therefore have decided to require intermediaries to do no more than what they practically can (unlike the EU proposal, which codifies the status quo, the US Act thereby anticipates future developments).[177] Thus the public interest in cheap, efficient and widely available and accessible electronic communications channels (which is expected to foster the development of e-commerce) has prevailed over the interests of potentially aggrieved parties in holding the intermediaries accountable.

References

J. Angel (1996), 'Legal Risks of Providing Services on the Internet', (1996) 1 *Communications Law* 105.

T. Aplin (1998), 'Internet Service Provider Liability for Moral Rights Infringement in Australia', <http://wwwlaw.murdoch.edu.au/dtlj/index.html>.

J. Band (1999), 'The Digital Millenium Copyright Act: a Balanced Result', (1999) 21 *EIPR* 92.

G. Bovenzi (1996), 'Liability of System Operators on the Internet', (1996) 11 *Berkeley Technology Law Journal* 93.

174 Markesinis 1994, p. 75. See also Pichler 1998, pp. 82-85. Pichler finds that operating as a hosting service provider constitutes such danger, since it is foreseeable that unlawful activities will be conducted on the provider's installations.

175 Panethiere 1997, p. 18.

176 See *supra* Section 2.

177 See Band 1999, p. 93 (stating that not deeming a service provider responsible for what is beyond its control is one of the underlying principles of the liability regulations of the DMCA).

J.J. Brinkhof, W.J.H.T. Dupont, F.W. Grosheide, E.J.M. Jeunink, J.J.C. Kabel, A. Kamperman Sanders, R.J.Q. Klomp, B.J. Lenselink, P. Mochel and A.B.E. dos Santos Gil (1998), 'Aansprakelijkheid van tussenpersonen in het Nederlandse intellectuele eigendomsrecht', in J.M. van Buren-Dee, F.W. Grosheide *et al.* (eds.), *Tussen de polen van bescherming en vrijheid, Aspecten van aansprakelijkheid*, Antwerpen/Groningen: Intersentia 1998, pp. 205–236.

F.W. Bulst (1997), 'Hear No Evil, See No Evil, Answer for No Evil: Internet Service Providers and Intellectual Property — The New German Teleservices Act', [1997] *EIPR* (Special Report on the Internet) 32.

C.C. van Dam (1989), *Zorgvuldigheidsnorm en aansprakelijkheid*, Deventer: Kluwer 1989.

U. Decker (1998), 'Haftung für Urheberrechtsverletzungen im Internet, Anforderungen an die Kenntnis des Host Providers', (1998) 1 *Multimedia und Recht* 7.

R.W.M. Dias (ed.) (1989), *Clerk & Lindsell on Torts*, London: Sweet & Maxwell 1989.

R.W.M. Dias and B.S. Markesinis (1984), *Tort Law*, Oxford: Clarendon Press 1984.

E.J. Dommering (1998a), 'De auteursrechtelijke aansprakelijkheid van intermediairs, het Kabelarrest revisited in de tijd van Internet', in D.W.F. Verkade and D.J.G. Visser (eds.), *Intellectuele eigenaardigheden*, Deventer: Kluwer 1998, pp. 75–84.

E.J. Dommering (1998b), 'De Grondwet in de informatiemaatschappij', in M.C. Burkens *et al.* (ed.), *Gelet op de Grondwet*, Deventer: Kluwer 1998, pp. 110–123.

J.M. van Dunné (1998), 'De historische ontwikkeling van het aansprakelijkheidsrecht. De grondslagenkwestie: schuld of aansprakelijkheid', in N.F. van Manen and R.H. Stutterheim (eds.), *Wie draagt de schade?*, Nijmegen: Ars Aequi Libri 1998, pp. 23–40.

G. Dworkin and R.D. Taylor (1989), *Copyright, Designs and Patents Act 1988*, London: Blackstone 1989.

N. Elkin-Koren (1995), 'Copyright Law and Social Dialogue on the Information Superhighway: The Case against Copyright Liability of the Bulletin Board Operator', (1995) 13 *Cardozo Arts & Entertainment* 345.

S. Emanuel (1991), *Torts*, Larchmont, NY: Emanuel Law Outlines, Inc. 1991.

S. Engel-Flechsig (1999), 'The German 1997 Multimedia Act — Overview and European Dimensions', (1999) 11 *Mediaforum* 45.

S. Engel-Flechsig, F.A. Maennel and A. Tettenborn (1997), 'Das neue Informations- und Kommunikationsdienste-Gesetz', (1997) 50 *Neue Juristische Wochenschrift* 2981.

I. Englard (1992), *The Philosophy of Tort Law*, Aldershot/Brookfield USA/Hong Kong/Singapore/Sidney: Darthmouth 1992.

J.E. Fesevur (1998), 'Aansprakelijkheid wegens onrechtmatige daad vanuit een Spinozische optiek', in J.M. van Buren-Dee, F.W. Grosheide *et al.* (eds.), *Tussen de polen van bescherming en vrijheid, Aspecten van aansprakelijkheid*, Antwerpen/Groningen: Intersentia 1998, pp. 3–23.

N.P. Flechsig and D. Gabel (1998), 'Strafrechtliche Verantwortlichkeit im Netz durch Einrichten und Vorhalten von Hyperlinks', 14 (1998) *Computer und Recht* 351.

W. Foster (1997), 'Copyright: Internet Service Provider Rights and Responsibilities', <http://gbnic.gb.com.cn/internet/1997/B1/B1_2.HTM>.

S. Gerbrandy (1988), *Kort commentaar op de Auteurswet 1912*, Arnhem: Gouda Quint 1988.

D. Gervais (1998), *The TRIPS Agreement: Drafting History and Analysis*, London: Sweet & Maxwell 1998.

N.W. Guenther (1998), 'Good Samaritan to the Rescue: America Online Free from Publisher and Distributor Liability for Anonymously Posted Defamation', (1998) 20 *Communications and the Law* 35.

A.S. Hartkamp (1998), *Verbintenissenrecht Deel III, De verbintenis uit de wet*, Deventer: Tjeenk Willink 1998.

B.A. Hepple and M.H. Matthews (1985), *Tort: Cases and Materials*, London: Butterworths 1985.

P.B. Hugenholtz (1998), 'Het Internet: het auteursrecht voorbij?', (1998) 128 *Handelingen NVJ* 197.

S.C. Huisjes (1998), 'Generiek aansprakelijkheidsrecht: ondermijning van vrije telecommarkt?', [1998] *Computerrecht* 20.

Institute for Information Law (K.J. Koelman) (1997), *Liability for Online Intermediaries*, Amsterdam: Institute for Information Law 1997.

C.H.M. Jansen (1996), *Monografiën Nieuw BW, Onrechtmatige Daad: algemene bepalingen*, Deventer: Kluwer 1996.

R. Julià-Barceló (1998), 'Liability for On-line Intermediaries: A European Perspective', (1998) 20 *EIPR* 453.

F.A. Koch (1997), 'Zivilrechtliche Anbieterhaftung für Inhalte in Kommunikationsnetze', (1997) 13 *Computer und Recht* 193.

K.J. Koelman (1998), 'Wat niet weet, wat niet deert: civielrechtelijke aansprakelijkheid van de Internet provider', (1998) 10 *Mediaforum* 204.

Ch. Koenig (1998), 'Regulierungsoptionen für die neuen Medien in Deutschland', [1998] *Beilage zu Multimedia und Recht* 12.

M. Lemley and E. Volokh (1998), 'Freedom of Speech and Injunctions in Intellectual Property Cases', <http://www.law.ucla.edu/faculty/volokh/copyinj.htm>.

B.S. Markesinis (1986), *A Comparative Analysis of the German Law of Tort*, Oxford: Clarendon Press 1986.

B.S. Markesinis (1994), *The German Law of Torts, a Comparative Introduction*, Oxford: Clarendon Press 1994.

J.R. McDaniel (1992), 'Electronic Torts and Videotex — At the Junction of Commerce and Communication', (1992) 18 *Rutgers Computer & Technology Law Journal* 773.

J. van der Meent (1997), 'Wettelijke limitering van aansprakelijkheid in de telecommunicatie-wereld?', [1998] *Computerrecht* 223.

M.B. Nimmer and D. Nimmer, *Nimmer on Copyright*, New York/San Francisco: Mathew Bender & Co, loose leaf.

C.J.C. van Nispen (1978), *Het rechterlijk verbod en bevel*, Deventer: Kluwer 1978.

W. Nordemann, K. Vinck and P.W. Hertin (1994), *Urheberrecht, Kommentar zum Urheberrechtsgesetz und zum Urheberrechtswahrnemungsgesetz*, Stuttgart/Berlin/Koln: Verlag W. Kohlhammer 1994.

D. Panethiere (1997), 'The Basis for Copyright Infringement Liability: The Law in Common Law Jurisdictions', [1997] *EIPR* (Special Report on the Internet) 13.

H.H. Perritt Jr. (1992), 'Tort Liability, The First Amendment, and Equal Access to Electronic Networks', (1992) 5 *Harvard Journal of Law & Technology* 65.

R. Pichler (1998), 'Haftung des Host Providers für Persönlichkeitsrechtsverletzungen vor und nach dem TDG', (1998) 1 *Multimedia und Recht* 79.

A.A. Quaedvlieg (1998), annotation with, *inter alia*, Court of Appeals Den Bosch 20.9.96, (1998) 22 *Informatierecht/AMI* 159.

W.V.H. Rogers (1989), *Winfield and Jolowicz on Tort*, London: Sweet & Maxwell 1989.

Th.A. de Roos (1998), 'Het concept voorstel computercriminaliteit II', [1998] *Computerrecht* 55.

M. Rütter (1992), 'Inhaltscontrolle und Inhaltsverantwortlichkeit bei Telekommunicationsdiensten aus der sicht der Deutschen Bundespost Telekom', [1992] *jur-pc* 1812.

G.A.I. Schuijt (1987), *Werkers van het woord, Media en arbeidsverhoudingen in de journalistiek*, Deventer: Kluwer 1987.

G.A.I. Schuijt (1998), 'Wet computercriminaliteit II: van uitgever en drukker naar tussenpersoon', (1998) 10 *Mediaforum* 70.

U. Sieber (1997a), 'Kontrollmöglichkeiten zur Verhinderung rechtswidriger Inhalte in Computernetzen (I)', (1997) 13 *Computer und Recht* 581.

U. Sieber (1997b), 'Kontrollmöglichkeiten zur Verhinderung rechtswidriger Inhalte in Computernetzen (II)', (1997) 13 *Computer und Recht* 653.

J.H. Spoor and D.W.F. Verkade (1993), *Auteursrecht*, Deventer: Kluwer 1993.

A. Waldenberger (1998), 'Der juristische Dauerbrenner: Haftung für Hyperlinks im Internet – ein Fall des LG Hamburg, (1998) 29 *AfP* 373.

H. Willekens (1998), 'Risico, aansprakelijkheid en de destructieve scheppingskracht van de markt', in N.F. van Manen and R.H. Stutterheim (eds.), *Wie draagt de schade?*, Nijmegen: Ars Aequi Libri 1998, pp. 65–80.

K. Zscherpe (1998), 'Urheberrechtsschutz digitalisierter Werke im Internet', (1998) 1 *Multimedia und Recht* 404.

II. Privacy, Data Protection and Copyright: Their Interaction in the Context of Electronic Copyright Management Systems

Lee A. Bygrave and Kamiel J. Koelman

1. Introduction

1.1 THE CENTRAL ISSUE

This chapter investigates the way in which legal rules for the protection of privacy and of related interests can impinge upon the design and operation of an electronic copyright management system (ECMS). Much of the discussion in the chapter, however, is also relevant for Internet-based systems of electronic commerce generally. The chapter does not canvass all rules for privacy protection; rather, it focuses upon rules that specifically regulate various stages in the processing (i.e. collection, registration, storage, use and/or dissemination) of personal data in order to safeguard the privacy of the data subjects (i.e. the persons to whom the data relate). By 'personal data' is meant data that relate to, and permit identification of, an individual person. The main body of these legal rules is found in legislation that commonly goes under the nomenclature of data protection, at least in European jurisdictions. Accordingly, it is with the application of data protection legislation to ECMS operations that this chapter is mainly (though not exclusively) concerned.

This chapter is divided into two main parts, along with the Introduction and Conclusion. In brief, the first part, written by Lee Bygrave, analyses the way in which the basic principles of privacy and data protection laws may apply to ECMS operations (Sections 2 and 3); in a separate section (Section 4) so-called privacy-enhancing technologies are discussed . The second part of the chapter, written by Kamiel Koelman, analyses the various legal and technological balances that have been struck between the privacy interests of consumers and the interests of copyright-holders, and considers the impact that an ECMS might have on these balances (Section 5).

Copyright and Electronic Commerce (ed. P. Bernt Hugenholtz; ISBN 90-411-9785-0; © Kluwer Law International, 2000; printed in Great Britain).

It is important to note at the outset that this chapter does not attempt to grapple with issues of jurisdiction and choice-of-law. Neither does it consider in detail problems related to the enforceability of legal rules on privacy and data protection.

1.2 BACKGROUND TO THE ISSUE

1.2.1 The nature of ECMS operations

Recent years have seen a marked growth in interest and opportunities for electronic commerce via distributed computer networks. The development of workable electronic copyright management systems is one part of this process. In a nutshell, these systems create a technological and organisational infrastructure that allows the creator of an original information product to enforce their copyright in the product when it is accessed online by other parties. An ECMS is usually predicated on the assumption that the process by which other parties acquire use of the copyrighted product is along the lines of a commercial contractual transaction; i.e. these parties purchase from the creator, via intermediaries, an online disseminated copy of, and/or certain usage rights with respect to, the product.

As intimated above, an ECMS typically involves the presence and interaction of one or more parties in addition to the creator, copyright-holder and purchaser. For example, the IMPRIMATUR WP4 Business Model (Version 2.0)[1] involves the actors and inter-relationships shown in Figure II.1.

In brief, the role of the *creation provider* is analogous to that of a publisher; i.e. he/she/it packages the original work into a marketable product. The role of the *media distributor* is that of a retailer; i.e. he vends various kinds of rights with respect to usage of the product. The role of the *unique number issuer* is analogous to the role of the issuer of ISBN codes; i.e. it provides the creation provider with a unique number to insert in the product as microcode so that the product and its rights-holders can be subsequently identified for the purposes of royalty payments.[2] The role of the *IPR database provider* is to store basic data on the legal status of the products marketed by the media distributor. These data concern the identity of each product and its current rights-holder. The main purpose of the database is to provide verification of a product's legal status to potential purchasers of a right with respect to usage of the

---

1 'IMPRIMATUR' stands for Intellectual Multimedia Property Rights Model and Terminology for Universal Reference. IMPRIMATUR is a project established by the Commission of the European Communities and co-ordinated by the UK Authors' Licensing and Collecting Society (ALCS). Version 2.0 of the IMPRIMATUR Business Model is available at <http://www.imprimatur.net/download.htm.>

2 It is envisaged that this number will be in the form of an International Standard Work Code (ISWC), which, in turn, may be inserted in a Digital Object Identifier (DOI).

product. As such, the IPR database is somewhat similar in content and function to a land title register. The role of the *monitoring service provider* is to monitor, on behalf of creators/copyright-holders, what purchasers acquire from media distributors. Finally, the *certification authority* is intended to assure any party to an ECMS operation of the authenticity of the other parties with whom he deals. Thus, the certification authority fulfils the role of trusted third party.

Figure II.1: IMPRIMATUR WP4 Business Model (Version 2.0)

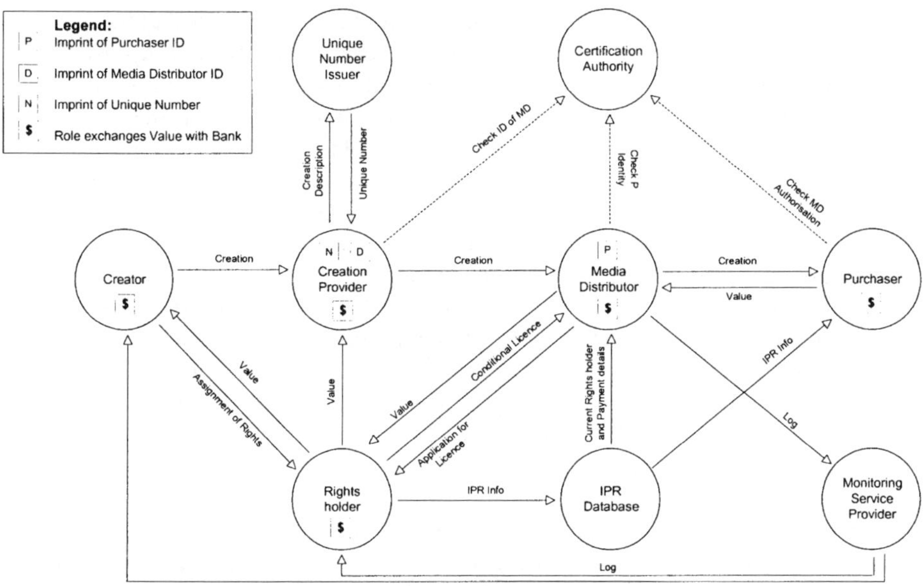

It is important to note that most electronic copyright management systems are still in the process of being designed. Accordingly, there is some uncertainty about the parameters of their operation when they are finally put into practice on a widespread basis. More specifically, there is some uncertainty about the exact functions and inter-relationships of some of the above-described actors. It is quite possible, for instance, that the functions of some of these actors could be taken over by just one actor (e.g. a creation provider could act as media distributor or monitoring service provider). Secondly, there is some uncertainty about the degree to which an ECMS will be 'fenced off' from other information systems. A pertinent question in this respect is to what extent and under what conditions data held within an ECMS will be accessible by external actors. Thirdly, the precise nature of the payment mechanisms to be employed in ECMS operations remains to be finalised. Fourthly, uncertainty exists over the amount and content of data that the various actors within an ECMS will register and further process.

It can be safely assumed, though, that at least some of the data processed by an ECMS will be person-related. One category of such data is the unique number (ISWC or the like), which enables identification of an information product's creator, author, editor, etc. This category of data will flow through most points of an ECMS. A second category of personal data is data relating to purchasers. These data will be primarily registered by media distributors and stored in their sales logs. There is another category of personal data which might be registered: these are data relating to browsers (i.e. persons who inspect or sample an information product without purchasing a particular right with respect to it). Like purchaser-related data, these data will be primarily registered and stored, if at all, by media distributors.

Of the above three categories of personal data, the first-mentioned raises few privacy problems for the data subjects, relative to the other two data categories. The creator, author, editor, etc. of copyrighted material must expect that this material, and their involvement with it, will receive considerable publicity. The same cannot be said for the purchaser and browser, however. Accordingly, this chapter focuses on the privacy rights of the latter two actors. It is important to note, though, that the first-mentioned category of data may still qualify for protection under some data protection laws and other legal rules on privacy.[3]

The amount and content of purchaser- and browser-related data which are registered in an ECMS, together with the manner in which these data are used and disseminated, will depend on a range of factors. One set of factors are legal. For example, data protection laws (as shown further below) set limits on the extent to which personal data may be registered and further processed.

Another set of factors are economic. For example, a media distributor might desire to register as much purchaser- and browser-related data as possible, in order to create detailed customer profiles that can be subsequently used (by the media distributor itself or by others) for cross-selling and other marketing purposes. Concomitantly, the media distributor could make purchases and browsing contingent upon the purchaser and browser disclosing a great detail of information about themselves. On the other hand, a media distributor might want to reduce its registration and usage of purchaser- and browser-related data in order to attract the custom of those who are seriously concerned about possible infringements of their privacy.

A third set of factors are technical-organisational. For instance, an entity operating as media distributor might sell a multiplicity of goods and services (e.g. food products, travel tickets, etc.) in addition to usage rights to copyrighted information. If a purchaser or browser has contact with the media distributor also in respect of these other goods and services, the media distributor will end up having

3 However, some such laws have exempted this sort of data from their protection: see e.g. Art. 2(1)(c) of the Netherlands' 1988 Act on Protection of Privacy in Connection with Personal Data Files; Art. 3(2)(3) of the Belgian 1992 Act on Protection of Personal Privacy in Relation to the Processing of Personal Data.

a great deal of information about the purchaser or browser's personal preferences. Concomitantly, a one-off sales transaction or 'shop visit' is likely to involve registration of fewer data on the purchaser or browser than in the case of frequent or regular transactions pursuant to some form of service subscription. To take another example, the amount of browser-related data which are registered by a media distributor will depend on, *inter alia*, the extent to which the latter's server utilises mechanisms for automatically registering such data (e.g. as 'cookies').[4]

This third set of factors, however, will tend to be ultimately derivate of the first two sets (i.e. legal and economic factors), with one *current* exception: at present, it is usually not possible to visit an Internet server without the browser software automatically revealing certain data to the server. These data are typically the network identity (hostname and IP address) of the browser's machine, the URL of the last page visited by the browser before coming to the present server, and whatever cookies are stored on the browser's computer.[5] Whether or not such data can be said to be 'personal' pursuant to data protection laws is an issue dealt with in Section 2.1 below.

At the same time, sight should not be lost of the fact that services are springing up which allow for the use of anonymising servers as intermediaries for browsing and/or purchasing transactions on the Internet.[6] Nevertheless, such servers will usually not guarantee full transactional anonymity as they will also record certain details about a browser's/purchaser's Internet activities — details which could be accessed by others under exceptional circumstances.[7] It is also an open question as to whether or not a media distributor in an ECMS would be willing to allow use of anonymising servers by purchasers or browsers.

In any case, anonymising servers highlight the fact that there are a number of technical and organisational tools being developed in order to safeguard the privacy and related interests of persons using the Internet. These tools often go under the nomenclature of 'privacy-enhancing technologies' or 'PETs'. The application of such tools to ECMS operations is an issue that will be addressed in Section 4 below.

1.2.2 Affected interests of the data subject

The registration and/or further processing of purchaser- and browser-related data in an ECMS may impinge on a multiplicity of interests of the data subjects. The most important of these interests for the purposes of this chapter may be summed up in

4 In brief, 'cookies' are transactional data about a browser's Internet activity which are automatically stored by an Internet server on the browser's computer. See further Mayer-Schönberger 1998.

5 Greenleaf 1996a, pp. 91–92.

6 See e.g. <http://www.anonymizer.com/faq.html>.

7 *Ibid.*

terms of privacy, autonomy and integrity. Each of these concepts are nebulous and often used in haphazard fashion.

For present purposes, the concept of privacy denotes a state of limited accessibility consisting of three elements: secrecy: 'the extent to which we are known to others'; solitude: 'the extent to which others have physical access to us'; and anonymity: 'the extent to which we are the subject of others' attention'.[8] It should be emphasised that privacy here is not delimited to apply only to those aspects of persons' lives that are considered as sensitive or intimate.

The concept of autonomy denotes self-determination; i.e. a person's capacity to live his life in accordance with his own wishes (including, of course, the capacity to use goods as he sees fit). In the context of this chapter, it is a person's self-determination on the informational plane that is of main importance. Many scholars (e.g. Westin 1967; Miller 1971) define privacy in terms of a person's ability to control the flow of information about himself to others; in this chapter, such informational self-determination is viewed as a precondition for, and result of, privacy (i.e. limited accessibility).

As for the concept of integrity, this is used here to denote 'a person's state of intact, harmonious functionality based on other persons' respect for him'.[9] A breach of integrity will therefore involve disruption of this functionality by the disrespectful behaviour of other persons.

In the context of an ECMS, a purchaser and browser's privacy will be diminished by the mere registration by a media distributor of data that can be linked back to them. Their autonomy will also be diminished insofar as the registration occurs without their consent or knowledge, or insofar as the registration causes them to behave along lines determined primarily by the media distributor or another ECMS actor. And their integrity will be detrimentally affected insofar as the registration or subsequent use of the data does not conform with their expectations of what is reasonable. For example, many persons are likely to view the non-consensual or surreptitious processing of data on them by others as integrity-abusive.

The mere registration of data will not be the only activity that can diminish the privacy, autonomy and/or integrity of data subjects. Other stages in the data-processing cycle will potentially affect these interests as well. Especially problematic will be the use, re-use and/or dissemination of data for secondary purposes; i.e. purposes that vary from the purposes for which the data were originally collected. A typical example here is when personal data originally registered in order to ensure non-repudiation of a particular transaction are subsequently used for the purposes of cross-selling or other marketing of products *vis-à-vis* the data subjects. Such 're-purposing' of data will be particularly problematic if it occurs without the data

8 Gavison 1980, pp. 428–436.
9 Bygrave 1999, p. 45.

subjects' prior consent or if it falls outside the data subjects' reasonable expectations. It will also be problematic, not just for the data subjects but also the data user, if it involves the application of data for purposes for which the data are not suited.

The latter point highlights the fact that safeguarding the privacy, autonomy and integrity interests of data subjects will not always conflict with the interests of data users. Moreover, people's readiness to enter into electronic commerce as consumers (or 'prosumers') will be largely contingent upon the degree to which they feel confident that their privacy, autonomy and integrity interests will be respected by the other actors in the market.[10] Indeed, an increasingly major task of data protection laws and related measures is precisely that of building up such confidence.[11]

Arguably, the most important point that should be emphasised here is that the development of electronic copyright management systems has the *potential* to impinge on the privacy, autonomy and integrity interests of information consumers to an unprecedented degree. In other words, such systems could facilitate the monitoring of what people privately read, listen to, or view, in a manner that is both more fine-grained and automated than previously practised. This surveillance potential may not only weaken the privacy of information consumers but also function as a form of thought control, weighing down citizens with "the subtle, imponderable pressures of the orthodox",[12] and thereby inhibiting the expression of non-conformist opinions and preferences. In short, an ECMS could function as a kind of digital Panopticon. The attendant, long-term implications of this for the vitality of a pluralist, democratic society are obvious.

1.2.3 The nature of data protection laws

Data protection laws emerged in the 1970s in response to a congeries of public fears about the potentially privacy-invasive consequences of computer technology. Well over 20 countries have now enacted such laws. Most of these countries are European. Important countries outside Europe (notably, the United States, Canada, Japan, Australia and New Zealand) also have data protection legislation

---

10 Samarajiva 1997, p. 282 ff.

11 See e.g. Industry Canada and Justice Canada, Task Force on Electronic Commerce, *The Protection of Personal Information: Building Canada's Information Economy and Society*, Ottawa: Industry Canada/ Justice Canada 1998, p. 6 ("In an environment where over half of Canadians agree that the information highway is reducing the level of privacy in Canada, ensuring consumer confidence is key to securing growth in the Canadian information economy. Legislation that establishes a set of common rules for the protection of personal information will help to build consumer confidence"); also available at <http://strategis.ic.gc.ca/privacy>.

12 The phrase is taken from the concurring opinion of Justice Douglas in *U.S. v. Rumely*, 345 U.S. 41 (1953), p. 58.

in place, though this is often less comprehensive and stringent than the European legislation.[13] In addition to national data protection laws, a range of data protection instruments have been adopted at an international level. The most influential of these have been worked out under the auspices of the European Union (EU), Council of Europe (CoE) and Organisation for Economic Co-operation and Development (OECD). These instruments are:

1. the European Community (EC) Directive on the Protection of Individuals with Regard to the Processing of Personal Data and on the Free Movement of Such Data,[14] adopted by the European Parliament and the Council on 24 October 1995;
2. the Council of Europe Convention for the Protection of Individuals with regard to Automatic Processing of Personal Data,[15] adopted by the CoE Committee of Ministers on 28 January 1981; and
3. the OECD Guidelines Governing the Protection of Privacy and Transborder Flows of Personal Data,[16] adopted by the OECD Council on 23 September 1980.

The United Nations has also issued Guidelines Concerning Computerized Personal Data Files,[17] adopted by the UN General Assembly on 4 December 1990. These guidelines, however, have received relatively little attention.

Each of the above international instruments are of general ambit. They have been supplemented by a range of instruments dealing with aspects of data processing within specified sectors. Some of these sectoral instruments have been drafted and adopted by the CoE as recommendations. Of particular relevance for this chapter are: Recommendation No. R(85) 20 on the protection of personal data used for the purposes of direct marketing, adopted on 25 October 1985; Recommendation No. R(90) 19 on the protection of personal data used for payment and other related operations, adopted on 13 September 1990; and Recommendation No. R(95) 4 on the protection of personal data in the area of telecommunications services, with particular reference to telephone services, adopted on 7 February 1995. Another sectoral instrument of particular relevance for this chapter is the EC Directive on the processing of personal data and the protection of privacy in the telecommunications sector.[18] Also of relevance are

13 See *infra* for examples.
14 Council Directive 95/46/EC, OJ L 281/31 ('EC Data Protection Directive' or DPD).
15 E.T.S. No. 108 ('CoE Data Protection Convention'). The Convention entered into force on 1 October 1985.
16 Guidelines Governing the Protection of Privacy and Transborder Flows of Personal Data (Paris: OECD, 1980).
17 Guidelines Concerning Computerized Personal Data Files (Doc E/CN.4/1990/72, 20 February 1990).
18 Directive 97/66/EC, OJ L 024/1 ('EC Telecommunications Privacy Directive' or TPD).

various sets of guidelines dealing specifically with the processing of personal information over the Internet.[19]

At a national level, special mention must be made of Germany's Teleservices Data Protection Act of 1997.[20] This is, to our knowledge, the first law to deal specifically with data protection issues in an Internet context. It can be expected to exert considerable influence on other countries' legislative activity in the field.

The central rules of data protection laws are built up around the following set of principles:

1. personal data should be gathered by fair and lawful means (the 'fair collection principle');
2. the amount of personal data gathered should be limited to what is necessary to achieve the purpose(s) of gathering the data (the 'minimality principle');
3. personal data should be gathered for specified and lawful purposes and not processed in ways that are incompatible with those purposes (the 'purpose specification principle');
4. use of personal data for purposes other than those specified should occur only with the consent of the data subject or with legal authority (the 'use limitation principle');
5. personal data should be accurate, complete and relevant in relation to the purposes for which they are processed (the 'data quality principle');
6. security measures should be implemented to protect personal data from unintended or unauthorised disclosure, destruction or modification (the 'security principle');
7. data subjects should be informed of, and given access to, data on them held by others, and be able to rectify these data if inaccurate or misleading (the 'individual participation principle').
8. parties responsible for processing data on other persons should be accountable for complying with the above principles (the 'accountability principle').

These are not the only principles manifest in data protection laws but they are the main ones. Another principle is worth noting too; this is that fully automated

19 See especially Working Party on the Protection of Individuals with Regard to the Processing of Personal Data, *Anonymity on the Internet*, Recommendation 3/97 adopted on 3 December 1997, available at <http://europa.eu.int/comm/dg15/en/media/dataprot/wpdocs/wp6en.htm ('Data Protection Working Party 1997'); and Information Infrastructure Task Force, Privacy Working Group, *Principles for Providing and Using Personal Information*, adopted on 6 June 1995, available at <gopher://ntiant1.ntia.doc.gov:70/h0/papers/documents/files/niiprivrin_final.html> ('Information Infrastructure Task Force 1995').

20 In force as of 1 August 1997. The Act was passed as part of a federal legislative package 'to Regulate the Conditions for Information and Communications Services'. An English translation of the entire legislative package is available at <http://www.iid.de/iukdg/iukdge.html>. For the German version, see <http://www.iid.de/rahmen/iukdgk.html>.

evaluations of a person's character should not be used to reach decisions that significantly impinge upon the person's interests. This principle is not yet manifest in the majority of data protection laws but will gain more prominence on account of it being embodied in Article 15 of the EC Data Protection Directive.[21]

While data protection laws enjoy common ground in terms of most of the above principles, they presently differ in terms of their ambit. Some countries' laws only apply to data processing by public sector bodies,[22] while most other countries' laws, and all of the international data protection laws, apply also to data processing by private sector bodies. Some countries' laws only apply to computerised/automated processing of data,[23] while most other countries' laws apply also to non-automated processing. Some countries' laws give express protection for data relating to legal/juridical persons (i.e. corporations and the like),[24] in addition to data relating to individual natural/physical persons, while most other countries' laws expressly protect only the latter data.

Differences occur also with respect to the regulatory regimes established pursuant to each law. For instance, while most countries' laws provide for the establishment of a special independent agency (the 'data protection authority') to oversee the laws' implementation, this is not the case with respect to the laws of the United States and Japan. To take another example, while most countries' laws contain express restrictions on the flow of personal data to other countries that lack adequate data protection safeguards, some countries' laws do not.[25] To take a third example, while some countries' laws do not allow certain data-processing operations to commence without the operations first being checked and licensed by the relevant data protection authority,[26] other countries' laws permit all or most operations to commence simply on the data protection authority first being notified of the operations.[27]

In this chapter, the main point of departure for legal analysis will be the international instruments on data protection set out above, in particular the EC Data Protection Directive. The latter instrument is likely to exercise the greatest influence on new data protection initiatives, both in and outside the EU. Member

---

21 The principle has its legal origins in Art. 2 of France's 1978 Act on Data Processing, Data Files and Individual Liberties. Article 15 of the Directive is presented *infra* in Section 2.5.2.

22 See e.g. the US federal Privacy Act 1974, Canada's federal Privacy Act 1982 and Australia's federal Privacy Act 1988.

23 See e.g. Sweden's Data Act of 1973 and the UK's Data Protection Act 1984.

24 See Norway's Personal Data Registers Act of 1978, Iceland's 1989 Act on the Registration and Handling of Personal Data, Austria's Data Protection Act of 1978, Luxembourg's Nominal Data (Automatic Processing) Act of 1979, Switzerland's Federal Data Protection Act of 1988, Italy's 1996 Act on the Protection of Individuals and Other Subjects with regard to the Processing of Personal Data, and Denmark's Private Registers Act of 1978.

25 See e.g. the US federal Privacy Act 1974 and Australia's federal Privacy Act 1988.

26 See e.g. Norway's Personal Data Registers Act of 1978 and Sweden's Data Act of 1973.

27 See e.g. Italy's 1996 Act on the protection of individuals and other subjects with regard to the processing of personal data.

States of the EU have been given, with a few exceptions, until 24 October 1998 to bring their respective legal systems into conformity with the provisions of the Directive (see Article 32(1) of the latter). If — as is likely — the Directive is incorporated into the 1992 Agreement on the European Economic Area (EEA), then countries that are not members of the EU but party to the EEA Agreement (i.e. Norway, Iceland and Liechtenstein) will also become legally bound to bring their respective laws into conformity with the Directive. In addition, the Directive is likely to exercise some political and legal influence over other countries outside the EU, not least because the Directive, with some exceptions, prohibits the transfer of personal data to these countries if they do not provide 'adequate' levels of data protection (see Article 25(1), discussed below in Section 2.8).

1.2.4 Other important legal provisions

The formal normative roots of data protection laws lie mainly in the right to privacy set down in international catalogues of fundamental human rights, particularly Article 17 of the 1966 International Covenant on Civil and Political Rights (ICCPR) and Article 8 of the 1950 European Convention for the Protection of Human Rights and Fundamental Freedoms (ECHR). Indeed, this is expressly recognised in many of the data protection instruments themselves.[28]

Article 17 of the ICCPR provides:

> "1. No one shall be subjected to arbitrary or unlawful interference with his privacy, family, home or correspondence, nor to unlawful attacks upon his honour and reputation.
> 2. Everyone has the right to the protection of the law against such interference or attacks".

Article 8 of the ECHR provides:

> "1. Everyone has the right to respect for his private and family life, his home and correspondence.
> 2. There shall be no interference by a public authority with the exercise of this right except such as is in accordance with the law and is necessary in a democratic society in the interests of national security, public safety or the economic well-being of the country, for the prevention of disorder or crime, for the protection of health or morals, or for the protection of the rights and freedoms of others".

---

28 See e.g. Art. 1 and Recital 10 of the EC Data Protection Directive and Art. 1 of the CoE Data Protection Convention.

Both provisions have been interpreted as capable of addressing data protection issues.[29] In prescriptory terms, however, the case law developed pursuant to these provisions adds nothing, so far, to what is found in ordinary data protection instruments. In other words, while these provisions operate, to some extent, as data protection instruments in their own right, they give little guidance on the legal requirements for processing personal data.

The most extensive relevant case law has been developed by the European Court of Human Rights pursuant to Article 8 of the ECHR, but even this case law is fairly meagre, particularly with respect to the data-processing practices of private sector bodies. Indeed, the Court has yet to have treated a case pursuant to Article 8 which involves the latter data-processing practices. Nevertheless, it is highly unlikely that such practices will be held as falling outside the protective scope of Article 8, given that CoE Member States, both nationally and internationally,[30] apply data protection rules to both the private and public sectors. It is also important to note that Article 17 of the ICCPR has been interpreted by the UN Human Rights Committee as requiring implementation of basic data protection guarantees in both sectors.[31] Thus, the processing of purchaser/browser-related data in the context of ECMS operations has the potential to impinge on purchasers'/browsers' rights laid down in Article 8 of the ECHR and Article 17 of the ICCPR — in addition to impinging on their rights set down in laws dealing specifically with data protection. A short analysis of the way in which Article 8 case law might apply to ECMS operations is given in Section 3 below.

It should also be noted that the constitutions of many countries contain provisions that require, expressly or implicitly, implementation of basic data protection principles. Arguably the most solid constitutional underpinning for data protection in a European country is provided by the Federal Republic of Germany's Basic Law (*Grundgesetz*) of 1949. The Basic Law contains several provisions which have been held to relate to data protection. Article 1(1) provides that "[t]he dignity of man shall be inviolable", while Article 2(1) states that "[e]veryone shall have the right to the free development of his personality in so far as he does not violate the rights of others or offend against the constitutional order or against morality". Article 10 states that "[p]rivacy of letters, posts and telecommunications shall be inviolable", and Article 13 upholds the inviolability of the home. In a famous and influential decision of 15 December 1983, the German Federal Constitutional Court (*Bundesverfassungsgericht*) held that Articles 1 and 2 of the Basic Law provide individuals with a right to 'informational self-determination' (*informationelle Selbstbestimmung*); i.e. a right for the individual "to decide for him/herself ... when and within what limits facts about his/her personal life shall be publicly

29 For a comprehensive analysis, see Bygrave 1998.

30 See e.g. the CoE Data Protection Convention.

31 See the Committee's General Comment 16, issued on 23 March 1988 (UN Doc A/43/40, pp. 181–183).

disclosed".[32] The Court went on to hold that this right will be infringed if personal data are not processed in accordance with basic data protection principles, including that of purpose specification (*Zweckbindung*).

2. Application of Data Protection Laws to ECMS Operations

In the following, we do not address the totality of ways in which data protection laws can be expected to apply to ECMS operations; rather, we focus on what we consider to be the most important points of application. These points concern the scope of the concept of 'personal data' in data protection laws (Section 2.1), who is primarily responsible for complying with these laws' obligations (Section 2.2), and the basic conditions these laws set down for the processing of personal data (Sections 2.3 to 2.9).

2.1 PERSONAL DATA

As intimated above, the ambit of data protection laws is restricted to situations in which *personal* data are processed. In other words, the design and operation of an ECMS may be affected by data protection laws only insofar as the ECMS processes such data. The concept of personal data is usually defined by the laws in a broad and flexible manner. For instance, Article 2(a) of the EC Data Protection Directive (DPD) defines 'personal data' as:

> "any information relating to an identified or identifiable natural person ("data subject"); an identifiable person is one who can be identified, directly or indirectly, in particular by reference to an identification number or to one or more factors specific to his physical, physiological, mental, economic, cultural or social identity".[33]

Domestic data protection laws contain broadly similar definitions of 'personal data' or 'personal information'. The focus of these definitions on the criterion of direct or indirect identifiability (i.e. on the potential of information to enable identification of a person) makes them capable in theory of embracing a great deal of data that *prima facie* have little direct relationship to a particular person. Thus, data may be

32 *Volkszählungsgesetz,* German Federal Constitutional Court, BverfGE 1983/65: 1, pp. 42–43.

33 Recital 14 in the Directive's preamble makes clear that this definition also encompasses sound and image data on natural persons.

'personal' even if they allow a person to be identified only in combination with other (auxiliary) data.[34]

At the same time, though, certain limitations are usually read into the identifiability criterion such that identification must be possible using methods that do not involve an unreasonably large amount of time, expense and labour. Paragraph 28 of the Explanatory Report for the CoE Data Protection Convention states that an 'identifiable person' is one "who can be *easily* identified: it does not cover identification of persons by means of *very sophisticated* methods" (emphasis added). Subsequent elaborations of the identifiability criterion in relation to the CoE's various sectoral recommendations on data protection introduce the factors of reasonableness, time, cost and resources. For example, para. 1.2 of Recommendation No. R(85) 20 on the protection of personal data used for the purposes of direct marketing, states, *inter alia*, that "[a]n individual shall not be regarded as 'identifiable' if the identification requires an unreasonable amount of time, cost and manpower". Some national laws which expressly qualify degree of identifiability employ similar criteria.[35] In the most recent CoE recommendations, explicit reference to the cost factor is omitted.[36] As for the EC Data Protection Directive, Recital 26 in the Directive's preamble lays down what appears to be a broader and more flexible criterion for identifiability: "to determine whether a person is identifiable, account should be taken of all the means likely reasonably to be used either by the controller or by any other person to identify the said person". Nevertheless, the Directive's criterion is probably similar in effect to the criteria laid down in the more recent CoE instruments.

Usually, data must be capable of being linked to a *particular individual* person before they are to be regarded as 'personal' pursuant to data protection laws. Thus, data which can only be linked to an aggregate of persons will normally fall outside the ambit of such laws. Some countries, though, have data protection legislation that expressly covers data on collective entities such as corporations, partnerships

34 See e.g. Commission of the European Communities, Amended Proposal for a Council Directive on the protection of individuals with regard to the processing of personal data and on the free movement of such data, COM (92) 422 final, ('EC Commission 1992') at p. 9 ("A person may be identified directly by name or indirectly by a telephone number, a car registration number, a social security number, a passport number or by a combination of significant criteria which allows him to be recognized by narrowing down the group to which he belongs (age, occupation, place of residence, etc.)").

35 For instance, a criterion of proportionality is read in to the identification process envisaged by Art. 3(1) of the FRG's Federal Data Protection Act of 1990 so as to exclude cases where identification is only possible through a data controller making an effort that is 'disproportionate' in relation to his 'normal' means and activities. This criterion of proportionality is derived from Art. 3(7) of the Act which defines 'depersonalized data' as information which "can no longer be attributed to [an identified or identifiable natural person] or only with a disproportionately great expenditure of time, money and labour".

36 See e.g. para. 1 of Recommendation No. R(97) 5 on the protection of medical data, adopted 13 February 1997.

and citizen initiative groups.[37] Nevertheless, such data are only covered if they can be linked back to one particular entity as opposed to a multiplicity of entities.

From the above, it can be seen that the legal threshold for what amounts to personal data is low. It is likely, therefore, that an ECMS will involve the processing of personal data, including data that can be linked to specific purchasers and browsers. However, exactly which types of data will be regarded as 'personal' is a question of fact that is impossible to answer conclusively at present. Of greatest interest in this regard is the extent to which e-mail addresses and/or machine addresses (i.e. IP numbers and domain names) can properly be said to amount to personal data. The answer to this issue will depend on the ease/probability of linking such addresses to a specific person. If, for instance, there is a readily accessible directory listing one particular person against one particular address, the latter is likely to be seen as personal data.[38] This will not be the case, however, if a multiplicity of persons are registered against that address. At the same time, though, the possibility of a multiplicity of persons sharing a machine with an address registered in the name of only one person will usually not disqualify that machine address from being treated as personal data. Many numbers (e.g. car registration and telephone numbers) which are formally registered against the name of one specific person are commonly treated as personal data even if the objects to which they directly attach are occasionally or regularly used by other persons.[39]

2.2 DATA CONTROLLERS AND DATA PROCESSORS

Primary responsibility for observing the rules laid down in data protection laws is given to those actors that control the means and purposes of the processing of data on other persons. In the nomenclature of the Data Protection Directive, such actors are termed 'controllers' (also called 'data controllers'). Article 2(d) of the Directive defines a 'controller' as the 'natural or legal person, public authority, agency or any other body which alone or jointly with others determines the purposes and means of the processing of personal data'.

Four points should be noted with respect to this definition. First, it envisages the possibility of there being more than one controller per data-processing operation (i.e. control can be shared). Secondly, a controller need not be in possession of the personal data concerned.[40] Thirdly, who is controller can change

37 See e.g. Art. 3(2) of Austria's Data Protection Act of 1978 and Art. 1(2)(c) of Italy's 1996 Act on the protection of individuals and other subjects with regard to the processing of personal data. Note that the EC Directive does not address the issue of whether or not data on collective entities are to be protected; hence, each EU Member State is able to arrive at its own decision on the appropriateness of such protection.

38 See also Greenleaf 1996b, pp. 114–115.

39 See e.g. the comments of the EC Commission, cited *supra* n. 36.

40 See also Terwangne and Louveaux 1997, p. 236 ("There is no requirement that the controller be in actual possession of the data; it is the concept of control that is important").

from one data-processing operation to another, even within one information system. Fourthly, what is decisive for determining who is controller is not the formal allocation of control responsibilities as set down in, say, contractual provisions, but the *factual* exercise of control. Thus, if a legal provision allocates control responsibilities to one party but the control is actually exercised by another party, it is the latter who must be regarded as the controller for the purposes of the Data Protection Directive.

In the context of an electronic communications network, Recital 47 in the preamble to the Data Protection Directive indicates that, for the purposes of the Directive, the person or organisation providing the transmission services is normally not to be regarded as the controller of personal data contained in a transmitted message. The controller will instead be the person or organisation 'from whom the message originates'. However, transmission service providers 'will normally be considered controllers in respect of the processing of the additional personal data necessary for the service'.

A controller is to be distinguished from what the Data Protection Directive terms a 'processor'. The latter is defined in Article 2(e) of the Directive as a person or organisation engaged in processing personal data 'on behalf of' a data controller. Under the Directive, controllers must ensure, through appropriate contractual or other arrangements, that processors carry out their tasks in accordance with the laws that are enacted pursuant to the Directive. Liability for a processor's non-compliance with these laws is put on the shoulders of the controllers. Accordingly, for the purposes of ECMS operations, it is more crucial to determine which actors are controllers than determining which actors are processors.

As noted in the Introduction, uncertainty still reigns over the exact powers and functions of each of the actors in an ECMS. A pertinent question here concerns which actors are to be regarded as controllers with respect to registration and other processing of purchaser-related data. Several possibilities exist. For instance, it could be that the creation provider and/or copyright-holder solely determine(s) the means and purposes of the registration of all (or some) of these data, with the media distributor and monitoring service provider acting simply as processors in this regard. Alternatively, either one of the latter actors will also be a controller with respect to those data if he co-determines the means and purposes of the data processing. As noted above, what will be decisive for determining who is controller with respect to a given data-processing operation is not the formal allocation of control responsibilities pursuant to contract, but the *factual* exercise of control.

Any of the above ECMS actors will be *sole* controllers with respect to processing operations of which they alone determine the means and purposes. It is not unlikely, for example, that the media distributor will be sole controller in relation to registration and further processing of *browser*-related data, given that such data are not of direct relevance for the interests of the creation provider, copyright-holder, monitoring service provider or certification authority.

2.3 Limits to data collection

2.3.1 Personal data generally

As indicated in the Introduction, a core principle of data protection laws is that personal data should be gathered by fair and lawful means. This principle is set out expressly in Article 6(1)(a) of the DPD. 'Lawful' is a criterion which is relatively self-explanatory. As for the criterion of 'fair', this is not specifically defined in the Directive and its exact ambit is uncertain. One can safely assume, though, that fairness embraces a requirement that personal data not be collected in a surreptitious or overly intrusive manner.[41]

The Data Protection Directive prohibits the collection and further processing of personal data unless the processing satisfies specified conditions. These are laid down in Article 7 as follows:

> "(a) the data subject has unambiguously given his consent [to the processing], or
> (b) processing is necessary for the performance of a contract to which the data subject is party or in order to take steps at the request of the data subject prior to entering into a contract, or
> (c) processing is necessary for compliance with a legal obligation to which the controller is subject, or
> (d) processing is necessary in order to protect the vital interests of the data subject, or
> (e) processing is necessary for the performance of a task carried out in the public interest or in the exercise of official authority vested in the controller or in a third party to whom the data are disclosed, or
> (f) processing is necessary for the purposes of the legitimate interests pursued by the controller or by the third party or parties to whom the data are disclosed, except where such interests are overridden by the interests or fundamental rights and freedoms of the data subject which require protection under Article 1(1)".

Of these conditions, paragraphs (a), (b), (c) and (f) are pertinent to the operation of an ECMS.

Regarding paragraph (a), this must be read in light of Article 2(h), which defines 'the data subject's consent' as 'any freely given specific and informed indication of his wishes, by which the data subject signifies his agreement to personal data relating to him being processed'. From this definition, it appears that consent need not be in writing. However, the express registration of consent on

---

41 See also Terwangne and Louveaux 1997, p. 239.

paper or electronic medium will aid in fulfilling the requirement in Article 7(a) that consent be 'unambiguous'. Arguably, the latter requirement will be met even if consent is not explicit (see below), but the data subject's actions must leave no doubt that he has given consent.

In the context of an ECMS, the simple fact that a purchaser takes the initiative to enter into a transaction with the media distributor could be seen as a manifestation of consent to the media distributor's registration of at least some data on the purchaser. However, this consent will only extend to the registration practices which the purchaser could reasonably expect or about which the purchaser is notified by the media distributor. Given the Directive's concern to ensure that data processing is carried out in a manner that is *fair* to the interests of data subjects,[42] notification of the purchaser will have to be done in such a way as to help ensure such fairness. Thus, notification will arguably need to occur *prior* to the purchase transaction taking place (i.e. during the browsing phase), and it will need to involve *active steps* on the part of the controller (i.e. through the latter creating screen-icons that can reasonably be said to catch the attention of potential purchasers).[43]

The same applies with respect to browsers. If a person decides to browse a media distributor's server *after* being made aware (e.g. by an appropriately formatted notice on the first server page visited) that the media distributor will register certain data on the person's browsing activity, the person should be taken as implicitly (and unambiguously) consenting to such registration.

However, the registration of the fact that a person accesses a media distributor's server — without the person necessarily going on to browse through the server's various pages — is not justifiable under paragraph (a), if the person is not given an opportunity to consent to that registration. Hence, if a media distributor's server operates with a mechanism for automatically creating and setting cookies at the time the server is first accessed, and if the cookies constitute personal data (see Section 2.1 above), the mechanism will fall outside the bounds of paragraph (a). Indeed, in the context of ECMS operations, it is hard to see that such a cookies mechanism will meet any of the other conditions in Article 7, except possibly those laid down in paragraphs (b) and (f).[44]

It goes without saying that if the processor or controller processes browser- / purchaser-related data along parameters that differ fundamentally from those parameters about which the browser/purchaser was first notified and to which the latter agreed (implicitly or explicitly), the processing will be unlawful unless consent is given anew or the processing meets the other conditions laid down in Article 7.

The condition set out in Article 7(b) will often be met with respect to the

---

42 See Art. 6(1)(a) set out at the beginning of this section. See also Arts 10 and 11(1) set out *infra* Section 2.6.

43 See also Terwangne and Louveaux 1997, pp. 239 and 241.

44 Note also Art. 3(5) of Germany's Teleservices Data Protection Act, set out *infra* Section 2.6.

processing of purchaser-related data in the context of an ECMS, given that there will exist a contract between the purchaser and the media distributor. The condition may also be satisfied with respect to the processing of browser-related data insofar as the processing is "in order to take steps at the request of the data subject prior to entering into a contract". The main point of concern is to determine which data processing is 'necessary' in both cases. Of particular interest here will be determining the extent to which Article 7(b) can properly be used as justification for the monitoring of purchasers' private activities after a contract is entered into, so as to check compliance with the contract.

The necessity criterion in Article 7(b) should be read as embracing two overlapping requirements: (1) that the processing corresponds to a pressing social or commercial need; and (2) that the processing is proportionate to the aim of the contract.[45] The stringency of these requirements will vary from case to case in accordance with the kind of data-processing involved. Thus, exactly which types of data-processing will meet the requirements is a question of fact that cannot be answered conclusively at present. It is clear, though, that the requirements will be met if a media distributor registers only those data as are necessary for enforcing the terms of a contract entered into with a purchaser. Such data would probably include the purchaser's name and address, the name and price of the purchased product, together with the date of purchase.

With respect to registration and further processing of browser-related data, the condition in paragraph (b) will not serve to justify this when the data subject is purely browsing. The condition will only be relevant once the data subject actively asks the media distributor to prepare for an imminent purchase transaction.

The condition set down in paragraph (c) could be relevant insofar as the controller (e.g. the media distributor) has legal obligations towards other ECMS actors (e.g. the creation provider and creator). At the same time, though, it could be argued that the term 'legal obligation' in paragraph (c) is to be construed narrowly, such that it does not cover purely contractual obligations. This argument is based on the fact that paragraph (c) otherwise could be used by data controllers to create at will a legal competence to process personal data simply by writing up a contract (to which the data subject is not party). The argument would also seem to be supported by the existence and wording of paragraph (b).[46]

If an appropriate legal obligation is found to exist between ECMS actors, a question of fact will again arise as to what data are necessary to process in order to comply with the obligation. The necessity criterion here will be the same as in relation to paragraphs (b), (d), (e) and (f). It is doubtful that the criterion will be

45 Cf. Art. 6(1)(c) of the Directive (personal data must be 'not excessive' in relation to the purposes for which they are processed). Note too that the European Court of Human Rights has interpreted the term 'necessary' in Art. 8(2) of the ECHR along similar lines: see further *infra* Section 3.

46 Note that Art. 7(c) in an earlier proposal for the Directive referred to an "obligation imposed by national law or by Community law". See EC Commission 1992, *supra* n. 34, pp. 17 and 72.

met in the case of registration and further processing of data relating to persons who only browse. Hence, the use of cookies mechanisms to register such data will fall outside the scope of paragraph (c).

The condition laid out in paragraph (f) is the most flexible and open-ended of the ECMS-relevant conditions in Article 7. The Directive provides little useful guidance on how the various interests in paragraph (f) are to be balanced. Who, for example, is intended to undertake the interest balancing? Recital 30 states that, in balancing the various interests, Member States are to guarantee 'effective competition'; Member States may also determine conditions for use of personal data 'in the context of the legitimate ordinary business activities of companies and other bodies', and for disclosure of data to third parties for marketing purposes. Otherwise, the Directive leaves it up to the Member States to determine how the interests are to be balanced.

An interesting issue in relation to paragraph (f) is the extent to which it may justify the use of cookies mechanisms that involve non-consensual registration of the fact that a person has accessed a media distributor's server. The issue is, of course, only pertinent insofar as the data registered (e.g. the address of the visitor's machine) can properly be viewed as 'personal' pursuant to Article 2(a) of the Directive. While such cookies mechanisms may serve the legitimate interests of, say, media distributors, it is difficult to see how they can be seen as 'necessary' for satisfying these interests, though the propriety of such an assessment all depends on how the interests are defined and on exactly what data are registered. If the interests are defined in terms of achieving 'best possible conditions for product marketing', the use of cookies mechanisms might be seen as necessary, even if those mechanisms only generate relatively coarse-grained data about consumer preferences. But even if such mechanisms are found necessary, they may well be 'trumped' by the data subjects' interests in privacy, integrity and autonomy. The strength of these interests will increase in tandem with the increase in detail and sensitivity of the data generated by the cookies mechanisms (see further the discussion in Section 2.3.2 below).

To sum up, the four conditions discussed above should, in combination, enable the registration and further processing of certain types of purchaser-related data by ECMS actors. They may also allow for the registration and further processing of certain types of browser-related data, though to a much lesser extent than in the case of data on purchasers.

2.3.2 Especially sensitive data

The conditions for lawful registration and further processing of personal data are sharpened by Article 8 of the DPD in relation to certain kinds of especially sensitive data. Most other data protection laws (but not all)[47] also contain extra safeguards for designated categories of especially sensitive data, but there is considerable variation in the way in which these data categories are described. The Data Protection Directive lists the following data categories as deserving extra protection: data on a person's "racial or ethnic origin, political opinions, religious or philosophical beliefs, trade-union membership, and ... health or sex life" (Article 8(1)). Data on "offences, criminal convictions or security measures" are also afforded extra protection under Article 8(5), though these are scarcely relevant in the context of ECMS operations.

There is some uncertainty whether the list of data categories in Article 8(1) is exhaustive or not. We will not go into this issue in detail. It suffices to say that there is nothing on the face of the Directive to indicate that the list is not exhaustive, though the loose way in which the categories are formulated makes it possible to interpret them broadly.

An ECMS might involve the processing of some of the above types of data inasmuch as certain personal preferences of purchasers and/or browsers are registered by a media distributor. If, for instance, a purchaser enters into a contractual transaction for the use of an information product that concerns a particular religious or sexual theme, and the product is registered against the purchaser's name (or pseudonym or other unique identifier), it could be argued that sensitive data about the purchaser have thereby been processed. But it could also be contended that the connection between the product's theme and the purchaser's personality in such a case is too remote: i.e. just because a person buys usage rights with respect to a particular product does not necessarily mean that the product reflects the person's own taste; he/she may simply be sampling or analysing a range of products. The strength of this contention will depend on several factors, including the nature of the product (e.g. an academic treatise on satanism will tend to say less about the purchaser's personal religious inclinations than, say, a video-clip depicting satanistic rituals for the purpose of viewer enthralment) and the nature of the transaction (e.g. a one-off transaction will also tend to say less about the purchaser's personal preferences than a series of transactions involving information products that focus on a similar theme). The same sort of analysis will apply with respect to registration of products in which a particular browser shows interest.

Article 8 of the Directive opens with a prohibition on the processing of the above categories of data, but follows up with a list (in Article 8(2)) of alternative exemptions to this prohibition. In the context of ECMS operations, the relevant exemptions are found in Article 8(2)(a) (i.e. processing may occur if the data subject explicitly consents to it, except where national laws override this condition), and Article 8(2)(e) (i.e. processing may occur if the data in question 'are manifestly made

47 See e.g. the data protection laws of the Pacific-rim countries.

public' by the data subject, or their processing is 'necessary for the establishment, exercise or defence of legal claims'.

With regard to the first-mentioned exemption, it should be noted that consent must be 'explicit' (cf. the more lenient criterion of non-ambiguity in Article 7(a)). This means that the process of requesting and providing consent must occur as a formally separate process to the actual purchase transaction. There must be a specific request by the media distributor for permission from the purchaser/browser to process the data in question, followed by a specific reply in the affirmative. Arguably too, there must be some sort of record made of the request and reply, with measures in place to keep the record secure from unauthorised access and modification. It is worth noting Article 3(7) of the German Teleservices Data Protection Act which allows for electronic declaration of consent if the teleservice provider ensures that:

1. such consent can be given only through an unambiguous and deliberate act by the user,
2. consent cannot be modified without detection,
3. the creator can be identified,
4. the consent is recorded, and
5. the text of the consent can be obtained by the user on request at any time.

These conditions apply even in relation to non-sensitive data.

As for the second-mentioned exemption in Article 8(2)(e), one issue concerns the meaning of 'manifestly made public'. Given the nature of the data involved, the phrase should arguably be interpreted fairly narrowly as indicating an *obvious and conscious readiness* by the data subject to make the data available to *any* member of the general public. The extent to which this condition will be satisfied in the context of an ECMS will depend on the data subject's understanding of the operational parameters of the particular ECMS. If the data subject believes that the ECMS operates as a closed system *vis-à-vis* other systems (i.e. that ECMS actors observe strict rules of confidentiality when handling purchaser-/browser-related data), it is difficult to see the condition being satisfied.[48]

Another issue in relation to Article 8(2)(e) concerns the meaning of 'legal claims'. Again, it is arguable that the phrase is not intended to cover claims arising from purely contractual obligations, for the same reasons as are given with respect to Article 7(c) (see Section 2.3.1 above). Indeed, the sensitive nature of the data involved is an extra ground for reading the phrase in this way. Nevertheless, it is

48 It is even difficult to see the condition being satisfied in relation to non-virtual shopping: while the purchase of, say, a book in a non-virtual shop will typically be a public act in the sense that any member of the public can incidentally witness the transaction, the purchaser will rarely intend a record of that transaction to be made available (in non-anonymous format) to any member of the public.

quite possible that national legislation implementing the Directive will allow for data processing in order for a data controller to defend a legal claim in the form of copyright, as the latter is statutorily anchored. Note, though, that the latter claim will attach primarily to the copyright-holder and not, say, the media distributor. Another issue, though, will be the extent to which such processing is 'necessary' (as defined in relation to Article 7) for the defence of such a legal claim. Here, the necessity criterion should be interpreted strictly since the data in question are regarded as especially sensitive. Thus, 'necessary' should be held as denoting a stringent standard of indispensability. For instance, while initial registration of such data might be found indispensable for ensuring that copyright is not breached, it will be incumbent on the media distributor (or whoever is data controller) to delete or anonymise the data once the relevant interests of the copyright-holder can be safeguarded in some other way.

Finally, it is worth noting that although the United States has not yet enacted data protection legislation regulating the private sector as comprehensively as the equivalent legislation does in West European countries, it has singled out for special regulation several sectors of what we might call the informational distribution industry. We refer here especially to the Video Privacy Protection Act 1988,[49] the Cable Communications Privacy Act 1984,[50] together with state legislation regulating the processing of library records.[51] All of these pieces of legislation aim at restricting the registration and further processing of data on information consumers' viewing/reading/listening habits. For our purposes, these laws serve to underline the fact that such data are generally regarded as deserving of special protection.

2.4 ANONYMITY

Article 6(1)(e) of the DPD provides for the anonymisation of personal data once the need for person-identification lapses; i.e. personal data must be 'kept in a form which permits identification of data subjects for no longer than is necessary for the purposes for which the data were collected or for which they are further processed'. The same rule is contained in many other data protection laws too. The rule should be seen in conjunction with the stipulation in Article 6(1)(c) — also found in numerous other data protection laws — that personal data be 'not excessive' in relation to the purposes for which they are processed.[52] Read together, these rules arguably embody a general principle requiring, as a point of departure,

49 Codified at para. 2710 of Title 18 of the United States Code (USC).
50 Codified at para. 551 of Title 47 of the USC.
51 See e.g. para. 4509 of the New York State Civil Practice Law and Rules. See further the references given in Cohen 1996, n. 214.
52 Note too the necessity criterion in Arts 7 and 8, discussed in the preceding sections.

transactional anonymity unless there are overriding legitimate interests to the contrary. Such a principle should also be read as requiring that active consideration be given to crafting technical solutions for ensuring transactional anonymity.

It is worth noting that the issue of transactional anonymity is expressly addressed in the German Teleservices Data Protection Act. The Act provides, *inter alia*, that "[t]he design and selection of technical devices to be used for teleservices shall be oriented to the goal of collecting, processing and using either no personal data at all or as few data as possible" (Article 3(4)). Further, the Act stipulates that a teleservice provider "shall offer the user anonymous use and payment of teleservices or use and payment under a pseudonym to the extent technically feasible and reasonable" and that the user "shall be informed about these options" (Article 4(1)).[53]

The issue of transactional anonymity is also specifically addressed in some policy documents issued recently. The Budapest-Berlin Memorandum on Data Protection and Privacy on the Internet, adopted on 19 November 1996 by the International Working Group on Data Protection and Telecommunications, states, *inter alia*, that, "[i]n general, users should have the opportunity to access the Internet without having to reveal their identity where personal data are not needed to provide a certain service".[54] Recommendation 3/97, adopted on 3 December 1997 by the Working Party on the Protection of Individuals with regard to the Processing of Personal Data ('Data Protection Working Party'), set up pursuant to Article 29 of the DPD, follows the thrust of the above Memorandum by urging the EC Commission to develop proposals for securing transactional anonymity on the Internet.[55] In the United States, the Information Infrastructure Task Force adopted on 6 June 1995 a set of Principles for Providing and Using Personal Information which stipulate, *inter alia*, that "[i]ndividuals should be able to safeguard their own privacy by having ... the opportunity to remain anonymous when appropriate" (Principle III.B.4).[56] The Australian Privacy Charter, adopted in December 1994, contains a principle of 'anonymous transactions' which states: "People should have the option of not identifying themselves when entering transactions".[57] None of these policy instruments, however, have the force of law. Nevertheless, they demonstrate an increasing concern in many countries to create conditions conducive to anonymity in cyberspace.

53 Note also Art. 4(4), set out *infra* Section 2.5.2.

54 See further International Working Group on Data Protection and Telecommunications, Budapest-Berlin Memorandum on Data Protection and Privacy on the Internet, adopted on 19 November 1996, available at <http://www.datenschutz-berlin.de/diskus/13_15.htm> ('International Working Group on Data Protection and Telecommunications 1996').

55 See Data Protection Working Party 1997, *supra* n. 19.

56 See Information Infrastructure Task Force 1995, *supra* n. 19.

57 The Charter is the private initiative of a group of concerned citizens and interest groups; it has not been conferred any official status by a government body.

In light of the above, it is advisable that those engaged in the design and establishment of an ECMS 'build in' possibilities for anonymising transactions wherever technically feasible and wherever the interest in purchaser/browser anonymity is not overridden by other legitimate interests.[58] There would appear to be, for instance, no overriding interests to justify the flow of transactional data from a media distributor to a monitoring service provider in other than anonymised (e.g. aggregate) form.

2.5 PURPOSE SPECIFICATION AND FINALITY

2.5.1 Generally

As noted in the Introduction, a central principle in most data protection laws is that of purpose specification (sometimes also termed the finality principle). The principle is expressed in Article 6(1)(b) of the DPD as follows:

> "[Member States shall provide that personal data must be] collected for specified, explicit and legitimate purposes and not further processed in a way incompatible with those purposes. Further processing of data for historical, statistical or scientific purposes shall not be considered as incompatible provided that the Member States provide appropriate safeguards".

In an ECMS context, this sort of rule has obvious repercussions for the secondary uses to which media distributors, creation providers and other ECMS actors will be able to put purchaser-/browser-related data. We can see the principle in Article 6(1)(b) as grounded partly in concern for ensuring that data are processed in ways that conform with data subjects' reasonable expectations.[59] We can also see the principle as grounded in concern for ensuring that data are used for purposes to which they are suited (i.e. a concern for adequate information quality).

From the wording of Article 6(1)(b), it is apparent that the purposes for which, say, a media distributor registers data on a purchaser or browser must be defined, documented and announced in advance of registration. They must also be notified to the data subject.[60] Further, they must be 'legitimate'. Arguably, the term 'legitimate' denotes a criterion of social acceptability which is broader than that of lawfulness, though it is difficult to determine how much it is broader. The

58 See further *infra* Section 4.

59 In this regard, note the Fairness Principle adopted by the US Information Infrastructure Task Force ("[i]nformation users should not use personal information in ways that are incompatible with the individual's understanding of how it will be used, unless there is a compelling public interest for such use"): see Information Infrastructure Task Force 1995, *supra* n. 19.

60 See also Arts 10 and 11 of the Directive set out *infra* Section 2.6.

conditions laid down in Articles 7 and 8 (see Section 2.3 above) provide some, but not exhaustive, guidance on the ambit of the legitimacy criterion. At the same time, it is apparent that a data controller cannot define the purposes of data processing in the same broad and diffuse terms as are found in Articles 7 and 8: use of the adjective 'specified' in Article 6(1)(b) indicates that the purposes need to be delineated more concretely and narrowly.

The phrase 'not incompatible' could be read as meaning simply 'compatible', though use of the double negative perhaps denotes a slightly less stringent standard than that of straight compatibility. However, if we accept that one of the underlying concerns of the purpose specification principle is to ensure that data are processed in conformity with data subjects' reasonable expectations, then any secondary purpose should not pass the test of compatibility/non-incompatibility unless the data subject is able, objectively speaking, to read that purpose into the purpose(s) first specified, or the secondary purpose is otherwise within the ambit of the data subject's reasonable expectations. It is doubtful, for example, that the purpose of marketing would satisfy this test if the primary purpose for the data processing were specified only in terms of billing.

The rule in Article 6(1)(b) is supplemented by Articles 6(1)(c) and 6(1)(d). The latter provision requires that data be "accurate and, where necessary, kept up to date", while Article 6(1)(c) stipulates that personal data must be "adequate, relevant and not excessive in relation to the purposes for which they are collected and/or further processed". The criteria in sub-paragraph (c) (particularly that of non-excessiveness) reinforce the necessity criterion in Articles 7 and 8. If, say, a media distributor announces that he/she/it registers purchaser-related data for the purpose of billing the data subjects, the rule in Article 6(1)(c) will not allow the media distributor to register more purchaser-related data than is necessary for billing purposes, unless the data subject consents otherwise.

The provisions of both the EC Telecommunications Privacy Directive (TPD) and Germany's Teleservices Data Protection Act signal an intention on the part of European legislators to enforce a fairly stringent version of the purpose specification principle in the relations between telecommunications service providers and service users/subscribers. Both laws severely restrict the purposes for which telecommunications service providers may store and utilise data on users/subscribers without the latters' consent. For instance, the Telecommunicatons Privacy Directive's basic point of departure is that traffic data on users/subscribers which are processed to establish 'calls' must be erased or made anonymous upon termination of the call (Article 6(1)).[61] Article 6(2) of the TPD permits service

61 From the use of the word 'call', it appears that this provision is intended to regulate ordinary telephone calls only, but this would seem inconsistent with the broad definition of 'telecommunications service' in Art. 2(d) of the TPD which refers to 'services whose provision consists wholly or partly in the transmission and routing of signals on telecommunications networks, with the exception of radio- and television broadcasting'.

providers to process only such data on users/subscribers as are necessary for billing purposes and interconnection payments. This processing is "permissible only up to the end of the period during which the bill may lawfully be challenged or payment may be pursued" (Article 6(2)). The data may only be used for the purpose of marketing the provider's own services if the subscriber has consented (Article 6(3)). Similar rules are found in sections 5 and 6 of Germany's Teleservices Data Protection Act.

2.5.2 Marketing

Some data protection laws (particularly those enacted recently) show an express concern to limit the extent to which data controllers can exploit personal data for the purpose of marketing goods and services *vis-à-vis* the data subjects. Two main sets of measures tend to be pursued. One set of measures is to give data subjects a right to object to direct marketing; the other set of measures is to restrict data controllers' ability to build up personality profiles of data subjects.

An important instance of the first-mentioned set of measures is Article 14(b) of the DPD. According to Article 14(b), EU Member States are to provide a data subject with two options: (1) "to object, on request and free of charge, to the processing of personal data relating to him which the controller anticipates being processed for the purposes of direct marketing"; or (2) "to be informed before personal data are disclosed for the first time to third parties or used on their behalf for the purposes of direct marketing, and to be expressly offered the right to object free of charge to such disclosures or uses". Member States are required to take "necessary measures to ensure that data subjects are aware of" the right to object pursuant to Article 14(b).

Another important instance of this sort of right to object is section 5(2) of Germany's Teleservices Data Protection Act which provides that "[p]rocessing and use of contractual data for the purpose of advising, advertising, market research or for the demand-oriented design of the teleservices are only permissible if the user has given his *explicit* consent" (emphasis added).

Of more global relevance are the Revised Guidelines on Advertising and Marketing on the Internet adopted 2 April 1998 by the International Chamber of Commerce (ICC). These Guidelines ('ICC Guidelines') contain provisions restricting unsolicited commercial messages over the Internet. Article 5(6) of the Guidelines states:

> "Advertisers and marketers should not send unsolicited commercial messages online to users who have indicated that they do not wish to receive such messages. Advertisers and marketers should make an online mechanism

available to users by which the users can make known to the advertisers that they do not wish to receive future online solicitations".[62]

In North America, the Individual Reference Services Industry Principles adopted on 10 June 1997 by CDB Infotek *et al* contain a principle dealing expressly with use of information on minors: "[w]here an individual is identified in the product or service as being under the age of 18, no Non-Public Information about that individual should be provided for non-selective commercial distribution without parental consent".[63]

Regarding the second set of measures (i.e. those concerned to restrict profiling), Germany's Teleservices Data Protection Act appears to provide the most restrictive regulations. The Act stipulates that teleservice providers are to take measures to ensure that "personal data relating to the use of several teleservices by one user are processed separately; a combination of such data is not permitted unless it is necessary for accounting purposes" (Article 4(2)(4)). Moreover, the creation of user profiles is allowed only if pseudonyms are employed, and the "[p]rofiles retrievable under pseudonyms shall not be combined with data relating to the bearer of the pseudonym" (Article 4(4)).

Also of relevance for profiling is Article 15(1) of the DPD. This provision grants a person the right "not to be subject to a decision which produces legal effects concerning him or significantly affects him and which is based solely on automated processing of data intended to evaluate certain personal aspects relating to him, such as his performance at work, creditworthiness, reliability, conduct, etc.". The right is not absolute; a person may be subjected to such decisions if they are, in summary, taken pursuant to a contract with the data subject or authorised by law, *and* provision is made for 'suitable measures' to safeguard the person's 'legitimate interests' (Article 15(2)). Note that the right does not restrict the creation of profiles by fully automated means; rather, it restricts certain *uses* of such profiles.

The above sorts of provisions dealing with profiling are not yet commonplace in data protection laws, though this is likely to change in the near future.

All of the provisions canvassed in this section will set limits on the purposes for which ECMS actors will be able to employ purchaser-/browser-related data. While there will exist some legal opportunities for using these data for purposes beyond what the data subjects might reasonably expect, it would be advisable that ECMS actors show reticence in exploiting such opportunities, not least in order to build up consumer trust and confidence in ECMS operations.

62 ICC, Revised Guidelines on Advertising and Marketing on the Internet, adopted 2 April 1998, available at <http://wwwiccwbo.org/Comm/html/Internet_Guidelines.html>, ('ICC 1998').

63 CDB Infotek, Database Technologies Inc, Experian, First Data Infosource, Donnelly Marketing, Information America, IRSC Inc, LEXIS-NEXIS and Metromail Corp, Individual Reference Services Industry Principles, 10 June 1997, available at <http://zeus.bna.com/e-law/docs/dbguide.html>, ('CDB Infotek *et al* 1997'). By 'Non-Public Information' is meant "[i]nformation about an individual that is of a private nature and neither generally available to the public nor obtained from a public record".

2.6 ORIENTATION OF DATA SUBJECTS

The EC Data Protection Directive sets down several sets of rules aimed at orienting persons about the processing of data on them. One set of rules grant persons the right to gain access to data kept on them by other persons and organisations. The most important formulation of this right is given in Article 12 as follows:

> "Member States shall guarantee every data subject the right to obtain from the controller:
> (a) without constraint at reasonable intervals and without excessive delay or expense:
> — confirmation as to whether or not data relating to him are being processed and information at least as to the purposes of the processing, the categories of data concerned, and the recipients or categories of recipients to whom the data are disclosed,
> — communication to him in an intelligible form of the data undergoing processing and of any available information as to their source,
> — knowledge of the logic involved in any automated processing of data concerning him at least in the case of the automated decisions referred to in Article 15(1)".

Broadly similar sets of access rights are a central feature of all data protection laws.

A second set of rules provides that data controllers must, of their own accord, inform data subjects about their data-processing practices. Article 10 of the Directive stipulates that when data are collected from the data subject, he/she must be informed of 'at least' the identity of the data controller and the latter's representatives, together with the intended purposes of the data processing (unless the data subject already has this information); other types of information may also be provided insofar as is 'necessary' in the circumstances 'to guarantee fair processing in respect of the data subject'. With a few exceptions, Article 11 contains similar requirements in cases when data are not collected directly from the data subject.

Such rules are not yet commonplace in data protection legislation but will become so under the influence of the Directive.

Germany's Teleservices Data Protection Act contains several provisions that elaborate upon and extend the rules in Articles 10 and 11 of the DPD. The first of these provisions states that a user of teleservices 'shall be informed about the type, scope, place and purposes of collection, processing and use of his personal data' (Article 3(5)). The provision goes on to address the use of cookies mechanisms, stipulating that, "[i]n case of automatic processing, which permits subsequent identification of the user and which prepares the collection, processing or use of personal data, the user shall be informed prior to the beginning of the procedure". Another provision of note requires that the user be informed about his/her right to withdraw his/her consent to a given data-processing operation (Article 3(6)). Finally, Article 4(1) requires the user to be notified of whatever options exist for making anonymous or pseudonymous use and payment of teleservices.

Also noteworthy is the following Notice Principle included in the data protection principles adopted by the US Information Infrastructure Task Force. This principle provides that:

> "[i]nformation users who collect personal information directly from the individual should provide adequate, relevant information about: 1) Why they are collecting the information; 2) What the information is expected to be used for; 3) What steps will be taken to protect its confidentiality, integrity, and quality; 4) The consequences of providing or withholding information; and 5) Any rights of redress".[64]

The ICC Guidelines provide that "[a]dvertisers and marketers of goods and services who post commercial messages via the Internet should always disclose their own identity and that of the relevant subsidiary, if applicable, in such a way that the user can contact the advertiser or marketer without difficulty" (Article 2). Further, "[a]dvertisers and marketers should disclose the purpose(s) for collecting and using personal data to users" (Article 5(1)).

2.7 SECURITY MEASURES

Data protection laws typically contain provisions requiring data controllers to take steps to ensure that personal data are not destroyed accidentally and not subject to unauthorised access, alteration, destruction and disclosure. A representative provision to this effect is Article 17(1) of the DPD which stipulates:

> "[Data controllers] must implement appropriate technical and organizational measures to protect personal data against accidental or unlawful destruction or accidental loss, alteration, unauthorized disclosure or access, in particular where the processing involves the transmission of data over a network, and against all other unlawful forms of processing. Having regard to the state of the art and the cost of their implementation, such measures shall ensure a level of security appropriate to the risks represented by the processing and the nature of the data to be protected".

---

64 Information Infrastructure Task Force 1995, *supra* n. 19. Cf. the more generally worded guideline in the Budapest-Berlin Memorandum ("[s]ervice providers should inform each potential user of the Net unequivocally about the risk to his privacy"); see International Working Group on Data Protection in Telecommunications 1996, *supra* n. 54.

A controller must also ensure — by way of contract or other legal act (Article 17(3)) — that data processors they engage provide "sufficient guarantees in respect of the technical security measures and organizational security measures governing the processing to be carried out" (Article 17(2)). The latter requirements are supplemented in Article 16 which provides that "[a]ny person acting under the authority of the controller or ... processor, including the processor himself, who has access to personal data must not process them except on instructions from the controller, unless he is required to do so by law".

Similar provisions are set out in Articles 4 and 5 of the TPD. Article 5 is especially relevant for ECMS operations. Amongst other things, it prohibits "listening, tapping, storage or other kinds of interception or surveillance of communications, by others than users, without the consent of the users concerned, except when legally authorised, in accordance with Article 14(1)" (Article 5(1)). This provision is sufficiently broad to impinge upon the ability of ECMS actors to monitor the activities of purchasers and browsers. We can see the provision as grounded partly in a concern to uphold the right to privacy of communications — a right embodied in, *inter alia*, Article 8(1) of the ECHR.[65]

At the same time, Article 14(1) permits derogation from Article 5(1) insofar as is "necessary ... to safeguard ... prevention, investigation, detection and prosecution of criminal offences". Moreover, Article 5(2) states that the prohibition in Article 5(1) "shall not affect any legally authorised recording of communications in the course of lawful business practice for the purpose of providing evidence of a commercial transaction or of any other business communication". Both derogations appear to derive from the criteria listed in Article 8(2) of the ECHR. Both may be relied upon to justify some monitoring of purchaser activities in an ECMS context, though probably not the activities of browsers.

2.8 TRANSBORDER DATA FLOWS

In the context of an ECMS, four situations could arise involving the flow of personal data on purchasers or browsers across national borders:

1. the purchaser/browser is situated in one EU Member State with the media distributor (or other ECMS actor) situated in another EU Member State;
2. the purchaser/browser is situated in an EU Member State and the media distributor (or other ECMS actor) is situated in a state outside the EU (i.e. a so-called 'third country');
3. the media distributor (or other ECMS actor) is situated in an EU Member State, while another ECMS actor is situated in a third country;

65 See further *infra* Section 3.

4. the purchaser/browser is situated in a third country, while the media distributor (or other ECMS actor) is situated in an EU Member State.

With regard to situation 1, the Data Protection Directive stipulates in Article 1(2) that the flow of personal data between EU Member States cannot be restricted for reasons concerned with protection of the 'fundamental rights and freedoms of natural persons, and in particular their right to privacy with respect to the processing of personal data'.

As for transfer of personal data to countries outside the EU (situation 2), this is regulated in Articles 25 and 26 of the Directive. The basic rule is that transfer "may take place only if . . . the third country in question ensures an adequate level of protection" (Article 25(1)). No definition or indication of the meaning of "adequate" is provided by the Directive, but it probably denotes a less stringent standard than that of equivalence.[66] Article 25(2) states that the 'adequacy' criterion cannot be fleshed out in the abstract; rather, "adequacy of the level of protection afforded by a third country shall be assessed in the light of all the circumstances surrounding a data transfer operation or set of data transfer operations". From this provision, it is clear that account is to be taken not just of the content and application of third countries' legislation that deals specifically with data protection; other rules and practices may also be relevant.

According to the Data Protection Working Party, the issue of adequacy essentially involves assessing the "degree of risk that the transfer poses to the data subject".[67] Interestingly (from an ECMS perspective), the Working Party includes in its list of data transfers that "pose particular risks to privacy" the following: "repetitive transfers involving massive volumes of data (such as transactional data processed over telecommunications networks, the Internet etc.)" and "transfers involving the collection of data using new technologies, which, for instance, could be undertaken in a particularly covert or clandestine manner (e.g. Internet cookies)".[68]

It is not entirely clear from the Directive if adequacy may be assessed on a sectoral as opposed to national basis; i.e. if the whole of the third country's legal regime on data protection is to be assessed or just those parts of the regime which deal specifically with the data concerned. The focus of Article 25(2) on particular 'data transfer operations' suggests that sector-specific as opposed to national assessment is possible.[69]

---

66 See also Schwartz 1995, pp. 473 and 487; Ellger 1991, p. 131.

67 Working Party on the Protection of Individuals with Regard to the Processing of Personal Data, *Transfers of Personal Data to Third Countries: Applying Articles 25 and 26 of the EU data protection directive*, Working Document adopted on 24 July 1998, available at <http://europa.eu.int/comm/dg15/en/media/dataprot/wpdocs/wp12en.htm>, ('Data Protection Working Party 1998'), ch. 1.

68 *Ibid.*, ch. 6.

69 See also *ibid.*, ch. 6; Greenleaf 1995, p. 106.

Some uncertainty reigns also over whether the standards in the Directive constitute the only point of reference for determining adequacy. Article 25(1) and Recital 60 suggest that the legislative standards adopted by an EU Member State pursuant to the Directive — standards which may be more stringent in certain respects than those set by the Directive — may constitute the primary point of departure for assessing the adequacy of data protection afforded by a third country.[70]

Derogations from the rule in Article 25(1) are set out in Article 26. Of particular relevance for ECMS operations, are the following derogations:

> "(a) the data subject has given his consent unambiguously to the proposed transfer; or
> (b) the transfer is necessary for the performance of a contract between the data subject and the controller or the implementation of precontractual measures taken in response to the data subject's request; or
> (c) the transfer is necessary for the conclusion or performance of a contract concluded in the interest of the data subject between the controller and a third party; or
> (d) the transfer is necessary or legally required on important public interest grounds, or for the establishment, exercise or defence of legal claims".

These conditions for transfer are broadly similar to some of the conditions for data processing laid down in Article 7, such that interpretation of the latter will be of relevance for interpretation of the former. Regarding the condition in Article 26(1)(a) (dealing with consent) the media distributor (or other ECMS actor) must take active measures to make the purchaser/browser aware of the fact that data will be transferred to a third country (i.e. consent must be given 'to the proposed transfer', not processing generally). The data subject must also be informed of the identity of the country of destination, together with the fact that the latter does not provide adequate protection.[71]

As for the condition laid down in paragraph (b) above, this should be met fairly easily in the context of situation 2. Otherwise we refer to what is written in relation to Article 7(b) in Section 2.3.1 above. It has been claimed that the condition in Article 26(b) will only be satisfied if the data subject is also "made aware that once the data has [*sic*] been transferred to the third country for the contract in question, there are no means of ensuring that the data will not be further used for other

---

70 See also Schwartz 1995, p. 487. Article 25(1) states that "transfer may take place only if, *without prejudice to compliance with the national provisions adopted pursuant to the other provisions of this Directive*, the third country... ensures an adequate level of protection" (emphasis added). According to Recital 60, "transfers to third countries may be effected only in full compliance with the provisions adopted by the Member States pursuant to this Directive".

71 See also Terwangne and Louveaux 1997, p. 244.

purposes".[72] From a data protection perspective, the latter requirement is sensible *de lege ferenda* but is by no means obvious from the wording of paragraph (b). Such a requirement, however, could be implied from the more general fairness criterion that is expressly embodied in Article 6(1)(a) of the Directive and particularised in the principles of purpose specification in Article 6(1)(b) and individual participation in Articles 10–12. There can be little doubt that this fairness criterion also permeates Articles 25 and 26.

The condition in paragraph (d) should be met fairly easily, inasmuch as the transfer serves to safeguard copyright. Purely contractual obligations will probably fall outside the scope of the phrase 'legal claims', for the same reasons as are given in relation to Articles 7(c) and 8(2)(e) in Section 2.3 above.

Another provision of note is Article 26(2), which permits transfer in derogation of Article 25(1):

> "where the controller adduces adequate safeguards with respect to the protection of the privacy and fundamental rights and freedoms of individuals and as regards the exercise of the corresponding rights; such safeguards may in particular result from appropriate contractual clauses".

It is arguable that 'appropriate contractual clauses' in this provision must be enforceable by data subjects. Thus, where doctrines on privity of contract apply, contracts to which data controllers/processors/recipients are the sole parties might be insufficient to result in 'adequate safeguards' for the purposes of Article 26(2). A possible solution to this problem is that the controller enters into a separate contract with the data subject, undertaking that he/she/it (the controller) remains liable for any harm to the data subject incurred by the data recipient's failure to fulfil the terms of the other contract.[73] More generally, the Data Protection Working Party has stated that contractual solutions "are probably best suited to large international networks (credit cards, airline reservations) characterised by large quantities of repetitive data transfers of a similar nature, and by a relatively small number of large operators in industries already subject to significant public scrutiny and regulation".[74] At least some ECMS operations could well fall within this sort of network category.

All in all, it is difficult to see that a transfer of personal data in the context of situation 2 will not meet one or more of the above derogations. In other words, the issue of what constitutes adequate protection pursuant to Article 25 is likely to be of marginal significance here.

---

72 *Ibid.*, p. 245.

73 Cf. the suggestion by the Data Protection Working Party 1998, *supra* n. 67, ch. 4.

74 *Ibid.*

Regarding situation 3, it should first be noted that Articles 25 and 26 will only apply insofar as the data transferred are 'personal' pursuant to Article 2(a). Thus, if the data flowing from a media distributor to a monitoring service provider are anonymised (which we argue should probably be the case: see Section 2.4 above), the Directive will not impinge on the flow whatsoever. If the data are not anonymised, and the data are intended to be transferred to a country that does not provide adequate protection pursuant to Article 25(2), the transfer could arguably be justified under Article 26(1)(c) or (d), or Article 26(2). A sticking point in relation to Article 26(1)(c) will be whether or not the transfer could properly be said to be in the interest of the data subject (i.e. the purchaser or browser).

As for situation 4, transfers of purchaser-/browser-related data will not be affected by the Directive because the flow of data will be *into* the EU — a situation not addressed by Articles 25 or 26. However, if these data are subsequently passed on to an ECMS actor in a third country (i.e. situation 3), the Directive will apply.

2.9 General derogations

The Directive gives EU Member States the opportunity of adopting legislative measures that derogate from the provisions in Articles 6(1), 10, 11, 12 and 21, if it is necessary to safeguard, *inter alia*, "the prevention, investigation, detection and prosecution of criminal offences" (Article 13(1)(d)), or "the protection of the ... rights and freedom of others" (Article 13(1)(f)).

Both exemptions are of relevance in an ECMS context, and could be used by copyright-holders or their representative organisations as leverage points for pressuring EU Member States into drafting data protection laws that are more 'ECMS-friendly' than Articles 6(1), 10, 11(1), 12 and 21 would *prima facie* allow.

Another such leverage point could be Article 9 which requires Member States to derogate from all of the Directive's provisions canvassed so far in this chapter, with regard to "processing of personal data carried out solely for ... the purpose of artistic or literary expression" but only if the derogations are "necessary to reconcile the right to privacy with the rules governing freedom of expression". Of course, Article 9 will only be relevant for ECMS operations insofar as the basic rationale of the latter can properly be characterised as the promotion of freedom of artistic or literary expression — a debatable point!

3. Application of Article 8 of the ECHR to ECMS Operations

As noted in the Introduction, there is a paucity of Article 8 ECHR case law dealing specifically with the data-processing activities of private sector bodies. Nevertheless, on the basis of the case law dealing with the practices of public authorities, it could be plausibly argued that the processing of purchaser/browser-related data in an ECMS context will interfere with the data subject's right to respect for private life under Article 8(1) if the following cumulative conditions are met:

1. the data reveal details about the data subject's personality (e.g. his/her preferences);
2. the data are processed without the data subject's knowledge or consent; and
3. the processing potentially casts the data subject in a negative light or could result in a restriction of the data subject's freedom of choice.[75]

An interference will also arise if a person's communications are monitored by others without his/her consent and the monitoring is not what the person could reasonably expect.[76]

Denial of access to information about oneself which is kept by others will ordinarily not amount to an interference with Article 8(1). Nevertheless, Article 8(1) does embody an interest for persons to be given access to information that is essential for their psychological well-being and understanding of personal identity.[77] Further, the protection of this interest can arise as a positive obligation on the part of State Parties to ensure respect for a person's right under Article 8(1).[78] However, it is doubtful that purchasers or browsers would be given, pursuant to Article 8, a right of access to information gathered about them by ECMS actors, as access to such information can probably not be regarded as essential for their personal development in the manner outlined above.

Article 8(2) sets down a number of conditions for justifying an interference with an Article 8(1) right. First, there must be some sort of legal authority (not necessarily statutory in character) for the interference. Secondly, the legal measure concerned must be accessible to the data subject and sufficiently precise to allow him/her reasonably to foresee its consequences.[79] Thirdly, the interference must have been carried out in order to achieve one or more of the aims listed in Article 8(2). The fourth and final justificative criterion is that the interference must be 'necessary in a democratic society'; i.e. it must 'correspond to a pressing social need' and be 'proportionate to the legitimate aim pursued'.[80] In applying these criteria, the European Court of Human Rights accords State Parties a 'margin of appreciation', allowing the judgement of what is appropriate in the circumstances of the particular

75 See further Bygrave 1998, p. 269.
76 *Halford v. United Kingdom* (1997) Reports of Judgements and Decisions 1997-III, 1004, paras 44–46.
77 *Gaskin v. United Kingdom* (1989) Publications of the ECHR, Series A, 160, para. 49.
78 *Ibid.*
79 See e.g. *Sunday Times v. United Kingdom* (1979) Publications of the ECHR, Series A, 30, para. 49.
80 See e.g. *Leander v. Sweden* (1987) Publications of the ECHR, Series A, 116, para. 58.

case to be determined to some extent by the national authorities.[81] It is important to note, however, that the conditions in Article 8(2) are only directly relevant with respect to interferences incurred by the actions of *public* authorities. It seems likely that ECMS operations will ordinarily be executed by private sector bodies only, though some ECMS actors might conceivably operate in a semi-public capacity.

If ECMS operations involve private sector bodies only, the main issue under Article 8 will concern the nature and extent of a State Party's positive obligations to ensure that these bodies respect the Article 8(1) right of purchasers/browsers. In assessing the character of such obligations, the Court will attempt to strike a 'fair balance' between the 'general interests of the community and the needs of the individual'.[82] In this process, the Court will have some regard to the aims specified in Article 8(2).[83] At the same time, it should be kept in mind that the Court is likely to give State Parties a broad margin of appreciation when assessing the obligations of public authorities in this context, because the data processing concerned will be carried out by a private actor. Motivating the Court's policy in this regard will be a desire not to prompt State intervention in the private sphere which could in turn curtail the very interests that Article 8 or other ECHR provisions (particularly Article 10) are intended to safeguard.[84] Nevertheless, it is very doubtful that the Court will refrain from obliging a State Party to enact legal rules embodying core data protection principles and to apply these rules to private bodies.[85] This assumes, of course, that these rules contain much the same exemption clauses as are found, say, in the Data Protection Directive.

4. Privacy-Enhancing Technologies

Privacy-enhancing technologies (PETs) are technical and organisational tools for reducing or eliminating the collection and further processing of data that can be used to identify an individual person.[86] Most focus has hitherto been placed on PETs that rely on the application of public-key/asymmetric methods of encryption. On the basis of these methods, it is possible to create mechanisms for allowing a

---

81 The extent of this margin of appreciation varies from case to case and depends on the Court's appraisal of a variety of factors. These include the importance of the right that is breached, the importance of the 'legitimate aim' for which the breach is committed, and the conformity of the breach to a relevant pan-European practice. For detailed discussion of these factors, see e.g. Harris *et al* 1995, pp. 290–301, 344–353.

82 See e.g. *Gaskin v. United Kingdom* (1989) Publications of the ECHR, Series A, 160, para. 42.

83 *Ibid.* One such aim is the 'prevention of crime'; another is the 'protection of the rights and freedoms of others'. Both aims are relevant for ECMS operations.

84 See further Clapham 1993, p. 220 ff.

85 See further Bygrave 1998, p. 258.

86 For general overviews of PETs, see Burkert 1997.

person, such as a purchaser in an ECMS, to operate relatively anonymously in his direct contact with another person/organisation, such as a media distributor. There are two main mechanisms of interest here: digital cash and digital pseudonyms.

Currently, several forms of digital cash exist or are in the process of being tested.[87] Some are more privacy-enhancing than others but all are aimed at making it more difficult to link the purchase of a particular good or service to the purchaser. Digital pseudonyms, on the other hand, are aimed not so much at disconnecting the purchase of a particular good or service from the purchaser, but at making it difficult to find the real identity of the latter. At the same time, both types of mechanisms permit accountability and authentication with respect to the transaction entered into between the parties concerned.

There seems little or no valid technological or organisational reason for not incorporating these types of mechanisms into an ECMS. Indeed, as suggested in Section 2.4 above, there is a legal (and ethical) need for such incorporation, derived partly from the principles of minimality and anonymity embodied in data protection laws. A system for identity escrow could be administered fairly easily by the certification authority. In such a system, the certification authority would act as a trusted third party for purchasers (and possibly browsers) as well as for the media distributor and other ECMS actors. As a trusted third party, the certification authority would issue digital pseudonyms and hold the 'master key' connecting these pseudonyms with the real identities of the pseudonym users.

In terms of data protection, it is important to note that PETs do not necessarily guarantee total transactional anonymity; as their name suggests, they merely augment the degree of privacy enjoyed by the data subjects.[88] Concomitantly, use of PETs will not necessarily result in the elimination of personal data as defined in, say, Article 2(a) of the DPD. A digital pseudonym is quite capable of being classified as 'personal data' pursuant to most data protection laws, as the pseudonym may be indirectly linked to a specific person via the master key held by the trusted third party. However, a stringent interpretation of the 'ease/probability-of-identification' criterion (see Section 2.1) *might* result in pseudonymous data being regarded as non-personal (anonymous) if the trusted third party holding the master key operates with very strict measures to prevent the key being accessed by others.

If the use of a PET is viewed as not eliminating the registration and other use of personal data, those ECMS operations in which the PET is applied will have to comply fully with the requirements of data protection laws; i.e. the use of the PET will not take the ECMS operations outside the ambit of those legal requirements. However, the use of the PET will go a long way towards fulfilling the rules and

87 For a useful overview, see Froomkin 1996, Part III.

88 Cf. Cohen 1996, n. 217. ("Anonymity objectives and privacy objectives overlap substantially. Nonetheless, the term 'anonymity' describes a particularly stringent variety of 'privacy', and achieving true anonymity, as opposed to mere confidentiality, presents unique technological and procedural challenges").

recommendations set out in Section 2.4 above. The use of the PET may also have legal relevance for processes whereby the interests of data controllers are to be weighed against the privacy interests of data subjects; i.e. the PET may make it easier for the former interests to win out over the latter interests. Moreover, the use of a PET for a given data-processing operation may be relevant for assessing the extent to which that operation meets the criteria of 'adequate protection' in Article 25(1) and 'adequate safeguards' in Article 26(2) of the DPD (see Section 2.8 above).

Finally, note should be taken of the possibility of configuring ECMS operations such that no personal data on purchasers or browsers are registered in the first place. For example, instead of registering such data as a means of enforcing copyright, each copyrighted information product could have microcode inserted into it which prevents purchasers or other users of the product from making more than one perfect copy of it. The privacy implications of such 'blocking' mechanisms are discussed further below in Section 5.4.2.

5. Copyright Versus Privacy

5.1 Introductory comments

Copyright and privacy may be considered as protecting similar interests. Obviously, the right to privacy may be viewed as a personality right. The same applies for the moral rights granted to the author under copyright law. Thus, it could be argued that copyright and the right to privacy are branches of the same tree.[89] The right to privacy can even be regarded as deriving from copyright; Warren and Brandeis, who could be called the 'inventors' of the right to privacy (at least in US law), drew partly upon the common law on copyright to support their thesis that English and US common law implicitly protected the individual's right to privacy.[90]

However, copyright and the right to privacy can conflict if they work to the advantage of opposite parties. The intersection of the right to privacy and copyright law in this regard has not yet been thoroughly researched. The issue has become of particular interest only now that new technologies, as embodied, for example, in ECMS operations, enable the copyright owner to monitor and control with relative ease the actual use that a person makes of a copyrighted work, thereby extending the reach of copyright-holders. Until fairly recently, neither copyright, nor copyright-holders, invaded the private sphere of users of copyrighted materials. Copyright covered only acts that constituted a commercial exploitation of a work.

89 See Hughes 1988, p. 355. Hughes observes that the *droit de divulgation* could very well be viewed as a privacy right. See also Zimmerman 1992, pp. 670–673, discussing *Salinger v. Random House, Inc*, 650 F. Supp. 413 (S.D.N.Y. 1986), rev.'d 811 F.2d 90 (2nd Cir.), and cert. denied, 484 U.S. 890 (1987).

90 Warren and Brandeis 1890, pp. 204–213; see also Zimmerman 1992, pp. 698–699.

Although user privacy tends not to be directly addressed in copyright law, the users' right to privacy has arguably played a role in copyright in the 'analogue' world.[91] When copyright first entered into the users' private sphere, both the copyright-holders' interests and the user's right to privacy were expressly taken into consideration. With regard to copyright in the digital environment, however, legislators seem to underestimate the users' privacy and autonomy interests. Here the copyright-holders' sphere of control manifestly overlaps the users' private sphere.

In this section we will describe recent developments and investigate the possible impact of ECMS operations on user privacy. The purpose of this analysis is not to give an exhaustive or definitive description of the issue, but merely to provide for a rarely-taken line of approach which may provoke discussion.

5.2 COPYRIGHT VERSUS PRIVACY IN THE ANALOGUE WORLD

Until recently, the private 'consumption' or use of copyrighted works fell outside the scope of copyright law. Copyright began as a form of trade regulation. The first copyright statute in England, the Statute of Anne of 1709, was intended to establish order in the publishing industry.[92] Traditionally, the allocation of profits made from a copyrighted work was one of the main purposes of copyright law.[93] This is reflected in the exclusive rights of the copyright-holder, which mainly involve acts associated with forms of commercial exploitation.[94] Private 'analogue' use of copyrighted works, including the making of reproductions for private use, was generally not considered a commercial activity, and therefore not covered by copyright law.[95] Even though the consumers' right to privacy tends not to be expressly considered in copyright law, copyright generally did not invade the private sphere of end-users.

In the following sections we will briefly describe the mechanisms incorporated in copyright law which have kept copyright outside the end-users' private sphere. Thereafter follows an examination of the extent to which privacy considerations may have influenced copyright law.

91 See generally Haeger 1962.
92 Zimmerman 1992, p. 686.
93 See Zimmerman 1992, p. 707. See also Patterson and Lindberg 1991, p. 179. Obviously, the protection of authors' moral rights is another main goal of copyright, at least in Europe.
94 Spoor 1996, p. 71; Hugenholtz 1996a, pp. 86–87.
95 See e.g. Art. 15(2) of the German Copyright Act of 1901 (replaced by the Copyright Act of 1965) which stated that to make "a copy for personal use [was] no infringement, if it [did] not have the purpose to derive any profit from the work". Cited from Reinbothe 1981, n. 9. See also Spoor 1996, p. 72 (observing that small-scale copying for private use was generally considered permissible).

5.2.1 Copyright and privacy do not conflict

The Berne Convention of 1886 (BC or 'the Convention') grants the rights of '*public* performance', of 'communication *to the public*' and of '*public* recitation',[96] while the WIPO Copyright Treaty of 1996 (WCT) grants the right to make a work available *to the public.*[97] Considering the wording of these rights (collectively 'the right of communication'), one might argue that the *private* performance, recitation and communication, as well as the making available of a work *within the private circle*, do not fall within the scope of these rights. However, privacy concerns do not appear to be the main reason for the creation of this limitation of copyright. Ricketson states that it is likely that the term 'public' is used to indicate that only communications to "those who are willing to pay for the benefit of hearing or seeing the work performed" should be viewed as restricted acts.[98] In other words, an economic rationale lies at the root of the wording of the Convention. A non-public communication would not affect the pecuniary interests of the copyright-holder.[99]

The right of communication does not, in effect, penetrate the users' private sphere because of the addition of the term 'public' to the definition of each restricted act. In the definition of the right of reproduction in Article 9(1) BC, or in corresponding national law, no such term is used. Therefore, private copying would only fall outside the scope of copyright if a specific exemption were applicable. In many continental jurisdictions, private copying by individual users is indeed explicitly statutorily exempted.[100] In the United States, however, a specific statutory exemption does not exist. According to Litman, who observes that many copyright exemptions are the result of multilateral bargaining among affected stakeholders, an explicit private copying exemption is missing because nobody showed up to ask for it.[101] Still, however, some commentators presume that private copying falls outside the reach of US copyright, either implicitly, following from the structure and principles of copyright law, or because private copying must be regarded as 'fair use'.[102]

Whether explicit or implicit, the limitations of national copyright law which allow private copying are based on Article 9(2) BC. This provision permits national legislators to implement exemptions to the right of reproduction 'in certain special cases', if this does not come into conflict with the 'normal exploitation of the work'

---

96 Articles 11, 11bis, 11ter and 14 BC as last revised by the Act of Paris of 1971.

97 Articles 6 and 8 WCT.

98 Ricketson 1987, pp. 432, 453.

99 Hugenholtz 1996a, p. 90.

100 For France, see Act on Intellectual Property of 1992, Art. L 122-5, 2; for Belgium, see Copyright Act of 1994, Art. 22 para. 1, 4; for the Netherlands, see Copyright Act of 1912, Art. 16b; and for Germany, see Copyright Act of 1965, s. 53.

101 Litman 1997b near n. 21. Other parties, such as libraries and educators, were present at the negotiations and were rewarded with specific exemptions to their advantage.

102 Patterson and Lindberg 1991, pp. 193–197. The fair use doctrine is codified in s. 107 of the US Copyright Act 1976.

and does not 'unreasonably prejudice the legitimate interests of the author'. Although it is not specifically mentioned, and even though the criteria in the provision reflect mainly the copyright-holders' interests, according to Ricketson, private copying is assumed to fall within the scope of the provision. When Article 9(2) was included in the Convention in 1967, it was acknowledged that authors' rights should not impinge upon what is done in the private sphere. Then, however, most existing legislation that allowed private copying (which the provision was intended to legitimise), was predicated upon the assumption that reproductions would be made by hand or by typewriter. Consequently, it was thought that private copying would not readily affect the normal exploitation of a work nor come into conflict with the copyright-holders' interests.[103] Concomitantly, the economic interests of the copyright-holder and the users' right to privacy would not collide.[104]

The economic criteria of Article 9(2) BC are often expressed in national copyright legislation through the prohibition against putting into circulation reproductions which are permitted on the basis of the private copying exemption.[105] Apparently, it is felt that private copies will not interfere with the copyright-holders' interests as long as they remain within the private sphere. If private copies could legally be distributed, the private copier would be in direct competition with the copyright-holder. Accordingly, one of the factors to be considered under the fair use doctrine in the United States is the 'effect of the use upon the potential market for or value of the copyrighted work'.[106]

5.2.2 Privacy considerations in copyright law

Although privacy considerations did not play — certainly at the international level — an important role in shaping copyright law, it seems that, almost by chance, copyright law was kept out of the users' private sphere. Communications within the private sphere and private copying were not regarded as significantly affecting the interests of copyright-holders because these acts were not considered economically significant.

However, with the emergence of modern audio and video-recording techniques, opinions on private copying began to shift. Individuals were now able easily to make exact copies in the intimacy of their homes. It is not hard to see that this

103 Ricketson 1987, p. 485.

104 Although, for reasons of brevity and clarity, we do not address neighbouring or performers' rights, it should be noted that Art. 15(1)(a) of the Rome Convention of 1961 grants full discretion to the Contracting Parties to treat any 'private use' as non-infringing. This provision has been superseded, however, by Art. 16 of the WIPO Performances and Phonograms Treaty of 1996, which contains the same criteria as Art. 9(2) BC. See Ficsor 1997, pp. 214–215.

105 For the Netherlands, see Copyright Act of 1912, Art. 16b(5); for Germany, see Copyright Act of 1965, Art. 53(5).

106 Section 107(4) of the US Copyright Act.

practice could come in conflict with the normal exploitation of copyrighted works or the interests of copyright-holders.[107] Thus, even though the private copier did not directly compete with the copyright-holder, it was argued that home taping should fall under the exclusive right of reproduction and that unauthorised home taping would therefore constitute infringement. To enforce their rights, however, copyright-holders would have to violate the right to privacy of the home.[108] Hence, the exercise of copyright began to conflict with the users' right to privacy. This collision of rights is addressed in several interesting decisions of the German Federal Supreme Court (*Bundesgerichtshof*).

In 1955, in view of the large profits lost through home taping, the Supreme Court was of the opinion that home audio-recording was not covered by the statutory exemption for private copying because it dated from 1901, and at that time the legislator could not have foreseen the technological developments leading to vast amounts of private copies being made.[109] Consequently, even though it seemed covered by the wording of the provision,[110] this type of private copying was considered to be an infringement of the right of reproduction. The Court added that, where the copyright owners' interests conflict with the privacy interests of the user of a work, the former must prevail, since, without the author's creative labour, the work would not have been available for copying in the first place. Therefore, a right to prohibit private recordings was granted. The decision was heavily criticised by many commentators. They argued that the legislators had foreseen copying by mechanical devices. Moreover, in their view, even if the legislators had not foreseen this type of copying, it was implicit from the structure of copyright law that the legislators intended copyright not to invade the users' private sphere. They found that the Court had attached too little importance to the users' personality rights, and particularly to their right to privacy.[111]

In 1964, the German Supreme Court reconciled its 1955 ruling with the opinions of its critics. It decided that, although home taping indeed constitutes an infringement of copyright, the invasion of user privacy while *enforcing* copyrights was barred by the constitutionally guaranteed inviolability of the home pursuant to Article 13 of the Basic Law of 1949 (set out in Section 1.2.4 above).[112] The German collecting society (GEMA) could not demand, therefore, that retailers of recording equipment require that purchasers identify themselves in order to enable GEMA to control whether they had acquired a licence to make private copies, because such control would only be possible by penetrating the private homes of users.

107 Davies 1984, p. 71.

108 Stewart and Sandison 1989, p. 83.

109 *Grundig Reporter*, German Federal Supreme Court, 18 May 1955, [1955] GRUR 492.

110 See *supra* n. 95.

111 See Haeger 1962, Hefermehl 1957 and Spitzbarth 1963, p. 882. Spitzbarth refers to several other authors who were of this view.

112 *Personalausweise*, German Federal Supreme Court, 25 May 1964, [1965] GRUR 104. The Court stated: "Soll die Namensübermittlung für die Kl. überhaupt einen durchgreifenden Sinn haben, so

Additionally, it would be impossible to enforce copyrights against individual users anyway. Similarly, in 1983, the Court found that an owner of a copy shop could not be required to monitor every copy made by his customers, because such control would conflict with the customers' constitutionally guaranteed general privacy rights under Articles 1 and 2 of the Basic Law,[113] and because such control would be impossible in practice.[114]

In accordance with these decisions, the German legislature considered that granting a right to prohibit home taping would not be appropriate because of, *inter alia*, privacy concerns, and instead implemented in 1965 a statutory right to equitable remuneration through the imposition of a levy on the sale of sound recording equipment.[115] Similarly, a levy on reprography equipment was introduced in 1985. Thus, the interests of the copyright-holders and the users' right to privacy were balanced and user privacy, albeit indirectly, addressed in copyright law. Many countries have comparable regimes,[116] which are often inspired by the German experience.[117] In several other jurisdictions, home taping remains wholly outside the scope of copyright.[118]

(Cont.)
kann dies nur der sein, daß die Kl. auf Grund ihrer Kenntnis von Namen und Anschriften der Geräteerwerber in deren persönlicher häuslicher Sphäre Kontrollmaßnahmen durchführen und auf diese Weise etwaige Rechtsverletzungen ahnden will. Da die Art. der Verwendung der Geräte nur an Ort und Stelle festgestellt werden könnte und die Kl. bereits die Möglichkeit angekündigt hat, die erforderlichen Feststellungen auf Mitteilungen von Wohnungsnachbarn, Portiers usw. hin zu veranlassen, würde hierdurch die Gefahr unangemessener Eingriffe in die Unverletzlichkeit des häuslichen Bereichs heraufbeschworen (Art. 13 GG)".

113 As stated *supra* Section 1.2.4, the German Federal Constitutional Court has found that a person's right to informational self-determination derives from the same constitutional provisions.

114 *Kopierläden,* German Federal Supreme Court, 9 June 1983, [1984] GRUR 54. The Court held: "Mit Recht hat jedoch das BerG ausgeführt, daß eine solche generelle Kontrollpflicht im allgemeinen durchgreifenden Bedenken begegnet. Es weist darauf hin, daß die Fotokopiergeräte der Bekl. auch zur Vervielfältigung privater Aufzeichnungen, Urkunden und dergleichen benutzt werden, deren Inhalt vielfach vertraulich und nicht zur Kenntnisnahme durch dritte Personen bestimmt ist. Eine umfassende Kontrolle – und nur sie käme überhaupt als eine wirksame Maßnahme in Betracht – würde den Anspruch des einzelnen Kunden auf Vertraulichkeit, der seine Grundlage in den verfassungsrechtlich geschützten persönlichen Freiheitsrechten (Art. 1, 2 GG) hat, in unerträglicher Weise beeinträchtigen".

115 Haeger 1962, pp. 68–69; see also Reinbothe 1981 and Visser 1997, p. 48. Additionally, a levy on audio and video tapes was imposed in 1985.

116 In almost all European countries, a comparable regime has been adopted with regard to home taping, except in the United Kingdom, Ireland, Sweden and Luxembourg. See Visser 1996, p. 209.

117 In the Netherlands, for example, the creation of the home taping regime is considered to be based on the protection of the users' private sphere. See Spoor and Verkade 1993, p. 189.

118 In the United Kingdom and the United States, for instance, the copyright-holder has neither the right to forbid the private reproduction of a work nor a right to equitable remuneration. In the United States, home taping onto analogue formats is considered 'fair use'. Home taping onto digital formats apparently is not; a levy is imposed on digital audio-tapes and recorders. See Visser 1996, p. 210. The District Court in the *Betamax* case considered that Congress did not find that the protection of copyright-holders' rights over reproduction of their works was worth the privacy and enforcement problems which would arise from the restraint of home-use recording. The Supreme Court, however, did not refer to any privacy concerns in its decision to consider home taping for the purpose of time

Even though the Berne Convention does not expressly provide that communications within the private circle fall outside the ambit of copyright, the copyright legislation of many countries explicitly states that an author may not object to the communication of his work within the 'family' or 'private' circle.[119] A decision of the Dutch Supreme Court indicates that the purpose of such provisions is to ensure that copyright does not invade the users' privacy. According to the Court, the Dutch legislators enacted such a provision because the scope of author's protection is intended to be limited by the freedom of the individual citizen.[120] Consequently, it could be argued that privacy concerns are at the root of this limitation of copyright, at least in some jurisdictions. According to Visser, it is not a coincidence that the sphere protected by the right to privacy is more or less similar to the sphere kept outside the reach of the right of communication. Therefore, this boundary of copyright would not only be the result of practical or economic considerations, but also of a choice of principle.[121]

Theoretically, a problem comparable to the one addressed by the German courts in the context of the right of reproduction may arise if a right of communication within the private circle were granted; copyright-holders would have to invade the private sphere of users to be able to detect infringements and to enforce copyrights. With regard to private performances and recitations, again it would be the right of inviolability of the home which could stand in the way of enforcement of copyright; with regard to (online) communications, even if not within the private circle, it could also be the right to privacy of communications — expressly guaranteed by many national constitutions in Europe and by Article 8 of the ECHR (see Section 3 above) — which could bar the monitoring and effective enforcement of copyright.[122]

(Cont.)
shifting a 'fair use'. The basis for its decision appears to be merely economic. See *Universal City Studios, Inc., v. Sony Corp.*, 480 F. Supp. 429, 444 (C.D. Cal. 1979), rev.'d, 659 F.2d 963 (9th Cir. 1981), rev.'d, 464 U.S. 417 (1984). Nimmer asserts that the District Court's reasoning is far from flawless. See Nimmer and Nimmer § 8B.01[D].

119 For France, see Act on Intellectual Property of 1992, Art. L 122-5, 1; for Belgium, see Copyright Act of 1994, Art. 22 para. 1(3); for the Netherlands, see Copyright Act of 1912, Art. 12(4); for the United States, see Copyright Act 1976, s. 101(1); and for Germany, see Copyright Act of 1965, s. 15(3).

120 *Buma v. De Zon*, Dutch Supreme Court, 1 June 1979, NJ 1979, p. 470.

121 Visser 1997, p. 133; see also Haeger 1962, pp. 52–53. Lucas emphasises that the term 'family circle' under copyright law is a narrower concept than the notion of 'private', for the purpose of applying the right to privacy of communications. The first requires some kind of familiarity, whereas the latter applies to any non-public communication. See Lucas 1997, p. 232

122 Visser 1997, p. 34.

5.3 COPYRIGHT VERSUS PRIVACY IN THE DIGITAL WORLD

When, with the emergence of home taping and reprography, copyright hesitantly took its first steps into the users' private sphere and thus outgrew the stage of merely protecting against direct competitors, copyright and user privacy were balanced in a way that did justice to both sides; even though copyright slipped into the users' private sphere, the copyrightholder was kept outside of it. In the digital environment, however, legislators appear not to attach much weight to the users' right to privacy; copyright bluntly strides into the private sphere of users. Instead of granting a right to exercise control over acts of commercial exploitation, a right to control the use of works is awarded. Moreover, the application of a levy scheme to balance both rights is, or may be, expressly prohibited.

5.3.1 Computer programs and databases

Until recently, copyright-holders had no legal action against the private 'consumption' of copyrighted works. Reading an unauthorised copy or viewing an illegal broadcast did not constitute restricted acts under copyright law. In the analogue environment, copyright-holders had to exercise their control at the level of exploitation, i.e. the reproduction, distribution and public dissemination level.[123] This situation has changed with regard to software and databases. Under Article 4(a) of the EC Software Directive,[124] temporary reproduction is expressly included among the restricted acts. Therefore, acts which are necessary to use or 'consume' software, such as the loading, running, transmitting and displaying of the software, are covered by copyright law, because, with the current state of technology, they require for a temporary copy to be made in the computer's random access memory (RAM). Similarly, under the copyright protection and *sui generis* right granted in Articles 5(a) and 7 of the EC Database Directive,[125] the temporary reproduction and 'transfer' of a substantial part of the contents of a database are restricted acts. To gain access to an electronic database implies a temporary transfer to, or reproduction in, a computer's RAM. Thus, the private use of a database may be prohibited by the copyright-holder.

The broadening of the right of reproduction may affect the users' 'privilege' to communicate privately a work. To make a work perceptible, even in the private circle, is, in effect, covered by the right of reproduction, as is the private online communication of the work. These regimes do not simply imply a right to exercise control at the exploitation level (as copyright traditionally did), they provide for a

123 Litman 1997a, p. 601; Patterson and Lindberg 1991, p. 193; Nicholson 1995, p. 168.
124 Council Directive 91/250/EEC of 14 May 1991 on the legal protection of computer programs OJ L 122/42.
125 Council Directive 96/9/EC of 11 March 1996 on the legal protection of databases OJ L 77/20.

right to control the *use* of the works concerned.[126] Furthermore, the possibility for EU Member States to exempt private copying or extraction from electronic databases is specifically excluded under the Database Directive,[127] just as it is forbidden under the Software Directive to provide for a private copying exemption to the broad right of reproduction.[128] Thus, the application of an equitable remuneration scheme, comparable to the home taping or reprography regimes, is impossible under both Directives.[129] Under either Directive, however, it is provided that the 'lawful' user does not require express authorisation to use the product 'in accordance with its intended purpose'.[130] This, however, is not equivalent to a private use exemption, since the latter would be applicable independently of how the user acquired the original copy, and of what is to be considered the 'intended purpose' of the program or database. Also, the 'lawful acquirer' of a computer program is statutorily permitted to make a back-up copy.[131] This again differs from a general private copying exemption, because the back-up copy must serve as a replacement, whereas the private copy might serve for any non-commercial private purpose.

While the home taping regime was implemented, at least partly, because it was considered undesirable for copyright-holders to invade users' privacy, the copyright-holder may now statutorily hold the 'unlawful' private user of a computer program or database accountable; i.e. the right-holder may now control the private use of these types of works. Apparently, there are no major objections to invading user privacy to enforce rights attached to software or databases; by definition, the interests of the copyright-holders seem to outweigh the users' right to privacy. To our knowledge, on the other hand, a private individual is yet to be sued for the non-commercial, but copyright infringing, private use of software.[132] One reason for this

---

126 Hugenholtz 1996a, p. 93; see also Spoor 1996, p. 75. Spoor is of the opinion that the reproduction right had to be broadened in respect of software because, given that one server may serve a whole battery of computers, the impact of loading a program in RAM would be so great that it must be covered by copyright. Visser, on the other hand, feels that it would be enough if the copyright-holders were able to exercise control over the making available of a copyrighted work on the server. See Visser 1997, pp. 176–177. Litman argues that a 'right of commercial exploitation' should be granted instead of a 'right to use'. See Litman 1997b, Part VI.

127 See Arts 5 and 7 of the Database Directive.

128 Articles 5 and 6 of the Software Directive are interpreted as providing an exhaustive enumeration of permitted exemptions. Private use is not one of those. See also paras 5.6.17 and 5.8.2(f) of the European Commission's Green Paper on 'Copyright and the Challenge of Technology', Brussels, 7 June 1988, COM (88) 172 final. There it is observed that instead of providing for a private copying exemption, it would be more appropriate to allow the legitimate user to make back-up copies without authorisation. The pros and cons of a private copying exemption with regard to software are considered. However, end-user privacy is apparently overlooked. The fact that 'genuine private copying' is made unlawful is considered to be a side effect which is taken for granted, as it would be impossible to police such copying anyway.

129 Hugenholtz 1996b, p. 133.

130 Admittedly, this is a simplification. This is not the place, however, to discuss this issue thoroughly. See Arts 5, 6 and 9 of the Software Directive and Arts 6, 8, 9 and 15 of the Database Directive.

131 See Art. 5(2) of the Software Directive.

132 Litman observes that the suing of non-commercial private users of any type of work is a rarity. See Litman 1997b, near n. 49. Of course, infringing private use of a database has never been challenged

may be the present difficulty of detecting copyright infringements that occur in the private sphere,[133] but the introduction of electronic copyright management systems might change that in the near future. Indeed, the Database Directive seems to anticipate the existence of technological measures which protect copyrighted works and enable direct licensing with each end-user.[134]

In the United States, the approach with respect to software is largely similar. Temporary reproductions in RAM may be covered by copyright.[135] Section 117 of the US Copyright Act 1976 states, however, that the 'owner' of a copy of a computer program may make a copy of the software provided that it is 'created as an essential step in the utilization' of the program. The 'owner' is understood to be the 'legitimate holder'. The copies must be made only for the owner's personal use.[136] The main difference with respect to the European software regime appears to be that the fair use exemption is not excluded in the United States, whereas private copying exemptions are ruled out under the EC Software Directive. Non-commercial use by consumers, even if inconsistent with the intent of the author, is presumed to be 'fair' in the United States.[137] To our knowledge, however, the fair use defence has never been applied to private use by a non-legitimate holder of a copy of a program.

5.3.2 Copyright Directive Proposal

Under Article 2 of the proposed European Copyright Directive (CDP),[138] the

---

(Cont.)
on the basis of the Database Directive in court either — the Directive is too recent for such a challenge to have been mounted.

133 To cope with this problem, the Business Software Alliance introduced an 'Anti-Piracy Hotline' through which software piracy could be reported. See Visser 1997, pp. 57–58. See also <http://www.nopiracy.com.>. In the Dutch House of Representatives (*Tweede Kamer*), the legality of the initiative was discussed. The Minister of Justice found that it might be unlawful to elicit the disclosure of information concerning private use but that this would be a question for the courts to decide. See Tweede Kamer 1995–1996, Aanhangsel nr. 927.

134 Hugenholtz 1996b, p. 133.

135 *MAI Sys Corp. v. Peak Computer, Inc.*, 991 F.2d 511 (9th Cir. 1993), cert. denied, 126 L. Ed. 2d. 640, 114 S. Ct. 671 (1994). See, however, Nicholson 1995, pp. 167–169 (arguing that the court's decision is incorrect, because granting a 'right to use' software goes beyond what was proposed by the National Commission on New Technological Uses (CONTU), which contemplated a revenue stream on the proliferation of permanent copies, not on the basis of use of computer programs).

136 See *Aymes v. Bonelli*, 47 F.3d 23, 26 (2d Cir. 1995) where the court followed CONTU, which had stated that the intent of s. 117 is to grant legitimate holders of a computer program permission to copy the program in order to use it.

137 Olson 1992, p. 909.

138 Proposal for a European Parliament and Council Directive on the harmonisation of certain aspects of copyright and related rights in the Information Society, Brussels, 10 December 1997, COM (97) 628 final; Amended proposal for a European Parliament and Council Directive on the harmonisation of certain aspects of copyright and related rights in the Information Society, Brussels, 21 May 1999, COM (1999) 250 final. Commentary in this chapter refers to the amended proposal.

temporary reproduction of any type of work will constitute a restricted act under copyright. Thus, the 'consumption' or use of any digitalised work would fall within the scope of copyright law. Under Article 5(1) of the CDP, however, acts of reproduction "which are an integral and essential part of a technological process ... whose sole purpose is to enable use to be made of a work or other subject matter" must be exempted in national copyright law. Therefore, unlike the database and software regimes, broadening the right of reproduction here would not, in principle, enable copyright-holders to exercise copyright *vis-à-vis* private users. It is added, however, that this mandatory exemption would apply only when the reproduction has 'no economic significance'. Consequently, the exemption is not absolute; an economic criterion would determine its applicability. If certain uses that require temporary reproductions are considered economically significant, an exclusive right to *use* copyrighted works privately may be granted on the basis of the proposed Directive. It is difficult to predict when use will be considered economically significant. The software and database examples could imply, however, that this hurdle is not too difficult to clear.[139]

Although the Explanatory Memorandum to the proposed Copyright Directive acknowledges that, in the context of home taping, it is "not even desirable to enforce an exclusive right in this area of private use for reasons of privacy", end-user privacy is not specifically treated as a factor of importance in relation to digital use. According to the Commission, the major reason for applying the private copying exemption to home taping is the practical impossibility of enforcing copyright against individual private users.[140] In conformity with Article 9(2) BC, the Commission seems to take mainly the copyright-holders' economic interests into account. This is exemplified by the fact that Recital 27 with the proposed Copyright Directive states that private copying exemptions 'should not inhibit the use of technological measures or their enforcement against circumvention'. Furthermore, Article 5(2)(b)(bis) of the CDP which allows for a limitation "in respect of reproductions on audio, visual or audio-visual digital recording media made by a natural person for private and strictly personal use and for non-commercial ends", is "without prejudice to operational, reliable and effective technical means capable of protecting the interests of the rightholders". This may imply that once such means (i.e. ECMS) are available, private copying may, or should, not be exempted by EU Member States.

---

139 It is not unlikely that technologies will soon exist that make a work disintegrate when it is accessed a fixed number of times. Then, each temporary reproduction that occurs while the work is accessed may be viewed as having economic significance. See Litman 1997a, p. 601.

140 Explanatory Memorandum, Comment 4 in Chapter 3, Part I A.

5.4 TECHNOLOGICAL MEASURES VERSUS PRIVACY

In sum, private use of digital works would seem to be brought within the copyright owners' sphere of control because of its economic significance, and because, contrary to the enforcement of private analogue use, the enforcement of private digital use through an ECMS is presumed not to conflict with the users' right to privacy. In any case, the issue is not expressly addressed. The impossibility of enforcing copyright against individual users is viewed to constitute the main reason for private copying exemptions. Until now, the effect of enforcing, through an ECMS, 'digital' copyrights within the private sphere has been merely a theoretical issue; even if copyright-holders were granted the right to exercise control at the level of the individual private user, they were unable to enforce their broadened right in practice. In the near future, however, an ECMS may enable them to monitor private usage and enforce copyright against any individual user. This may not only impinge upon the users' right to informational privacy, but also the users' private sphere could be invaded, albeit electronically. One option to cut back on this potential would be to block private use through the construction of 'electronic fences' that the end-user cannot cross. These sorts of technological measures are briefly described below.

5.4.1 Monitoring

New techniques currently under development would enable the copyright-holder to monitor easily the use of his work and to detect copyright infringements and violations of licence terms even when these occur within the user's private sphere. Some techniques would utilise a software module attached to a digitalised copy of the work which is disseminated online. The module would record everything that happens to the copyrighted material. Each time the work is used, the module would send a message to the copyright owner, thus providing the rights-holder with an audit trail.[141] The licensor would then be able to bill the user for each specific use, or spot violations of the terms of the licence. Obviously, the data must be processed in accordance with data protection regulations. In addition to informational privacy, the more general right to privacy may also be violated. Even though such electronic monitoring is more subtle than a physical search-and-seizure procedure, from the above-mentioned decisions of the German Federal Supreme Court could follow that penetrating the users' domestic or private sphere by such monitoring may be barred by the users' right to privacy.[142] This would especially be the case if alternative, less privacy-invasive solutions are available. The availability of such

141 Clark 1996, p. 143; See also Cohen 1996, n. 10.

142 Notably, the '*pax computationis*', as an equivalent of the formal sphere of secrecy of the home is protected in several jurisdictions. See Koelman and Helberger, elsewehere in this volume, p. 203.

solutions was one of the reasons why the German Supreme Court did not acquiesce to GEMA's demand in 1964.[143]

Although the monitoring of non-commercial private use of copyrighted works in order to ensure compliance with licence terms is unprecedented, it is an established practice in the context of pay-per-view television to bill the viewer for each actual use of the service. By paying a subscription fee, the customer gains access to the TV programme. The system does not prevent taping of the programme and viewing it countless times, or sharing a copy within a private circle. The above-mentioned monitoring technique would go a step further. Even after the purchase of a copy, the copyright-holder would be able to keep track of each private use made of a work. Interestingly, the legislature in the United States felt it was necessary to protect the informational privacy of subscribers to cable services through the Cable Communications Privacy Act 1984, which is applicable to pay-per-view services. The Act allows the collection of personally identifiable information to detect unauthorised reception of cable communications. It is, however, only the unauthorised first access that can justify an intrusion on the right to privacy, and not the private copying or private communication of the work.

5.4.2 Blocking

Another technological measure to protect copyrighted works would be to encrypt copyrighted material and thus block access to such works, or certain uses of them, unless an access key is acquired. Thus, copyright and compliance with the terms of a licence could be effectively enforced, even without the licensor having to obtain knowledge of the actual use that is made of a work. If no personal data are acquired or disclosed, there can be no violation of data protection laws, and the only aspect of the right to privacy which can be breached is the right to the privacy of the home; the copyright owner would be 'blindly trespassing' into the users' private sphere. Mackaay observes that technological blocking measures can be compared to fences protecting real property.[144] In this case, the measures could be seen as negatively 'fencing in' the users' private sphere. Admittedly, these analogies are not entirely accurate (as analogies rarely are),[145] and somewhat far-fetched. It may be more accurate to say that a measure like blocking will constrict user *autonomy* rather than privacy. Certainly, such a measure will interfere with the users' autonomy more than

143 *Supra* n. 112. The German Supreme Court considered that the imposition of a levy scheme, such as existed with regard to public performances, would provide an alternative solution. In this case, the principle of proportionality was applied in the context of what could be considered '*zumutbar*' (i.e. what could reasonably be expected of the defendants to avoid endangering the rights of others). The criterion of proportionality also applies under Art. 8 ECHR: see *supra* Section 3.

144 Mackaay 1996.

145 See Litman 1997b, near n. 42. Litman rightly observes that analogies are often misappropriated in assessing the consequences of regulations in the digital environment.

copyright has done traditionally. For example, a multimedia product could be designed to prevent the making of print-outs, thus blocking the possibility of making reproductions for private, non-commercial purposes.

Some commentators assume that private copying exemptions are particularly aimed at protecting the individual's private sphere.[146] The German copyright scholar Kohler saw a connection between the ability to copy for private, non-commercial purposes and the freedom of thought.[147] Moreover, when Article 9(2) was introduced into the Berne Convention, the normative position was taken that copyright should not impinge on what is done in the private sphere.[148] If the intention of the private copying exemptions is to have neither copyright nor the copyright-holders interfere with user privacy or autonomy, the question may be posed whether it is desirable for private uses to be effectively blocked as soon as the work is used in the digital environment. From a pure privacy perspective, however, blocking is still preferable to the monitoring of private use.[149]

5.5 STATUTORY PROTECTION OF TECHNOLOGICAL MEASURES

On top of the protection already provided by copyright, contract law and technological measures, an additional layer of protection is currently in the making: the legal protection of technological measures intended to protect copyrighted works.[150] In the following, we examine whether the legal protection schemes that are adopted or proposed for this purpose are in line with the balance between copyright and the users' right to privacy which presently exists in 'analogue' copyright law. In other words, we consider whether tampering with technological measures for the purpose of private, non-commercial use of copyrighted works or of safeguarding user privacy, is outlawed.[151]

The WIPO Copyright Treaty (WCT), which is intended to supplement the Berne Convention, was signed in 1996. Articles 11 and 12 WCT oblige the Contracting Parties to provide legal protection for ECMS.[152] Article 11 states:

---

146 Hugenholtz 1996a, p. 94; Hefermehl 1957, p. 65; Haeger 1962.

147 See Spoor 1996, pp. 73–74; see also Cohen 1996, Part IV. Cohen argues that the close interdependence between the receipt and expression of information and between reading and freedom of thought, would make recognition of a right of anonymous access to reading materials 'sound constitutional policy'. Note too the Proceedings of the First IMPRIMATUR Consensus Forum (1996), available at <http://www.imprimatur.alcs.co.uk/download.htm>, ('Proceedings of the First IMPRIMATUR Consensus Forum 1996'), p. 86 (agreeing that user privacy is closely related to the freedoms of expression, association and assembly).

148 See *supra* Section 5.2.1.

149 See also Cohen 1997, p. 185.

150 See extensively Koelman and Helberger elsewhere in this volume, p. 165 ff.

151 Cf. Cohen 1996, Part V (arguing that anti-tampering provisions which are contrary to fundamental rights would not be constitutional, and therefore not enforceable).

152 In Arts 18 and 19 of the WIPO Performances and Phonograms Treaty of 1996, similar provisions are included with respect to neighbouring rights.

> "Contracting Parties shall provide adequate legal protection and effective legal remedies against the circumvention of effective technological measures that are used by authors in connection with the exercise of their rights under this Treaty or the Berne Convention and that restrict acts, in respect of their works, which are not authorized by the authors concerned or permitted by law".

Clearly, the act of circumventing technological measures by an end-user is covered by the provision.[153] However, by its wording, Article 11 WCT only applies to measures that "restrict acts ... not ... permitted by law". If private copying as well as communicating within the private circle are acts permitted under copyright law, the Contracting Parties would not have to provide for legal remedies against the circumvention of technological measures for the purpose of performing these acts. Moreover, because the provision mentions 'law' in general, and not copyright law in particular, it would seem that even the circumvention of technological measures to perform acts that are not permitted under copyright law itself, but permitted on the basis of other areas of the law (e.g. the rights to privacy or freedom of expression), may be allowed.[154]

According to a WIPO document, Articles 11 and 12 WTC were introduced because it was felt that in a digital environment "no rights may be applied efficiently without the support of technological measures of protection and rights management information necessary to license and monitor uses", and that appropriate legal provisions were needed to protect the use of such measures and information.[155] Apparently, measures which are designed to *monitor* the uses of copyrighted works are intended to fall within the scope of the provisions, even though the monitoring of the use of a work does not necessarily 'restrict acts', and, hence, does not seem to be covered by Article 11 WTC. Also, because there is no such thing as an exclusive right to monitor the use of copyrighted works, the WCT does not prescribe the protection of monitoring devices. Because the act of circumvention may be allowed on the basis of the law in general, it would seem that the provision could be interpreted as permitting the Contracting States not to outlaw the circumvention of technological measures the purpose of which is to monitor the private use of copyrighted works, if such monitoring would conflict with the right to privacy.

---

153 Cf. Art. 13 of the Basic Proposal for the Substantive Provisions of the Treaty on Certain Questions Concerning the Protection of Literary and Artistic Works to be Considered by the Diplomatic Conference of 30 August 1996, WIPO document no. CRNR/DC/4, which would have made unlawful not the act of tampering itself but the manufacturing, distribution and possession of devices that enable circumvention. Thus, circumvention for private purposes would not have been covered. Moreover, n. 13.05 stated that the Contracting Parties could take into consideration "the need to avoid legislation that would impede lawful practices".

154 See also Cohen 1997, p. 176.

155 WIPO National Seminar on Digital Technology and the New WIPO Treaties, document no. WIPO/CNR/SER/97/1, at p. 7.

Article 11 WCT is implemented in Article 6 of the proposed Copyright Directive as follows:

> "1. Member States shall provide adequate legal protection against the circumvention without authority of any effective technological measures designed to protect any copyright or any rights related to copyright as provided by law or the sui generis right provided for in Chapter III of European Parliament and Council Directive 96/9/EC, which the person concerned carries out in the knowledge, or with reasonable grounds to know that he or she pursues that objective.
> 2. Member States shall provide adequate legal protection against any activities, including the manufacture or distribution of devices, products or components or the provision of services, carried out without authority, which:
> (a) are promoted, advertised or marketed for the purpose of circumvention of, or
> (b) have only a limited commercially significant purpose or use other than to circumvent, or
> (c) are primarily designed, produced, adapted or performed for the purpose of enabling or facilitating the circumvention of,
> any effective technological measures designed to protect any copyright or any right related to copyright as provided by law or the sui generis right provided for in Chapter III of European Parliament and Council Directive 96/9/EC.
> 3. The expression 'technological measures', as used in this Article, means any technology, device or component that, in the normal course of its operation, is designed to prevent or inhibit the infringement of any copyright or any right related to copyright as provided by law or the sui generis right provided for in Chapter III of European Parliament and Council Directive 96/9/EC. Technological measures shall be deemed 'effective' where the access to or use of a protected work or other subject matter is controlled through application of an access code or any other type of protection process which achieves the protection objective in an operational and reliable manner with the authority of the rightholders. Such measures may include decryption, descrambling or other transformation of the work or other subject matter".

Even though, in conformity with copyright tradition, it is stressed in the Explanatory Memorandum that the real danger to intellectual property rights will not be single acts of circumvention by individuals,[156] the provision clearly covers such acts. Whether it intends to target only circumvention for the purpose of infringing copyrights, i.e. whether circumvention is allowed if it serves a copyright

156 See the comments with respect to Art. 6.

exemption, is not entirely clear.[157] In any case, from Recital 27 it seems to follow that circumvention of a technological measure that prevents private copying must be prohibited by the Member States. Moreover, if temporary reproduction were regarded as a restricted act because of its economic significance, then the circumvention by individuals to enable uses which require an ephemeral reproduction would be outlawed as well.[158]

Although end-user privacy does not appear to have been a factor of importance when the Commission considered the scope of copyright, the Commission acknowledges that enforcing copyright through an ECMS may conflict with the users' right to privacy. The proposed Copyright Directive's Explanatory Memorandum states:[159]

> "Since technological identification and protection schemes may, depending on their design, process personal data about consumption patterns of protected subject matter by individual consumers and thus may allow for tracing of on-line behavior, it has to be ensured that the right of privacy of individuals is respected. Therefore, such technological measures must incorporate in their technical functions privacy safeguards in accordance with the Data Protection Directive".

When Clark stated that "the answer to the machine is in the machine", he was thinking of the answer to the threat to the copyright-holders' interests posed by the use of copyrighted works in the digital environment.[160] Now the Commission places hopes on machines to provide the answer to the threat that the answering machines pose to the users' right to informational privacy. It is noteworthy that only informational privacy is considered; the general right to privacy (i.e. interference with the users' private sphere) is not addressed. It is assumed that the users' informational privacy will be properly protected through the application of PETs. As is shown in Section 2.3.1 above, the EC Data Protection Directive allows processing of personal data if it is necessary for the performance of a contract or for the establishment, exercise or defence of legal claims. If these categories are interpreted broadly, the Data Protection Directive perhaps does not afford protection against the processing of data concerning private use of works that are acquired and licensed through an ECMS. In any case, the Data Protection Directive does not regulate the way that data are collected, except for the rather vague requirement of fairness in Article 6(1)(a).[161] Whereas the relationship between

157 See Koelman and Helberger elsewhere in this volume, p. 189 ff.
158 See *supra* Section 5.3.2.
159 See Comment 1 in Chapter 3, Part III A.
160 Clark 1996.
161 See *supra* Section 2.3.1.

copyright and privacy is a problem with broad implications,[162] and whereas user privacy and autonomy is perhaps already addressed in copyright law,[163] the extent to which the users' private sphere may be invaded while enforcing copyright through an ECMS should arguably not be left to a general regulatory instrument like the Data Protection Directive, but be addressed more explicitly in copyright law.[164] To what extent should copyright-holders be permitted to process data concerning individual usage of copyrighted works, or to otherwise interfere with the users' private sphere? Do the copyright-holders' interests justify such interference?[165]

In the US Digital Millennium Copyright Act of 1998 (DMCA), circumvention of a system that *protects a copyright* is not prohibited. Only the production and distribution of devices that enable circumvention of a technological measure that protects a copyright are prohibited. Thus, circumvention for the purpose of enabling private use is permitted, even if the use were covered by copyright law. If the use constitutes an infringement it will be actionable on the basis of general copyright law. The DMCA does, however, target the act of circumventing a technological measure that *controls access.*[166] The Act contains several explicit exceptions to the prohibition on circumventing such systems. One of the exceptions permits circumvention for the purpose of protecting privacy. Article 1201(i) of the DMCA allows the disabling of access controlling measures that collect or disseminate information reflecting the online activities of a person (e.g. cookies), if conspicuous notice is not given and the data subject is not provided the ability to prevent the collection and dissemination of the information. Additionally, the act of circumvention must have the sole effect, and be carried out solely for the purpose, of preventing the collection and dissemination.[167] However, although it is permitted to circumvent under these circumstances, it is prohibited to provide the tools that enable such circumvention. Thus, it remains to be seen what effect the permission will have in practice.

---

162 To process data concerning the use of information products may not only have privacy implications. These are *information* products. As Cohen shows, a right to read anonymously may not only derive from the right to privacy but also from the rights to freedom of expression and of association: see Cohen 1996. Moreover, the fact that in the United States (which lacks an omnibus data protection law) informational privacy in the area of video rental, cable communications and library services (see *supra* Section 2.3.2) is specifically regulated, indicates the sensitive nature of data regarding the information one consumes.

163 See *supra* Section 5.2.2.

164 See also Cohen 1996, Part VI ("Rather than penalizing legitimate and constitutionally protected individual conduct, the government could enact legislation that would outlaw intrusive, anonymity-destroying practices by copyright owners").

165 Interestingly, Art. 60 of the Greek Copyright Act of 1993 specifies that, by decree, the application of mechanisms limiting the use of copyrighted works may be imposed *as long as this does not unjustifiably violate the interests of the users.* See Lucas 1997, n. 41.

166 See Koelman and Helberger elsewhere in this volume, p. 178.

167 See US House of Representatives, Digital Millennium Copyright Act of 1998, Report and Additional Views to Accompany H.R. 2281, 22 July 1998, Report 105-551, Part 2, pp. 27–28.

5.6 STATUTORY PROTECTION OF COPYRIGHT MANAGEMENT INFORMATION

The IMPRIMATUR Business Model does not envisage the implementation of any of the above-mentioned, far-reaching 'technological measures'. In the Business Model, copyright-holders will rely on the monitoring of works sold through the media distributor and on the imprint of an identifier of the work, the media distributor and the work's purchaser.[168] These imprints will facilitate the monitoring of the 'flow of works' within the system and could serve as an article of evidence against the purchaser if a licensed work pops up somewhere in violation of the terms of the licence. Also, by applying search engines to search for an imprinted identifier, it could be fairly easy to monitor whether or not a work is made available on a network. Implementation in national legislation of Article 12 WTC would protect so-called 'rights management information', which is defined as:

> "information which identifies the work, the author of the work, the owner of any right in the work, or information about the terms and conditions of use of the work, and any numbers or codes that represent such information, when any of these items of information is attached to a copy of a work or appears in connection with the communication of a work to the public".

Neither the Imprinted Media distributor ID nor the Purchaser ID appear to fall within the meaning of any of the enumerated kinds of information. Therefore, these IDs do not appear to be covered by the provision. Consequently, if the provision were directly implemented in national legislation, removing these imprints or knowingly distributing or communicating to the public works from which such imprints have been removed or altered would not necessarily be prohibited. However, if a work is licensed to be used by a single user, perhaps the identity of that user could be part of the 'conditions of use of the work' as mentioned in Article 12 WCT.

In Article 7 of the proposed Copyright Directive the Member States are required to provide legal protection against any person who removes or alters rights management information. The definition of rights management information does not specifically include information concerning the purchaser. According to the Explanatory Memorandum with the Proposal, Article 7 only "aims at the protection of electronic rights management information, and does not cover all kinds of information that would be attached to the protected material". Moreover, the Explanatory Memorandum states that the provision does not cover removal or alteration that occurs with 'authority', i.e. is permitted or even required by law (e.g. the EC Directive on data protection).[169]

---

168 See *supra* Section 1.2.1.

169 See Comments 1 and 2 with respect to Art. 7.

Similarly, in the DMCA, information regarding the purchaser of a work is not included in the definition of rights management information. Moreover, user privacy is expressly addressed; Article 1202(c) of the DMCA stipulates that the Act does not protect personally identifiable information about a user of a work. Therefore, removal or alteration of such information is not unlawful on the basis of the DMCA.[170] Apparently, the legislature found that it would be disproportionate, with respect to end-users' privacy rights, to protect imprinted information regarding the purchaser.

5.7 LICENCES

One of the purposes of an ECMS is to enable direct licensing to each individual end-user. The user would not only obtain an online disseminated copy of the work, but also an accompanying licence, which would only allow certain uses of the work. Thus, not only copyright, but also contract would constitute a legal ground for enforcement. Obviously, to enforce the terms of a valid contract against an individual is possible in any jurisdiction. An argument could then be that it is necessary to know the user and to monitor the actual use of a work in order to monitor compliance with the terms of the licence. In the EC Data Protection Directive, the processing of personal data is expressly allowed if necessary for the performance of a contract.[171]

Still, the question remains how far one can go in monitoring the extent to which a contract is observed when this monitoring involves physical or virtual penetration into the purchaser's private/domestic sphere. The 1964 and 1983 decisions of the German Federal Supreme Court and the subsequent adoption of the home taping and reprography regimes can be interpreted to imply that it would go too far to conclude licences with each private user of copyrighted works. Although copyright may invade the private sphere, the rights-holder should remain outside it.[172] On the basis of the 1964 *Personalausweise* decision, it could even be argued that the requirement of user identification so as to enforce copyright within the private sphere after the occurrence of an infringement, would be disproportionate in relation to the copyright-owners' interests because, in the end, to enforce copyright actual private use will have to be monitored, thus invading the users' private sphere.[173] From the European software and database regimes and the

170 See De Kroon elsewhere in this volume, p. 255.

171 See *supra* Section 2.3.1.

172 Article 29 of the Dutch Copyright Act of 1912 could serve as an illustration. It states that the seizure of infringing items permitted under Art. 28, is not allowed with respect to persons who do not make it a business to trade in the infringing items, and who have acquired the items only for private use, unless they have themselves infringed copyright.

173 See also Proceedings of the First IMPRIMATUR Consensus Forum 1996, *supra* n. 147, p. 88 (agreeing that a reader should only be identified in a transaction if required by a specific law).

proposed Copyright Directive, however, a conclusion to the contrary might be drawn.

Until recently, copyright contracts were concluded mainly between a copyright-holder and a party intending to exploit commercially a copyrighted work. The private use of copyrighted works can hardly qualify as an act of commercial exploitation, although, as the home taping controversy shows, it could be regarded as conflicting with the normal exploitation of a work or the legitimate interests of the copyright-holder. However, in practice copyright-holders have already begun to contract directly with private end-users. It has become common practice to include so-called shrink-wrap licences with hard copies of computer software or multimedia products.[174] To our knowledge, however, a shrink-wrap licence is yet to be enforced against an individual who used the work privately and non-commercially,[175] probably because it is virtually impossible to detect a violation of licence terms which occurs in the private sphere.

If tampering with technological measures to enable private use or the removal of imprinted information concerning the user were not declared unlawful, the copyright-holder would have to rely on the user's contractual obligation as the legal basis for holding him accountable for these acts. If the balance that exists in the analogue world is to be maintained, the question arises whether clauses in a licence which forbid removal of a purchaser ID or the circumvention of copyright for the purpose of private use, should be enforceable. Here, the heavily debated issue of the overridability of the limitations of copyright comes into play. Are such licences pre-empted by copyright law? Can other areas of the law be invoked in court to invalidate these licences? There are no clear-cut answers to either question.[176]

An argument in favour of contractual freedom in this respect could be that consumers are always free to reject a contract, or to turn to another information provider. Market forces would determine whether such limitations and contracts are acceptable to users. In this context, however, it should be considered that copyright, in effect, gives the copyright-holder a monopoly over the work concerned, and that the consumer will usually not be the information provider's equal in bargaining power.[177] Perhaps, therefore, some kind of consumer protection would be desirable. It may be further argued that, even if the copyright-holder had no legal action against removal or circumvention, most consumers would lack the technical ability

174 See Trompenaars elsewhere in this volume, p. 267 ff.

175 The validity and enforceability of shrink-wrap licences has been disputed several times. In the United States, see e.g. *Vault Corp. v. Quaid Software*, 847 F.2d 255 (5th Cir. 1988); *Step-Saver Data Systems, Inc. v. Wyse Technology*, 939 F.2d 91 (3rd Cir. 1991); *Arizona Retail Systems, Inc. v. Software Link, Inc.*, 831 F. Supp. 759 (D. Ariz. 1993); *ProCD, Inc. v. Zeidenberg*, 86 F.3d 1447, (7th Cir. 1996). For the United Kingdom, see *Beta Computers (Europe) Ltd. v. Adobe Systems (Europe) Ltd.* [1996] FSR 367. For the Netherlands, see District Court Amsterdam, 24 May 1996, [1997] Computerrecht 63.

176 For extensive treatment of these topics, see Guibault, elsewhere in this volume, p. 125 ff; Elkin-Koren 1997; Bell 1998, pp. 608–614.

177 See also Elkin-Koren 1997, p. 109; Cohen 1996, Part III.

to perform these acts. Therefore, if the above-mentioned balance should be upheld, it could be argued that the copyright owners should be forbidden from using technological measures that block or monitor private use or imprint user information in an acquired work.[178]

On the other hand, it is unclear in what direction the market will develop. If copyright-holders would become unable to receive adequate remuneration due to a vast growth of private, uncontrolled use of copyrighted works, granting them a right to exercise control over private use may be considered necessary. Moreover, to be able to pay for each individual, private use of a work may be favourable to consumers, despite the fact that their privacy is invaded. They might, for instance, appreciate customer-tailored services provided through consumer profiles. Furthermore, the losses that copyright-holders currently suffer due to private use are presently passed on to those consumers who do pay for the use of copyrighted works. Bell argues that the application of electronic copyright management systems may therefore create a world where information costs less than under the existing fair use doctrine.[179] But, then again, perhaps efficiency and wealth maximisation are not very appropriate criteria to apply where a fundamental right is at stake.[180]

5.8 MAINTAINING THE BALANCE

If, in order to respect the private sphere of users, communications within the private circle as well as private copying are left outside the reach of copyright law, the question may be posed whether the emerging possibility of licensing with each individual user and of monitoring and controlling the private use of a work can justify delimiting user privacy by enforcing copyright to a greater extent than is possible under 'analogue' copyright law. Should privacy, as Geller argues, be given priority over copyright in cases of conflict, since the former is a basic human right intimately connected with the freedom of expression?[181] A counter-argument could be that copyright also promotes freedom of expression.[182] In any case, legislators are not only obliged under international copyright law to take into account copyright-holders' interests, they are also bound by their respective constitutions and by international treaties to protect their citizens' privacy. Neither the right to

178 See also Cohen 1996, as quoted *supra* n. 164.

179 Bell 1998.

180 See also Zimmerman 1992, p. 713 (arguing that economic theories are a poor source to consult when considering the relationship between freedom of speech and copyright).

181 Geller 1996, p. 35. See also Proceedings of the First IMPRIMATUR Consensus Forum 1996, *supra* n. 147, p. 86 (agreeing that, as a general point of departure, a state of privacy is to be preferred rather than a state of no privacy). Cf. Cohen 1996 (arguing that a "right to read anonymously" may derive, other than from the right to privacy, also from the right to freedom of information and expression and the right to associate anonymously).

182 See Haeck 1998, pp. 35–37.

privacy, nor copyright, nor, for that matter, any property right, is an absolute right.[183] It would seem, therefore, that neither right prevails by definition.

Up until some 30 years ago copyright and users' right to privacy did not conflict. When it was felt that they did, as a result of the development of home taping, both rights were nevertheless balanced by imposing a levy on copying equipment and blank tapes rather than granting a right to prohibit the private copying of copyrighted works. Should this balance be upheld now that we have entered the digital networked environment? In Recital 21 of the proposed Copyright Directive, the European Commission considers that a 'fair balance' between copyright-holders and users of protected subject matter must be safeguarded. This 'fair balance' need not necessarily replicate the balance achieved in the analogue environment. The peculiarities of the digital environment may mean that the equilibrium should shift to one side or the other. The European software and database regimes, for example, appear to reflect the need for an extension of copyright to cover the unlawful private 'consumption' or use of copyrighted products in the digital environment, although, to our knowledge, such an extended right has not yet been invoked to prohibit non-commercial, private use by an 'unlawful' acquirer. The proposed Copyright Directive would permit the Member States to abolish the private copying exemption with respect to digital copying of those works not covered by the software and database regimes, and to broaden the right of reproduction to cover the use of these works when such use is considered economically significant. Apparently, the copyright-holders' interests gain more weight when a work is to be used in the digital environment. However, the users' right to privacy appears to be mostly overlooked when the scope of copyright and the reach of the copyright-holder in the digital environment are considered.[184] Remarkably, user privacy seems to carry greater weight in the context of the legal protection of rights management information. The fact that a blind eye is turned to the users' right to privacy where digital use of copyrighted works is concerned seems to follow from a presumption that enforcement through an ECMS will not unduly

---

183 As noted *supra* Section 1.2.4, Art. 8(2) of the ECHR states, *inter alia*, that the right to privacy may be limited if necessary for the protection of the rights of others. In its *Kirchen- und Schulgebrauch* decision, the German Federal Constitutional Court stated that copyright is a property right and thus protected under Art. 14 of the Basic Law of 1949 which allows for property rights to be restricted in the public interest: German Federal Constitutional Court (*Bundesverfassungsgericht*) 7 July 1971, [1972] GRUR 481. Similarly, Art. 1 of the 1st Protocol to the ECHR (which protects the 'peaceful enjoyment' of possessions), provides that a State Party may "enforce such laws as it deems necessary to control the use of property in accordance with the general interest". In the United States, the situation is apparently comparable; see Cohen 1996, near n. 162.

184 See Legal Advisory Board for the Information Market, *Reply to the Green Paper on Copyright and Related Rights in the Information Society*, Brussels 1995, available at <http://www2.echo.lu/legal/en/ipr/reply/reply.html> ('LAB 1995'), under "Human Rights" (noting that informational privacy considerations are practically absent from the Green Paper (Commission of the European Communities, Green Paper on 'Copyright and Related Rights in the Information Society', Brussels, 19 July 1995, COM (95) 382 final).

impinge upon the users' private sphere and that the main reason for exempting private copying is the practical impossibility of enforcing copyright against individual users. Even if the latter view is correct, enforcement of copyright through an ECMS will delimit user privacy and autonomy to a greater extent than 'analogue' copyright does. Given the importance of privacy and freedom of information and expression in a democratic society, and given the fact that copyright, in effect, constitutes a form of information policy, it will be desirable to undertake a careful and explicit balancing of interests to determine the extent to which the users' right to privacy may be interfered with in order to enforce copyright through an ECMS.[185]

6. Conclusion

This study shows that the development of electronic copyright management systems has the potential to impinge on the privacy and related interests of purchasers/users of copyrighted information products to an unprecedented degree. At the same time, various safeguards—legal, technological and organisational—do exist which may reduce this potential. Ultimately, the stringency of these safeguards in practice will be determined by the outcome of interest-balancing processes.

On the legal-ethical plane, the interest-balancing process will mainly consist of an assessment of what is necessary/proportionate for ensuring the effective enforcement of copyright-holders' legitimate interests in the light of the privacy and related interests of purchasers/users. On the commercial-political plane, the interest-balancing process will mainly take the form of a struggle between, on the one hand, copyright-holders and their representative organisations and, on the other hand, consumer groups, for the sympathies of legislators.

On both planes, however, the most important thing will be to secure balanced and thorough public debate about how best to weigh up the above interests. It is undesirable that the outcome of the interest-balancing be determined, in effect, by technological fiat or by one-eyed lobbying. This chapter may hopefully contribute to preventing such an outcome.

185 See also LAB 1995, *ibid.*, under "Human Rights" ("the right to privacy and the freedom of expression and information are clearly affected and therefore need careful consideration. The LAB therefore recommends that the Commission give sufficient attention and weight to issues of privacy protection and freedom of expression and information when undertaking any initiative in the area of intellectual property rights in the digital environment").

References

T.W. Bell (1998), 'Fair Use vs. Fared Use: The Impact of Automated Rights Management on Copyright's Fair Use Doctrine', (1998) 76 *North Carolina Law Review* 557.

C.J. Bennett (1992), *Regulating Privacy: Data Protection and Public Policy in Europe and the United States*, Ithaca/London: Cornell University Press 1992.

H. Burkert (1997), 'Privacy-Enhancing Technologies: Typology, Critique, Vision', in P.E. Agre and M. Rotenberg (eds.), *Technology and Privacy: The New Landscape*, Cambridge, Massachusetts/London: MIT Press 1997, pp. 125-142.

L.A. Bygrave (1998), 'Data Protection Pursuant to the Right to Privacy in Human Rights Treaties', (1998) 6 *International Journal of Law and Information Technology* 247.

L.A. Bygrave (1999), 'Data Protection Law: Approaching its Rationale, Logic and Limits', doctoral thesis on file with author, to be published mid-2000.

Canadian Association of Internet Providers (1997), *Code of Conduct*, available at <http://caip.ca/caipcode.htm>.

A. Clapham (1993), *Human Rights in the Private Sphere*, Oxford: Clarendon Press 1993.

C. Clark (1996), 'The Answer to the Machine is in the Machine', in P. B. Hugenholtz (ed.), *The Future of Copyright in a Digital Environment*, The Hague/London/Boston: Kluwer Law International 1996, pp. 139–148.

J. E. Cohen (1996), 'A Right to Read Anonymously: A Closer Look at "Copyright Management"' (1996) 28 *Connecticut Law Review* 981-1039.

J. E. Cohen (1997), 'Some Reflections on Copyright Management Systems and Laws Designed to Protect Them', (1997) 12 *Berkeley Technology Law Journal* 161.

G. Davies (1984), *Private Copying of Sound and Audio-Visual Recordings*, Oxford: ESC Publishing 1984.

N. Elkin-Koren (1997), 'Copyright Policy and the Limits of Freedom of Contract', (1997) 12 *Berkeley Technology Law Journal* 93.

R. Ellger (1991), 'Datenschutzgesetz und europäischer Binnenmarkt (Teil 2)', [1991] *Recht der Datenverarbeitung* 121.

M. Ficsor (1997), 'The Spring 1997 Horace S. Manges Lecture — Copyright for the Digital Era: The WIPO "Internet" Treaties', (1997) 21 *Columbia VLA Journal of Law & the Arts* 197.

M. Froomkin (1996), 'Flood Control on the Information Ocean: Living with Anonymity, Digital Cash, and Distributed Databases', (1996) 15 *University of Pittsburg Journal of Law and Commerce* 395.

M. Froomkin (1997), 'The Internet as a Source of Regulatory Arbitrage', in B. Kahin and C. Nesson (eds.), *Borders in Cyberspace: Information Policy and the Global Information Infrastructure*, Cambridge, Massachusetts/London: MIT Press 1997, pp. 129–163.

R. Gavison (1980), 'Privacy and the Limits of Law', (1980) 89 *Yale Law Journal* 421.

P.E. Geller (1996), 'Conflicts of Law in Cyberspace: International Copyright in a Digitally Networked World', in P. B. Hugenholtz (ed.), *The Future of Copyright in a Digital Environment*, The Hague/London/Boston: Kluwer Law International 1996, pp. 27–48.

G. Greenleaf (1995), 'European Privacy Directive and data exports', (1995) 2 *Privacy Law & Policy Reporter*) 105.

G. Greenleaf (1996a), 'Privacy and cyberspace — an ambiguous relationship', (1996) 3 *Privacy Law & Policy Reporter* 88.

G. Greenleaf (1996b), 'Privacy principles — irrelevant to cyberspace?', (1996) 3 *Privacy Law & Policy Reporter* 114.

J.F. Haeck (1998), *Idee en Programmaformule in het Auteursrecht*, Deventer: Kluwer 1998.

S. Haeger (1962), 'Die Einbruch von Nutzungsrechten in die Privatsphäre', (1962) 37 *Archiv für Urheber- Film- Funk- und Theaterrecht* 45.

D.J. Harris, M. O'Boyle and C. Warbrick (1995), *Law of the European Convention on Human Rights*, London/Dublin/Edinburgh: Butterworths 1995.

W. Hefermehl (1957), 'Magnetton-Aufnahmen urheberrechtlich geschützter Werke zum persönlichen Gebrauch', (1957) 24 *Archiv für Urheber- Film- Funk- und Theaterrecht* 56.

P.B. Hugenholtz (1996a), 'Adapting Copyright to the Information Superhighway', in P.B. Hugenholtz (ed.), *The Future of Copyright in a Digital Environment*, The Hague/London/Boston: Kluwer Law International 1996, pp. 81–102.

P.B. Hugenholtz (1996b), 'De Databankrichtlijn eindelijk aanvaard, een zeer kritisch commentaar', [1996] *Computerrecht* 131.

J. Hughes (1988), 'The Philosophy of Intellectual Property', (1988) 77 *The Georgetown Law Journal* 287.

J. Litman (1997a), 'Symposium: Copyright Owners' Rights and Users' Privileges on the Internet: Reforming Information Law in Copyright's Image', (1997) 22 *Dayton Law Review* 587.

J. Litman (1997b), 'New Copyright Paradigms', in L.N. Gassaway (ed.), *Growing Pains: Adapting Copyright for Libraries, Education and Society*, Littleton, Co.: Rothman 1997, available at <http://www.msen.com/~litman/paradigm.htm>.

A. Lucas (1997), 'Copyright Law and Technical Protection Devices', (1997) 21 *Columbia VLA Journal of Law & the Arts* 225.

E. Mackaay (1996), 'The Economics of Emergent Property Rights on the Internet', in P.B. Hugenholtz (ed.), *The Future of Copyright in a Digital Environment*, The Hague/London/Boston: Kluwer Law International 1996, pp. 13–26.

V. Mayer-Schönberger (1998), 'The Internet and Privacy Legislation: Cookies for a Treat?' (1998) 14 *Computer Law & Security Report* 166.

A.R. Miller (1971), *The Assault on Privacy: Computers, Data Banks, and Dossiers*, Ann Arbor: University of Michigan Press 1971.

B.J. Nicholson (1995), 'The Ghost in The Machine: Mail Systems Corp. v. Peak Computer, Inc. and the Problem of Copying in RAM', (1995) 10 *Berkeley Technology Law Journal* 147.

M.B. Nimmer and D. Nimmer, *Nimmer on Copyright*, New York/San Francisco: Mathew Bender, looseleaf.

J. Nouwt and H.A.C.M. Vorselaars (1996), 'Privacy in Cyberspace', in V. Bekkers, B.-J. Koops and S. Nouwt (eds.), *Emerging Electronic Highways: New Challenges for Politics and Law*, The Hague/London/Boston: Kluwer Law International, 1996, pp. 103–120.

E.W. Olson (1992), 'Galoob v. Nintendo: Subject Matter Fixation and Consumer Fair Use Define the Scope of Copyright Protection for Interoperable Works', (1992) 18 *Rutgers Computer & Technology Law Journal* 879.

L.R. Patterson and S.W. Lindberg (1991), *The Nature of Copyright, A Law of Users' Rights*, Athens/London: The University of Georgia Press 1991.

S. Ricketson (1987), *The Berne Convention for the Protection of Literary and Artistic Works: 1886–1986*, London/Reading: The Eastern Press 1987.

J. Reinbothe (1981), 'Compensation for Private Taping Under Sec. 53(5) of the German Copyright Act', [1981] *International Review of Industrial Property and Copyright Law* 36.

R. Samarajiva (1997), 'Interactivity As Though Privacy Mattered', in P.E. Agre and M. Rotenberg (eds.), *Technology and Privacy: The New Landscape*, Cambridge, Massachusetts/London: MIT Press 1997, pp. 277–309.

P. Schoning (1998), 'Danish Report, In Response to François Dessemontet's Questionnaire', in G. Roussel (ed.), *Conference Proceedings of the ALAI Conference 1997*, Cowansville: Les Éditions Yvon Blais 1998 , pp. 174–180.

P.M. Schwartz (1995), 'European Data Protection Law and Restrictions on International Data Flows', (1995) 80 *Iowa Law Review* 471.

R. Spitzbarth (1963), 'Der Streit um die private Tonbandaufname', (1963) 16 *Neue juristische Wochenschrift* 881.

J.H. Spoor (1996), 'The Copyright Approach to Copying on the Internet: (Over)Stretching the reproduction Right?', in P. B. Hugenholtz (ed.), *The Future of Copyright in a Digital Environment*, The Hague/London/Boston: Kluwer Law International 1996, pp. 67–80.

J.H. Spoor and D.W.F. Verkade (1993), *Auteursrecht,* Deventer: Kluwer 1993.

S.M. Stewart and H. Sandison (1989), *International Copyright and Neighbouring Rights*, London/Boston/Sydney: Butterworth 1989.

C. de Terwangne and S. Louveaux (1997), 'Data Protection and Online Networks', 13 *Computer Law & Security Report* (1997), pp. 234–246.

D.J.G. Visser (1996), 'Auteursrechtvergoedingen in Europa en de VS', *ITeR deel 2,* Alphen aan den Rijn/Diegem: Samson Bedrijfsinformatie 1996, pp. 202–321.

D.J.G. Visser (1997), *Auteursrecht op toegang, De exploitatierechten van de auteur in het tijdperk van digitale informatie en netwerkcommunicatie*, The Hague: VUGA 1997.

S.D. Warren and L.D. Brandeis (1890), 'The Right to Privacy', (1890) 4 *Harvard Law Review* 193.

A.F. Westin (1967), *Privacy and Freedom*, New York: Atheneum 1967.

D.L. Zimmerman (1992), 'Information as Speech, Information as Goods: Some Thoughts on Marketplaces and the Bill of Rights', (1992) 33 *William & Mary Law Review* 665.

III. Contracts and Copyright Exemptions

Lucie M.C.R. Guibault

1. Introduction

Contracts are legal instruments essential to the exploitation of copyrights, from the moment of creation of a work to its end use by the consumer. But while the vast majority of copyright contracts are beyond doubt enforceable, the validity of the few contracts that attempt to bar precisely those activities that copyright law permits should be examined closely.[1] Indeed, the grant of exclusive exploitation rights under copyright law, including the limitations imposed on their exercise, is thought to reflect a balance carefully drawn by the legislator to encourage creation on the one hand and dissemination of new material, on the other.[2] Any contractual expansion of rights beyond what is provided for under copyright law risks disrupting this balance of interests, which may ultimately stifle creation.

In practice, the threat of seeing contracts rule out some or all of the users' rights has dramatically increased, since digital technology now easily allows copyright owners to impose their terms of use, often through non-negotiated agreements. The tendency to have transactions for information governed by contractual terms raises the issue of the overridability of copyright limitations in more acute terms in the digital environment than in the analogue world, where everyone relied on copyright law to set the limits of permitted action. This aspect of the boundary between copyright law and contract law has recently been the object of much attention in the United States, particularly during the drafting process of proposed Article 2B of the Uniform Commercial Code. In view of the controversy around it, the National Conference of Commissioners on Uniform State Laws eventually adopted the text not as an article of the Uniform Commercial Code but as a separate document, the Uniform Computer Information Transactions Act (UCITA). Once implemented into State law the new regime will not only validate shrink-wrap and other mass-market licences of information, but will also set out

1 See Nimmer, Frischling and Brown 1998.
2 Guibault 1996, p. 210.

Copyright and Electronic Commerce (ed. P. Bernt Hugenholtz; ISBN 90-411-9785-0; © Kluwer Law International, 2000; printed in Great Britain).

rules on electronic contracting for information products and services.[3] In the wake of the highly criticised decision of the Court of Appeal for the Seventh Circuit in *ProCD v. Zeidenberg,*[4] negotiations over the draft of UCITA have been marked by intense discussions on the necessity to include a specific section on pre-emption, which would, in addition to the constitutional Supremacy Clause[5] and section 301 of the US Copyright Act,[6] ensure precedence of the copyright limitations over contractual provisions to the contrary.

In the European Union, however, pre-emption issues have rarely been examined. This may be due to the fact that copyright rules are not subject to constitutional pre-emption in any of the Member States, and no provision similar to section 301 of the US Copyright Act has been enacted as a consequence. In rare cases, the legislator has avoided possible conflicts between contract law and copyright law by expressly providing that copyright rules have precedence over contractual provisions to the contrary. This is the case of the Directives on computer programs and databases, which both contain provisions stating that contractual provisions which prevent users from accomplishing specific acts allowed therein, are null and void.[7] In the absence of specific language from the legislator, the assessment of whether other statutory copyright limitations override contractual provisions to the contrary must follow a careful examination of the basis of each limitation. Some limitations may find their justification in competing bodies of law, such as the European Convention on Human Rights or the competition rules of the EC Treaty, while others may result from national public interest considerations or serve as a remedy to market failure. Public policy reasons may thus warrant the mandatory application of a number of these limitations, for fear of disrupting the

3 Samuelson 1998, p. 1; see Trompenaars, elsewhere in this volume, p. 277 ff.

4 86 F.3d 1447 (7th Cir. 1996); see Trompenaars, elsewhere in this volume, p. 270. In this case, the Court enforced a mass market licence restriction permitting only 'home use' of a CD-ROM of telephone directory information, despite the fact that telephone directory information had been declared non-copyrightable subject matter by the US Supreme Court in *Feist Publications, Inc. v. Rural Telephone Service Co., Inc.*, 499 U.S. 340 (1991). Main critics consider that the *ProCD* decision goes against federal copyright policy not to protect purely factual information and that the mass market licence should have been pre-empted under s. 301 of the US Copyright Act.

5 According to Karjala 1997, p. 533, "pre-emption can also occur under the Supremacy Clause of the Constitution, where the state law 'stands as an obstacle to the accomplishment and execution of the full purposes and objectives of Congress'".

6 Section 301(a) of the US Copyright Act of 1976 reads as follows: "On and after January 1, 1978, all legal or equitable rights that are equivalent to any of the exclusive rights within the general scope of copyright as specified by section 106 in works of authorship that are fixed in a tangible medium of expression and come within the subject matter of copyright as specified by sections 102 and 103, whether created before or after that date and whether published or unpublished, are governed exclusively by this title. Thereafter, no person is entitled to any such right or equivalent right in any such work under the common law or statutes of any State".

7 Council Directive 91/250/EC of 14 May 1991 on the Legal Protection of Computer Programs, OJ L 122/42, Art. 5 ('Computer Programs Directive'); and Directive 96/9/EC of the European Parliament and of the Council of 11 March 1996 on the Legal Protection of Databases, OJ L 77/20, Art. 6 ('Database Directive').

balance struck by copyright law.

The question of copyright overridability is not merely theoretical. As transactions relating to digital information are increasingly being completed through licensing agreements, practical problems are likely to arise as to the validity of the conditions of use of copyrighted material set out in such licences. Moreover, given the global nature of digital networked transactions, it is to be expected that, now that the UCITA has been adopted, some pressure will be exercised on foreign countries to adopt similar provisions.

This chapter is divided in two sections. The first examines the statutory limitations on the exercise of exclusive rights and their grounds for implementation, as well as a number of possible limitations found outside copyright law, for example in constitutional law, civil law, consumer protection law and competition law. We will also have a brief look at the current draft of Article 5 of the Proposal for a European Directive on the harmonisation of certain aspects of copyright and related rights in the Information Society. The second section concentrates on the issue of copyright overridability. On the basis of the findings in the first section, we will attempt to draw the boundary between copyright and contract law by trying to determine the legal status of the statutory copyright limitations in relation to contracts. Are the copyright limitations imperative or default rules? Are the copyright exemptions, like the right to reproduce a work for private research, the right to quote and the library privilege, mandatory provisions that pre-empt any contractual clause to the contrary? If statutory copyright exemptions are simply default rules which can be excluded from the application of a fully negotiated contract, does this hold true in the case of non-negotiated contracts, such as shrink-wrap licences, as well?

2. Limitations on the Exercise of Exclusive Rights

Like any other type of private property right, copyrights are not absolute rights. Even the countries most committed to the advancement of author's rights recognise the need for restrictions or limitations upon these rights in particular circumstances.[8] There are several reasons to restrict the scope of copyright, all of which are designed to maintain a balance between the rights of copyright holders and users, respectively.[9] Some limitations are based on fundamental principles of law, some on public interest considerations, and others on economic factors. The justifications for

8 See Bochurberg 1994, p. 31; Schricker 1997, p. 139.

9 See e.g. the preamble to the WIPO Copyright Treaty 1996: "The Contracting Parties, recognising the need to maintain a balance between the rights of authors and the larger public interest, particularly education, research and access to information, as reflected in the Berne Convention have agreed as follows".

the creation of such limitations are not static however: limitations based today on public interest considerations may eventually be justified as remedies to market failure, and likewise, limitations which are currently implemented in response to perceived market failure may take a public interest dimension in the future. It is also quite possible that certain limitations have more than one ground of justification.

2.1 LIMITATIONS FOUND IN COPYRIGHT LAW

While most exemptions to copyright find their origin in international instruments like the Berne Convention, states have always maintained full sovereignty to decide whether and how to implement their international obligations in the national legal order. Differing policy orientations, distinct drafting techniques and judicial interpretation have resulted in a variety of copyright limitations found among the countries of the Berne Union, ranging from the minimal exemptions allowed under the French Intellectual Property Code, to the extensive list of limitations recognised under the United Kingdom Copyright, Designs and Patents Act 1988.[10] Solutions to the same problem also tend to vary from one country to another. A particular use may be carved out from the scope of protection in one country, and take the form of a statutory licence, with or without remuneration, in another.

In any case, limitations imposed on the exercise of exclusive rights under copyright law have been divided, for the purpose of this chapter, into four categories: (1) limitations based on the defence of fundamental rights; (2) limitations based on competition law considerations; (3) limitations based on public interest considerations; and (4) limitations based on market failure. At the end of this section we will have a brief look at Article 5 of the Proposal for a Directive on the harmonisation of certain aspects of copyright and related rights in the Information Society,[11] adopted by the European Commission in December 1997.

2.1.1 Limitations based on the defence of fundamental rights

In October 1997, the European Parliament passed a Resolution containing its main guidelines and recommendations for the elaboration of a Directive on copyright and the Information Society. The safeguard of the public's fundamental rights

10 Hugenholtz 1996, p. 93.

11 Proposal for a Directive on the harmonisation of certain aspects of copyright and related rights in the Information Society, Brussels, 10 December 1997, COM (97) 628 final ('Proposal for a Directive' or 'the Proposal'). Following discussions in the European Parliament an amended proposal was adopted by the European Commission on 21 May 1999, COM (99)250 final. Commentary in the present chapter refers to the original proposal.

constitutes an important preoccupation for the European Parliament. Among other points, the Parliament stresses "that it is essential to make a distinction between the protection of copyright and related rights and the protection of individual freedoms, such as freedom of expression and, in general terms, the interests of the general public, the right to respect for human dignity and privacy or the public's right to be informed".[12] At paragraph 19 of the Resolution, the Parliament adds that, in support of the principles expressed in the Ministerial Declaration of July 1997, "rules on responsibility relating to copyright and neighbouring rights must take into account their impact on freedom of speech, respect public and private interests and not impose disproportionate burdens on actors".

Freedom of expression and right to information

The individual's freedom of expression and the public's fundamental right to information are guaranteed under several international instruments. The most significant among these is perhaps the Universal Declaration on Human Rights of 1948,[13] in particular its Article 19 on the freedom of opinion and expression and the freedom to seek, receive and impart information. In addition, Article 27 not only recognises everyone's right to the protection of the moral and material interests resulting from any scientific, literary or artistic production of which he is the author, but recognises also the right to participate freely in the cultural life of the community. These two provisions of the Universal Declaration have been incorporated in Article 19 of the International Covenant on Civil and Political Rights[14] and Article 15 of the International Covenant on Economic, Social and Cultural Rights,[15] respectively, whereas Article 10 of the European Convention for the protection of Human Rights and fundamental freedoms (ECHR)[16] essentially repeats Article 19 of the Declaration on the freedom of opinion and expression.

Protection is guaranteed to all members of society, whether authors, performers, or simple users of protected material. But the rights-holders' freedom of expression, which materialises ultimately in copyright protection of their works, is not absolute; it is counterbalanced by the public's same fundamental rights and freedoms. Hence, rights-holders must, in making use of their own rights, take account of those of others.[17] The balance between the rights of the creators and

12 Resolution on the Communication from the Commission: European Parliament, Follow-up to the Green Paper on Copyright and Related Rights in the Information Society, of 23 October 1997, para. 12.

13 Adopted unanimously by the United Nations General Assembly on 10 December 1948.

14 Signed on 16 December 1966, reproduced in (1976) 999 United Nations Treaty Series, p. 187.

15 Signed on 16 December 1966, reproduced in (1976) 999 United Nations Treaty Series, p. 13.

16 European Convention for the Protection of Human Rights and Fundamental Freedoms, Rome, 4 November 1950, Art. 10.

17 Spoor and Verkade 1993, p. 187.

those of the public contributes to maintaining the free flow of information within society.

The fact that, as a principle, copyright law only protects the form of expression and not the underlying ideas certainly tends to limit the possible impact of copyright on freedoms of speech and the right to information. Following this principle, anyone may publish or reproduce the ideas of another contained in copyrighted material, provided that the form of expression is not also reproduced.[18] While the freedom to use another's ideas contributes substantially to the freedom of public debate and news reporting, there may be circumstances where it is important to be able to use not merely a person's ideas, but also his form of expression in order to have effective reporting or criticism of his/her thoughts. For example, it may be important to capture the mood, the tone or the nuances in an address, which may not be possible without reproducing a substantial part of the speaker's form of expression.[19]

Whether from the *droit d'auteur* or copyright tradition, most countries have enacted some measures designed to safeguard the individual's freedom of speech and the public's right to information, and to promote the free flow of information. These limitations are established within the boundaries set by the Berne Convention and the Rome Convention. The Berne Convention makes the right to quote mandatory, but leaves the decision to Member States whether to adopt exemptions in favour of the press and to exclude official texts, political speeches and speeches delivered in the course of legal proceedings from copyright protection. The adoption of limitations on the exercise of copyright is implicitly permitted, or even required, under Article 10(2) of the ECHR and Article 19(3) of the International Covenant, whereby states may impose statutory restrictions on the freedom of expression and information that are necessary in a democratic society for the protection of the rights of others.

To make a list of all possible limitations adopted for this purpose pursuant to the Berne Convention proves very difficult, particularly in view of the many nuances brought by national legislators and by linguistic subtleties. Some limitations relate to the informational character of the protected material, such as political speeches and other similar public addresses, while others regulate the manner in which protected material may be used without the rights-holder's consent. Most limitations are subject to strict conditions of application. However, uses allowed under these provisions often, but not always, do not entail monetary compensation for the rights-holders. It is generally deemed in the general public interest that such material or such uses be allowed without the authorisation of the rights-holder and without payment of a fee.[20] Among the numerous limitations that may be

18 Johnston 1996, p. 6.
19 Kéréver 1996, p. 323.
20 Schricker 1997, p.161.

introduced into national legislation for the promotion of the free flow of information are the following:

1. the right to quote works of critic, polemic, informational or scientific character for purposes of criticism, news reporting;[21]
2. the right to reproduce press reviews, news reports, miscellaneous reports or articles concerning current economic, political or religious topics that have appeared in a daily or weekly newspaper or weekly or other periodical or works of the same nature that have been broadcast in a radio or television programme;[22]
3. the right to reproduce, make available or broadcast political speeches and other public addresses;[23]
4. the right to reproduce individual articles, reports or other texts which have appeared in a daily or weekly newspaper or weekly or other periodical, or short passages from books, pamphlets or other writings, in so far as they are scientific works;[24]
5. the right to record, show or announce a literary, scientific or artistic work in public in a photographic, film, radio or television report, provided this is necessary in order to give a proper account of the current affairs that are the subject of the report;[25]
6. the right to reproduce works for purposes of parody.[26]

These limitations have all been implemented into national legislation in some form or another for the purpose of promoting political, social, economic and cultural debate, as an integral part of a free and democratic society.

Right to privacy

Traditionally, copyright owners have never held absolute control over the use of their works. They were never able to prevent personal use of their works, that is to prevent someone from reading, listening to or viewing a work for his or her own learning, enjoyment, or sharing with a colleague or friend, as long as the work being used had been previously made public and as long as there was no motive for profit

---

21 French Intellectual Property Code (*Code de la propriété intellectuelle*), Art. L. 122-5, 3° (a); German Copyright Act (*Urheberrechtsgesetz*), BGBl. I S. 1273, 9 September 1965, s. 51; Dutch Copyright Act of 1912, Art. 15a; Belgian Copyright Act, (*Loi du 30 juin 1994 relative au droit d'auteur et aux droits voisins,* Moniteur belge, 27 July 1994), p. 19297, Art. 21.

22 Dutch Copyright Act of 1912, art. 15; German Copyright Act, s. 49; French Intellectual Property Code, Art. L. 122-5, 3° (b).

23 German Copyright Act, s. 48; French Intellectual Property Code, art. L. 122.5,3°(c).

24 Dutch Copyright Act of 1912, Art. 17.

25 Dutch Copyright Act of 1912, Art. 16a; German Copyright Act, s. 50; Belgian Copyright Act, Art. 22 s. 1, 1°.

26 French Intellectual Property Code, Art. L. 122-5, 4°; Belgian Copyright Act, Art. 22 para. 1, 6°.

behind the private use.[27] It is generally thought that copyright and neighbouring rights do not protect against acts of consumption or reception of information.[28] However, there is under the Berne Convention no limitation allowing the performance or broadcast of an author's work in the family circle[29] or to its reproduction for private use.[30]

Nevertheless, such limitations have long been introduced in the legislation of many countries partly on the basis that copyright and neighbouring rights do not extend to the private sphere of individuals, and partly on the basis that reproduction for private use does not affect the interests of the rights-holders. It has been argued that the wording and the structure of some of the exclusive rights granted to authors, performers and phonogram producers implies that rights-holders are not meant to control the use made of their work in people's homes. Under the copyright laws of many countries, rights-holders have indeed been granted the exclusive right to perform in 'public', to communicate to the 'public', and to present a work at a 'public' exhibition.[31] Consequently rights-owners may not prohibit the accomplishment of these acts, if they are completed strictly within the private circle. Admittedly, these provisions raise some controversy in case law, as to the proper definition of 'public' and 'private' and as to what can be considered a close family tie or an intimate friendship of the participants to a performance.[32] Furthermore, to be generally considered lawful, no admission fee must be charged on the audience of such a representation. In other words, there must be a motive for profit.

The basis of the right to make reproductions for private purposes follows the same grounds of analysis as those set out above, despite the fact that the reproduction right covers all reproductions of a work in any manner or form, notwithstanding any possible distinction between the private and the public sphere. It was initially thought that hand-copying or typewriting of a manuscript did not affect the normal exploitation of the work, and that such practice could therefore be considered lawful.[33] On this basis, many statutes still provide that a reproduction is lawful if it is realised for personal or private purposes and if it is made without any

---

27 Gordon 1989, p. 1383; and Patterson and Lindberg 1991, p. 193.

28 Legal Advisory Board 1995.

29 See French Intellectual Property Code, Art. L. 122-5, 1°; Belgian Copyright Act, Art. 22 para. 1, 3°.

30 See French Intellectual Property Code, Art. L. 122-5, 2°; Belgian Copyright Act, Art. 22 para. 1, 4° and 5°; Dutch Copyright Act of 1912, Art. 16(b); German Copyright Act, s. 53.

31 See e.g. French Intellectual Property Code, Art. L. 122-2: "La représentation consiste dans la communication de l'oeuvre au *public* par un procédé quelconque, et notamment: 1° Par récitation *publique*, exécution lyrique, représentation dramatique, présentation *publique*, projection *publique* et transmission dans un lieu *public* de l'oeuvre télédiffusée; 2° Par télédiffusion. La télédiffusion s'entend de la diffusion par tout procédé de télécommunication de sons, d'images, de documents, de données et de messages de toute nature. Est assimilée à une représentation l'émission d'une oeuvre vers un satellite"(emphasis added).

32 Bertrand 1991, p. 193; Del Bianco 1951, p. 127 and ff.

33 Wistrand 1968, p. 320.

motive for profit.[34] Other statutes will require in addition that the user must not resort to the services of a remunerated third party to make the copies.[35] It is understood that these reproductions must not be put into circulation so as to reach the public in any way, or they would otherwise come in conflict with the normal exploitation of the work. Generally, reproductions made for personal use are required to be short and should not exceed one or two copies.[36]

The considerations at the root of the right to make single copies of a work were soon put to the test with the development of more sophisticated techniques of reproduction. At the time of the Stockholm Conference for the revision of the Berne Convention in 1967, home taping of sound recordings was becoming widespread. And although no consensus could emerge on the introduction of a specific limitation on private use, delegations agreed to the adoption of the 'three-step-test' of Article 9(2) and to specify, in Article 9(3), that "any sound or visual recording shall be considered as a reproduction for the purposes of this Convention". As Ricketson explains, the Main Committee I of the Stockholm Conference has interpreted these provisions, both as a justification for the existence of the private use exemption and as the basis for the adoption of home taping regimes:

> "This clearly envisages that exceptions under Article 9 (2) may take the form of either absolute exceptions or compulsory licences, depending essentially on the number of copies made ... As a matter of language, it also makes sense. The power under Article 9(2) is to permit the reproduction of works in certain special cases, and there is nothing in the wording of the provision which forbids the imposition of conditions on the grant of such permission, such as an obligation to pay for it (or to acknowledge the source of the work reproduced, for that matter)".[37]

A few years before the negotiations at the Stockholm Conference took place, it had already become evident that the practice of home taping of sound recordings was severely affecting the normal exploitation of works as well as the economic interests of rights-holders. Home taping conflicts with the normal exploitation of the work as the loss of a sale deprives the author of his royalties. In 1955, in view of the profits lost by large-scale home taping, the German collecting society GEMA brought action against producers of tape recorders on two grounds: (1) to enjoin these producers from selling the recorders, unless they made customers aware of their

34 For a complete account of the law in force on this subject in 18 European countries, see Hugenholtz and Visser 1995.

35 Bertrand 1991, p. 194. See French Intellectual Property Code, Art. L. 122-5, 2°: "Lorsque l'oeuvre a été divulguée, l'auteur ne peut interdire: les copies ou reproductions strictement réservées à l'usage privé du copiste et non destinées à une utilisation collective", where the term 'copiste' has been interpreted as the physical person making the copies for himself.

36 Stewart and Sandison 1989, p. 250.

37 Ricketson 1987, p. 484.

obligations under copyright law; and (2) to obtain damages for past infringement.[38] The German Supreme Court granted GEMA's motion on all points except the claim for damages.[39]

Following the decision of the German Supreme Court, concerns over the safeguard of the individual's fundamental right to privacy arose, as rights-owners expressed their intention to start monitoring the use of their works in the private sphere.[40] Indeed, in order to know whether people were infringing copyrighted works through private copying, owners would have had to physically enter, search and possibly seize material in individual's homes, which was both highly intrusive and practically unenforceable. Again in 1964, the Supreme Court of Germany decided on the same grounds, that the collecting society GEMA could not oblige sellers of home taping equipment to request from their customers that they reveal their identity so as to enable the society to verify the legality of their activities.[41]

Such actions would have conflicted with the fundamental right to privacy of each individual, which is not only guaranteed under the German Basic Law, but also under Article 8 of the ECHR and Article 17 of the International Covenant on Civil and Political Rights. The German Supreme Court's decisions and their effects strongly influenced the preparatory work for a reform of the German copyright law. The new German Copyright Act was adopted in 1965. It introduced the first known statutory right to equitable remuneration in favour of authors, performers and phonogram producers for home taping, through the imposition of a levy on the sale of sound recording equipment.[42]

The German experience has influenced to a great extent the future legislative actions undertaken in other countries with respect to the establishment of home taping regimes,[43] originally with respect to sound recordings, and eventually to audio-visual works. Such regimes have been put in place in a number of countries for two reasons: first, to provide rights-holders with monetary compensation for profits lost in the hands of private use, and secondly, to protect the citizens' fundamental right to privacy,[44] as guaranteed under Article 8 of the ECHR. But in the absence of international provisions on the subject, the regulation of home taping is left to national legislation. Not surprisingly then, the structure of these regimes varies significantly from one country to another, if and where such regime is in place at all. In view of the circumstances surrounding their creation, non-voluntary licences for home taping may also be seen as a cure to market failure.

---

38 *Grundig Reporter*, German Supreme Court, 18 May 1955, [1955] GRUR 492.
39 Wistrand 1968, p. 368.
40 Reinbothe 1981, p. 39.
41 *Personalausweise*, German Supreme Court, 29 May 1964, [1965] GRUR 104. See Bygrave and Koelman elsewhere in this volume, p. 101.
42 Wistrand 1968, p. 364.
43 Visser 1996, at p. 50.
44 Spoor and Verkade 1993, p. 189, where the authors specifically acknowledge the fact that the creation of home taping regimes is based originally on the protection of the user's private sphere.

2.1.2 Limitations based on competition law considerations

In the field of computer software and databases, specific copyright limitations have been implemented on the basis of competition law considerations, to prevent any abuse of dominant position within the industry.[45] Under the EC Directive on the legal protection of computer programs, lawful owners of a copy of a computer program have the right to make, in the absence of specific contractual provisions, a permanent or temporary reproduction of the program as well as to make a translation, adaptation, arrangement or any other alteration. These acts are allowed under the sole condition that they are necessary for the use of the computer program in accordance with its intended purpose, including for error correction. Lawful users may also make one back-up copy of the computer program. The right to a back-up copy may not be prevented by contract insofar as it is necessary for that use. The Directive further provides that the rightful owner of a copy of a computer program may, without the authorisation of the right-holder, observe, study or test the functioning of the program in order to determine the ideas and principles which underlie any element of the program. Such unauthorised reproduction of a computer program is allowed if it is accomplished while performing any of the acts of loading, displaying, running, transmitting or storing the program which the owner of the copy is entitled to do.[46] More directly concerned with the workings of a competitive software market, Article 6 of the Directive states that:

> "The authorisation of the rightholder shall not be required where the reproduction of the code and translation of its form within the meaning of Article 4(a) and (b) are indispensable to obtain the information necessary to achieve the interoperability of an independently created computer program with other programs, provided that the following conditions are met:
>
> (a) these acts are performed by the licensee or by another person having a right to use a copy of a program, or on their behalf by a person authorised to do so;
> (b) the information necessary to achieve interoperability has not previously been readily available to the persons referred to in subparagraph (a); and
> (c) these acts are confined to the parts of the original program which are necessary to achieve interoperability".

The Directive offers an imaginative solution to ensure that users can achieve computer interoperability. Whenever the original developer does not provide the

45 See Kroker 1997.
46 Computer Programs Directive, Art. 5.

necessary information on a voluntary basis, the lawful owner of a copy may obtain it through decompilation, under the conditions specified in the Directive. Any attempt on the part of the original developer to prevent the lawful owner of a copy of the computer program to decompile it for purposes of interoperability may justify the institution of procedures, for practices running foul of Articles 81 and 82 (ex Articles 85 and 86) of the EC Treaty. Of course, the information obtained through decompilation should not be used for goals other than to achieve interoperability of the independently created computer software, nor should it be given to others, nor should it be used for the production of a substantially similar computer program. For more certainty, this provision of the Directive is subject to the criteria of the 'three-step-test' of Article 9(2) of the Berne Convention.

Authorised users of databases protected under the new European Directive on the legal protection of databases are also entitled to accomplish similar acts with respect to databases, without the rights-holder's authorisation.[47]

In the United States, the right to reverse engineer is not expressly provided for in the Copyright Act. Section 117 of the Act deals strictly with the right to make another copy or adaptation of a computer program either as an essential step in the utilisation of the computer program in conjunction with a machine, or for archival purposes. However, courts have now admitted the fact that for creators of computer programs, achieving interoperability with particular computers and operating systems is necessary for commercial survival. Case law has thus allowed the making of a reproduction of a computer program for purposes of reverse engineering as fair use when the information could not otherwise be obtained and when this information was used to achieve interoperability.[48] The commercial importance of maintaining the public's ability to reverse engineer a computer program has been further recognised by Congress when it recently implemented the WIPO Copyright Treaty. The new provisions prohibiting the use of anti-circumvention measures do not apply when the circumvention is accomplished for the sole purpose of reverse engineering a lawfully obtained copy of a computer program, if it is necessary to

47 Database Directive, Art. 6: "1. The performance by the lawful user of a database or of a copy thereof of any of the acts listed in Article 5 which is necessary for the purposes of access to the contents of the databases and normal use of the contents by the lawful user shall not require the authorization of the author of the database. Where the lawful user is authorized to use only part of the database, this provision shall apply only to that part. 2. Member States shall have the option of providing for limitations on the rights set out in Article 5 in the following cases: in the case of reproduction for private purposes of a non-electronic database; where there is use for the sole purpose of illustration for teaching or scientific research, as long as the source is indicated and to the extent justified by the non-commercial purpose to be achieved; where there is use for the purposes of public security of for the purposes of an administrative or judicial procedure; where other exemptions to copyright which are traditionally authorized under national law are involved, without prejudice to points (a), (b) and (c)".

48 *Sega Enterprises Ltd. v. Accolade, Inc.*, 977 F.2d 1510 (9th Cir. 1992); *Atari Games Corp. v. Nintendo of America Inc.*, 975 F.2d 832 (Fed. Cir. 1992).

achieve interoperability of an independently created computer program with other programs.[49]

2.1.3 Limitations based on public interest considerations

Although not founded on the defence of fundamental rights and freedoms or competition law considerations, some limitations are nevertheless adopted on the basis of major public interest considerations, such as the promotion of education and culture. Statutory provisions passed to this end encompass a wide range of measures designed to allow institutions like schools, libraries, museums and archives,[50] to make specific unauthorised uses of protected material. Some of these restrictions have been implemented pursuant to Article 10(2) of the Berne Convention, which gives full discretion to the countries of the Union to regulate the "utilisation of works by way of illustration" for teaching purposes. In countries where special measures have been introduced with respect to schools and other educational institutions, the most frequent limitations to be found are the following:

1. the right to make compilations of only short works or of short passages of works by one and the same author and, in the case of artistic works, photographs or drawings, only a small number of those works, for purposes of teaching;[51]
2. the right to reproduce parts of works in publications or sound or visual recordings made for use as illustrations for teaching;[52]
3. the right to communicate to the public parts of works by broadcasting a radio or television programme made to serve as an illustration for teaching purposes;[53]
4. the right to perform and display a work in the course of teaching activities.[54]

---

49 Digital Millennium Copyright Act, Public Law 105-304, 112 Stat. 2860, 28 October 1998, where Art. 1201(f)(1) reads as follows: "Notwithstanding the provisions of subsection (a)(1)(A), a person who has lawfully obtained the right to use a copy of a computer program may circumvent a technological measure that effectively controls access to a particular portion of that program for the sole purpose of identifying and analysing those elements of the program that are necessary to achieve interoperability of an independently created computer program with other programs, and that have not previously been readily available to the person engaging in the circumvention, to the extent any such acts of identification and analysis do not constitute infringement under this title".

50 See Copyright, Designs and Patents Act 1988, UK Statutes, c. 24, ss 37-42; German Copyright Act, ss 46, 47, 53(5).

51 US Copyright Act, s. 107; German Copyright Act, s. 46; Dutch Copyright Act, Art. 16 (3). See Spoor and Verkade 1993, p. 212 ff.

52 Dutch Copyright Act of 1912, Art. 16(1)(a).

53 US Copyright Act, s. 110; German Copyright Act, s. 47; Dutch Copyright Act of 1912, Art. 16(1)(b).

54 US Copyright Act, s. 110; German Copyright Act, s. 52.

Such reproductions and other uses are usually allowed under the condition that the work, which is reproduced or used, has been lawfully communicated to the public and that such reproduction or use be in conformity with that which may be reasonably accepted in accordance with social custom. As in the case of citations, the source must be clearly indicated, together with the indication of the author if it appears in the source. Furthermore, the law often provides for the payment of an equitable remuneration to the author or his successors in title.

The public lending of works by libraries was harmonised at the European level through the adoption of the Council Directive on rental right and lending right and on certain rights related to copyright in the field of intellectual property.[55] The Directive grants to authors, as a basic principle, the exclusive right to authorise or prohibit the public lending of their works, but at the same time offers Member States the possibility to opt for a right to remuneration instead. The choice between an exclusive right and a remuneration right, provided by Article 4, was initially intended to allow Member States' to adapt the copyright rules to their cultural policies, in particular to the need to guarantee access for consumers to public libraries. This option also served, at the time of its adoption, as an element of compromise between the Member States, which had strongly diverging provisions, if any, on lending rights.[56]

Unlike other European copyright acts, Article 38 of the United Kingdom Copyright, Designs and Patents Act 1988 provides for very extensive and complex library privileges. Subject to the provisions of this Act and of the applicable statutory instruments, public librarians may supply to any of their patrons one copy of one article from an issue of a periodical publication or one copy of a reasonable proportion of a work other than an article. In order to receive a copy, the user must provide the librarian with sufficient evidence that such copy will serve for purposes of research or private study only. Section 108 of the US Copyright Act contains a similar provision, allowing employees of public libraries "to reproduce no more than one copy or phono record of a work, or to distribute such copy or phonorecord", under the conditions specified in the Act. This right also extends to the reproduction and distribution of a work for purposes of archival copies, replacement copies, articles and short excerpts for users, out-of-print works for scholarly purposes, news programmes and inter-library loans.[57] The applicability of these limitations to the digital networked environment raises important concerns however, both on the part of the rights-holders and on that of the users.

Libraries, schools, archives and museums may also benefit from limitations allowing for reprographic reproduction. However, contrary to the specific exemptions adopted to facilitate teaching and education, reprography regimes are

---

55 92/100/EEC of 19 November 1992, OJ L 346/61.

56 Reinbothe and Lewinski 1993, p. 34.

57 Information Infrastructure Task Force, *Intellectual Property and the National Information Infrastructure*, Washington DC, September 1995, pp. 85-88.

based on and must conform to the 'three-step-test' of Article 9(2) of the Convention. Whereas an individual's private use of a work is allowed under the conditions described above, multiple reproductions made by schools, libraries, and other such institutions do not fall under the private use exemption.[58] Unauthorised copying by such institutions violates the owner's exclusive right of reproduction, because it inevitably leads to copies that are intended for collective use, the collective body in question being that formed by the pupils, the students or the library patrons. Be that as it may, with the development of reprographic techniques in the early 1970s, the number of photocopies made within educational institutions, libraries and other public and private organisations have grown drastically. Although such reproductions may have followed public interest objectives, they became very damaging for the normal exploitation of works and the legitimate interests of rights-holders.

In a number of countries, the reprographic use of protected material by educational institutions, libraries and other institutions is allowed under a non-voluntary licence regime. Under such a regime, a fixed levy is imposed on domestic manufacturers, importers or acquirers of reprographic equipment. The law may also provide for (additional) payment per page reproduced, from physical and legal persons making the copies or, as the case may be, from entities who make such equipment available to others. The sums paid under these reprography regimes are administered by a collective society, often on a mandatory basis.[59] In many cases, the reprography regimes cover not only the reproductions made by schools and libraries, but also all reproductions made by governmental organisations, enterprises, administration offices and copy shops where reprographic equipment is available.[60]

A number of other limitations are justified under general public interest considerations. Among these are limitations of the reproduction right adopted in favour of the physically handicapped and those adopted for administrative and judicial purposes, both of which were already envisaged during the negotiations of the Stockholm Conference in 1967 concerning Article 9(2) of the Berne Convention.[61]

2.1.4 Limitations based on market failure considerations

Other copyright limitations have been implemented in view of alleviating the perceived market failure in the production and exploitation of protected material.

---

58 See e.g. *CB-infobank I*, German Supreme Court, 16 January 1997, [1997] GRUR 459, where the Court decided that reproductions made by a research service for purposes of archiving are not admissible under the personal use exemption when the reproductions are intended to be used by third parties.

59 Belgian Copyright Act, Art. 61; German Copyright Act, s. 54(6).

60 Spoor and Verkade 1993, p. 242.

61 Ricketson 1987, p. 485 ff.

Market failure can best be described in cases where market conditions make bargaining between individual copyright owners and potential users of copyrighted material impossible or prohibitively costly, or where copyright owners are unable in practice to enforce their rights effectively against unauthorised users.[62] In such circumstances, economic efficiency demands that alternate ways be found to make up for the absence of negotiations between rights-holders and users and to compensate the unenforceability of the exclusive rights for the unauthorised uses made of works. Most limitations based on market failure take the form of non-voluntary licences, such as the home-taping levy on blank cassettes and recording equipment for sound and audio-visual works,[63] or that of a remuneration right for the broadcast of sound recordings.[64] However, it is also possible that this type of limitations consists simply in a restriction of the exclusive right in favour of users, without any kind of monetary compensation to the rights-holders.

With the arrival on the market of audio and video-recorders allowing users to make inexpensive and good quality copies of sound recordings and films for private purposes, rights-owners have lost an important part of their revenues on sales and royalties. As indicated earlier in this chapter, both the enforcement of exclusive rights and the direct negotiation of licences with users are practically impossible in the case of home copying. In consequence, several national legislatures have set up non-voluntary licence regimes to the benefit of authors, performing artists and phonogram producers. These provisions are intended to grant copyright-holders compensation for the exploitation of their protected works by means of private home taping.[65] The solution has been applied in other instances as well, whenever the collective enforcement of rights makes more sense or is the only possible method in comparison to individual enforcement.

The fate, in the digital environment, of limitations initially adopted in view of alleviating the symptoms of market failure is the subject of heated debate. Many consider that since electronic copyright management systems and other digital techniques allow rights-holders to license directly for the use of their works and to receive payment for the authorised uses, the main cause of market failure is eliminated and, consequently, a number of copyright limitations could be abrogated.[66] The European home-copying regimes and the American fair use defence have come under fire lately, especially where the latter is applied as a private use exemption. Indeed, the grounds underlying the fair use defence are disputed: some authors and courts find its basis in the notion of public interest, while others

62 Adelstein and Peretz 1985, p. 211.

63 See German Copyright Act, s. 54 ff.; French Intellectual Property Code, Art. L. 122-5, 2° and Art. L. 211-3, 2°; Copyright Act of Canada, R.S.C. (1985), c. C-42 as last amended by S.C. 1997, c. 24, s. 79 ff.

64 Belgian Copyright Act, Art. 55; French Intellectual Property Code, Art. L. 241-1.

65 Schricker 1997, p. 163.

66 Hugenholtz 1996, p. 94.

see it strictly as a remedy for market failure. The fair use defence has in fact been admitted for uses that the copyright owner would have licensed but for insurmountable transaction costs, as well as for uses, even in the absence of transaction costs, whose social benefit outweighs the loss to the copyright owner.[67]

The Federal Court for the Second Circuit has indeed suggested, in the case of *American Geophysical Union v. Texaco*, that the availability of means for paying rights-holders for the use of their works would reduce or even eliminate the need to invoke the fair use defence. In the Court's opinion, the absence of mechanism to compensate authors would justify a fair use defence, whereas such defence would hardly be admissible in the presence of such a mechanism:

> "Despite Texaco's claims to the contrary, it is not unsound to conclude that the right to seek payment for a particular use tends to become legally cognizable under the fourth fair use factor when the means for paying for such a use is made easier. This notion is not inherently troubling: it is sensible that a particular unauthorized use should be considered 'more fair' when there is no ready market or means to pay for the use, while such an unauthorized use should be considered 'less fair' when there is a ready market or means to pay for the use".[68]

When considering the appropriateness of the private use and home copying exemptions in the digital environment, governments and courts must take several factors into account. First, the economic impact of the digital networked environment on the exploitation of works is not yet fully known. Secondly, it is felt that eliminating the private use exemption could disrupt the traditional balance between rights-holders and users, where the latter have always been able to read, listen to or view publicly available works for their own learning, and enjoyment. A corollary question to be asked is what constitutes a 'normal exploitation of a work' in the digital networked environment. Do all types of private uses of lawfully obtained copies of works constitute a 'normal exploitation' of a work, merely because technology allows the control of each and every single use? While copyright owners should be able to extract revenue from the commercial exploitation of their works in the digital networked environment, users should retain the possibility, as part of their autonomy as consumers, to make reproductions in well-defined circumstances for private purposes without the owner's consent. And, as Michael Hart explains:

67 Davies 1993, p. 66.

68 *American Geophysical Union, et al v. Texaco Inc.*, 37 F.3d 881 (2d Cir. 1994), affd 60 F.3d 913 (2d Cir. 1995).

> "The call from some quarters that there should be no private copying exception in relation to digital technology is clearly absurd. People will still want to be able to record a television programme of interest when they go out, if they cannot get home in time, to watch when they return, irrespective of whether the television or video recorder is digital or analogue. An improved and clarified definition of private copying which takes proper account of the digital environment, supported by some specific instances of what type of private copying should be lawful (e.g. timeshifting), is needed which makes it clear that it is restricted to purely private and non-commercial copying of which is a part of a person's reasonable use and enjoyment of a work rather than a substitute for a sale".[69]

Of course, the private use exemption should be eliminated only if one considers that the sole basis for adoption of these exemptions is market failure. However, in our opinion, home-copying regimes may still be justified as a means to protect the public's fundamental right to privacy, even in the digital environment.

2.1.5 Proposal for a Directive on copyright and related rights in the Information Society

In December 1997, the European Commission presented its Proposal for an EC Directive on copyright and related rights in the Information Society. According to the Background Document, the Proposal would adjust and complement the existing legal framework, and would particularly harmonise the rules pertaining to the right of reproduction, the right to communicate to the public, and the distribution right. The Proposal is also meant to implement the main obligations of the new WIPO Copyright Treaty and Performers and Phonograms Treaty, in view of their ratification by the Community.

The structure of the rights and limitations provided for by the Proposal differs somewhat from that of the WIPO Treaties. Contrary to the WIPO Treaties which contain no specific limitations besides the general reference to the 'three-step test', the Proposal would introduce an *exhaustive* list of limitations in addition to the test. Member States would not be allowed to maintain or enact any exemptions other than those enumerated in Article 5. According to the Commission, without adequate harmonisation of the exemptions to the reproduction right and to the right to communicate in public, as well as of the conditions of their application, Member States might continue to apply a large number of different limitations and exemptions, to the detriment of the Internal Market. The prohibition to impose limitations other than those included in the list would apply both to future 'digital'

69 Hart 1998, p. 170. See also Dreier 1997, p. 23.

and existing 'analogue' provisions.

Although Article 1(2) of the Proposal states that, 'unless otherwise provided, the Proposal shall apply without prejudice to existing Community provisions relating to' copyright and related rights, the relationship between the Proposal and limitations currently existing in the Member States is not clear. For instance, it is safe to assume that the specific exemptions of the Computer Programs Directive and of the Database Directive would continue to apply.[70] However, there is no indication as to the intended fate of 'minor reservations', which exist in some countries on the basis of local public interest considerations. Would these minor limitations have to be abolished, even if they have no economic significance for the Internal Market?[71]

Article 5 of the Proposal is divided into four paragraphs, the fourth one providing that all limitations included in the previous three paragraphs would be subject to the 'three-step test'. The first and second paragraphs would provide for limitations relating to the reproduction right, whereas the exemptions of the third paragraph would be applicable to both the reproduction right and the right to communicate to the public. Article 5(1) would introduce the only mandatory limitation, according to which "temporary acts of reproduction referred to in Article 2 which are integral to a technological process made for the sole purpose of enabling a use of a work or other subject matter and have no independent economic significance, shall be exempted from the right set out in Article 2". This provision would cover purely technical and ancillary reproductions, made for the sole purpose of accomplishing other acts of exploitation of works, and which have no separate significance of their own. If this provision were adopted, courts would come to examine first, whether a particular act of reproduction is 'temporary', secondly whether it falls within the category of those accomplished as an "integral [part of] a technological process made for the sole purpose of enabling a use of a work" and thirdly, whether such act has an "independent economic significance". All three criteria are foreign to current European copyright law. Instead of prescribing a limitation strictly directed to technical processes, which may prove insufficient in the long term, countries that wish to do so should be allowed to adopt a 'fair use' type limitation. Such a limitation would have the advantage of being more flexible to adapt to similar situations, which are not expressly listed in the law as permitted acts, but which might justify an exemption under certain circumstances. Furthermore, the introduction of a 'fair use' type limitation could incorporate the more familiar and more elaborate criteria of evaluation developed in the United States.

70 Proposal for a Directive, Recital 31: "Whereas such a harmonised legal protection should not inhibit decompilation permitted by Directive 91/250/EC".

71 See e.g. Dutch Copyright Act of 1912, Art. 17(c), which reads as follows: "Congregational singing and the instrumental accompaniment thereof during a religious service shall not be deemed an infringement of the copyright in a literary or artistic work".

The second paragraph of Article 5 of the Proposal lists three optional limitations to the reproduction right: (1) the reproduction on paper or similar support by using any kind of photographic technique or other processes with similar effects ('reprography'); (2) the reproduction on audio, visual or audio-visual recording media made by private individuals for private use and non-commercial ends ('home taping'); and (3) specific acts of reproduction made by public libraries, museums and other establishments accessible to the public, which are not for direct or indirect economic or commercial advantage ('library privilege'). In its Explanatory Memorandum, the Commission writes that the limitation concerning reprography does not focus on the technique used but rather on the result obtained, which has to be in paper form. The background document to the Proposal further explains that:

> "The effect of these optional exceptions would be that Member States could, for example, maintain their current systems for compensating right holders for *private copying* or photocopying (e.g. levies on sales of blank tapes and audio and video recorders, levies on photocopiers and photocopies). The Directive would not, therefore, introduce any obligation on Member States to introduce such private copying or photocopying levies or harmonise their level".

Hence, the essential purpose of Article 5(2) would be to ensure the legality of such limitations, whether current or future, and to subject them to the 'three-step-test'. Interestingly, the Commission stresses, in the Explanatory Memorandum, that the limitation concerning reprographic reproduction is left as an option in the Proposal, despite existing differences between Member States that provide for such limitations, as their effects are in practice rather similar. The Commission then goes on to say that "the Internal Market is far less affected by these minor differences than by the existence of schemes in some Member States and their inexistence in others", and that "those Member States that already provide for a remuneration should remain free to maintain it, but this proposal does not oblige other Member States to follow this approach".[72] Clearly, to be consistent with its wish to harmonise all limitations to the reproduction right so as to effectively eliminate barriers inside the Internal Market, the Commission would have to make the adoption of this limitation mandatory.

Under Article 5(3) of the Proposal, Member States would also have the option of applying further exemptions to both the reproduction right and the right to communicate to the public. Such limitations would be permitted, provided that they conform to the 'three-step-test', in the following five circumstances:

72 *Ibid.*, p. 36.

1. use for the sole purpose of illustration for teaching or scientific research as long as the source is indicated and to the extent justified by the non-commercial purpose to be achieved;
2. for uses to the benefit of visually-impaired or hearing-impaired persons, which are directly related to the disability and of a non-commercial nature and to the extent required by the specific disability.
3. use of excerpts in connection with the reporting of current events, as long as the source is indicated, and to the extent justified by the informatory purpose;
4. quotations for purposes such as criticism or review, provided that they relate to a work or other subject matter which has already been lawfully made available to the public, the source is indicated, their making is in accordance with fair practice and to the extent required by the specific purpose;
5. use for the purposes of public security or for the purposes of the proper performance of an administrative or judicial procedure.

These limitations would apply to any category of work. They are modelled either on the provisions of the Berne Convention or those found in the law of the Member States. In the Commission's view, these limitations are of only limited economic importance. Article 5(3) therefore merely sets out minimum conditions for their application, and it is for the Member States to define the detailed conditions of their use, albeit within the limits set out by the provision.

The structure of Article 5 of the Proposal inspires three major comments. First, concerning the *exhaustive* character of the list of limitations, we believe, along with the Legal Advisory Board, that harmonisation does not necessarily mean uniformity.[73] Rules should be converging, but should also allow distinctive features found in national legislation to subsist, as long as they do not hinder the Internal Market. The history of Article 9(2) of the Berne Convention provides a good example. The possibility of adopting a more complete list of exemptions, which would have been exhaustive, was examined at the Stockholm Conference. However, this proposal was rejected for two main reasons. First, because in order to encompass all the principal exemptions existing in national laws, such a list would have had to be very lengthy, and it would still not have been comprehensive. The second reason was the fact that not every country recognised all possible exemptions, or that some of them were granted only subject to the payment of remuneration under a compulsory licence. It was feared that by including an exclusive list of limitations, states would be tempted to adopt all the limitations allowed and abolish the right to remuneration, which would have been more

73 Legal Advisory Board, 'Commentaires du Legal Advisory Board sur la Communication de la Commission du 20 novembre 1996: Suivi du Livre vert "Le droit d'auteur et les droits voisins dans la société de l'information" sous l'éclairage des travaux de la Conférence diplomatique de l'OMPI (WIPO) de décembre 1996', Brussels, 1997, available at <http://www2.echo.lu/legal/fr/proprint/labcomment.html>.

prejudicial to the rights-owners.[74] These remarks hold true today in respect of the Proposal for a Directive.

Secondly, if proposed Article 5 only covers the right of reproduction and the right of communication to the public, what limitations, if any, may be implemented with respect to the distribution right? And thirdly, considering the *exhaustive* character of the list of limitations included in the Proposal, the manner in which these limitations are intended to interact with pre-existing limitations is not obvious from the text of the Proposal. Are the limitations listed in the Proposal to abrogate and replace all prior rules? As mentioned above, Article 1(2) of the Proposal sheds no light on the fate of the 'minor reservations' applied by some Member States. What room would be left under the Proposal for Member States to legislate on purely local public policy matters? In any case, like others have pointed out, we have serious doubts as to the ability of the current Proposal to meet the twin objectives of harmonisation and adaptation of copyright to the digital environment.[75] A 'fair use' type limitation may prove more efficient and flexible in the short and middle term or at least, until the impact of the digital networked environment on the rights of copyright owners and users is better known.[76] At that time, law-makers would be able to determine with more precision the extent of the possible limitations to adopt in favour of users.

2.2 LIMITS FOUND OUTSIDE COPYRIGHT LAW

A number of legal rules may serve as additional means to ensure fair dissemination of information. These restrictions originate from diverse sectors of the law, namely constitutional law, civil law, consumer protection law and competition law. All share a common objective, to safeguard the public interest. These norms have not been created to apply primarily to copyright matters. Nevertheless, they constitute a precious safety net for users of protected material, against rights-holders who misuse their copyrights to the detriment of the public interest. They are also invoked periodically to justify the adoption of particular copyright limitations.

This is the case in Germany, where the validity of several copyright limitations has been challenged before the Federal Constitutional Court as being contrary to Article 14(1) of the Basic Law *(Grundgesetz)*, which secures private property. Interestingly, this provision also guarantees that the public interest is taken into account in the use of private property. Paragraph 14(2) provides that 'property imposes duties. Its use should also serve the public interest', whereas paragraph 14(3) states that expropriation of private property is allowed only in the public

74 Ricketson 1987, p. 480.
75 Hart 1998, at p. 169.
76 Alberdingk Thijm 1998, p. 148 ff.

interest and subject to compensation.[77] Hence, in the leading case, known as the 'School-book case',[78] the Federal Constitutional Court found that while the Basic Law in principle guarantees the attribution of the economic value of a copyrighted work to the author, it does not provide a constitutional safeguard for any and all kinds of exploitation. The Court recognised the legislature's power to decide the appropriate standards, which guarantee an exploitation of the exclusive rights that is proportionate to the nature and social importance of copyright. In this instance, the Court believed that the interest of the general public in easy access to cultural objects justified the incorporation, without the author's consent, of copyright material into compilations intended for religious, school or instructional use. This did not mean however that the use of the copyrighted works would have to be free of charge.[79]

In our opinion, constitutional law could serve in certain circumstances as an additional limit on the exercise of exclusive rights, in cases where restrictions imposed by copyright owners on the use of protected material affect users' fundamental rights and freedoms.[80] To our knowledge, the European Commission of Human Rights has rendered only one decision on the conflict between copyright and freedom of information.[81] The matter concerned the control exercised by the copyright owner over lists of television programmes and the defendant's right to use the lists as part of his freedom to impart information, guaranteed under Article 10 of the ECHR. Unfortunately, the Commission did not directly consider the weight to give each legal norm, but came to a rather obscure and much criticised conclusion on the issue.[82]

In the Netherlands, Article 10 of the ECHR was also raised as a defence against allegations of copyright infringement.[83] In this case, the District Court of Amsterdam ruled that the newspaper *De Volkskrant* and two of its journalists had

77 German Basic Law, Art. 14 which reads as follows: "(1) Property and the right of inheritance are guaranteed. Their content and limits shall be determined by the laws. (2) Property imposes duties. Its use should also serve the public interest. (3) Expropriation shall be permitted only in the public interest. It may be effected only by or pursuant to a law which shall provide for the nature and extent of the compensation. Such compensation shall be determined by establishing an equitable balance between the public interest and the interests of those affected. In case of dispute regarding the amount of compensation, recourse may be had to the ordinary courts".

78 *Kirchen- und Schulgebrauch*, German Constitutional Court, 7 July 1971, [1972] GRUR 481.

79 See Davies 1993, p. 124.

80 See Hugenholtz 1989, p. 150 ff.; and Fraser 1998, p. 51 where the author writes: "The argument for bringing a First Amendment privilege outside of the confines of the fair use doctrine is that the purposes of the Copyright Act, although alleged to act as the engine of the First Amendment, do not always coincide with the basis underlying the First Amendment. Furthermore, maintaining the First Amendment privilege within the fair use doctrine leaves the impression that the interests found in the *Bill of Rights* can be balanced away every time the price to copyright holders is too high".

81 *De Geïllustreerde Pers v. De Staat der Nederlanden*, European Commission of Human Rights, 6 July 1976, [1978] NJ 1978 237.

82 Hugenholtz 1989, p. 164.

83 *De Volkskrant v. M.A. van Dijk en de Stichting Beeldrecht*, District Court of Amsterdam, 19 January 1994, [1994] Informatierecht/AMI 51.

infringed the plaintiff's copyright in a work of plastic art, when they published, as illustration to the text of an interview, the photograph of a Dutch personality showing the plaintiff's work in the background. The Court considered that, in the protection of the 'rights of others', guaranteed under the second paragraph of Article 10 of the ECHR, lies the recognition that copyright constitutes a legitimate restriction of the freedom of expression. Whether in the case at hand such a restriction was really necessary in a democratic society depended, according to the Court, first, on the balance of the relevant interests under the Copyright Act and secondly, on the seriousness of the violation of the freedom of expression.

The District Court of Amsterdam reminded that, subject to the limitations set out in the law, the Copyright Act grants the author of a literary, scientific or artistic work an exclusive right to publish or reproduce it, and that the statutory limitations of the Copyright Act could be partly understood as concessions in favour of the freedom of expression. Although the literature has assumed for a long time that the legislator has taken account of the proper balance of interests within the framework of the Copyright Act, an unmistakable current of opinion has emerged since the 1980s according to which the exclusive rights guaranteed under the Act can, in certain circumstances, come into conflict with Article 10 of the ECHR, especially because the narrow formulation of the system of statutory limitations does not provide sufficient guarantees for the freedom of expression. On the basis of these considerations, the Court came to the conclusion however that, in the circumstances, the exercise of the rights-holder's exclusive rights on his work of plastic art did not violate the newspaper's or the journalist's freedom of expression.

Civil law offers a further mode of control over the manner in which copyright owners make use of their exclusive rights, namely through the application of the concept of abuse of right. Abuse of right was initially understood as the intentional misuse of a right by its owner, which results in a prejudice to others, thereby giving rise to damages. Today, the notion has evolved so as to encompass any fault, whether intentional or not, in the exercise of a right. Abuse of right may therefore be invoked to limit a copyright owner's abuse of his rights to the detriment of users.[84] According to a French author, any abuse of the exclusive rights which the law grants him constitutes a violation of the conditions of their safeguard.[85] Moreover, Article L. 122-9 of the French Intellectual Property Code provides that a tribunal may order any appropriate measure to be taken in the case of 'notorious' or 'manifest' abuse in the use or non-use of the exploitation rights of a deceased author by his representatives.[86]

84 See Strowel 1993, p. 166 where the author refers to the decision of the European Court of Justice in Grundig-Consten, of 13 July 1966, [1966] ECR 299, involving the misuse of trademarks. See also Krikke 1995, pp. 103-110; and Stein 1993, pp. 123-126.

85 Carreau 1996, p. 31.

86 See *Affaire Foujita*, Civ. 1st, 28 February 1989, [1991] 148 RIDA 107.

In certain jurisdictions, general principles of civil law may also serve as the basis for the recognition of limitations outside of the copyright system. In *Dior v. Evora*,[87] the Dutch Supreme Court relied on an interpretation of Article 6:1 of the Civil Code to admit the legality of an unauthorised reproduction of photographs of consumer products for advertising purposes. The relevant provision of the Civil Code states that "obligations exist only insofar as they result from the law". Indeed, it had been previously interpreted by the same Court as meaning that, in cases which are not specifically regulated under the law, the solution which fits in the legal regime and which does connect to cases provided for in the law must be acceptable.[88]

Consumer protection rules are likely to play an increasing role in transactions relating to the dissemination of information. Considering the conditions under which copyright material is now available on or offline, one can easily assimilate copyright owners to merchants and users to consumers. In our opinion, consumer protection rules could be made applicable to the digital networked environment, in all cases where copyright owners' licensing practices unreasonably encroach upon the user's legitimate rights and interests as a consumer. This was the objective pursued by the European Parliament and the Council when they adopted the recent Directive on the protection of consumers in respect of distance contracts, as suggested by Recitals 4 and 13.[89]

Many of the situations which give rise to the application of the notion of abuse of right or of the rules of consumer protection law are likely to involve an element of antitrust or unfair competition. Some copyright licensing practices have indeed been challenged before national courts as well as before the European Court of Justice, as contrary to (European) competition rules. One of the most important cases of the recent years, in which the licensing practices of a copyright owner were examined under Articles 81 and 82 (ex Articles 85 and 86) of the EC Treaty, is the *Magill* Case.[90] On appeal, the European Court of Justice agreed with the decision of the Court of First Instance of the European Communities that by refusing to licence a third party to publish the advance weekly listings of their television and radio

---

87 *Christian Dior v. Evora*, Supreme Court of the Netherlands, 20 October 1995, [1995] IER 223.

88 Grosheide 1996, p. 46.

89 Directive 97/7/EC of the European Parliament and of the Council of 20 May 1997 on the protection of consumers in respect of distance contracts, OJ L 144/19, Recitals 4 and 13 which read as follows: "(4) Whereas the introduction of new technologies is increasing the number of ways for consumers to obtain information about offers anywhere in the Community and to place orders; whereas some Member States have already taken different or diverging measures to protect consumers in respect of distance selling, which has had a detrimental effect on competition between businesses in the internal market; whereas it is therefore necessary to introduce at Community level a minimum set of common rules in this area; (13) Whereas information disseminated by certain electronic technologies is often ephemeral in nature insofar as it is not received on a permanent medium; whereas the consumer must therefore receive written notice in good time of the information necessary for proper performance of the contract". See Trompenaars, elsewhere in this volume, p. 297.

90 *Radio Telefis Eireann v. E.C. Commission*, Court of First Instance of the European Communities, 10 July 1991, [1993] 24 IIC 83, confirmed by *RTE and ITP v. Commission*, European Court of Justice, 6 April 1995, Joint Cases C-241/91 and C-242/91, [1996] 27 IIC 78.

programmes, the applicants were abusing a dominant position contrary to Article 82 (ex Article 86) of the EC Treaty. The compulsory licence which was imposed by the European Commission as a remedy for the abuse was upheld. On the impact of this decision on future licensing practices, Vinje commented:

> "While no wholesale attacks on traditional and accepted licensing practices are to be expected, the ECJ's judgment in *Magill* preserves the necessary flexibility to apply competition law to situations, such as those that may arise with respect to the 'information superhighway', where the industrial context and new technological constraints make third parties dependent on licensing from dominant undertakings in order to participate in legitimate competitive activities".[91]

Competition law considerations are also at the heart of the adoption of the restrictions to the rights granted under the EC Directive on the legal protection of computer programs,[92] concerning computer system interoperability. Interoperability is considered by the industry as essential for the development of new products and for the compatibility of existing software. Consequently, besides the restrictions provided by Articles 5 and 6 of the Directive, Recital 27 specifically states that its provisions are without prejudice to the application of the competition rules under Articles 81 and 82 (ex Articles 85 and 86 of the EC Treaty), if a dominant supplier refuses to make information available which is necessary for interoperability as defined in the Directive.[93]

It is generally not a defence to a copyright infringement claim in the United States that the rights owner is violating the US federal antitrust laws. However, a number of antitrust lawsuits brought by the Government on the grounds that a copyright-holder has abused his monopoly grant through anti-competitive practices have resulted in the approval by courts of consent decrees. One of the first major antitrust cases involving copyright, which was litigated between 1941 and 1950, opposed the US Government to the collective licensing society American Society of Composers, Authors and Publishers (ASCAP). ASCAP was accused of anti-competitive behaviour in its licensing of musical compositions and distribution of royalties.[94] The consent decree still governs the manner in which ASCAP licenses the use of its repertoire and distributes the royalties to its member composers, lyricists, and publishers. In recent years the Microsoft Corporation has been under

91 Vinje 1995, p. 297.

92 Computer Programs Directive, Arts 5 and 6.

93 Kroker 1997, p. 249.

94 *United States of America v. American Society of Composers, Authors and Publishers et al.*, Amended Final Judgement, Civil Case No 13-95, 14 March 1950, United States District Court (SDNY), last modified by an Order of 19 February 1993, 832 F.Supp. 82 (SDNY 1993), aff'd 32 F.3d 727 (SDNY 1994).

attack from the Antitrust Division on charges of abuse of a dominant position, contrary to the provisions of the Sherman Act. This has led to the approval of a consent decree in 1995, which prohibits the software manufacturer from tying sales of 'other products' to its market-dominant PC operating system Windows 95.[95] Although it has scored a temporary victory against the Department of Justice in June 1998,[96] the problems of Microsoft are far from over, since several motions are still pending in relation to Microsoft's licensing of its web-browser, operating systems and office productivity software.

3. Copyright Versus Contract Issues

Legislation regarding copyright contracts is not unusual. In several countries, publisher's agreements and contracts for the production of sound and audiovisual works are subjected to specific rules of form and content.[97] Where specific legislation has not been enacted, courts are often called in to temper the unbalance resulting from the strict application of the principle of freedom of contract.[98] Usually, rules on contractual relations in copyright matters aim at protecting the traditionally weaker party to the negotiations: the author. It is somewhat of a reversal of fortune that we should now look at protecting the interests of users of copyright material, for fear that copyright owners try to unduly extend their rights through mass market licences.

Generally, freedom of contract is the rule, and contractual restraints the exception. Whether under the copyright regime or the *droit d'auteur* regime, parties to a contract are generally free to negotiate the content, nature and scope of any copyright licence agreement, as long as they remain within the bounds of public order. A contract whose object is prohibited by law or contrary to public order is null and void. However, norms of public order take many faces and vary from one country to another. The question is then whether copyright limitations constitute imperative rules around which parties may not contract.[99] Or, as one author puts it:

---

95 *United States of America v. Microsoft Corporation*, 56 F.3d 1448 (DC Cir. 1995).

96 *United States of America v. Microsoft Corporation*, US Court of Appeals for the District of Columbia Circuit, of 23 June 1998, No. 97-5343 (where the majority held that Microsoft's Internet Explorer browser and its Windows 95 operating system appeared to be an 'integrated system' and could be marketed together without violating the anti-tying restrictions agreed to in the 1995 Justice Department consent decree).

97 See French Intellectual Property Law, Art. L. 132-1 ff.; Publishers Act (*Gesetz über das Verlagsrecht)*, of 19 June 1901 (RGBl. S. 217, as subsequently modified); Belgian Copyright Act, Art. 20 ff.

98 Strowel 1993, p. 32.

99 See e.g. Directive 97/7/EC of the European Parliament and of the Council of 20 May 1997 on the Protection of Consumers in Respect of Distance Contracts, Art. 12(1) which reads: "The consumer may not waive the rights conferred on him by the transposition of this Directive into national law".

"Under what circumstances would limiting freedom of contract be justified when contractual arrangements expand copyrights?"[100]

In the United States, copyright overridability—or copyright pre-emption, as it is called there—is regulated under section 301 of the US Copyright Act. Section 301(a) governs general conflicts arising between federal copyright law and State law. It pre-empts "all legal or equitable rights that are equivalent to any of the exclusive rights within the general scope of copyright as specified by section 106 in works of authorship that are fixed in a tangible medium of expression and come within the subject matter of copyright as specified by sections 102 and 103".[101] This pre-emptive standard hinges on three factors: (1) the right must be equivalent to a right under copyright law; (2) the subject matter must be a work of authorship fixed in a tangible medium of expression; and (3) the subject matter must be within the scope of copyright.[102] Pre-emption may also be based on the federal Supremacy Clause, according to which a particular cause of action may be pre-empted if its enforcement would stand as an obstacle to the accomplishment of the full purposes and objectives of Congress.[103]

In Europe, the rights of users have been expressly protected on two occasions by the European legislature, through the adoption of the EC Directive on the legal protection of computer programs and the Directive on the legal protection of databases. The right of any lawful user of a computer program to make a back-up copy of the program, "insofar as it is necessary for that use", may not be set aside by contract, nor can the right to observe, study or test the functioning of the program. The same is true for the right of a lawful user to decompile the program to achieve interoperability.[104] This follows from Article 9(1), which provides that 'any contractual provisions contrary to Article 6 or to the exceptions provided for in Article 5(2) and (3) shall be null and void'.[105] The Directive on the legal protection of databases contains a similar provision in Article 15. Accordingly, any contractual agreement contrary to the right of the lawful user to reproduce the database for the purpose of normal use, or to extract and re-utilise insubstantial parts of the database for any purposes whatsoever, shall be null and void.[106]

Besides the rights given to users under the Computer Programs Directive and the Database Directive, the question of overridability has been the object of little

---

100 Elkin-Koren 1997, p. 105.

101 17 U.S.C. § 301(a) which goes on to state that "no person is entitled to any such right or equivalent right in any such work under the common law or statutes of any State". See Karjala 1997, p. 525.

102 R. Nimmer 1998, pp. 2-38.

103 D. Nimmer et al. 1998, pp. 1-10.

104 Computer Programs Directive, Art. 5(2) and (3), and Art. 6.

105 See also Recital 26 of the Directive: "Whereas protection of computer programs under copyright laws should be without prejudice to the application, in appropriate cases, of other forms of protection; whereas, however, any contractual provisions contrary to Article 6 or to the exemptions provided for in Article 5(2) and (3) should be null and void". See: Mauro 1995(I), pp. 27-39, and Mauro 1995(II), pp. 29-44.

106 Database Directive, Arts 6(1) and 8.

attention from legislators and authors in Europe.[107] Moreover, whereas both Directives specify which exemptions may not be set aside by contractual agreement, the Proposal for a Directive on the harmonisation of certain aspects of copyright and related rights in the Information Society remains silent on this issue. In its Explanatory Memorandum, the Commission puts much importance on contractual relationships, as a means for information producers, intermediaries and end-users to determine directly the conditions of use of protected material. As the Legal Advisory Board pointed out in its Reply to the Green Paper, "there is good reason to expect that in the future much of the protection currently awarded to information producers or providers by way of intellectual property, will be derived from contract law". However, there is also reason to fear that, without appropriate contractual boundaries, users may be forced to forego some of the privileges recognised by law in order to gain access to protected material.

Absent precise indications from the legislator, the question of whether specific copyright provisions constitute imperative or default rules must be determined essentially in light of public interest considerations.[108] Except for the widely accepted notions of fundamental rights and freedoms and of freedom of competition, public interest matters are mostly a question of national policy: what is in the public interest in one country, is not necessarily in the public interest in another. Thus limitations based on the notion of public interest differ from one country to the next and can hardly be aggregated to reflect what is in the 'global' public interest. Admittedly, not only the nature and content of public interest considerations vary from one country to another, but the solutions put in place at the national level to deal with public interest considerations vary as well. Of course, public interest considerations are an integral part of the copyright system. In principle, laws are enacted only if they are, or thought to be, in the public interest. Following this principle, the structure of the copyright system owes a lot to the legislator's acknowledgement of and response to public interest concerns, in its effort to encourage both creation and dissemination of original works. The copyright system as whole is thus believed to establish a balance between the interests of the creators and those of the public, in furtherance of the common good. However, the focus is here on the collective interests of society, as a counterbalance to the individual interests of the copyright-holder. There may be, outside the copyright regime itself, particular instances where the needs of the majority justify overriding those of the individual, and where the citizen should

---

107 One notable exception is the Legal Advisory Board; see Legal Advisory Board 1995.

108 See Lemley 1995, p. 1274 where the author writes: "The case of enforcing the terms of federal intellectual property law in the face of a contradictory contract depends heavily upon the nature of the federal interest at stake. There must be some affirmative governmental policy benefit in order to justify overriding the public and private interests in enforcing contracts. In the context of intellectual property law, therefore, it matters greatly whether the federal statutes were intended as default rules or whether there is a public interest in enforcing the rights of vendors and users as the laws are written".

relinquish any thoughts of self-interest in favour of the common good of society as a whole.[109]

In some jurisdictions, the notion of public interest constitutes a separate rule of judicial interpretation, while in others it is an element of substantive law which courts must take into consideration in their rulings. In the United Kingdom, while the common law defence of public interest is considered outside and independent of any statute and not limited to copyright cases, it has nevertheless been codified in the 1988 Act in these words: "Nothing in this Part affects any rule of law preventing or restricting the enforcement of copyright, on grounds of public interest or otherwise".[110] An often-quoted comment taken from an earlier British case would summarise the matter as follows: "Public interest, as a defence in law, operates to override the rights of the individual (including copyright) which would otherwise prevail and which the law is also concerned to protect".[111] In Germany, the acknowledgement of public interest considerations is guaranteed under Article 14(2) of the German Constitution, in relation to the use of private property. In relation to copyright, the Federal Constitutional Court noted in the 'School-book case', that:

> "The legislature is not only obliged to secure the interests of the individual; rather, it is also charged with drawing bounds on the individual rights and powers that are necessary in the interest of the general public; it must bring about a just balance between the sphere of the individual and the interests of the public. Thus, the constitutionality of the contested provision ... hinges upon its justification by the public interest".

Similarly, in the United States, the public interest has been the background consideration on numerous occasions, and in relation to a wide range of copyright issues. On conflicts between copyright protection and public interest matters, the Congress Report of the Register of Copyrights on the General Revision of the US Copyright Law of July 1961 stated that:

> "The primary purpose of copyright is to stimulate the creation and dissemination of intellectual works, thus advancing 'the progress of science and useful arts'. The grant of exclusive rights to authors is a means of achieving this end, and of compensating authors for their labors and their contributions to society.
>
> Within limits, the author's interests coincide with those of the public. Where they conflict, the public interest must prevail. The ultimate task of the

109 Davies 1993, p. 2.
110 UK Copyright, Designs and Patents Act 1988, s. 171(3).
111 *Beloff v. Pressdram*, [1973] 1 All E.R. 241.

> copyright law is to strike a fair balance between the author's right to control the dissemination of his works and the public interest in fostering their widest dissemination".[112]

Clearly, the public interest must prevail in certain circumstances, where the rights of copyright owners and the interests of users collide. However, how this translates into practice is not entirely clear. In Europe, the lack of guidance by the legislator, apart from the two Directives mentioned above, and the lack of relevant case law prevents us from reaching a conclusive decision on the weight to give copyright limitations in respect of contractual agreements. One could well argue that, although the law makes no express mention of the mandatory nature of the copyright limitations, the copyright system has been carefully designed so as to incorporate public interest considerations and that, consequently, any agreement enjoining the user from performing certain acts that are otherwise allowed under copyright law would go against public interest. It may be further contended that if parties were to agree to such a provision, the violation of the user's obligations would in such a case amount at most to a breach of contract. But before deciding whether to enforce such a contract against a particular user, courts would first need to examine whether this contractual agreement runs contrary to established copyright policy and whether its enforcement would be in the public interest.

On the issue of the compatibility of contractual agreements with copyright policy, we believe that a number of copyright restrictions are not merely default rules and that it would indeed go against copyright policy if parties were to override them through contract. Limitations based on universally recognised fundamental rights and freedoms, such as the right to make reproductions for purposes of study, research, criticism, news reporting and parody, undeniably constitute imperative rules of copyright law whose application cannot be waived by parties to a contract. Contractual agreements preventing users making reproductions for such purposes would, in our opinion, violate Article 10 of the European Convention on Human Rights and the First Amendment. This assertion holds true as well for the digital networked environment. The information highway is rapidly becoming a privileged medium for political, social, economic and cultural debate, where most major newspapers and broadcasting enterprises around the world are already engaged in online activities, such as real-time communication of news reports and electronic publishing. It is thus important that users be allowed to make quotations of works in the digital networked environment, and that they have the possibility of reporting current events, even if contractual obligations would not permit it. The same would hold true in our opinion for the private use exemption, which is partly justified by the need to protect the users' right to privacy and their individual autonomy. We believe that, as long as the use is strictly limited to a single copy made for the

112 87th Congress, 1st Session, at p. 6.

personal use of a private individual, it should not be possible to set the exemption aside by contract.

In contrast, limitations favouring schools, libraries, archives and museums should not be immune to contractual overrides. Of course, education, research, and learning contribute to the general welfare. But, in our opinion, limitations of this type do not pursue objectives so fundamental to the defence of individual freedoms and the free flow of information that they should be considered imperative rules from which parties may not deviate by contract, under any circumstances. Moreover, one might well argue that individual or collective licensing schemes specifically crafted to suit the needs (and budgets) of these categories of users would suffice to fulfil the intended policy goals. This would be all the more true in the digital environment, where the involvement of public libraries in the sphere of electronic document delivery is increasingly considered as directly competing with the services of publishers or other commercial information providers, thereby affecting the normal exploitation of works and the legitimate interests of rights holders.[113] Because of the lack of current information on the economic impact of the activities of public libraries on the electronic exploitation of protected works,[114] it is difficult to determine the proper form and scope of any possible limitation intended to benefit public libraries with respect to the digital environment. Ultimately, such a limitation, if needed at all, would have to take into account the interests of the rights owners, as well as the information and cultural policies at the root of the public library system. In the meantime however, many believe that the existing limitations should not apply in the case of electronic document delivery, activity that would therefore be subject to the rights owner's authorisation. This last position is in fact the one adopted by the European Commission in the framework of the Proposal for a Directive.

Clearly, contractual provisions that attempt to override mandatory limitations should be declared null and void, and courts should refuse to enforce such contracts against users. In the case of non-mandatory limitations the validity and enforceability of restrictive user contracts may depend on whether the contractual obligations stem from a fully negotiated agreement or from a standard form contract. Of course, the principle of freedom of contract should be maintained whenever possible, as a matter of public policy. Consequently, the validity of freely negotiated agreements that restrict the user's freedom under a non-imperative limitation should be upheld.

On the information highway however, current licensing practices tend to take the form of all-encompassing, hard-to-read, interminable 'click-on' agreements imposed by the copyright-holder. Because licensors rarely know whether the

113 Hugenholtz and Visser 1995, p. 1.

114 European Commission, *Explanatory Memorandum on the Proposal for a Directive on the harmonisation of copyright and neighbouring rights in the information society*, Brussels, December 1997, p. 38.

purchaser is an individual user or a potentially competing enterprise, these agreements often prohibit the acquirer from making any reproduction for any purpose whatsoever, thereby expanding the copyright owner's monopoly over the licensed material beyond what is normally recognised under copyright law.

The question of the validity and enforceability of mass-market standard software licence agreements, such as 'shrink-wrap' licences, has given rise to a lively debate, particularly in the United States. Discussions were triggered in 1995 following the decision of the Court of Appeals for the Seventh Circuit in *ProCD v. Zeidenberg.*[115] In this case, the plaintiff sought to enforce a mass-market software licence agreement on the use of a CD-ROM containing all telephone listings throughout the United States. In a highly criticised decision, the Court of Appeal for the Seventh Circuit enforced the licence. In many authors' opinion, the Court of Appeal should have rejected the plaintiff's action on the following grounds: since telephone listings had been declared non-copyright subject matter by the Supreme Court a few years earlier for lack of originality,[116] ProCD's cause of action should have been pre-empted under section 301 of the Copyright Act, as going against federal copyright policy.[117] Furthermore, the Seventh Circuit's peremptory statement that "a simple two-party contract is not 'equivalent to any of the exclusive rights within the general scope of copyright' and therefore may be enforced", is likely to lead, if followed, to an unwarranted expansion of rights owners' control over the dissemination of information. The fact is that, as Reichman explains, in the case of non-negotiated terms in information contracts, "rights between parties to the agreement" *are equivalent* to "rights against all the world". When owners have the technological power to block access to information goods combined with the power to impose non-negotiated terms of use, it produces contracts that are roughly equivalent to private legislation that *is* valid against the world.[118]

The threat of seeing rights owners extend their reach over information beyond the boundaries of copyright law is all the more real in view of the recent adoption in the United States of the Uniform Computer Information Transactions Act (UCITA), formally known as (draft) Article 2B of the Uniform Commercial Code.[119] Once implemented in the laws of each State, the UCITA would indeed validate shrink-wrap licences imposed on very broadly defined 'information'. Copyright pre-emption issues are one of the many topics that have generated intense discussions for a great part of the drafting process. Strong lobby of consumer groups and intellectual property scholars have had much influence

115 86 F.3d 1447 (7th Cir. 1996). See Trompenaars, elsewhere in this volume, p. 270.
116 *Feist Publications, Inc. v. Rural Telephone Service Co.*, 499 U.S. 340 (1991).
117 D. Nimmer et al. 1998, p. 3-34.3; Reichman and Samuelson 1997, p. 144; Karjala 1997, p. 526.
118 Reichman and Franklin 1998, p. 17.
119 See Trompenaars, elsewhere in this volume, p. 277. The final text of the UCITA was not yet available at the time of writing; commentary refers to earlier drafts of Art. 2B UCC.

towards the inclusion in the draft of a provision, which would go beyond the mere statement that 'a provision of this article which is preempted by federal law is unenforceable to the extent of that preemption'. It is worth noting that, in the December 1998 version of the draft, the paragraph in the Reporter's notes that deals with federal pre-emption has been entirely rewritten. The fact that the argument below was altogether withdrawn denotes an important concession on the part of the drafters:

> "There are many sources of federal preemption. Some stem from intellectual property law. Section 301 of the Copyright Act preempts any state law that creates rights equivalent to copyright. That rule will seldom apply to contracts since a contract deals with the relationship between parties to an agreement, while property law in the Copyright Act deals with interests good against persons with whom the property owner has not dealt. Contracts control many aspects of the commercial distribution of information".[120]

The consumer and academic lobby has also succeeded in introducing several additional subsections to the draft of Section 2B-105 to serve as caveats for courts confronted with questions of trade secret law, unfair competition law, consumer protection law or the validity of electronic contracts. For our purposes, the most significant change is the inclusion of subsection (b), which states that:

> "If a term of a contract violates a fundamental public policy, the court may refuse to enforce the contract, or it may enforce the remainder of the contract without the impermissible term, or it may so limit the application of any impermissible term as to avoid any result contrary to public policy, in each case, to the extent that the interest in enforcement is clearly outweighed by a public policy against enforcement of that term".

The public policies most likely to be applicable to transactions within this article are those relating to innovation, competition and fair comment. According to the Reporter's notes:

> "innovation policy recognizes the need for a balance between conferring property interests in information in order to create incentives for creation and the importance of a rich public domain upon which most innovation ultimately depends. Competition policy prevents unreasonable restraints on publicly available information in order to protect competition. Rights of free expression

120 Uniform Commercial Code Art. 2B: Software Contracts and Licenses of Information, NCCUL and ALI Council Draft, August 1998, p. 38.

may include the right of persons to comment, whether positively or negatively, on the character or quality of information in the marketplace".[121]

To our knowledge, there are only few precedents in European law where a copyright owner attempted to expand his monopoly beyond the terms of the Copyright Act through a non-negotiated licence. It happened at least on one occasion in the Netherlands, before the age of shrink-wrap licences, that the Supreme Court flatly refused to enforce a plaintiff's non-negotiated licence. In the well-known *Leesportefeuille* case,[122] a magazine publisher had put a notice on his publications prohibiting the legal acquirer from re-using the printed material in subsequent 'reading portfolios'. The defendant disregarded the notice, published a portfolio and distributed it to his clients. Plaintiff filed suit on the grounds of copyright infringement. The Supreme Court found in favour of the defendant, considering that the plaintiff's copyrights were exhausted as soon as he had made his magazines available to the public, and had therefore no right to restrict the user's subsequent actions. The notice prohibiting further reproduction was contrary to the exhaustion doctrine found under the Dutch Copyright Act. In any case, shrink-wrap licences have not attracted in Europe the amount of attention that they have in the United States. It is generally believed that shrink-wrap licences are enforceable, subject to the rules governing adhesion contracts which find application in matters of copyright licences just as they do in other civil matters.[123]

4. Concluding Comments

In the digital networked environment, rights-holders have the means to exercise tight control over the use made of their works, through a combination of technological measures, contractual practices and copyright law principles. In fact, contracts constitute a key element in the way information is exchanged in the new environment, serving as the tool through which authors determine the extent of authorised uses. Contracts are also seen as a means to discourage infringement. Effective control over the use of protected works is certainly desirable: creators should be able to exercise and enforce their rights to the full extent necessary to recoup the cost of investment made in the production of works and to generate reasonable profit from their commercial exploitation. Without an adequate level of

121 *Ibid.*, p. 38.

122 *De N.V Drukkerij «de Spaarnestad» v. Leesinrichting «Favoriet»,* Supreme Court of the Netherlands, 25 January 1952, [1952] NJ 95.

123 See *Beta Computers (Europe) Limited v. Adobe Systems (Europe) Limited,* [1996] FSR 367; Westerdijk and Klaauw 1991, p. 24; Schneider 1996, p. 663; and Girot 1998, p. 7. See Trompenaars, elsewhere in this volume, p. 267 ff.

protection, creators may not have the necessary incentive to produce new works. But as much as creators need protection, users must be able, in the interest of the free flow of information, to make use of lawfully obtained copies of works including, in certain well-defined circumstances, the capacity to make limited uses of those works without the consent of the rights-holder.

Concerns arise from the possibility that an unbridled use of technological measures coupled with anti-circumvention legislation and contractual practices would permit rights owners to extend their rights far beyond the bounds of the copyright regime, to the detriment of users and the free flow of information. The copyright bargain reached between granting authors protection for their works and encouraging the free flow of information would be put in serious jeopardy if, irrespective of the copyright rules, rights owners were able to impose their terms and conditions of use through standard form contracts with complete impunity. If this were the case, the copyright regime would succumb to mass-market licences and technological measures. Unless the legislator clarifies the issue, these concerns may become all too real with the gradual implementation of electronic copyright management systems, whose workings are based on technology and contractual relations, with the generalisation of mass-market licences as the main vehicle for transactions in information over the information highway and with the implementation of the UCITA, which would validate mass-market licences in the United States. The Proposal for a Directive would certainly be a good opportunity for the European Commission to make its position clear on the overridability of copyright limitations.

References

R.P. Adelstein and S.I. Peretz (1985), 'The Competition of Technologies in Markets For Ideas: Copyright and Fair Use in Evolutionary Perspective', (1985) 5 *International Review of Law and Economics* 209.

Chr. A. Alberdingk Thijm (1998), 'Fair use: het auteursrechtelijk evenwicht hersteld', (1998) 22 *Informatierecht/AMI* 145.

A. Bertrand (1991), *Le droit d'auteur et les droits voisins*, Paris: Masson 1991.

L. Bochurberg (1994), *Le droit de citation*, Paris: Masson 1994.

C. Carreau (1996), 'Propriété intellectuelle et abus de droit', in *Mélanges en l'honneur de André Françon*, Paris: Dalloz 1996.

J.E. Cohen (1996), 'A Right to Read Anonymously: A Closer Look at "Copyright Management" in Cyberspace', (1996) 28 *Connecticut Law Review* 981.

G. Davies (1993), *Copyright and the Public Interest*, Munich: VCH Verlagsgesellschaft 1993.

E. Del Bianco (1951), *Le droit d'auteur et ses limites*, Lausanne: Nouvelle Bibliothèque de Droit et de Jurisprudence 1951.

T. Dreier (1997), *Copyright Law and Digital Exploitation of Works* — The Current Copyright Landscape in the Age of the Internet and Multimedia, Munich: IPCC 1997.

N. Elkin-Koren (1997), 'Copyright Policy and the Limits of Freedom of Contract', (1997) 12 *Berkeley Technology Law Journal* 93.

S. Fraser (1998), 'The Conflict between the First Amendment and Copyright Law and its Impact on the Internet', (1998) 16 *Cardozo Arts & Entertainment Law Review* 1.

C. Girot (1998), 'La validité des licences de logiciel sous plastique en droit français: les enseignements du droit comparé', [1998] 1 *Droit de l'informatique et des télécoms* 7.

W. Gordon (1989), 'An Inquiry into the Merits of Copyright: The Challenges of Consistency, Consent, and Encouragement Theory', (1989) 41 *Stanford Law Review* 1343.

F.W. Grosheide (1996), 'De commercialisering van het auteursrecht', (1996) 20 *Informatierecht/AMI* 43.

L. Guibault (1996), 'La propriété intellectuelle et la technologie numérique: à la recherche d'un compromis satisfaisant', (1996) 8 *Cahiers de Propriété Intellectuelle* 203.

M. Hart (1998), 'The Proposed Directive for Copyright in the Information Society: Nice Rights, Shame about the Exceptions', [1998] 5 *EIPR* 169.

P.B. Hugenholtz (1989), *Auteursrecht op informatie*, Deventer: Kluwer 1989.

P.B. Hugenholtz (1996), 'Adapting Copyright to the Information Superhighway', in P.B. Hugenholtz (ed.), *The Future of Copyright in a Digital Environment*, The Hague: Kluwer Law International 1996, pp. 81-96.

P.B. Hugenholtz, and D.J.G. Visser (1995), *Copyright problems of electronic document delivery*, Luxembourg: Report to the Commission of the European Communities 1995.

G. Johnston (1996), 'Copyright and Freedom of the Media: A Modest Proposal', [1996] 1 *EIPR* 6.

D. Karjala (1997), 'Federal Preemption of Shrinkwrap and On-Line Licenses', (1997) 22 *University of Dayton Law Review* 511.

A. Kérëver (1996), 'Note — *Vladimir Jirinovski c. Didier Daeninckx*, Tribunal de Grande Instance de Paris, 3° Chambre, 10 mai 1996', (1996) 170 *RIDA* 323.

J.I. Krikke (1995), 'Auteursrecht in de maat', (1995) 19 *Informatierecht/AMI* 103.

E.R. Kroker (1997), 'The Computer Directive and the Balance of Rights', [1997] 5 *EIPR* 247.

Legal Advisory Board (1995), *Reply to the Green Paper on Copyright and Related Rights in the Information Society*, Brussels 1995.

M.A. Lemley (1995), 'Intellectual Property and Shrinkwrap Licenses', (1995) 68 *Southern California Law Review* 1239.

C. Mauro (1995(I)), 'Ordre public et contrats internationaux en matière de logiciels — Partie I', [1995] 1 *Computer & Telecoms Law Review* 27.

C. Mauro (1995(II)), 'Ordre public et contrats internationaux en matière de logiciels — Partie II', [1995] 2 *Computer & Telecoms Law Review* 29.

D. Nimmer, G.N. Frischling, and E.Brown (1998), 'The Metamorphosis of Contract into Expand', paper presented at the Boalt Conference on Intellectual Property & Contract in the Information Age: The Impact of Article 2B of the UCC on the Future of Transaction in Information & Electronic Commerce, held at University of California at Berkeley, on 24-25 April 1998.

M.B. Nimmer and D. Nimmer (1998), *Nimmer on Copyright*, New York: Matthew Bender 1998.

R. Nimmer (1998), *Information Law*, Boston: Warren, Gorham & Lamont 1998.

R. Patterson and S.W. Lindberg (1991), *The Nature of Copyright* — A Law of Users' Rights, London/Athens: The University of Georgia Press 1991.

J.H. Reichman and J.A. Franklin (1998), 'Privately Legislated Intellectual Property Rights: The Limits of Article 2B of the UCC', paper presented at the Boalt Conference on Intellectual Property & Contract in the Information Age: The Impact of Article 2B of the UCC on the Future of Transaction in Information & Electronic Commerce, held at University of California at Berkeley, on 24-25 April 1998.

J.H. Reichman and P. Samuelson (1997), 'Intellectual Property Rights in Data?', (1997) 50 *Vanderbilt Law Review* 51.

J. Reinbothe (1981), 'Compensation for Private Taping Under Sec. 53(5) of the German Copyright Act', [1981] *International Review of Industrial Property and Copyright Law* 36.

J. Reinbothe and S. von Lewinski (1993), *The E.C. Directive on Rental and Lending Rights and on Piracy*, London: Sweet & Maxwell 1993.

S. Ricketson (1987), *The Berne Convention for the Protection of Literary and Artistic Works: 1886-1986*, London: Kluwer 1987.

P. Samuelson (1998), 'Legally Speaking: Does Information Really Have To Be Licensed?', *Communications of the ACM* September 1998, available at: <http://sims.berkeley.edu/~pam/papers/acm_2B.html>.

D.A. Schneider (1996), 'Vertragsschluß bei Schutzhüllenverträgen', (1996) 11 *Computer und Recht* 657.

G. Schricker (ed.) (1997), *Urheberrecht auf dem Weg zur Informationsgesellschaft*, Baden-Baden: Nomos Verlagsgesellschaft 1997.

J.H. Spoor and D.W.F. Verkade (1993), *Auteursrecht*, 2nd edn., Deventer: Kluwer 1993.

P.A. Stein (1993), 'Misbruik van auteursrecht', (1993) 17 *Informatierecht/AMI* 123.

S.M. Stewart and H. Sandison (1989), *International Copyright and Neighbouring Rights*, 2nd edn., London: Butterworths 1989.

A. Strowel (1993), *Droit d'auteur et copyright* — Divergences et convergences, Paris: L.G.D.J. 1993.

T.C. Vinje (1995), 'The Final Word on Magill', [1995] 6 *EIPR* 297.

D.J.G Visser (1996), 'Copyright Exemptions Old and New: Learning from Old Media Experiences', in P.B. Hugenholtz (ed.), *The Future of Copyright in a Digital Environment*, The Hague: Kluwer Law International 1996, pp. 49-56.

R. Westerdijk and F.v.d. Klaauw (1991), 'De shrink-wrap licentie', (1991) 1 *Computerrecht* 18.

H. Wistrand (1968), *Les exceptions apportées aux droits de l'auteur sur ses oeuvres*, Paris: Editions Montchrestien 1968.

IV. Protection of Technological Measures

Kamiel J. Koelman and Natali Helberger

In the online environment consumers no longer have to leave their homes to buy copies of information products, but can purchase and acquire them online. However, since it is not often that people will pay for what they can obtain at no cost, 'electronic fences', in the form of firewalls, copy-protection systems or encryption techniques are applied by service providers and copyright-holders. Well known examples are the scrambling technologies that are used in connection with pay-TV services and the anti-copying devices that are sometimes included in software products. This chapter deals with the legal protection of such technologies from circumvention.

The chapter consists of seven sections. The first section describes four categories of technological measures protecting copyright ('TMs'). TMs may be categorised in accordance with their functions: providing access control, usage control, integrity protection or usage metering. The second section provides an in-depth analysis of present and future legislation, on the national, European and international level, in respect of TMs protecting copyright. The legislative developments at the European level (the proposed Copyright Directive) and in the United States (the Digital Millennium Copyright Act) are dealt with in most detail. Thereafter, we will examine how these protection schemes relate to 'traditional' copyright protection, i.e. in what way the legal protection of technological measures and the availability of these technologies affect the extent of a rights-holder's control over the use of information. Next, the legal protection of technological measures will be related to other rights and areas of the law protecting comparable interests. This may shed some light on the nature and necessity of the specific legal protection for technologies that protect copyrighted works, an issue which will be addressed in Section 4. The fifth section concentrates on the legal protection of conditional access services, a topic intimately connected to the one discussed in Sections 2 to 4, but generally ignored in copyright doctrine. Here the focus is on the European Conditional Access Directive. In addition, Section 6 contains an overview of the law of conditional access as it stands in a number of European Member States. Then, finally, both types of protection will be compared. Sections 1-4 and 7-8 were written by Kamiel Koelman, Sections 5 and 6 by Natali Helberger.

Copyright and Electronic Commerce (ed. P. Bernt Hugenholtz; ISBN 90-411-9785-0; © Kluwer Law International, 2000; printed in Great Britain).

1. Technological Measures

Technological measures take many shapes. Several classifications of TMs have been proposed.[1] For the purpose of this survey, we will distinguish four categories of TMs: measures that control access, measures that control particular uses, technologies that protect the integrity of a work, and TMs that enable metering of access to or use of information. Of course, this description is not exhaustive. Moreover, in practice the various categories will often overlap and undoubtedly other technologies and functions will be developed in the (near) future.

1.1 ACCESS CONTROL

The first category (TMs that prevent access to and use in general of the information) can be subdivided into four kinds of measures: technologies that control access at the online outlet, measures that control access within the physical sphere of control of the user, measures that control access to an acquired copy, and measures that do not prevent initial access, as do the other three types of access controlling measures, but control access in other ways.

1.1.1 Technologies that control access at the online outlet

This type of measure is often used by providers of subscription-based information services, e.g. to control access to a website. TMs of this kind can best be compared to a door or a gatekeeper in the real world; if the user applies the proper key, which often comes in the form of a password, the technology will 'let him in'. TMs of this type protect access to a *service* inasmuch as they protect access to the content provided.

1.1.2 TMs that control access at the level of the user or receiver of the information

Currently, the signal of most pay-TV systems can be received by everyone. However, to access the information that the signal contains one needs a key or device (a decoder) in order to decrypt or descramble the signal and obtain access to the

1 Smith classifies TMs into two broad categories. The first covers measures that prevent interception of a work by unauthorised recipients; the second contains TMs that limit the use and/or further distribution of works. See Smith 1997, p. 425. Schlachter distinguishes measures that are put in place before distribution (pre-infringement), measures that ensure payment prior to or at the time of the use of the work (metering) and technologies that are used to discover infringement and thus to enhance enforcement (post-infringement). See Schlachter 1997, pp. 38-45.

information.[2] This method can also be used with regard to information distributed through an online service (possibly in combination with the above-mentioned access-controlling technology) in which case the decrypting device may be a 'plug-in' (i.e. a software application which the user has to install on his computer).[3] Although with this type of TM access control occurs further 'downstream', the effect of the technology in both cases is similar — the barring of *initial access* to the TM-protected content without authorisation. Again, this category of TMs protects both services (e.g. pay-TV) and content.

1.1.3 Measures that control access to an already acquired copy of a work

This category covers measures protecting, for example, a CD-ROM or a copy downloaded from a network. These technologies also control access. As in the second category, access is controlled within the physical sphere of control of the end-user. A conceptual difference between this category and the two discussed above is that access-prevention in relation to an acquired copy does not protect a service. In this context the notion of 'access' can have two distinct meanings. One might qualify installing the product on the user's PC as constituting (initial) access. It could, however, also be argued that each time the content of a copy is consulted the user 'accesses' the information.

1.1.4 Measures that prevent subsequent access

Here, initial access remains unprotected, but subsequent access is controlled by technical means. For instance, it is now common practice to post a version of a computer program on the Internet so that potential customers can download it, and try it out. After having run for a certain time the program will disintegrate or shut itself off, having given the user a taste of the program and leaving him with the urge to purchase a copy that will last longer. Similarly, it may become possible in the near future to construct applications that will make a work disintegrate after it has been accessed a fixed number of times, thus enabling the rights-holder to bill per use.[4] Other technologies do not prevent access totally, but, for instance, merely prevent users from accessing the protected material simultaneously on several terminals.

2 See for an overview of encryption technologies, Institute for Information Law 1998, pp. 7-16.
3 Schlachter 1997, p. 41; Stefik 1997, p. 139.
4 Schlachter 1997, p. 39; Litman 1997a, p. 601. These applications are often called 'date bombs'.

1.2 CONTROL OF CERTAIN USES

By controlling access one can control the *use in general* of information; if material cannot be accessed, it cannot be used. The second main category of TMs prevents *certain uses* being made of the work after it has been accessed. A multimedia product may, for example, be designed to prevent the making of print-outs, the making of copies of the product in its entirety, or its use in a network. An early example of such a TM is the 'dongle' (or hardware lock) that is used in connection with software. The making of copies of the program is not prevented by this protection method, but because the program can only be run and accessed if the dongle is inserted into the computer's parallel port, the technology prevents simultaneous use of copies of the purchased original.[5] This example indicates that controlling access and certain uses may come down to the same thing.

Copy protection is the predominant function of this type of TM. A well-known example is the Serial Copy Management System (SCMS), which prevents the making of digital copies of digital copies. As a result, a copy of a digital work cannot serve as a 'master' for subsequent digital copies.[6] Another method of preventing copying is to plant a 'worm' in a computer program, which detects efforts to copy the program and 'counterattacks' by erasing the copied files.[7] Also, a product can be designed to prevent the making of print-outs or copies of the product in its entirety, by blocking these functions through software routines. These and other copy-protection mechanisms were widely used in connection with computer software in the 1980s, but because consumers resented the inconvenience and the mechanisms were easy to break, copy-protection technologies are no longer very popular.[8]

1.3 INTEGRITY PROTECTION

A third set of measures are those that protect the integrity of the work by preventing a work from being altered. In fact, these TMs also prevent certain uses, but because in copyright doctrine moral rights are generally distinguished from economic rights, we place these measures in a separate category. To our knowledge, integrity-protecting technologies are not yet widely used in the context of copyright (or moral rights) protection. Until now, the issue of the integrity of electronic information has mainly been addressed as a problem of 'authentication': to what extent does an electronic document or signature constitute valid proof of a transaction?

5 Wand 1996, p. 902; Raubenheimer 1996, p. 69.
6 Under US law these SCMSs must be built into DAT recorders. See US Audio Home Recording Act of 1992; ss 1001-1010 of the US Copyright Act (AHRA).
7 Palmer 1989, p. 289.
8 Schlachter 1997, p. 39.

1.4 USAGE METERING

A fourth category consists of TMs that do not prevent or inhibit access or use, but merely meter or track the frequency a work is accessed, or monitor other uses made (e.g. copying). These measures do not directly protect copyrighted works or copyrights or prevent unauthorised access, but merely facilitate the exploitation of copyrights. TMs may, for instance, provide the rights-holder with an audit trail (either measured at the online outlet or by a software module incorporated in a disseminated copy) of the actual usage made of a work, which enables him to bill for each specific use or to spot violations of the terms of a licence.[9] A next step would be to enable automatic and simultaneous payment to the rights-holder for each actual use made of a work, through online transaction schemes.

These methods could support so-called superdistribution, i.e. they would provide the rights-holder with continuing revenue regardless of who holds the copy of the work to which the module is attached. If the original purchaser were to disseminate it further, the module would provide the rights-holder with data on subsequent usage. Moreover, the rights-holder might automatically receive compensation for each use of the work by subsequent holders of the copy.[10]

1.5 ELECTRONIC COPYRIGHT MANAGEMENT SYSTEMS

Advanced TMs of the latter type may be qualified as full-blown 'Electronic Copyright Management Systems' (ECMSs). The term ECMS normally covers more than measures merely preventing access or use. These systems are intended to facilitate the trade in copyrights or copyrighted works within a networked environment. An ECMS would provide the complete infrastructure necessary for rights-holders to license directly users of copyrighted works.[11] The TMs mentioned here are not necessarily part of such an ECMS. However, it is not unlikely that some of the techniques described above will be applied.

2. Protection of Technological Measures in the Copyright

The main focus in this section is on the legal protection of TMs in the context of copyright, in particular Article 11 of the WIPO Copyright Treaty of 1996 (WCT),[12]

---

9 Clark 1996, p. 143; Schlachter 1997, p. 41; Elkin-Koren 1997, p.104.
10 Bell 1998, pp. 566-567.
11 See <http://imprimatur.net> ; Bechtold 1998, p. 19.
12 WIPO document CRNR/DC/94 of 23 December 1996, available at <http://www.wipo.org/eng/diplconf/distrib/94dc.htm>.

Article 6 of the proposed European Copyright Directive (CD)[13] and the relevant sections in the US Digital Millennium Copyright Act of 1998 (DMCA).[14] Article 11 WCT has its counterpart in Article 18 of the WIPO Performances and Phonograms Treaty. Since both provisions are very much alike, we will limit our discussion to Article 11 WCT. Both the proposed Directive and the DMCA are intended to implement the obligations following from the WIPO Treaties.

The initial US proposals concerning the protection of technological measures were included in the National Information Infrastructure Copyright Protection Bill of 1995,[15] and were based upon the White Paper.[16] Thereafter, several other bills were introduced in the House of Representatives and the Senate. The Bill on which the legislative work eventually concentrated, and that was signed into law, is the DMCA.[17] The provisions on the protection of technological measures are included in the WIPO Copyright and Performances and Phonograms Treaties Implementation Act of 1998, which is part of the DMCA. The European Commission issued its first proposal for a Copyright Directive in December 1997. After the first reading by the European Parliament in February 1999,[18] the Commission published its Amended Proposal in May of the same year.[19]

Prior to the WIPO Treaties a modest body of anti-circumvention law has been developed in a number of countries in the context of copyright. In most instances these legal regimes do not protect all types of measures, or are limited to technological measures that protect only certain kinds of works. The most important provisions in this context, that will be dealt with in this section, are the US Audio Home Recording Act (AHRA),[20] Article 296 of the UK Copyright, Designs and Patents Act (CDPA) and Article 7(1)(c) of the European Software Directive.[21] Also, we will discuss existing case law on the liability of persons who provide the means that facilitate copying, e.g. video recorders or photocopying machines. TMs that protect conditional access services, as opposed to copyrighted

---

13 European Commission, Proposal for a European Parliament and Council Directive on the Harmonisation of Certain Aspects of Copyright and Related Rights in the Information Society, Brussels, 10 December 1997, COM (97) 628 final.

14 Public Law 105-304, 28 October 1998.

15 S 1284 and HR 2441, 104th Congress.

16 Information Infrastructure Task Force, Intellectual Property and the National Information Infrastructure: The Report of the Working Group on Intellectual Property Rights, Washington: Library of Congress 1995 ('White Paper').

17 S 2037 and HR 2281, 105th Congress.

18 Proposal for a European Parliament and Council Directive on the harmonisation of certain aspects of copyright and related rights in the Information Society, COM (97) 628, A4-0026/99, Minutes of 10 February 1999 (Provisional Edition).

19 Amended Proposal for a European Parliament and Council Directive on the harmonisation of certain aspects of copyright and related rights in the Information Society, Brussels, 21 May 1999, COM(99) 250 final.

20 Codified in ss 1001–1010 of the US Copyright Act.

21 Council Directive 91/250/EEC of 14 May 1991 on the Legal Protection of Computer Programs, OJ L 122/42.

works, are protected in some countries as well. The latter protection schemes will be addressed extensively in Sections 5 and 6, but we will discuss these regimes and other existing law in this section whenever relevant to the above-mentioned WIPO, EU and US initiatives.

Below we will describe the rules adopted in the WIPO Treaty, proposed in the European Union and enacted in the DMCA, and compare them to existing law. First, we will describe which measures are protected. Secondly, we will analyse which activities are prohibited and which actors are targeted. Thirdly, certain specific requirements for liability under these regimes will be examined in detail. Fourthly, we will identify the persons that can apply for legal protection of TMs, and finally we will briefly investigate to what extent both the WIPO Treaty and the proposed Directive oblige Contracting and Member States to amend or supplement their existing laws.

2.1 MEASURES PROTECTED

As TMs take many forms, it is not surprising that legislators have difficulty defining them. Moreover, because these provisions are designed to deal with technologies not yet in existence, they need to be technology-neutral, which further enhances the vagueness of the definitions.[22]

2.1.1 WIPO

Article 11 WCT requires the Contracting States to protect:[23]

> "effective technological measures that are used by authors in connection with the exercise of their rights under this Treaty or the Berne Convention and that restrict acts, in respect of their works, which are not authorised by the authors concerned or permitted by law".

Four elements can be distinguished here; measures must be (1) effective, (2) used by authors, (3) to exercise copyright and (4) restrict acts not authorised by the authors or permitted by law.[24]

22 See US House of Representatives, Digital Millennium Copyright Act of 1998, Report and Additional Views to Accompany H.R. 2281, 22 July 1998, Report 105-551, Part 2, p. 24.

23 This provision is the implementation of an amendment proposed by the African delegation to the WIPO Conference; see WIPO document CRNR/DC/56 of 6 December 1996.

24 See WIPO Summary Minutes, Main Committee I, document CRNR/DC/102, 26 August 1997, No. 519; Greenstein 1996.

What exactly constitutes an 'effective' measure is unclear. At the very least this element indicates that not all TMs need be protected.[25] The European Commission interprets it as leaving room for discretion to the Contracting Parties.[26] Possibly, it has been inserted to clarify that only measures that actually require intentional acts of circumvention are protected. If a measure can be circumvented 'by accident', it is clearly not effective. Also, it may mean that the rights-holder must put some effort into protecting his works in order to deserve legal protection against circumventing.[27] All (proposed) implementations of the provision define the term 'effective'.

The third and, particularly, the fourth element imply that the measure must restrict the very same acts the 'law' prohibits. Thus, circumventing for the purpose of performing an act permitted by copyright law or other areas of the law (e.g., the right to privacy or the freedom of information), need not be outlawed.[28] Apparently, TMs that only meter usage or merely enable a transaction to take place are not covered, since they do not necessarily 'restrict acts'.

Moreover, mere access-controlling technologies do not appear to fall within the scope of the WCT provision, since neither the WCT nor the Berne Convention (BC) provide for an exclusive right to control individual access to a work. Of course, this is different if the TM would restrict the 'making available to the public' of a protected work, an act aimed at exploiting a work and covered by Article 8 WCT.[29]

2.1.2 EU

Article 6(3) of the Amended Proposal defines protected TMs as:

> "any technology, device or component that, in the normal course of its operation, is designed to prevent or inhibit the infringement of any copyright or any right related to copyright as provided by law or the sui generis right provided for in Chapter III of European Parliament and Council Directive 96/9/EC".

---

25 See Vinje 1996a, p. 433 (stating that the EU and US proposals that were incorporated in the Basic Proposal and simply protected any TM were too broad, and calling for a limit to the types of TMs covered by legal protection schemes).

26 Explanatory Memorandum with the Copyright Directive Proposal, Comment 1 in respect of Art. 6.

27 See Lucas 1998b, p. 274. In respect of the effectiveness criterion, Lucas argues that: "Elle s'explique probablement par l'idée que le droit n'a pas à venir au secours de celui qui n'utilise pas toutes les ressources de la technique".

28 Lucas 1998a, p. 13.

29 Cf. Saito 1998, pp. 1–2: "[I]n the digital environment we can recognize a closer relationship of exploitation to access, but we can still distinguish exploitation from access, in keeping with the analogue environment". One could argue that providing customers with a key in order to access a work may contribute to, or even constitute, an act of making a work available to the public. However, a person who subsequently uses the key to access a work does not commit such an act.

Only measures specifically 'designed' to protect copyrights are covered. Whether protection is limited to instances where the TM actually prevents a copyright infringement remains unclear. From the wording of the provision it may follow that it is enough if the measure is merely designed to inhibit infringements. From the Explanatory Memorandum to the Proposal, however, it can be concluded that only when a measure prevents acts that the copyright-holder can prohibit on the basis of copyright law does it need to be protected. Thus, the copyright limitations would limit the scope of the protection of TMs as well.[30]

Apart from being designed to prevent copyright infringements, technologies must be 'effective' in order to be protected under the Amended Proposal. With respect to 'effectiveness' the provision states:

> "Technological measures shall be deemed "effective" where the access to or use of a protected work or other subject matter is controlled through application of an access code or any other type of protection process which achieves the protection objective in an operational and reliable manner with the authority of the rightholders. Such measures may include decryption, descrambling or other transformation of the work or other subject matter".

The test of 'effectiveness' stems from the WCT. According to the Explanatory Memorandum to the Proposal, it implies that in order to obtain protection, rights-holders have the burden of proving that the technology chosen is effective.[31] Remarkably, in the first proposal only measures that prevent access were held to be 'effective' and thus protected. The other categories of TMs (e.g. copy-protection devices, measures that enable metering, etc.) therefore appeared to fall outside the definition. If a civil action could be brought against the circumvention of measures enabling the copyright owner to allow access only upon authorisation, it may be said to, in effect, amount to a 'right to control access'. A person could then be held accountable for circumventing an access-controlling TM without authorisation.[32]

Because the provision in the first Proposal considered 'effective' access-controlling technologies only, it suffered from a conceptual deficiency. If the scope of the provision was limited to measures that (1) merely prevent copyright infringement, and (2) merely prevent access, it is hard to understand which measures (if any) were to be protected under Article 6 CD. These criteria may be mutually exclusive; gaining access to a published work is not as such a restricted act, and

30 See Explanatory Memorandum with the CD, *supra* n. 26, Comment 3 in respect of Art. 6: "Finally, the provision prohibits activities aimed at an infringement of a copyright ...: this would imply that not any circumvention of technical means of protection should be covered, but only those which constitute an infringement of a right, i.e. which are not authorized by law or by the author". See *infra* Section 3.2.

31 Explanatory Memorandum with the CD, *supra* n. 26, Comment 2 in respect of Art. 6.

32 See also *infra* Section 4.2.

therefore does not amount to a copyright infringement.[33] Not surprisingly therefore, the Amended Proposal provides that not only access preventing technologies, but also 'any other type of protection process which achieves the protection objective in an operational and reliable manner' may be considered 'effective' for the purpose of Article 6.

However, the question remains how access control can be reconciled with the scope of copyright. It may be that the Commission has the right of temporary reproduction in mind, as granted by the Software and Database Directives and proposed in Article 2 CD (and limited in Article 5(1) CD), which may imply an exclusive right of access (or use), since in order to access a work it must be temporarily reproduced in the computer's random access memory.[34] On the other hand, in the Explanatory Memorandum to its proposal for a Conditional Access Directive, discussed below in Section 5, the Commission clarifies that that the protection of access preventing technologies must be distinguished from copyright protection, because "[e]ven though, from an economic point of view, rightholders will certainly benefit from such measures, this will be an indirect effect, and their interests remain distinct". Moreover, the Commission points out that:[35]

> "the 'cable and satellite' Directive, while providing rules on satellite broadcasting and cable retransmission of protected works, does not assist operators in their fight against illicit reception. This is because *reception does not constitute a relevant 'act' for the purposes of copyright law, which traditionally covers communication as opposed to reception* [or, in other words, mere access]" (emphasis added).

2.1.3 United States

When drafting legislation to protect TMs, contrary to the European Commission, the US legislature has taken into account that copyright does not (expressly) grant a right to control access. Two kinds of measures are distinguished in the DMCA: (1) measures that 'effectively' *control access*, and (2) TMs that 'effectively' *protect copyrights*. According to the Act[36]

> "a technological protection measure 'effectively *controls access* to a work' if the measure, in the ordinary course of its operation, requires the application of

33 See also *infra* Section 2.2. The US legislature expressly acknowledges this.

34 See Bygrave and Koelman elsewhere in this volume, p. 104.

35 European Commission, 'Communication from the Commission to the European Parliament, the Council and the Economic and Social Committee, Proposal for a European Parliament and Council Directive on the Legal Protection of Services based on, or consisting of, Conditional Access', Brussels, 9 July 1997, COM(97) 356 final, p. 6.

36 See s. 1201(a)(3)(B) DMCA.

> information, or a process or a treatment, with the authority of the copyright owner, to gain access to the work" (emphasis added).

A TM is considered 'effectively' to control access if due to the measure access can ordinarily not be obtained without the rights-holder's permission. Only TMs that control access to a 'work' are protected. Consequently, access prevention to non-copyrightable material does not fall within the scope of the provision. The legislature explains that the provision is only about 'initial access'.[37] What exactly is meant by this remains unclear. Elsewhere, circumventing an access-controlling TM is likened to breaking into a locked room in order to obtain a copy of a book.[38] This could imply that not each act of consultation is covered. Thus, measures preventing access to an obtained copy would not be protected.

Concerning the second category of TMs the Act provides that:[39]

> "a technological protection measure 'effectively *protects a right* of a copyright owner under this title' if the measure, in the ordinary course of its operation, prevents, restricts, or otherwise limits the exercise of a right of a copyright owner" (emphasis added).

A measure is presumed 'effective' if, due to the TM, the ability to perform acts that would infringe copyright is limited. The House Committee on Commerce considered effective only those measures that require the use of a 'key' provided by the rights-holder.[40] Thus, for example, measures that meter use are not covered. Measures that protect the integrity of the work, however, do fall within the scope of the definition, insofar as moral rights are protected in the United States and the ability to alter a work is made dependent on a key.[41] Because only measures that protect copyrights are considered 'effective', a TM is not protected when it prevents acts that constitute fair use or are otherwise permitted under copyright law. The same is true for TMs that protect material that is not subject to copyright in the first place.

---

37 US House of Representatives, WIPO Copyright Treaties Implementation and On-line Copyright Infringement Liability Limitation, Report to Accompany H.R. 2281, 22 May 1998, Report 105-551, Part 1, p. 19; US Senate, The Digital Millennium Copyright Act of 1998, Report and Additional Views to Accompany S. 2037, 11 May 1998, Report 105-190, p. 29.

38 House Report, *ibid.*, p. 17.

39 See s. 1201(b)(2)(B) DMCA.

40 House Report, *supra* n. 22, pp. 39–40. Note that this refers not only to TMs that protect a right, but also to those that control access.

41 See s. 106A of the US Copyright Act.

2.1.4 Existing law

Existing rules on TM protection are drafted mainly in technology-specific terms. Article 7(1)(c) of the Software Directive protects measures 'that protect a computer program'. In this Directive the *subject matter of the right* (the work) is considered protected by the technology, not the *right*, as in the proposed Copyright Directive and the DMCA. Whether this is a symptom of a conceptual difference or merely a slip of the drafter's pen, is unclear.

Article 296 of the UK CDPA follows a different approach. Protection is available only for TMs that protect against a specific act, i.e. copying. The provision states:

> "References in this section to copy-protection include any device or means intended to prevent or restrict copying of a work or to impair the quality of copies made".

Taken literally, the scope of the UK provision is extremely broad; protection is not limited to measures inhibiting potentially infringing behaviour.[42]

In contrast, the scope of the US Audio Home Recording Act is very narrow. It is limited both to a certain type of TMs and to a specific class of works (i.e. musical works). 'Serial copy management systems' and devices that have the same functional characteristics are covered. These TMs are not themselves defined in the Act. However, from the definitions that do appear in the Act it can be concluded that it protects only TMs that prevent a digital copy of a purchased digital musical recording from being used as a 'master' for subsequent copies.[43]

2.2 ACTS PROHIBITED AND ACTORS TARGETED

In this section we will describe which acts are targeted and, concomitantly, which actors may become liable for infringing the TM-protection schemes. The main distinction that can be made is between provisions that address the actual 'circumventor' and those that aim at preparatory activities to circumvention, such as the manufacturing or providing of devices or services that enable circumvention.

---

42 See Goddard 1998, p. 11.

43 Section 1001(11) of the US Copyright Act provides: "The term 'serial copying' means the duplication in a digital format of a copyrighted musical work or sound recording from a digital reproduction of a digital musical recording. The term 'digital reproduction of a digital musical recording' does not include a digital musical recording as distributed, by authority of the copyright owner, for ultimate sale to consumers". See Nimmer and Nimmer, § 8B.03[B].

2.2.1 WIPO

Existing statutory TM-protection schemes in copyright law target the preparatory activities to circumvention, not the actual act of circumventing. Accordingly, Article 13 of the WIPO Basic Proposal prohibited only the commercial trade in 'protection-defeating devices' and the provision of services 'having the same effect'.[44] The WIPO Treaties depart from this approach. To our knowledge, Article 11 WCT is the first provision directly aimed at the actual circumvention of a TM that protects a copyright. Apparently, the final wording of the provision is the result of successful lobbying by producers of (consumer) electronics. The main rationale for limiting the scope of the provision to the act of circumvention as such is not to hinder the manufacture, development and use of multipurpose devices, such as computers, computer software and video and audio recorders.[45]

2.2.2 EU

There seems to have been some confusion as to which activities ought to be covered by Article 6 CD. The first Commission proposal and its accompanying texts were not unambiguous as to this issue. An unofficial DG XV document suggested that only 'preparatory activities', not the act of circumventing itself, were to be prohibited.[46] Article 6 CD initially covered:

> "any activities, including manufacture or distribution of devices or the performance of services, which have only limited commercially significant purpose or use other than to circumvent".

Evidently, the provision aimed at the commercial dealing in circumvention devices or the provision of services commercially. In general, it dealt with "any activities . . . which have only limited commercially significant purpose other than to circumvent". Was the act of circumvention included in the words 'any activities'?[47]

---

44 WIPO Basic Proposal for the Substantive Provisions of the Treaty on Certain Questions Concerning the Protection of Literary and Artistic Works to be considered by the Diplomatic Conference, document CRNR/DC/4, 30 August 1996, Art. 13.

45 See Vinje 1996b, p. 587; Vaidyanatha Ayyar 1998, pp. 28-29; see also Greenstein 1996 and Browning 1997 (stating that Japan and other Asian nations opposed the Basic Proposal because it might have outlawed personal computers, which are, after all, the most common hacking devices). See also the *Consolidated Recommendations of International Non-Governmental Organizations and Associations*, available at <http://www.hrrc.org/pp_12-16.html>.

46 European Commission, Background to the Proposal for a Directive on Copyright and Related Rights in the Information Society, Brussels 1998, available at <http://europa.eu.int/comm/dg15/en/intprop/intprop/1100.htm#lega>.

47 See e.g. Von Lewinsky 1998, p. 138. Von Lewinsky apparently interprets the provision as applying to the act of circumvention as well as to the preparatory activities.

The Explanatory Memorandum suggested it was.[48] Recital 30, however, suggested otherwise.[49] Clearly, Article 6 CD was drafted with mainly the preparatory acts in mind, as is illustrated by the Explanatory Memorandum:[50]

> "the real danger for intellectual property rights will not be the single act of circumvention by individuals, but the preparatory acts carried out by commercial companies that could produce, sell, rent or advertise circumventing devices".

In conclusion, it remained unclear whether the act of circumvention as such was effectively protected by Article 6. In the Amended Proposal, however, it is undoubtedly both the act of circumvention and the preparatory activities that are covered. Article 6 now states:

> "(1) Member States shall provide adequate legal protection against the circumvention without authority of any effective technological measures designed to protect any copyrights or any rights related to copyright as by law or the sui generis right provided for in Chapter III of European Parliament and Council Directive 96/9/EC, which the person concerned carries out in the knowledge, or with reasonable grounds to know that he or she pursues that objective.
> (2) Member States shall provide adequate legal protection against any activities, including the manufacture or distribution of devices, products or components or the provision of services, which:
> (a) are promoted, advertised or marketed for the purpose of circumvention, or
> (b) have circumvention as their sole or principal purpose or as their commercial purpose, or
> (c) are primarily designed, produced, adapted or performed for the purpose of enabling or facilitating the circumvention of, any technological measures designed to protect any copyright or any right related to copyright as provided by law or the sui generis right provided for in Chapter III of European Parliament and Council Directive 96/9/EC".

2.2.3 United States

As does the Amended Proposal, the DMCA expressly aims at the act of circumvention, which is dealt with separately from any preparatory acts. However,

48 Explanatory Memorandum with the CD, *supra* n. 26, Comments in respect of Art. 6.
49 The Recital states that legal protection must be provided "against any activity enabling or facilitating the circumvention without authority of such measures". The act of circumvention is not mentioned.
50 Explanatory Memorandum with the CD, *supra* n. 26, Comment 1 in respect of Art. 6.

actual circumvention is only outlawed in respect of TMs that *control access*, not with regard to measures that *protect a copyright*. The Senate Report with the DMCA explains:[51]

> "there is no prohibition on conduct in 1201(b) akin to the prohibition on circumvention [of TMs that control access] in 1201(a)(1). The prohibition in 1201(a)(1) is necessary because prior to this Act, the conduct of circumvention was never before made unlawful ... The copyright law has long forbidden copyright infringements, so no new prohibition was necessary [in 1201(b)]".

Apparently, it was felt necessary to cover the act of circumventing measures that control access, because controlling access is not an act restricted by copyright. Does the DMCA deliberately create a 'right to control access'? The Senate Report sheds some light on this interesting question:[52]

> "Subsection (a) applies when a person has not obtained authorised access to a copy or a phonorecord of a work that is protected under the Copyright Act ... Paragraph (a)(1) establishes a general prohibition against gaining unauthorised access to a work by circumventing a technological protection measure put in place by the copyright owner ... In order to provide meaningful protection and enforcement of *the copyright owner's right to control access* to his or her copyrighted work, paragraph (a)(2) supplements the prohibition against the act of circumvention in paragraph (a)(1) with prohibitions on creating and making available certain technologies ... Unlike subsection (a), which prohibits the circumvention of access control technologies, subsection (b) does not, by itself, prohibit the circumvention of effective technological copyright protection measures. It is anticipated that most acts of circumventing a technological copyright protection measure will occur in the course of conduct which itself implicates the copyright owners rights under title 17. This subsection is not intended in any way to enlarge or diminish those rights. Thus, for example, where a copy control technology is employed to prevent the unauthorised reproduction of a work, the circumvention of that technology would not itself be actionable under section 1201, but any reproduction of the work that is thereby facilitated would remain subject to the protections embodied in title 17" (emphasis added).

Apparently, the reasoning is that circumvention of a TM that protects a copyright need not be covered, since (in most cases) the rights-holder will be able to take legal action against the infringer under existing copyright law. It is considered

51 Senate Report, *supra* n. 37, p. 12.
52 Senate Report, *supra* n. 37, pp. 28-29.

undesirable that rights-holders be unable to hold accountable those circumventing a TM that controls access. Therefore, a specific 'right to control access to TM-protected works' is created. This is a concept new to copyright law. Perhaps the rationale is that, as argued by Smith, controlling access is important for controlling copying, since it prevents many infringements from ever taking place, and it facilitates the control of copying by permitting use only by authorised, known users.[53]

Circumvention of a TM that *controls access* is defined as:[54]

> "to descramble a scrambled work, to decrypt an encrypted work, or otherwise to avoid, bypass, remove, deactivate, or impair a technological measure, without the authority of the copyright owner".

While the provision prohibits obtaining access to a work without the rights-holder's authorisation, it is, in effect, an exclusive right to authorise access to a technologically protected work.[55]

Since the act of circumventing a measure which *protects a copyright* is not itself prohibited, the definition of this act merely describes which capabilities a device must have in order to be prohibited. Such a device must enable "avoiding, bypassing, removing, deactivating, or otherwise impairing a technological measure".[56] Apart from the act of circumvention, the DMCA declares unlawful the commercial manufacturing and providing of services or devices that enable the circumvention of *both types* of TMs.[57]

2.2.4 Existing law

As noted above, none of the existing statutory provisions that specifically protect technologies that protect copyright covers the act of circumvention. The AHRA, Article 7(1)(c) of the Software Directive and Article 296 of the UK CDPA all prohibit only activities preparatory to circumvention. However, contrary to the Conditional Access Directive, some of the existing legislation on the protection of conditional access services in Member States does target the act of unauthorised access or reception of, e.g. pay-TV services, by fraudulent means.[58]

---

53 Smith 1997, p. 418.
54 See s. 1201(a)(3)(A) DMCA.
55 See *infra* Section 4.2.
56 See s. 1201(b)(2)(A) DMCA.
57 The Act makes it unlawful to 'manufacture, import, offer to the public, provide, or otherwise traffic in any technology, product, service, device, component, or part thereof'. See s. 1201(a)(2) and (b)(1) DMCA.
58 See *infra* Section 6.

The provisions of the Software Directive that grant exclusive rights may in certain circumstances provide for protection against the act of circumvention. According to a German court of appeals the act of circumventing a dongle in order to run a program,[59] which involved an adaptation of the software, was actionable under Article 69(c)(2) of the German Copyright Act (which implements Article 4(b) of the Software Directive).[60] According to Raubenheimer, such an act of circumvention would also constitute infringement of the right of reproduction granted in Article 69(c)(1) of the German Copyright Act (the equivalent of Article 4(a) of the Software Directive), because it would necessarily involve unlawful temporary copying.[61] On the basis of the latter right, not only a person actually adapting the software, but also a person running software of which a TM is circumvented by a third party may be held a copyright infringer.

2.3 PURPOSE OF DEVICE

Electronics manufacturers and software producers risk being affected by provisions that outlaw the dealing in circumvention-enabling devices.[62] Such regulations might inhibit the manufacture and trade in products that, until today, have been entirely lawful. To deal with this problem, the EU and US protection schemes include a 'purpose requirement'.

2.3.1 WIPO

In order 'to achieve the necessary coverage', Article 13 of the Basic Proposal covered devices of which the 'primary purposes or primary effect' is to circumvent TMs,[63] rather than devices 'specifically designed or adapted' to circumvent such measures.[64] Obviously, the latter criterion would have covered fewer devices. The Basic Proposal focused on the *effect* of a device; a manufacturer would incur liability if a device happened to be used for circumvention purposes, even though he could not possibly have foreseen this use.[65] The Proposal was heavily opposed at the

59 See *infra* Section 4.2.

60 *OLG Karlsruhe*, [1996] NJW-CoR 186; see Wand 1996, p. 903.

61 Raubenheimer 1996, p. 76.

62 Representatives of consumer electronics manufactures testified that, if the DMCA were enacted, it would possibly block the introduction of now legitimate products that could be perceived as being circumventing devices. See *BNA Electronic Commerce and Law* 1998/23. See also *BNA Electronic Commerce and Law* 1998/14 (manufacturing prohibitions might apply to personal computers).

63 This criterion stems from the US White Paper; see White Paper, *supra* n. 16, p. 230. It also applies under the AHRA.

64 Note 13.06 Basic Proposal, *supra* n. 44. The latter criterion is apparently inspired by s. 296 of the UK CDPA.

65 See Vinje 1996a, pp. 434-436.

Diplomatic Conference in 1996.[66] Several delegations suggested inserting the more stringent 'sole intended purpose' criterion used in Article 7(1)(c) of the European Software Directive.[67] In the end, Article 11 WCT as adopted does not aim at manufacturers of devices at all, and thus no longer contains any purpose requirement. It simply states that the remedies provided for must be 'adequate', thereby leaving the Contracting States with ample room for discretion.[68]

2.3.2 EU

The Copyright Directive, as first proposed by the Commission, did target preparatory activities, such as the manufacturing and providing of circumvention-enabling devices. It encompassed the dealing in devices or providing of services that "have only limited commercially significant purpose or use other than to circumvent".[69] The application of a broad criterion ('use' instead of 'effect') obviously worked to the advantage of the manufacturers; if a device coincidentally has an unintended use besides circumvention, it would not be outlawed. Arguably, this was to be understood as an objective criterion, i.e. a court would have to consider the apparent purpose of the device, since proof of intent (a subjective criterion) was expressly required separately.[70]

The Amended Proposal declares unlawful devices or services that (1) are promoted, advertised or marketed for the purpose of circumvention, (2) have circumvention as their sole or principle purpose or as their commercial purpose — a criterion similar to that used in the Software Directive — or, (3) are primarily designed, produced, adapted or performed for the purpose of circumventing a TM that protects a copyright. The first and third criteria focus on the activities of the manufacturer or dealer. The second is concerned with the apparent purpose of the device.[71] Recital 30*bis* clarifies that no obligation to design devices to correspond to technological measures is implied.

2.3.3 United States

The DMCA prohibits devices that are "primarily designed or produced for the purpose of circumventing". Again, this is probably an objective criterion.

66 See Greenstein 1996.
67 See Summary Minutes, *supra* n. 24, Nos 517, 526.
68 See Vaidyanatha Ayyar 1998, pp. 28-29.
69 See *infra* Section 3.4.
70 See *infra* Section 2.4.
71 See, however, Vinje 1996a, p. 435 (stating that devices do not themselves have purposes, and that the criterion included in the Basic Proposal, therefore, must refer to the purpose of the manufacturer or the user).

Alternatively, the 'limited commercial significance or use' criterion which was also used in the Directive's first proposal may apply.[72] As is the case in the amended EU proposal, to satisfy producers of general-purpose electronics, it is not required for a designer of consumer electronics, telecommunications or computing products to provide for a response to any TM.[73]

2.3.4 Existing law

To clarify the meaning of the tests applied in the DMCA, the US legislature repeatedly refers to the US Supreme Court's *Betamax* decision. The Court held that the provider of technology capable of 'substantial non-infringing uses', such as video recorders, is not liable for contributory copyright infringement. Thus, according to the Court, a balance is struck between the rights-holders' legitimate demand for effective protection and the right of others to engage freely in substantially unrelated areas of commerce.[74] Referring to this decision, in the *Vault* case an appellate court found that a producer of software that could be used to undo a copy-prevention system cannot be held liable because the software was capable of substantial non-infringing uses, as it enabled the making of back-up copies, which is allowed under the US Copyright Act.[75] From this case law the US Green Paper concluded that, under the *Betamax*-doctrine, even manufacturers of devices that are rarely or never actually put to non-infringing uses, will not incur liability.[76]

The Committee on Commerce of the US House of Representatives expressly understood the criteria proposed in the DMCA to imply that the Supreme Court's criterion is equivalent to those of the DMCA. Thus, consumer electronics would not be affected.[77] However, even though the intention may be to apply the Court's test, a device is still more likely to be found to have 'substantial non-infringing uses' than to have 'only limited commercial purpose other than circumvention', because the copyright exemptions are not applicable to the prohibition on circumventing TMs that control access and the specific exemptions on the prohibition to circumvent an access controlling TM cover fewer situations.[78]

72 See ss 1201(a)(2)(A) and (B) and 1201(b)(1)(A) and (B) DMCA.

73 See s. 1201(c)(3) DMCA. Remarkably, however, s. 1201(k) DMCA prescribes that certain copy-preventing technologies be included in analogue video recorders.

74 *Sony Corp. of America v. Universal City Studios, Inc.* 464 US 417 (1984). The test applied stems from patent law; see Samuelson 1996, pp. 7-9; Cohen 1997, pp. 172-173.

75 *Vault Corp. v. Quaid Software, Inc.*, 665 F. Supp.750 (E.D. La. 1987), aff'd, 847 F. 2d 255 (5th Cir. 1988); see Samuelson 1996, pp. 9-10.

76 Working Group on Intellectual Property, Preliminary draft of the Report of the Working Group on Intellectual Property (1994) ('US Green Paper'), text accompanying n. 354; see also Samuelson 1996, p. 14.

77 House Report, *supra* n. 22, p. 38.

78 See *infra* Section 3.3.

Surprisingly, the purpose of the device has not been raised as an issue in the context of the protection of conditional access services. The European Conditional Access Directive (CAD) covers the manufacturing of and dealing in "any equipment or software designed or adapted to give unauthorised access to a protected service".[79] This criterion is somewhat comparable to the Amended Proposal's and the DMCA's 'primarily designed or produced for the purpose of circumvention' test.

2.4 State of Mind and Liability

As mentioned above, the purpose of a device may affect liability under the various TM-protection schemes. Additionally, some (proposed) legislation contains specific requirements as to the state of mind of the provider of the circumvention enabling device and of the circumventor for him to be liable.

2.4.1 WIPO

The Basic Proposal contained an objective knowledge requirement. Only a person putting into circulation a device while knowing or having reasonable grounds to know that it will be used for circumvention might incur liability. Article 11 WCT simply requires that 'adequate' legal remedies be made available, thus leaving it up to the Contracting Parties to decide under what circumstances these remedies would be appropriate.

2.4.2 EU

The first Commission proposal applied the criterion of the Basic Proposal.[80] Clearly, in order to hold persons performing preparatory activities liable, some form of fault had to be shown. Whether the requirement also applied where an actual 'circumventor' was concerned remained unclear — just as it was not entirely clear whether the latter was targeted at all. The wording of Article 6 CD suggested that fault need not be proven.[81] The Explanatory Memorandum, on the other hand,

79 See *infra* Section 5.4.

80 Explanatory Memorandum with the CD, *supra* n. 26, comments in respect of Art. 6.

81 The provision states that remedies must be provided against "activities ... which the person concerned carries out in the knowledge, or with reasonable grounds to know, that they will enable or facilitate without authority the circumvention" of TMs. Since the knowledge criterion is connected to the enabling or facilitating of circumvention and not to the act of tampering itself, it apparently does not relate to the latter.

implied that it did.[82] The Amended Proposal reverses the situation. Now, legal protection must be provided against circumvention 'which the person concerned carries out in the knowledge, or with reasonable grounds to know that he or she pursues that objective'. However, a similar knowledge requirement is absent from the paragraph (Article 6(2)) dealing with preparatory activities, which merely states that 'adequate legal protection' must be provided against such activities. Does this mean that Member States may hold a provider of circumvention enabling devices strictly liable, but not a person circumventing a TM?

2.4.3 United States

The DMCA expressly holds strictly liable persons who circumvent TMs in order to obtain unauthorised access to a work. Similarly, in respect of the manufacturer of a device, no proof of knowledge or intent is required. The person who merely markets the device, on the other hand, violates the Act only if it can be shown that he actually knows it can be used for circumvention.[83] Smith presumes that a manufacturer or direct facilitator should be on notice, and therefore knowledge of the fact that the device will be used for unlawful purposes can be assumed (and easily proven), whereas a mere distributor is more likely to be ignorant of its purpose, especially if it is included in a product with other purposes and uses.[84] A criminal offence will be found only if the offender wilfully violated the DMCA.[85]

2.4.4 Existing law

Under Article 296 of the UK Copyright Act the manufacturer or trafficker of circumvention devices may be held liable if he knows or has reason to believe that it will be used to make infringing copies. The provisions protecting SCMSs in the US Copyright Act, however, do not contain a knowledge requirement.[86] A possible explanation might be that the SCMS regime is limited to a specific technology that protects a specific type of works.[87] Therefore, devices enabling circumvention of these technological measures are likely to have been designed specifically (intentionally) for that purpose. Concomitantly, a more stringent criterion may be appropriate.[88] In the United States, where direct copyright infringers are held

---

82 Explanatory Memorandum with the CD, *supra* n. 26, Comment 2 in respect of Art. 6 (stating that "[t]he provision adds an element of knowledge by the party liable for the circumvention").

83 See s. 1201(a) and (b) DMCA.

84 Smith 1997, p. 428.

85 See s. 1204 DMCA.

86 See s. 1002(c),Title 17 USC.

87 See *infra* Section 2.1.

88 Samuelson 1996, p. 17; Vinje 1996a, p. 433.

strictly liable, indirect infringers — such as contributory infringers — are not. To incur contributory liability, actual knowledge or a reason to know of the infringing nature of the activity is required.[89] Clearly, any new statute holding strictly liable the producer or provider of the means to infringe copyrights departs from existing doctrine.[90]

2.5 WHO CAN APPLY FOR PROTECTION?

Since the protection schemes that are discussed in this section specifically aim at protecting TMs that protect copyright or prevent access to protected works, one would expect that the remedies provided are available only to rights-holders. However, several commentators have suggested otherwise.

2.5.1 WIPO

The Basic Proposal leaves open to whom the right to object must be awarded; it merely states that 'appropriate and effective remedies' have to be provided for. Liedes, who drafted the Basic Proposal, saw the protection against the provision of tampering devices as "more akin to public law",[91] thus implying that it could be implemented in, for example, criminal law. The decision to prosecute would then be left to the public prosecutor. He stressed, however, that the Contracting Parties would be free to choose appropriate legal remedies according to their own legal traditions.[92]

The Berne Convention grants rights specifically to the 'author' of a work.[93] Article 11 WCT does not; it does, however, provide that only TMs 'used by authors in connection with their rights protected under this Treaty or the Berne Convention' require protection and that acts of circumvention 'not authorised by the authors' be outlawed. Although this could be read as implying that the remedies are available to 'authors', it does not necessarily mean that they are not available to others. Moreover, like the Basic Proposal, the WCT leaves the Contracting States free to implement this provision not in copyright law but, for instance, in criminal law.[94]

89 See Koelman elsewhere in this volume, p. 17.
90 See Samuelson 1996, p. 13.
91 Basic Proposal, *supra* n. 44, n. 13.03.
92 Basic Proposal, *supra* n. 44, n. 13.04.
93 See Arts. 9, 11, 11bis, 11ter and 14 BC. In the Berne Convention the term 'author' is undefined. It can be concluded, however, that the author is the person who has made a 'work'. In most jurisdictions, the author is a natural person, while in others copyright may vest initially in a legal entity. See Ricketson 1987, pp. 157-159.
94 Lucas 1998a, p. 13.

2.5.2 *EU*

The proposed Copyright Directive approaches the problem in a similar way. It states that 'adequate legal protection' must be provided for. It deliberately does not specify to whom remedies should be available, and whether the protection should be provided under civil, criminal or administrative law, thus enabling Member States to implement the provision following their respective legal traditions.[95] On the other hand, from Article 8 CD read in conjunction with the Explanatory Memorandum it may be concluded that copyright-holders must be able to take legal action to recover damages, and apply for an injunction and seizure.[96] It is therefore uncertain whether the CD Proposal effectively prescribes that a civil action is open only to rights-holders.

Article 7 of the Software Directive applies an approach similar to Article 6 CD. It merely states that 'appropriate remedies' must be provided for. In some Member States the rights owner can bring civil proceedings in this respect (e.g. Germany),[97] whereas others have implemented the provision in criminal law (e.g. the Netherlands).[98] If the proposed Copyright Directive leaves similar room for discretion, similar differences may result upon implementation.

2.5.3 *United States*

The DMCA provides for civil remedies as well as criminal sanctions.[99] The provisions of substantive law simply prohibit circumvention and preparatory activities. The DMCA specifies that 'any person injured' by a violation may bring a civil action in court. It appears this remedy is open to persons other than rights-holders (e.g. mere information service providers), as it is under the existing US Audio Home Recording Act. The AHRA provides that any 'interested copyright party' may bring a civil action for statutory damages and/or injunctive relief, while

95 Explanatory Memorandum with the CD, *supra* n. 26, Comment 1 in respect of Art. 6.

96 See Explanatory Memorandum with the CD, *supra* n. 26, Comment 2 in respect of Art. 8: "As has been stressed in the relevant provisions in the two new WIPO Treaties, the remedies in order to be effective have to be expeditious to prevent infringements and deter further infringements ... As regards copyright and related rights protection in general, such measures will already exist to a large degree but may need to be complemented notably in relation to the rights given in Articles 8 (Technological measures) and 10 (Rights Management Information) of this proposal". Presumably, these references to Arts 8 and 10 must be read as referring to Arts 6 and 7. Murray understands Art. 8 CD to imply that the remedies mentioned in Art. 6 CD must include being able to sue for damages and to apply for an injunction, in other words, that a civil action must be available to rights-holders. See Murray 1998, p. 192. From Comment 4 in respect of Art. 8 it can be concluded that these remedies must be open to rights-holders.

97 Art. 69(f) of the German Copyright Act.

98 Art. 32a of the Dutch Copyright Act.

99 See ss. 1203 and 1204 DMCA.

'any person injured' may bring a civil action for actual damages incurred as a result of a violation of the Act.[100]

2.6 OBLIGATION TO SUPPLEMENT EXISTING LAW

Both the WIPO Treaty and the future Directive are aimed at national legislators. To what extent do these international instruments oblige the Contracting and Member States to supplement their national laws?

2.6.1 WIPO

In Article 18 WCT the Contracting Parties take it upon themselves to assume all of the obligations provided for under the Treaty. Consequently, they agree to provide 'adequate legal protection and effective legal remedies' against the circumvention of effective TMs that protect rights granted under the Berne Convention and the WCT. In other words, only TMs that inhibit acts that are restricted under the Berne Convention and the WCT need be protected. Consequently, the determination of the circumstances under which TMs must legally be protected, is closely related to the rights these international legal instruments grant. If, for instance, private copying were allowed (which it may be, in certain circumstances),[101] the Contracting States would not have to protect TMs that prevent private copying. Moreover, whereas neither the Berne Convention nor the WCT appears to grant an exclusive 'right to control access to published works',[102] the WCT certainly does not prescribe the protection of technologies that merely prevent individual access.[103] As mentioned in Section 2.5 above, the WCT leaves room to implement its provisions in either civil or public law.

Since it is left for the Contracting States to determine what level of protection is 'adequate',[104] a state may decide that an (additional) specific statutory provision is unnecessary, if it finds that its existing national laws offer the necessary protection.[105] The Treaty prescribes protection against 'circumvention'. Does this oblige the Contracting Parties to actually prohibit the act of circumvention, or may

---

100 See Nimmer and Nimmer, § 8B.07[A] and [B].
101 See Bygrave and Koelman elsewhere in this volume, p. 100.
102 See *supra* Sections 2.1 and 2.2.
103 US House Member Coble finds otherwise; see Coble 1998, p. 332.
104 See *supra* Section 2.5.
105 Samuelson, for example, believes that the existing US doctrine of contributory infringement provides the required 'adequate and effective' remedies. See Cohen 1997, p. 169 n. 31. Similarly, the Dutch Copyright Advisory Board (*Commissie Auteursrecht*) finds that Art. 11 WCT does not necessitate any changes to Dutch law, since TMs are protected by, *inter alia*, provisions on computer crime and unfair competition law. See Commissie Auteursrecht, *Advies over auteursrecht, naburige rechten en de nieuwe media*, The Hague, August 1998, p. 50.

they decide that TMs are 'adequately' protected against circumvention if preparatory acts are prohibited? If not, the US legislation would not comply with the WCT, since it does not as such target the act of circumventing a TM that protects a right.

2.6.2 EU

In general, EU directives need not be implemented literally. In principle, directives are merely aimed at achieving a result; how that is achieved is a matter for the individual Member States.[106] The Amended Proposal seems to leave Member States with similar discretion as does the WCT by merely obliging them to provide 'adequate legal protection'. However, the CD may require that civil action be available to copyright-holders. Also, it remains unclear whether the TM protection which Member States must provide would have to coincide with the scope of copyright.[107]

3. Technological Measures and the Boundaries of Copyright

Under copyright law a rights-holder cannot statutorily control *each* use of a protected work. Arguably, to pursue certain socio-economic goals, the interests of the copyright owners and those of the general public and copyright users are balanced by limiting the scope of the exclusive rights. The introduction of TMs and their legal protection may upset the balance that copyright law has achieved between the interests of rights-holders and the interests of users. We will begin by briefly outlining several different views put forward on the rationale of the balance presently existing in copyright law. Thereafter, we will investigate what effect the introduction of technological measures and their legal protection may have on this equilibrium.

3.1 BALANCE

From a socio-economic point of view, the rationale of copyright and its boundaries may be summarised as follows. To remedy the market failure arising from the inability of producers of information to exclude its use efficiently, copyright law grants to the rights-holder a statutory monopoly over the use of a work, thus

---

106 Lauwaars and Timmermans 1994, pp. 95-96.
107 See *supra* Sections 2.1 and 2.5.

ensuring that he can recoup his investments. In this way copyright provides an incentive to create. Presumably, the production and dissemination of works will thus be promoted, thereby benefiting society as a whole. However, granting a monopoly causes another market failure. If the rights-holder's monopoly were unlimited, competition would be stifled and the creation of new works based upon preceding works would be impeded.[108] Thus, the total production of information and the public access to works would decrease, which would be to society's disadvantage.[109] Copyright limitations serve to off-set the disadvantages of a total monopoly over copyrighted information. In the words of the US Supreme Court:[110]

> "The limited scope of the copyright holder's statutory monopoly, like the limited copyright duration required by the Constitution, reflects a balance of competing claims upon the public interest: creative work is to be encouraged and rewarded, but private motivation must ultimately serve the cause of promoting broad public availability of literature, music, and the other arts. The immediate effect of our copyright law is to secure a fair return for an 'author's' creative labor. But the ultimate aim is, by this incentive, to stimulate artistic creativity for the general public good" (references omitted).

As the Supreme Court's reasoning illustrates, under the US system of copyright law it is generally accepted that the extent and limitations of copyright law are based on economic efficiency and public interest considerations. Under the European *droit d'auteur* regimes this is not as clearly established, but, even though principles of natural law appear as their main foundation, economic efficiency and public interest considerations play a significant role in the analyses of copyright matters under these regimes as well.[111]

Through the use of TMs the rights-holder's practical inability to exclude others from using his work will disappear. TMs provide rights holders with a tool to 'fence in' information, just as the owner of tangible goods can lock them up.[112] Indeed, TMs may provide for a 'property right' in the economic sense of the term, in enabling the person who holds the key to decide about the use of the 'fenced-in'

---

108 See also Mackaay 1996, p. 22. Cf. Landes and Posner 1989, pp. 332 and 360: "[I]f all borrowing from previously copyrighted works were deemed infringement, the number of new works might fall"; and Palmer 1989, p. 302: "[I]t is clear that a good deal of great art works would not have been produced under a strict copyright regime".

109 Elkin-Koren 1997, pp. 98-101; Landes and Posner 1989, p. 326.

110 *Twentieth Century Music Corp. v. Aiken*, 422 US 151, 156, 45 L. Ed. 2d 84, 95 S. Ct. 2040 (1975).

111 Guibault, elsewhere in this volume, pp. 154–155; Quaedvlieg 1992, p. 380; from Recitals 8 and 9 of the proposed Copyright Directive it can be concluded that the European Commission, which by now may be viewed as the 'supreme European copyright legislator', finds the main justification for copyright protection in public interest and economic efficiency considerations. Furthermore, in Recital 21 it is stressed that a 'fair balance' must be maintained. See Dietz 1998, pp. 440-441; see also Explanatory Statement with the EP Amendment to the proposed CD, *supra* n. 26, Comment 2.

112 Mackaay 1996; Palmer 1989, p. 285.

material.[113] Presumably, rights-holders will be tempted to exercise this *factual* monopoly (as opposed to the (limited) *statutory* monopoly that copyright grants) by fencing in more material, and precluding more uses by technical means than copyright law enables them to. Thus, the countervailing effect of the copyright limitations is undermined. Consequently, if the law were to sanction the circumvention of these technological 'fences' under all circumstances, the balance that was (presumably) struck to the benefit of society will be upset.[114]

However, Bell argues that (some) copyright limitations, rather than healing market failure resulting from over broad protection, in fact follow from the market failure existing in the practical impossibility to license the work. In his opinion, what matters is the availability for use; uses which under current law are deemed 'fair' need not necessarily be *free* uses in order to pursue copyright's broader goal. While he acknowledges the necessity of encouraging progress by enabling access to and 'building on' earlier works, he argues that:[115]

> "[t]he costs of avoiding infringement by obtaining permission to use a copyrighted work, and thus avoiding infringement claims, often exceed the benefits of the desired use. Such transaction costs threaten to prevent many socially beneficial uses of copyrighted works from taking place. The [copyright limitations] cure this particular market failure by excusing as non-infringing a limited ... class of uses of copyrighted works".

TMs and ECMSs may heal the market failure by facilitating licensing, and thus bring down transaction costs. As a consequence, the main justification for the copyright exemptions would no longer be valid and their scope could be reduced. Moreover, according to Bell, by permitting the control of uses that are currently seen as 'fair', information may ultimately become cheaper and more accessible, and thus net social wealth may increase.[116] However, even in this view exemptions may still be called for in certain circumstances, e.g. for purposes of parody or criticism.[117]

The limitations of copyright may be regarded as mere exceptions to the exclusive rights.[118] Some commentators, on the other hand, view them — the statutory exemptions in particular — as actually granting rights to copyright users.[119] Others perceive the copyright limitations as deriving from or closely related to the fundamental rights of users (e.g. the freedom of expression and information

---

113 Mackaay 1996, p. 15.
114 Bell 1998, p. 560.
115 Bell 1998, p. 583.
116 Bell 1998, pp. 585-591.
117 Bell 1998, pp. 592-596.
118 Lucas asserts that, in France, the exemptions must be regarded as exceptions, *inter alia*, because rights-holders have *rights* while copyright users only have *interests*. Lucas 1998b, pp. 170-175.
119 See Elkin-Koren 1997, pp. 98-101; Samuelson 1996, p. 22; Bell 1998, p. 393; Lucas 1998b, pp. 173-175.

and the right to privacy). According to this view, the balance expressed in copyright law is not (only) based on criteria of economic efficiency, but (also) reflects the equilibrium legislators have struck between the property right of the rights-holder and the fundamental rights of users.[120] Then, arguments of wealth maximisation are insufficient both in determining the scope of the rights-holder's subjective right, and in setting aside the copyright limitations.[121] Another approach would be to determine whether each (type of) limitation or exemption is based upon market failure considerations, a fundamental right, or other public interest concerns.[122]

Whatever the origin of the copyright limitations, the control over the use of protected material statutorily granted to the rights-holder is not absolute.[123] All legislative bodies that have taken on the protection of TMs stress that the balance that is struck in copyright law between the interests of the rights-holders and the users must be maintained. The Preamble to the WCT states that the Treaty is drafted while:

> "Recognizing the need to maintain a balance between the rights of authors and the larger public interest, particularly education, research and access to information, as reflected in the Berne Convention".

Similarly, in Recital 21 of the proposed EU Directive it is considered that a 'fair balance' must be safeguarded. Also, the US legislature underscores that a balance between the interests of both parties must be struck where the protection of TMs is concerned.[124] Indeed, all (proposed) legislation on the protection of TMs intends to take into account the balance that is reflected in copyright law by not prohibiting certain acts of circumvention and allowing certain circumvention-enabling devices.

3.2 PERMITTED CIRCUMVENTION

The WCT merely prescribes protection against circumvention for copyright infringing purposes.[125] Thus, it appears that a TM preventing acts that under the

120 See Guibault, elsewhere in this volume, p. 128; see on limitations of copyright possibly deriving from the right to privacy, Bygrave and Koelman, elsewhere in this volume, p. 100; see also Reinbothe 1998, p. 437; Bell 1998, p. 586.

121 See Quaedvlieg 1992, pp. 391–392: "[E]conomics can inform us about the effect of legal rules, but not about their justice — at least, if one does not . . . promote efficiency itself as a moral maxim. In some cases, justice is inefficient; subjective rights are worth more than their economic return".

122 Hugenholtz 1996, p. 94; Lucas 1998b, pp. 175–185; Guibault elsewhere in this volume, p. 128 ff.

123 See Bygrave and Koelman elsewhere in this volume, p. 118 (observing that neither fundamental rights, nor copyright, nor any other property rights, are absolute).

124 See House Report, *supra* n. 22, pp. 24–26. Commenting on the proposed TM-protection scheme, the House Report states that the provisions concerned "prohibit certain actions and create exceptions to permit certain conduct deemed to be in the greater public interest, all in a way that balances the interests of copyright owners and users of copyrighted works".

125 Several Delegates at the WIPO Diplomatic Conference in 1996 stressed that activities which are lawful or concern materials in the public domain should not be made subject to the TM-protection scheme. See Summary Minutes, *supra* n. 24, Nos 518, 523, 535-537, 541.

circumstances would not constitute copyright infringement may lawfully be circumvented. Whether Article 6 CD has a similar intention is not entirely clear. From the Explanatory Memorandum it can perhaps be concluded that it does.[126] As mentioned earlier in Section 2.1 above, TMs that are 'designed' to inhibit copyright infringement must be protected. This could imply that as long as the technology was initially designed to protect copyright protection is required, regardless of whether it actually protects a copyright. If this interpretation is correct, circumvention must also be made unlawful if the TM protects, for instance, public domain material, as long as the TM was originally intended or designed to inhibit acts restricted under copyright.

However, Member States are only required to provide adequate legal protection against circumvention 'without authority'. This additional requirement perhaps implies that the scope of TM protection is affected by the limitations of copyright. If an exemption 'authorises' certain use, the circumvention enabling that use would then not be prohibited. However, in the wording of the Proposal, it is *the circumvention* which may be authorised, *not the subsequent use.* As it stands, the copyright exemptions permit, e.g., the reproduction of a work or making it available to the public under certain circumstances, they do not — directly — 'authorise' certain acts of circumvention. Therefore, it may be that in the current version of the Proposal permission to circumvent does not follow from the limitations of copyright.

Article 11 WCT, in contrast, does not require the prohibition of circumvention, if the *acts that the measure restricts* are 'permitted by law'. Here it is not the circumvention as such, but the subsequent acts which may be 'authorised'. Clearly, under the Treaty the limitations of copyright do affect the extent to which TMs are protected.

According to Recital 27 of the Amended Proposal, private copying exemptions may not affect the protection of TMs. Thus, it appears that at least these limitations cannot 'authorise' circumvention. The European Parliament had proposed at first reading to insert a sentence in Article 5(4) CD, which would have implied that none of the copyright exemptions would have an impact on the protection of TMs:

> "[The copyright] exceptions and limitations must not prevent the use of technical means to protect works with the aim of safeguarding the interests of the rightholders, nor prejudice the protection of these means as referred to in Article 6".

The Commission, however, decided not to incorporate this amendment in its Amended Proposal. Perhaps from this refusal it can be concluded that, except for

126 Explanatory Memorandum with the CD, *supra* n. 26, Comment 3 in respect of Art. 6.

the private copying exceptions, all other copyright exemptions do prejudice the protection of TMs.

The DMCA does not prohibit the act of circumventing a TM that protects a right. It does, however, declare unlawful the act of circumventing a measure that controls access to copyrighted works. Circumvention for the purpose of gaining access to non-copyright-protected material is permitted.[127] However, to use copyrighted material 'fairly' one first needs to access it. For this purpose, the DMCA introduces certain specific exceptions to the prohibition on circumventing access-controlling TMs.

3.3 PERMITTED CIRCUMVENTION TO OBTAIN ACCESS

The DMCA's prohibition on the protection of measures that control access does not relate to activities that constitute copyright infringement. An explicit right to control access to published works has never existed. Since gaining access to a work does not (explicitly) amount to infringement, it would not be enough simply to refer to circumvention for the purpose of infringement in order to limit the 'right to control access'.[128] Moreover, section 107 of the US Copyright Act, which codifies the fair use doctrine, expressly refers to sections 106 and 106A, and consequently limits only 'traditional' copyrights, as do the more specific exemptions in the US Copyright Act. Thus, only the exemptions specifically mentioned in the DMCA will apply.

Libraries, archives and educational institutions may, under certain circumstances, circumvent in order to determine whether to acquire a copy of the protected work. Also, law enforcement and intelligence agencies will not be liable if they tamper with a TM. Furthermore, to achieve interoperability of computer programs and to enable encryption research or security testing, circumvention is allowed. Additionally, circumvention for the purpose of protecting minors is permitted. Lastly, it is permitted to circumvent a TM that collects information reflecting the online activities of a natural person.[129] For some of these purposes it is expressly allowed to design and produce circumvention-enabling devices. However, it appears that libraries, for example, that can lawfully circumvent under the 'shopping right', are not permitted to develop circumvention-enabling devices. Also it is prohibited to manufacture or provide the means for (lawfully) tampering with a TM in order to protect online privacy. Therefore, it remains to be seen whether these 'circumvention exemptions' will have much effect in practice.[130]

---

127 See *supra* Section 2.1.
128 See *supra* Section 2.2.
129 See s. 1201(d) to (j) DMCA.
130 See also *infra* Section 3.4.

A general fair use-like exemption to the right to control access did not appear in the DMCA's early drafts. In the House Committee on Commerce such a provision was proposed, but eventually rejected by the majority.[131] As a compromise, and because the serious implications of granting a right to control access were acknowledged (i.e. it may "dramatically diminish public access" or "create a pay-per-use society"),[132] the final version of the DMCA provides that the prohibition on circumvention takes effect only two years after enactment of the Act. Also, an exemption that is potentially open to any user of copyrighted works was added:[133]

> "The prohibition [on circumventing TMs that control access] shall not apply to persons who are users of a copyrighted work which is in a particular class of works, if such persons are, or are likely to be in the succeeding 3 year period, adversely affected by virtue of such prohibition in their ability to make non-infringing uses of that particular class of works under this title, as determined under subparagraph (C)".

During the two-year delay, the Librarian of Congress is to determine in regard of which 'particular class[es] of works' the ability to make non-infringing uses will be 'adversely affected'. This must be reassessed, and a renewed list must be published after each subsequent period of three years. In determining whether non-infringing uses are adversely affected, the Librarian must specifically take into account the availability for use of the class of works, the impact of the prohibition on criticism, comment, news reporting, teaching, scholarship or research, and the effect of circumvention on the market for or value of copyrighted works.[134]

Through these factors, a fair use-like exemption is introduced. The enumerated types of use will typically be considered 'fair' and non-infringing under the traditional fair use exemption. The effect on the market and value of the work is a factor that courts must take into consideration when determining whether a particular use is 'fair'.[135] However, since circumvention in order to access all classes of works will probably not be exempted, the scope of this exemption is likely to be narrower than that of the general fair use exemption. Moreover, by its wording the provision only allows the circumvention of access-controlling TMs, not the production or making available devices or services that enable such permitted circumvention. If this strict interpretation of the provision is correct, the permission to circumvent may be of little relevance in practice.

131 House Report, *supra* n. 22, p. 86.
132 See House Report, *supra* n. 22, pp. 25-26.
133 See s. 1201(a)(1)(B) DMCA.
134 See s. 1201(a)(1)(C) and (D) DMCA.
135 See s. 107(4), Title 17 USC.

3.4 PERMITTED PREPARATORY ACTIVITIES

In practice, technological protection measures are likely to be used in respect of both protectable and non-protectable material.[136] Moreover, the application of most copyright exemptions (e.g. fair use) depends upon the circumstances. Therefore, it is hard to see how TMs can be designed to prevent only non-infringing uses.[137] Circumventing may be lawful in one situation and unlawful in another. However, in order to be able to exercise their 'right' to circumvent, persons who do not have considerable technological abilities will be dependent on the availability of devices or services that enable circumvention.

In the *Vault* case, the US Court of Appeals held that providing a circumvention-enabling device that facilitates acts that are permitted by copyright law does not result in contributory liability, because such a device is capable of substantial non-infringing uses. If this decision were followed, and the proposed EU and US provisions were mere equivalents of the 'substantial non-infringing use' criterion,[138] providing the means that enable circumvention for non-infringing uses may be permitted, even if they could be used for infringing purposes as well. Consequently, not only 'multipurpose' devices of which the multiplicity of purpose exists in the enabling of circumvention and other, unrelated purposes (e.g. computer hardware), but also devices of which the multiplicity of purpose may be found in enabling circumvention for infringing as well as non-infringing purposes, would be allowed.[139] If this interpretation is correct, not many circumvention-enabling devices will actually be outlawed.

The question remains how this would fit in with the requirement that devices have 'only limited commercially significant purpose or use other than circumvention' in order to be found unlawful.[140] Should this be read as 'only limited commercial purpose or use other than *lawful* circumvention'?[141] The other tests in the DMCA and those of the Amended Proposal suffer from a similar problem; they all prohibit the production, dealing in or marketing of devices of which the primary, sole, intended (etc.) purpose is to enable circumvention *in general*, rather than circumvention *for lawful purposes.* Article 6(2) CD, however, does require that

136 Samuelson 1996, p. 19.

137 Smith 1997, p. 429.

138 See the speech of House Member Bliley of 12 October 1998, Congressional Records E2137. Bliley states that the criteria of the DMCA will only be fulfilled if "devices [have] no substantial non-infringing uses [and] are expressly intended to facilitate circumvention".

139 The US legislature appears to consider only 'multipurpose devices' in the former sense of the term; see Senate Report, *supra* n. 37, p. 29.

140 See *supra* Section 2.3.

141 Section 1201(b) DMCA prohibits the performance of preparatory activities that enable the circumvention of an 'effective' TM, where a measure only 'effectively protects a right' for the purpose of the DMCA if it prevents the performance of a restricted act (see *supra* Section 2.1). Thus, the prohibition on preparatory activities appears to be linked to the scope of copyright. It is unclear whether a similar connection is envisaged in Art. 6 CD.

preparatory activities be "carried out without authority". However, even if it can be argued that the copyright limitations may 'authorise' acts of circumvention, which is doubtful,[142] they certainly do not, as such, 'authorise' activities enabling circumvention.

As mentioned in Section 3.3 above, not all the DMCA's specific exemptions to the prohibition on circumventing access-controlling TMs are accompanied by an exemption allowing preparatory activities. Thus, devices that enable lawful circumvention cannot always be made available to persons who may lawfully circumvent a TM.

In regulating the protection of TMs the legislature has taken on a hard task.[143] On the one hand, it presumes that to provide 'meaningful protection' it is necessary to prohibit products and services used to defeat TMs,[144] while on the other hand it attempts to maintain the balance embodied in copyright law.[145] Unless technologies will eventually be developed that can automatically distinguish between exempted and infringing uses (which is highly unlikely), these goals are hard to reconcile.[146]

3.5 TECHNOLOGICAL MEASURES, COPYRIGHT LIMITATIONS AND CONTRACTS

The problem of reconciling TM-protection regimes with copyright exemptions is closely related to the question whether, or to what extent the 'traditional' limitations of copyright may be overridden by contractual agreement.[147] Both the EU and the United States are still struggling with the status of statutory limitations; are they mandatory or simply default rules?[148] If the limitations on copyright are not mandatory, then presumably the limitations on the protection of TMs that follow from the boundaries of copyright might also be contractually overridden, as can the specific 'circumvention exemptions' in the DMCA.

The ability to contract directly with users and the possibility of preventing unlicensed access by 'technological fencing' provide the rights-holder with the leverage to act as a monopolist, i.e. to impose his conditions on each end-user.[149]

---

142 See *supra* Section 3.2.

143 See (House member) Coble 1998, p. 333: "It is not easy to draw the line between legitimate and non-legitimate uses of decoding devices and to account for devices which serve legitimate non-infringing purposes".

144 See House Report, *supra* n. 22, pp. 38-39.

145 See *supra* Section 3.1.

146 Cf. Lucas 1998b, pp. 273–274: "Comment organiser une protection technique assez rigide pour dissuader des utilisateurs malveillants, et assez souple pour se prêter à l'exercise des facultés, aux contours souvent incertains, reconnues aux utilisateurs au titre du *fair use*, de l'exeption de citation, de la parodie, etc.?"

147 See Guibault, elsewhere in this volume, p. 125 ff; Elkin-Koren 1997.

148 Interestingly, in Belgium a new Art. 23bis has recently been added to the Copyright Act stating that the statutory copyright exemptions are all of a mandatory nature.

149 See Elkin-Koren 1997, pp. 104 and 107.

Thus, the rights-holder can shape his own rules and construct 'private legislation' that would not necessarily take account of the balance reflected in copyright law.[150] The factual protection layer provided by the TM, circumvention of which may be permitted by the law, could be supplemented with an additional layer of protection consisting of a contract that would override the law's permission to circumvent a TM or to use the material. The rights-holder could, for example, oblige the consumer not to reveal the work to any third party, thus creating a situation comparable to that existing after the conclusion of a know-how agreement. Clearly, this would affect public access.[151]

3.6 OBLIGATION TO DESIGN TMS ACCORDING TO LIMITATIONS?

The question of the status of the copyright exemptions is also linked to TM-protection in another way. If the copyright limitations may not be contractually overridden, one could argue that the principles underlying such prohibition similarly prevent the technical inhibition of uses permitted by copyright law.[152] However, the WCT and the Proposed Directive appear to follow a different approach. As it stands, information providers remain free to 'fence in' any information and restrict any type of usage by technological means, while at the same time users may (presumably) circumvent a measure if it serves a copyright limitation.

An alternative way of safeguarding the equilibrium would be to prohibit the application of TMs that prevent acts permitted under copyright law, or that block access to non-protectable material, altogether. In doing so, the limitations of copyright would directly determine which uses may or may not be technically blocked.[153] The US White Paper finds such an approach nonsensical:[154]

> "[T]he fair use doctrine does not require a copyright owner to allow or to facilitate unauthorised access or use of a work. Otherwise, copyright owners could not withhold works from publication; movie theatres could not charge admission or prevent audio or video recording; museums could not require entry fees or prohibit the taking of photographs".

---

150 Cohen 1997, pp. 179-183; Vinje 1996a, p. 437. Cf. Bell 1998, p. 577: "Increasingly, consumers in all probability will find that access to information in digital intermedia comes subject to contractual provisions that aim to secure rights more broad than those provided by the Copyright Act".

151 Samuelson 1996, pp. 23-25.

152 See Spoor 1998, pp. 24-25, noting that the French and Greek respondents to the ALAI questionnaire consider unlawful technological prevention of uses permitted by copyright law. Other reporters, however, state that in their national laws overriding the statutory exemptions is permitted, while excluding uses that are lawful under copyright through technological means is not. In other countries, the opposite situation is suggested to exist.

153 See Cohen 1996, Part VI; DePeiza 1997, text accompanying n. 31.

154 White Paper, *supra* n. 16, p. 231.

This reasoning, however, may not be entirely flawless. Copyright owners can indeed withhold works from *first* publication, but if a work is published it is available for fair use.[155] Moreover, since copyright has never before granted a right to control access, it is not surprising that the fair use doctrine did not limit the possibility of preventing access or setting conditions upon access to published works. Furthermore, as copyright holders simply *could not* prevent access to or use of published works in practice, there was obviously no need to contemplate a fair use exemption that would oblige a rights-holder to enable access to or use of copyrighted works. Finally, the authority of museums and movie theatres to set conditions on access is not based upon copyright law, but upon the possession of the venue and the doctrine of trespass.[156] These concepts, however, are not specifically developed to deal with information (as is copyright), and therefore do not take into account the public interest considerations that are embodied in copyright law.

A regime that has a somewhat similar function in the exploitation of information products as has the doctrine of trespass is that protecting conditional access services.[157] This is a regime specifically designed to deal with services that consist of the provision of information. Perhaps, therefore, the drawbacks of excessive access-control are taken into account in the EU Conditional Access Directive, which states that its provisions are:[158]

> "without prejudice to possible future Community or national provisions meant to ensure that a number of broadcasting services, recognised as being of public interest, are not based on conditional access".

Note that national legislators are permitted to set limitations on access control if this is in the public interest, which is reminiscent of the socio-economic rationale for the copyright limitations. One of the 'future Community provisions' the Directive refers to is the Television without Frontiers Directive, as recently amended. The Directive may serve as an example of a prohibition on blocking access, as it allows Member States to draw up lists of 'events' to which public access may not be prevented (i.e. by 'capturing' the event exclusively for pay-TV).[159] In this respect the

---

155 See *infra* Section 4.1.

156 See *NOS/KNVB*, Dutch Supreme Court (*Hoge Raad*), 23 October 1987, [1998] NJ 310. The Dutch Supreme Court decided that the Dutch Football Association (KNVB) can legally control TV coverage of a match on the basis of associated clubs' ownership of the stadium.

157 See *infra* Section 4.1.

158 Recital 9 with the CAD.

159 Article 3a(1) of European Parliament and Council Directive 97/36/EC of 30 June 1997 amending Council Directive 89/552/EEC on the coordination of certain provisions laid down by law, regulation or administrative action in Member States concerning the pursuit of television broadcasting activities, OJ L 202/60, states: "Each Member State may take measures in accordance with Community law to ensure that broadcasters under its jurisdiction do not broadcast on an exclusive basis events which are regarded by that Member State as being of major importance for society in

Directive is somewhat comparable to the DMCA that allows the circumvention of access-controlling TMs in respect of *certain classes* of works.[160] An important difference between the two instruments, however, is that under the Directive access may not be blocked at all, whereas the DMCA merely permits circumvention. In any case, these developments illustrate that legislatures are becoming aware of the dangers of access-inhibiting technologies to the free flow of information.

In theory, the freedom to impart and *receive* information as laid down in Article 10 of the European Convention on Human Rights could play a role in safeguarding the public domain. However, to our knowledge, a court has never explicitly decided that a private entity was under an obligation to disclose information pursuant to the freedom of expression and information.[161] Under special circumstances competition law may serve as an alternative instrument in gaining access to information. To enable the creation of new works, the limitations of copyright allow for existing works to be 'built upon'.[162] Similarly, it may be considered an abuse of a dominant position under Article 82 (ex Article 86) of the EC Treaty, if a party refuses access to information that is essential to a new, competing product and no substitute is available. Abuse of a monopoly will, however, only be found in 'exceptional circumstances'.[163] Furthermore, the doctrine of abuse will apply only where competition is hindered; mere individual access to information is not covered.

Reidenberg has demonstrated that, just as the law determines what can and cannot be done, technology imposes limitations on those who use it.[164] According to Reidenberg the *Lex Informatica*, i.e. the rules that follow from technology, should

---

(Cont.)
such a way as to deprive a substantial proportion of the public in that Member State of the possibility of following such events via live coverage or deferred coverage on free television. If it does so, the Member State concerned shall draw up a list of designated events, national or non-national, which it considers to be of major importance for society. It shall do so in a clear and transparent manner in due and effective time. In so doing the Member State concerned shall also determine whether these events should be available via whole or partial live coverage, or where necessary or appropriate for objective reasons in the public interest, whole or partial deferred coverage". Remarkably, from Recital 18, it can be concluded that especially sports events are considered.

160 See *supra* Section 3.3.

161 Moreover, the Dutch Supreme Court considered that the freedom to receive information of Art. 10 ECHR does not encompass the reception of a broadcasting service that is encrypted in order to ensure payment by those who receive the information (i.e. access to conditional access services). *Groeneveld v. TDS,* Dutch Supreme Court, 17 December 1993, [1994] NJ 274; see Hugenholtz 1998, p. 253.

162 See *supra* Section 3.1.

163 *Radio Telefis Eireann and Independent Television Publications Ltd. v. Commission*, European Court of Justice, 6 April 1995, Joined Cases C-241 and 242/91P; *Tiercé Ladbroke SA v. EC Commission*; European Court of Justice, 1997, Case T-504/93; see Vinje 1995, p. 299; Stamatoudi 1998, pp. 158-159 and 175; Hugenholtz 1998, p. 257.

164 Reidenberg 1998, pp. 568-569; see also Reidenberg 1996, p. 917: "System design imposes rules of order on an information society. Technical choices are policy decisions that have inherent consequences for network participants".

develop freely. These rules would have the advantages of flexibility, independence of national borders and self-enforcement; in addition they have the capability of monitoring compliance automatically.[165] Certainly, these characteristics would make exercising copyrights by means of TMs far more easy than through the courts. Reidenberg concedes, however, that in situations where fundamental public interests are at stake this is not the right approach. Especially if copyright exemptions are viewed as (closely related to) fundamental rights,[166] instead of protecting TMs the legislature should focus on safeguarding the interests of users. Then again, copyright itself may also be viewed as a fundamental (property) right.[167]

4. A New (Copy) Right?

In this section we will address several rights or legal doctrines that pursue similar interests as do the (proposed) TM-protection schemes. In other words, we will examine to what extent other areas of the law may protect the interests concerned in a comparable way.[168] Thereafter, we will briefly consider the nature of the legal protection of TMs.

4.1 RIGHTS PROVIDING SIMILAR PROTECTION AND RELATED RIGHTS

4.1.1 Copyright

If technological measures are only to be protected if they 'protect a copyright', protection against circumvention and copyright protection will overlap; a rights-holder can only apply for TM-protection in a situation that is also covered by copyright law. Of course, this may be different in respect of preparatory activities or where the protection of TMs that control access is concerned.

4.1.2 Right of temporary reproduction and right to use

The DMCA expressly prohibits circumvention for the purpose of accessing a work. Thus, effectively, a new 'right to control access' is created for the benefit of rights-

---

165 Reidenberg 1998, pp. 577-581.
166 See *supra* Section 3.1.
167 Reinbothe 1998, p. 436.
168 See Lucas 1998b, p. 273 (arguing that criminalising the act of circumvention should be regarded in the context of the areas of the law which protect similar interests, and not viewed isolated in the context of copyright).

holders that apply TMs.[169] This new right differs substantially from rights traditionally protected under copyright, such as the right to perform, distribute or display a work to the public or the right of reproduction. These traditional rights have effect at the level of exploitation; the mere act of accessing a work is not an act of exploitation.[170] Because a digitalised work can only be used if it is accessed first, both the right of temporary reproduction and the new 'right to control access' may effectively create an exclusive *right to use or to 'consume'* copyrighted works.[171] Due to the right of temporary reproduction granted under the Software and Database Directives, such a right already exists in respect of computer programs and databases.[172]

4.1.3 Droit de divulgation

A right to control access to published works is a concept new to copyright law. Admittedly, authors have always enjoyed a (moral) right to prohibit the first publication of their work (the *droit de divulgation*). Copyright exemptions generally do not apply *before* a work is published.[173] However, this moral right is different in nature from the right to control access that the EU and US legislation entails: first, because the novel right would also apply to published works; secondly, because the right to control access is merely based upon economic considerations,[174] whereas the right of first publication is rooted in the right to privacy.[175]

4.1.4 Protection of conditional access services

Theatres in the 'real world' are able to set conditions upon access to the works they exploit based upon possession of the venue and the doctrine of trespass.[176] Access to a performance of a work can be controlled, not access to a *work*. Copyright-holders, in turn, have the bargaining power to demand a share of the profits, because they are granted the right to prohibit the performance of their works. Their interests are indirectly involved in a theatre's ability to control access, since the price an exploiter is willing to pay for the right to perform a work depends upon the income he can generate, and the fact that he can exclude others from attending the performance enables him to generate revenues.

---

169 See *supra* Sections 2.1, 2.2 and 2.4.
170 Bygrave and Koelman, elsewhere in this volume, p. 99.
171 See Lucas 1997, p. 343; Cohen 1997, p. 176.
172 See Bygrave and Koelman elsewhere in this volume, p. 104; Hugenholtz 1992, p. 232.
173 Nimmer and Nimmer, § 13.05[A][2][b]: "the scope of the fair use doctrine is considerably narrower with respect to unpublished works that are held confidential". See also Spoor 1998, pp. 16-17.
174 D. Nimmer 1998, pp. 511-512.
175 See Hughes 1988, p. 355; Zimmerman 1992, pp. 670-673.
176 See generally on the doctrine of trespass under US law, Trotter Hardy 1996, pp. 9-10; Page Keeton 1984, p. 67 ff.

The relationship between conditional access service providers and rights-holders may very well be compared to that between more conventional exploiters of copyrighted works and copyright owners.[177] Legal remedies against unauthorised access to, for instance, pay-TV services protect providers of such services in a way that is somewhat comparable to access-control based upon the common law doctrine of trespass on land. Since circumventing a fence or bypassing the box-office only becomes unlawful if it is followed by trespassing on another's property, one could say that the service provider is granted a 'quasi-property right'.

Conditional access services are currently protected under a variety of legal regimes. In some jurisdictions the act of receiving information provided by a conditional access service without authorisation (i.e. the trespasser or 'circumventor') is declared unlawful, whereas in others only preparatory activities, i.e. enabling unauthorised access to such a service, are addressed. Provisions of the Conditional Access Directive and existing national law will be discussed in detail in Sections 5 and 6 below.

4.1.5 Computer crime

In many jurisdictions, the law covers what might be called 'digital trespass'. Unauthorised access to a computer is expressly covered by legislation that protects the *pax computationis* (an equivalent of the formal sphere of secrecy of the home). Some laws criminalise the 'mere' access to computer systems, others punish access only where the data are protected by security measures.[178] Circumvention of access-controlling TMs applied at the server of the information provider (the online outlet) are probably covered by these regimes. However, since a TM-protected copy of a work will most likely not qualify as a 'computer system', circumventing the TM that prevents access to the copy will probably not fall within the scope of these provisions, nor will circumvention of an access-controlling technology within the sphere of control of the end user (e.g. unauthorised decryption of a scrambled TV-signal). Other regimes in penal law that may protect against circumvention of TMs are those protecting the privacy of communications. In some countries unauthorised access to encrypted messages is made a punishable offence, independent of whether they are truly private communications. These provisions

---

177 See European Commission, Green Paper on Legal Protection for Encrypted Services, Brussels, 6 March 1996, COM (96) 76 def, p. 16: "Since the fees paid to rightholders generally also take into account the potential audience, the fact that encrypted programmes are picked up via illicit reception deprives rightholders of the income they would have received from subscription revenue if the customer had purchased an authorized decoder instead. Moreover, when negotiations take place regarding rights in respect of subsequent (in clear) broadcasts, rightholders will find it more difficult to secure high levels of remuneration because of illicit reception which had already occurred when the material was broadcast on the encrypted channel".

178 Sieber 1998, pp. 63-66.

may offer protection against the circumvention of TMs protecting pay-TV services.[179]

4.1.6 Contract law

ECMSs enable the establishment of direct contractual relationships between information providers and each individual information user. Thus it will be possible to oblige each user contractually not to circumvent a TM that protects information disseminated online. An example of a contract intended to control the use of information that is not based upon a statutory (intellectual property) right is the know-how agreement. A know-how licence typically involves an agreement that the licensor reveal information to its counter-party in exchange for undertaking by the latter not to reveal it to third parties.[180] The licensor has the leverage to impose this condition because he has factual control over the (secret) information. A rights owner who applies an access-controlling technology may be in a similar position.

Interestingly, both under EU and US anti-trust law, clauses in agreements concerning the use of information that would hamper progress by limiting the ability of the licensee to develop or market competing products may be invalid.[181] The extent to which *factual* control may be used to impose restrictions that are detrimental to society is thus limited. Note that, as is the case under copyright law, public interest considerations determine the scope of control that can be exercised over the use of information.[182]

4.1.7 Unfair competition law

Most of the above-mentioned areas of law cover acts of circumvention and do not target the preparatory activities to circumvention, the main exception being regimes that protect conditional access services.[183] Apart from these regimes, dealing in

179 See *infra* Section 6.2.

180 Palmer 1989, p. 264; see generally Bender 1986.

181 See Art. 3(2) of the European Commission Regulation 240/96 of 31 January 1996 on the application of Article 85(3) of the Treaty to certain categories of technology transfer agreements, OJ L 31/2, and sections 3.4 and 4.1.1 of the Antitrust Guidelines for the Licensing of Intellectual Property issued by the U.S. Department of Justice and the Federal Trade Commission, 6 April 1995, available at <http://www.usdoj.gov/atr/public/guidelines/ipguide.htm>.

182 Interestingly, a US Court of Appeals has decided that, even if anti-trust law is not violated, a copyright-holder 'misuses' copyright if he uses the leverage provided by the limited *statutory* monopoly copyright law grants to control, by way of contract, competition in an area outside of copyright, because copyright is then being used in a 'manner violative of the public policy embodied in copyright law'. *Lasercomb America, Inc. v. Reynolds*, 911 F.2d 970 (4th Cir. 1990). See Davidson and Engisch 1995. The Court drew upon the 'misuse of patent' doctrine, which, contrary to the 'misuse of copyright' doctrine, is recognised by the US Supreme Court.

183 See *infra* Sections 5 and 6.

devices that enable circumvention of TMs has mostly been dealt with in the context of unfair competition law. Several German courts, for instance, have held that the provision of programs (devices) that enable the circumvention of a dongle[184] amounts to unfair competition. This activity was regarded as unlawful because the providers of the circumvention-enabling device unfairly obstructed the plaintiff's sales of the original software.[185] Unfair competition law may provide remedies not only against trading in TM-circumventing technology, but also against dealing in devices that circumvent measures protecting conditional access services.[186]

4.2 NATURE OF PROTECTION OF TECHNOLOGICAL MEASURES

What is the legal nature of the protection of TMs? The answer will depend on whether the law targets the act of circumvention or preparatory activities. In the former case, the law deals with acts related to works, as does copyright, in the latter it will be more like unfair competition law. The outcome also differs depending on the type of TM that is considered; one could say that the protection of rights-protecting measures merely boosts existing copyright protection, whereas the protection of access-controlling measures, arguably, constitutes a new exclusive right. Below we will briefly describe what conclusions may be drawn from the US, EU and WIPO legislative initiatives discussed in this section.

4.2.1 United States

The US Green Paper described the legislation it proposed as follows:[187]

> "Copyright owners who use anti-copying systems to protect their works may bring actions for infringement against persons who, inter alia, manufacture or distribute devices whose primary purpose or effect is circumvention of those systems".

---

184 See *supra* Section 2.2.

185 See Raubenheimer 1996, pp. 77-78 (commenting on several decisions of lower courts); German Federal Supreme Court, 9 November 1995, (1996) 2 CR 79.

186 See *infra* Section 6.1.

187 US Green Paper, *supra* n. 76, text accompanying n. 358. It was proposed that a new s. 512 be inserted in the Copyright Act, stating: "No person shall import, manufacture or distribute any device, product, or component incorporated into a device or product, or offer or perform any service, the primary purpose or effect of which is to avoid, bypass, remove, deactivate, or otherwise circumvent, without authority of the copyright owner or the law, any process, treatment, mechanism or system which prevents or inhibits the exercise of any of the exclusive rights under section 106". Additionally, it was proposed to add the following to s. 501: "Anyone who violates section 512 is an infringer of the copyright in a work that utilizes the process, treatment, mechanism or system which the violator's device, product, component or service circumvents".

Apparently, something like an exclusive 'right to produce TM-bypassing devices' was envisaged. The US White Paper approached the issue differently. It proposed the introduction of specific remedies and sanctions separate from traditional copyright remedies.[188] Indeed, the DMCA provides for separate civil remedies and criminal sanctions,[189] which suggests that TM protection should, perhaps, not be viewed as a copyright.

In a letter sent to the US Congress by several US copyright law professors it was stated that:[190]

> "[the] enactment of [anti-circumvention provisions] would represent an unprecedented departure into the zone of what might be called paracopyright — an uncharted new domain of legislative provisions designed to strengthen copyright protection by regulating conduct which traditionally has fallen outside the regulatory sphere of intellectual property law".

Acting upon this statement, the Committee on Commerce of the House of Representatives proposed to remove the anti-circumvention provisions from the Copyright Act and establish them as free-standing provisions of law.[191] In the DMCA, as it was subsequently signed into law by the President, however, the provisions concerned are still part of the Copyright Act (as they were in the Senate version and the DMCA's predecessor in the House).

The DMCA provides for a *mere prohibition* of circumvention and preparatory activities; it does *not* explicitly grant the *exclusive right* to perform a certain act. Presumably, the right to authorise access to a work that is TM-protected is not separately transferable, as are 'true' copyrights. The difference with traditional copyrights is exemplified in that the DMCA grants remedies to 'any injured party', whereas copyright remedies are available, in principle, only to an actual rights-holder.[192]

On the other hand, although the DMCA does not explicitly grant a right, in effect it empowers the rights-holder exclusively to authorise access to a work that is protected by a TM. Whereas copyright similarly empowers the rights-holder exclusively to authorise the performance of certain acts in relation to a work, in this respect the statutory TM protection may very well be compared to a copyright. According to the Senate Committee on the Judiciary the prohibition on circumvention to gain access would, indeed, amount to a right; the Senate Report states that the DMCA deals with 'the copyright owner's right to control access to

188 White Paper, *supra* n. 16, pp. 230-234 and 8-11 of Appendix 1.
189 See *supra* Section 2.5.
190 Cited from House Report, *supra* n. 22, p. 25.
191 House Report, *supra* n. 22, p. 26.
192 See Chapter 5 of Title 17 USC.

his or her copyrighted work'.[193] Another similarity is that a person who circumvents an access-controlling TM—and even the manufacturer of a circumvention-enabling device—can be held strictly liable, just like a copyright infringer.[194]

4.2.2 WIPO

According to Liedes, who prepared the Basic Proposal for the WCT, a prohibition on the provision of circumvention-enabling devices is more akin to public law than to intellectual property.[195] Indeed, Article 11 WCT obliges the Contracting States to merely provide for 'adequate legal protection and effective legal remedies', leaving the Contracting States the freedom to find legislative solutions outside the realm of copyright.[196]

4.2.3 EU

The Explanatory Memorandum to the proposed Directive suggests that the act of circumvention constitutes copyright infringement:[197]

> "[N]ot any circumvention of technical means of protection should be covered, but only those which constitute an infringement of a right, i.e. which are not authorised by law or by the author".

However, Article 6 CD does not expressly require Member States to grant an exclusive right, nor does it specify in which area of the law TM protection and remedies must be introduced.[198] Consequently, it will depend upon the legislative solutions the Member States apply when implementing Article 6 CD whether or not TM-protection will be comparable to copyright.

Member States have previously implemented the similar obligation of Article 7(1)(c) of the Software Directive in different areas of law. In Germany, for instance, the rights-holder is explicitly granted remedies under civil law in Article 69(f) of the German Copyright Act. Raubenheimer concludes that the unlawful manufacturing of and trade in circumvention-enabling devices constitutes copyright infringement

---

193 See Senate Report, *supra* n. 37, pp. 28-29.
194 See *supra* Section 2.4.
195 Basic Proposal, *supra* n. 44, n. 13.04.
196 Lucas 1998a, p. 13; see also Lucas 1998b, p. 274: "Elle devrait logiquement conduire les États à insérer les disposition pertinents dans la législation sur le droit d'auteur ... plutôt que dans celle relative aux télécommunications, ou dans le droit pénal général. Mais les traités de l'OMPI n'imposent rien à cet égard".
197 Explanatory Memorandum with the CD, *supra* n. 26, Comment 3 in respect of Art. 6.
198 See *supra* Section 2.5.

because it is actionable under 'ordinary' copyright rules.[199] In the Netherlands, on the other hand, dealing in circumvention-enabling devices is penalised as a criminal offence and may therefore be analysed differently.[200]

5. Protection of Measures that Protect Conditional Access Services

In November 1998, the Conditional Access Directive (CAD) was adopted.[201] The Directive deals with the legal protection of technological measures which are applied in order to secure the remuneration interests of service providers. By focusing on the legal protection of conditional access devices, the Directive raises issues such as access to media and commercialisation, convergence, consumer protection and law enforcement as well as its relation to Article 6 of the proposed Copyright Directive. The emphasis in this section is on the scope of and background to the CAD. In Section 6, the approaches of various legislatures to the protection of conditional access techniques will be briefly discussed.

5.1 MEASURES PROTECTED

The CAD protects 'conditional access devices', which are defined as:[202]

> "any equipment or software designed or adapted to give access to a protected service in an intelligible form".

'Conditional access' is described as:[203]

> "any technical measure and/or arrangement whereby access to the protected service in an intelligible form is made conditional upon prior individual authorisation".

The repeated use of the requirement that access to the protected service be given 'in an intelligible form' may imply that the CAD targets only services that are conditionally accessible because of the use of encryption or scrambling techniques.

199 See Raubenheimer 1996, p. 76.
200 Article 32a of the Dutch Copyright Act.
201 European Parliament and Council Directive 98/84/EC of 20 November 1998 on the Legal Protection of Services Based on, or Consisting of, Conditional Access, OJ L 320/54.
202 Article 2(c) CAD.
203 Article 2(d) CAD.

However, the wording probably is a relict from former approaches, such as that adopted in the Green Paper on Encrypted Services.[204] From the Explanatory Memorandum with the Proposal for the CAD it can be concluded that the intention is to cover any type of conditional access system, either a mere 'gatekeeper' applied at the online outlet that grants access if the proper key is inserted, or a system based on encryption that controls access at the other end, i.e. the consumer's set-top box.[205] Thus, the legal protection in the Directive is not made conditional upon prior encryption of the transmitted signal.

5.2 PROTECTED SERVICES

Under the (proposed) copyright regimes a TM will only be protected if it is used in relation to a 'work'. Somewhat similarly, the CAD applies only to services that are considered 'protected' under the Directive. These services are enumerated in the CAD;[206] they are TV and radio-broadcasting services as well as so-called 'Information society services' in so far as these are provided against remuneration and on the basis of conditional access. The term 'Information society services' is defined as:

> "any service provided at a distance, by electronic means and on the individual request of a service receiver".

Clearly, interactive services provided over the Internet are covered. In this context, 'service' means any performance normally provided for against payment, as defined in Article 50 (ex Article 60) of the EC Treaty.[207] The term includes the provision of all kinds of services on individual demand such as online professional services (e.g., banking, distance-learning, stockbrokers, solicitors), interactive services (video-on demand and games), online information services, electronic databases, electronic retailing and electronic newspapers. According to the Commission, traditional telecommunication services are not 'Information society services', since telecommunication services are not provided by 'electronic means' (i.e. electronic processing systems).[208] By including online services, the Directive goes further than many of

---

204 European Commission, Green Paper on the Legal Protection of Encrypted Services in the Internal Market, Brussels, 6 March 1996, COM (96) 76 ('Green Paper').

205 European Commission, Explanatory Memorandum with the Proposal for a European Parliament and Council Directive on the Legal Protection of Services Based on, or Consisting of Conditional Access, 22 September 1997, COM (97) 356 final, Comments in respect of Art. 1(b).

206 Article 2(a) CAD.

207 Schweitzer and Hummer 1996, para. 1186.

208 The term 'Information society services' was first introduced as a legal concept in the Proposal for a European Parliament and Council Directive amending for the third time Directive 83/189/EEC laying down a procedure for the provision of information in the field of technical standards and regulations

the existing national regulations on the protection of conditional access devices, which are generally confined to broadcasting services.[209] Interestingly, the CAD protects providing conditional access to one of the above-mentioned services as 'a service in its own right'.[210] Apparently, the Directive applies to services that merely provide access (to information services), such as, for instance, Internet access providers who do not themselves provide information services.

To be afforded protection under the Directive, the listed service must be provided 'against remuneration'.[211] One might conclude that conditional access is protected only insofar as it serves remuneration interests. In most cases a TM will be applied to ensure that consumers can only access the service if they have subscribed to it, which will often be against payment. By concentrating on the remuneration interest of service providers, the CAD excludes a wide range of other reasons for controlling access, such as security, privacy, integrity or copyright protection.[212] These may, however, be protected by regimes aimed at preventing computer crime, privacy (of communications) and, of course, TM-protection in the context of copyright law.[213] When exactly a service is to be considered as provided 'against remuneration' remains unclear under the Directive. The payment a service provider obtains directly from the customer in exchange for access to the service will probably constitute 'remuneration'. The term could also be understood in a broader sense as any potential financial gains a service provider receives, directly or indirectly and irrespective from whom. Would, for instance, the provision of personal data — as many website operators require — also be considered 'remuneration' for the purpose of the Directive? Could a provider be said to provide a service 'against remuneration' if it derives income from advertisements, even though it is the advertising, rather than the access, that is paid for?[214]

(Cont.)
and providing for regulatory transparency in the internal market for information society services, *Bulletin EU* 7/8-1996, which led to Council Directive 83/189/EEC laying down a procedure for the provision of information in the field of technical standards and regulations, OJ L 109/10. The latest specification of the meaning of the term can be found in Directive 98/48/EC of the European Parliament and Council of 20 July 1998, amending Directive 98/34/EC laying down a procedure for the provision of information in the field of technical standards and regulations, OJ L 217/18.

209 Only a few Member States, including the Netherlands, Finland, the United Kingdom and Sweden, have also included services other than broadcasting services in their protection schemes.

210 Article 2a CAD.

211 Article 2a CAD.

212 Another option would have been to protect services based on conditional access in general; see Anastassopoulos, Report A4-0136/98 of the Committee on Legal Affairs and Citizen's Rights on the Proposal for a European Parliament and Council Directive on the legal protection of services based on, or consisting of, conditional access, COM (97) 356, available at <http://www.cl.cam.ac.uk/~mgk25/ca-law/>. Anastassopoulos proposes to dispense with the Proposal's requirement that conditional access systems be protected only insofar as they ensure a remuneration interest of the service provider.

213 See *supra* Section 2.

214 Helberger 1999a, p. 90.

5.3 UNLAWFUL ACTIVITIES

Contrary to the rules that protect TMs that protect (access to) copyrighted works, the CAD focuses exclusively on devices and preparatory activities that enable circumvention, rather than on the act of circumvention itself.[215] The CAD declares unlawful:[216]

> "the manufacture, import, distribution, sale, rental or possession for commercial purposes of illicit devices;
> the installation, maintenance or replacement for commercial purposes of an illicit device;
> the use of commercial communications to promote illicit devices".

National legislators are left free to require an additional element of fault for liability to arise, e.g., actual knowledge or reasonable grounds to know that the device in question was illicit.[217] The scope of the CAD appears to be narrower than that of the US and EU copyright regimes. This is not only because the CAD aims only at preparatory activities, but also by virtue of the fact that the possession, manufacturing or distribution of equipment or software *for non-commercial purposes* are not considered unlawful.[218] However, the CAD leaves the Member States with discretion to declare unlawful the private possession of illicit devices.[219] The question remains whether national legislatures may additionally target the *use* of such devices (the unauthorised circumvention, access or reception), as do the copyright regimes discussed. A considerable number of Member States (including Ireland, Italy, the United Kingdom, Finland, the Netherlands and the French community in Belgium) also consider unauthorised access to be unlawful. The legislation in these Member States does not focus exclusively on preparatory activities, such as the manufacture and distribution of pirate cards and decoding devices, but also on the use of such devices in order to access a service without payment.

The decision to leave private non-commercial possession outside the ambit of the CAD is based upon a Recommendation of the Council of Europe on the Legal Protection of Encrypted Television Services, which considered that the enforcement of provisions aimed at private behaviour would conflict with the right to privacy

---

215 See *supra* Section 2.2.

216 Article 4 CAD.

217 Recital 22 with the CAD.

218 Consequently, making a decoding program available to the public on a non-commercial website is not unlawful. The same is true for the private downloading of illicit information (e.g. passwords) or programs.

219 Recital 21 with the CAD.

and would, moreover, be impossible to enforce.[220] According to the European Commission such provisions would conflict with the principle of proportionality as laid down in Article 5 (ex Article 3b) of the EC Treaty, which limits Community action to that which is necessary in order to achieve the Treaty's objective, viz. the free movement of services.[221] The question then arises why the proposed Copyright Directive does seek to target the act of circumvention as such. Arguably, considerations of user privacy should equally play a role in the context of the Copyright Directive.

5.4 ILLICIT DEVICES

Under the CAD, it is unlawful to deal commercially in 'illicit devices'. An 'illicit device' is defined as:[222]

> "any equipment or software designed or adapted to give access to a protected service in an intelligible form without the authorisation of the service provider".

The definition of 'illicit devices' encompasses pirate cards and various programs for replacing passwords. An interesting question is whether the password itself can be considered an 'illicit device' in a situation where the user is not authorised to use the password. Currently, online services which are based on conditional access generally do not require the application of any hardware or software for the service to be accessed, but instead involve the feeding into the system of a password and/or a credit card number. The password is neither equipment nor software; it is information needed by the equipment or software to allow access. As a result, many online services might not be protected under the Directive. Some Member States, such as the Netherlands and the United Kingdom, explicitly prohibit the abuse of passwords.[223] The Copyright Directive and the DMCA also cover the illegal supply of passwords, since they prohibit the provision of *services* that enable unauthorised circumvention.

In order not to unduly hamper the general equipment market, the CAD introduces an element of purpose, as do the TM-protection schemes in copyright

---

220 See Council of Europe, Recommendation R(91)14, The Legal Protection of Encrypted Television Services, 27 September 1991, Explanatory Memorandum with the CAD, *supra* n. 205, paras 82 and 84.

221 See Explanatory Memorandum with the CAD, *supra* n. 205, Art. 3.

222 Article 2(e) CAD.

223 Article 326c of the Dutch Penal Code, unlike the Conditional Access Directive, prohibits the unauthorised reception of a service "by technological means or by means of false signals".

law.[224] However, similar problems as under the latter regimes may arise.[225] Can a personal computer running software to access a digitally encrypted TV-signal be said to be 'adapted to give unauthorised access' and therefore fit the definition?

5.5 SANCTIONS AND REMEDIES REQUIRED

Article 5(1) CAD requires Member States to provide sanctions and remedies with respect to the activities listed in Article 4 CAD. Sanctions are to be 'effective, dissuasive and proportional to the potential impact of the infringing activity'. The vague wording of Article 5 CAD gives the national legislator considerable freedom to decide what sanctions are appropriate. Moreover, Member States are free to choose in which field of law the provisions of the Directive are to be transformed. On the basis of Article 5(2) CAD, however, the Member States must make available action for damages and injunctions and 'where appropriate applying for disposal outside commercial channels of illicit devices'. Clearly, this may be read to imply that civil action should be open to conditional access service providers. From Recital 23 it can be concluded that the obligations of the Directive need not necessarily be implemented under criminal law.

The right to bring an action is available exclusively to 'providers of protected services'. Thus, third parties, whose interests may be affected by the marketing of illicit devices, such as holders of intellectual property rights, cannot file an action in court. The European Commission explains that "[al]though, from an economic point of view, rights holders will certainly benefit from such [legal] measures, this will be an indirect effect, and their interests remain distinct".[226] In its Opinion on the proposal for the Directive, the Economic and Social Committee of the European Parliament criticised this approach.[227] The Committee proposed to expand the right to institute proceedings to anyone who can prove a direct interest.[228] The Committee on Legal Affairs and Citizen's Rights explicitly proposed to extend the right to bring proceedings to copyright owners. Many existing national regulations already grant legal remedies to anyone whose rights are affected, as does the DMCA, which grants a right to 'any person injured' to sue for the damages for violation of the protection of TMs that control access to

224 See *supra* Sections 2.2 and 3.4.
225 See *supra* Section 2.2.
226 Amended Proposal, Explanatory Memorandum, Art. 1 (g).
227 Opinion of the Economic and Social Committee on the Proposal for a European Parliament and Council Directive on the Legal Protection of Services Based on or Consisting of Conditional Access, 25 February 1998, OJ C 129/16.
228 See Anastassopoulos, *supra* n. 212, proposing to recognise the rights set out in Art. 4(2) of the proposed Conditional Access Directive as attaching to owners of intellectual property rights.

copyrighted works, thereby including copyright-holders and mere service providers.[229]

It may be argued that the decision to grant the right to bring legal proceedings to service providers alone is in keeping with the existing information value chain. The copyright-holder can prohibit *the performance* of a work, whereas the organiser of the performance (i.e. the theatre) — the equivalent of the conditional access service provider — authorises the public to *attend* the performance.[230] However, there may be situations where the interests of the service provider and the rights-holder do not coincide. Suppose, for example, that a scrambled TV-signal is broadcast by satellite and can be received in several countries while the conditional access service provider seeks only to exploit the national market. The service provider would have little incentive to act against the distribution of illicit decryption devices in other countries. The rights-holders of the works contained in the service, on the other hand, may wish to exploit their rights on a territorial basis, and would therefore have an interest in preventing the illicit reception of the service. One solution may be for rights-holders to oblige service providers contractually to take legal action against the producers of illicit devices. Copyright-based TM-protection may also apply in such circumstances.

6. Existing Law on the Protection of Conditional Access Services

The aim of the CAD is to harmonise the protection of conditional access services in Europe. Indeed, Member States have already provided for legal protection of conditional access systems in various ways. Insofar as specific national legislation exists, the national laws differ considerably in structure, scope and procedure. Pursuant to the CAD, Member States may either have to adopt new specific rules or, where specific rules are already enacted, may have to adapt the existing legislation to the provisions of the Directive.

Most of the specific national laws currently in place focus on broadcasting services. Only a few Member States (e.g. the Netherlands and the United Kingdom) have legislation that covers 'Information society services'. Member States that have passed legislation targeting the act of unauthorised reception of a service, often include additional provisions concerning activities involving decoding equipment. Where national regulations focus on preparatory activities, they generally prohibit the possession, manufacture, importation and distribution of such equipment.

The legal protection of conditional access services differs also from country to country in respect of the chosen field of law. National rules applicable to

229 See *supra* Section 2.4.
230 See *supra* Section 4.1.

conditional access services can be found in several areas of the law, such as unfair competition, copyright, penal, broadcasting and telecommunications law.

6.1 UNFAIR COMPETITION LAW

Where specific rules do not exist, national courts generally apply the rules on unfair competition to activities that enable or prepare for the unauthorised reception of conditional access services. Unfair competition law applies only to commercial activities, since the existing laws on unfair competition generally require the existence of a commercially competitive situation. Therefore, the mere possession of decoding equipment, as well as the unauthorised circumvention, access or reception of the service by an end-user generally are not considered unlawful under unfair competition law.

Most commonly, merely taking advantage of a competitor's performance does not in itself constitute an act of unfair competition unless additional circumstances can be established. Nevertheless, until now national courts have regarded as such additional circumstances the actual hindrance of a competitor,[231] unfairly profiting from the development and manufacturing expenses incurred by the service provider[232] as well as the amount of damages or the factual destruction of the business of a closed pay-TV subscription system. Thus, courts have found that the manufacture and marketing of decoders or pirate cards with the intention of enabling third parties to access services without authorisation may constitute unlawful unfair competitive behaviour.[233] Whether the trading in general purpose equipment, capable of serving other purposes than decoding encrypted signals, is 'unfair' remains to be seen.[234] Under unfair competition law, service providers may claim civil remedies including damages and costs and seek injunctions.

6.2 COMPUTER CRIME

Some penal law provisions may protect conditional access services. One could argue that unauthorised access to the information contained in a scrambled signal constitutes a form of 'theft'. However, in many jurisdictions this is conceptually problematic, because the general provisions on theft often require that tangible property be taken away and the victims therefore no longer have the property at

---

231 Court of Appeal Frankfurt (*Oberlandesgericht*) 13 July 1995, [1995] CR 533.

232 *Ibid.*

233 *Firma Teleclub,* Court of Appeal Munich (*Oberlandesgericht*) 7 December 1989, [1990] ZUM 198; Court of Appeal Brussels (*Cour d'Appel*) 20 April 1990, J.L.M.B. 1991, 1079, J.T. 1990, 642; *Teleclub,* Austrian Supreme Court (*Oberster Gerichtshof Österreich*) 25 October 1988, Wbi 1988/56.

234 *Firma Teleclub,* Court of Appeal Munich (*Oberlandesgericht*) 7 December 1989, [1990] ZUM 198.

their disposal, whereas if information is appropriated there is no physical removal of property and the owner can still use the information.[235] Other provisions that may be applicable to (the enabling of) unauthorised access, although not necessarily specifically written for that purpose, are those protecting the secrecy of communications or those relating to forms of computer fraud or 'digital deceit'.[236]

German law, for example, contains no specific provisions on the legal protection of conditional access services, but the unauthorised decoding of such services is probably covered by a provision in the chapter on the protection of the private sphere and communications secrecy in the German Penal Code. The provision prohibits accessing electronically encrypted data of which one is not the intended recipient, or enabling such access.[237] The supply of pirate cards and the unauthorised reception of a digitally encrypted TV-programme may fall within the scope of this provision.[238]

The Dutch Criminal Code regards the application of technical means or false signals in order to use a service "offered to the general public via telecommunications", with the intent of avoiding payment, as a form of deceit. Clearly, online services may be covered by the provision, but 'over the air' broadcasting services probably are not. According to the Dutch approach, the party fraudulently accessing the service is the primary offender. A person enabling such access is regarded as an accomplice. Therefore, preparatory activities enabling the unauthorised use of the service are subject to smaller fines than is the unauthorised use itself, except where the activities are carried out in the course of business.[239]

6.3 BROADCASTING LAW

Contrary to Germany and the Netherlands, where the circumvention of a conditional access device may be punishable on the basis of general criminal law and civilly actionable under unfair competition law, certain Member States have legislation in place specifically aimed at protecting conditional access services. In most cases these laws deal exclusively with broadcasting services and are made part of broadcasting law (e.g. in Ireland and France).[240] Generally, these provisions make it criminally punishable to use and deal in devices that enable fraudulent reception of encrypted services where those services are offered against payment. In Ireland,

235 Sieber 1998, p. 67.
236 See extensively Sieber 1998.
237 Article 202a of the German Penal Code.
238 See extensively Helberger 1999b, p. 295.
239 Article 326c of the Dutch Penal Code.
240 Article 9 of the Irish Broadcasting Act 1990; Art. 79-1 to 79-6 of the French Broadcasting Act. Previously, conditional access services were protected by Art. 429 of the French Penal Code, which was implemented in 1987; see on the provision of the French Penal Code, Beucher and Engels 1998, p. 107.

in contrast, it is simply declared an offence to receive a service without authorisation, or to enable such reception. Often, provisions embodied in broadcasting law include civil remedies.

Pursuant to the Directive, these Member States may have to adopt additional regulations on the legal protection of 'Information society services'. This will raise the question of whether these services can be regarded as 'broadcasting services' for the purpose of broadcasting law, or have to be treated outside broadcasting law. Furthermore, the existing rules concentrate on encrypted signals whereas the Conditional Access Directive presumably prescribes the protection of other forms of access-control as well.

6.4 TELECOMMUNICATIONS LAW

Telecommunications law may be another area of the law where rules relevant to the protection of conditional access services can be found. Indeed, Finland's Telecommunications Market Act prohibits the unauthorised decoding of encrypted signals, including broadcasting and radio signals.[241] Besides Finland only Belgium has adopted specific provisions in telecommunications law. The Belgian rules, although part of telecommunications law, nevertheless exclusively address broadcasting services.[242]

One aspect which prevents Member States from adopting specific provisions within the context of telecommunications law may be that this field of the law generally focuses on point-to-point communications, whereas services based on conditional access are naturally directed to the general public, albeit that the access is conditional. In Germany as a federal state, for example, the question is whether pay-TV and online services directed to the public fall under the competence of the federal government, which has legislative powers in the field of telecommunications, or that of the States (*Länder*) that are responsible for legislation in the field of broadcasting. This underscores the fact that the convergence of 'Information society services', broadcasting and telecommunications will require new legislative solutions that relinquish the traditional distinction between individual telecommunications and broadcasting services.

6.5 COPYRIGHT LAW

Exceptionally, the United Kingdom deals with the unauthorised reception of broadcasting services in the framework of copyright law. Apart from a provision

---

241 Article 25 of the Finnish Telecommunications Market Act (No. 396) of 1997.
242 Article 43, Decree of the French Community on Audiovisual Services.

explicitly protecting technological measures that prevent copying,[243] the UK Copyright, Designs and Patents Act 1988 contains a provision which declares the 'dishonest' reception of a broadcast or cable programme service an offence, if the service is provided from a place in the United Kingdom and the intention is to avoid payment.[244] When the provision was introduced, it was acknowledged that copyright does not confer an exclusive right to control reception as such. Therefore, a separate criminal offence was created.[245] It is provided that an encrypted transmission shall be deemed to be received with authorisation only if the decoding equipment is made available by the service provider.[246] Any person who charges for reception as well as any person who sends encrypted transmissions has a civil action against the circumventor, but also against a person who enables the unlawful access, either by supplying devices or information (e.g. passwords).[247] Interestingly, in the *Shetland Times* case a Scottish court considered linking to a copyrighted work in a web page to constitute the infringing act of 'inclusion of a programme in a cable programme service' for the purpose of the CDPA. Thus, the UK provisions might apply to online information services.[248]

7. Comparative Analysis

Clearly, the impact of the CAD will depend upon the way it will be implemented. Similarly, the TM-protection schemes in copyright law (particularly the proposed Copyright Directive) leave unanswered many questions as to their exact meaning and scope. Nevertheless, some general observations on the relationship between TM-protection under copyright law and conditional access protection schemes can be made.

At first glance, conditional access regimes and copyright-based TM-protection rules appear to treat two different aspects of the communication of a work. Traditionally, copyright law covers acts of exploitation of a work, rather than its access or 'consumption'.[249] Existing conditional access regimes in EU Member States, on the other hand, explicitly aim at inhibiting the act of unauthorised (or fraudulent) individual reception or access. However, recent developments have caused the distinction between the two regimes to blur. First, accessing a digitised

243 Article 296 CDPA.
244 Article 297 CDPA.
245 Dworkin and Taylor 1989, pp. 200-201. Article 298(5) CDPA implies that the right to bring action on the basis of the conditional access regime is not a 'copyright'.
246 Article 6(2) CDPA.
247 Article 298 CDPA.
248 *Shetland Times Ltd. v. Wills, et al*, 24 October 1996, [1997] SLT 669. See Art. 7 CDPA; see also Beucher and Engels 1998, p. 107.
249 Wand 1996, pp. 897, 903; see also *supra* Sections 2.1 and 4.1.

work may implicate the right of (temporary) reproduction. Secondly, protection of copyright law now extends to access to TM-protected works and activities preparatory to such access (the DMCA does so explicitly, but access control appears to play a part in the proposed Copyright Directive as well). Thirdly, if both regimes grant a civil action to any interested or injured party, as does the DMCA and as the CD may permit Member States to do, aggrieved parties may often be able to apply for protection under both schemes.

The most obvious distinction between the two regimes is that the copyright rules prohibit circumvention of a TM that protects *works*, whereas the conditional access regimes protect *services*. However, as many services will consist of copyrighted works, accessing the work and the service may often amount to one and the same act.[250] The distinction results in difference in scope of protection for TMs under either regime. Under copyright, TMs that inhibit access to or use of public domain material (presumably) are not protected, whereas the CAD covers technologies that protect access to any information (service). However, the copyright regimes are broader in scope in that they may also protect TMs that inhibit the use of, or access to, a work *after* it has been obtained, whereas the protection of conditional access services exclusively deals with first access.

The US legislature has felt it necessary to limit the protection of TMs that control access to copyrighted works, because an overbroad 'right to control access to TM-protected works' may unduly limit public access and therefore be detrimental to society. Of course, limitations on the control which a rights-holder can exercise over protected information are not new in copyright law, where, certainly in the United States, public interest considerations determine the extent of the right to preclude the use of information.[251] In this context, the question may be posed whether similar limitations would be justified where access control to (information) services is concerned. A first symptom of such a limitation can be found in the amended Television without Frontiers Directive that prohibits capturing certain 'events' exclusively for pay-TV.[252] In this respect the TV Directive goes further than the DMCA. Under the US Act there are no restrictions on blocking access to information, but access-controlling TMs may, under certain circumstances, be circumvented. The TV Directive allows Member States to prohibit access-control in the first place. The CAD takes into account the amended Directive and other "possible future Community or national provisions meant to ensure that a number of broadcasting services, recognised as being of public interest, are not based on conditional access".[253] Thus, the CAD in effect allows

250 Explanatory Memorandum with the CD, *supra* n. 26, Comment 4 in respect of Art. 6. According to the European Commission, the CAD deals with the "protection against unauthorized reception of a conditional access service, which may or may not contain or be based upon intellectual property".

251 See *supra* Section 2.1.

252 See *supra* Section 3.6.

253 Recital 9 with the CAD.

national legislators to set limitations upon access control, if, as is the case with the limitations of copyright, this is in the public interest.

Interestingly, neither the CAD nor the proposed Copyright Directive or the DMCA target the act of unauthorised access as such; they apply only if a technological layer of protection is added to the work or the service.[254] These technologies enable new modes of exploitation of information and (information) services. The main rationale behind the CAD appears to be the fostering of these new business models. This is expressed by the fact that the CAD requires that the TM be applied to a service provided 'against remuneration', and only targets commercial activities. Similarly, one of the main purpose of copyright is to ensure that the rights-holder is able to obtain adequate compensation for his efforts, thus gaining incentive to create.[255] TM-protection under copyright, however, was not initially designed to encourage the creation of new markets, but rather to uphold the existing level of copyright protection, which was presumably undermined by the copyright-holders' vulnerability in the electronic environment.[256] Nevertheless, the rationale of the new copyright regime as it turned out is similar to that of the CAD. This is exemplified by the (apparent) inclusion of access-control, which was never explicitly a copyright, and by the fact that the proposed Copyright Directive brings private use expressly within the sphere of control of the rights-holder, at least partly, because new technologies are expected to enable the exercise of copyrights against private users.[257]

As was explained in Section 4.2 above, the DMCA's prohibition on circumventing access-controlling TMs may be seen as an exclusive copyright-like right to control access. How the European TM-protection schemes (of the Copyright Directive and the CAD) should be regarded will largely depend on the way they will eventually be implemented. The approach of the CAD, however, has much in common with unfair competition law, as it aims at commercial preparatory activities to unauthorised access and only becomes applicable if a TM is used to guarantee the protection of a remuneration interest. However, conditional access protection schemes already existing in a few Member States do target acts of unauthorised access, circumvention or reception. Some of these regimes make it a criminal offence 'dishonestly' or fraudulently to access a service by using false

---

254 Similarly, traditional copyright law does not cover the act of unauthorised access itself. Some of the existing conditional access service protection schemes of EU Member States, however, do explicitly target the acts of unauthorised circumvention, access or reception. See *supra* Section 6.

255 See *supra* Section 3.1.

256 See, e.g. House Report, *supra* n. 22, p. 25: "[T]he Committee also recognizes that the digital environment poses a unique threat to the rights of copyright owners, and as such, necessitates protection against devices that undermine copyright interests. In contrast to the analog experience, digital technology enables pirates to reproduce and distribute perfect copies of works — at virtually no cost at all to the pirate. As technology advances, so must our laws. The Committee thus seeks to protect the interests of copyright owners in the digital environment". See also Summary Minutes, *supra* n. 24, No. 525.

257 See Bygrave and Koelman, elsewhere in this volume, p. 107.

information or technical means with the intent of evading payment, thereby indicating that such access is a form of criminal deceit. Enabling such 'deceit' would then make the supplier of devices an accomplice. Insofar as these regimes grant a civil action, one could argue that a 'quasi-property right' is created.[258]

8. Concluding Remarks

The newly created TM-protection schemes are predicated on the assumption that they are necessary to safeguard the interests of the protected actors. It is by no means certain, however, that technological use prevention will in fact be widely applied in the digital environment. The practice of 'copy-protecting' computer programs, which began rather promisingly in the 1980s, has now been almost completely abandoned.[259] DAT recorders, containing SCMSs prescribed by US law, are yet to become a commercial success. Perhaps, it may be concluded that consumers do not like information products that are protected by technology. However, access-controlling TMs will probably be applied by information service providers as equivalents of the physical control that bookstores and theatres are able to exercise in order to obtain remuneration for their efforts. Probably, these business models would be seriously endangered if access control techniques were to be circumvented *en masse*.

Particularly controversial is the protection of technological measures in copyright law. Whether legal protection against circumvention is really necessary, is unclear. No empirical data exist on the need for protection.[260] If TM protection is limited to acts of circumvention which enable copyright infringement, existing copyright remedies may suffice. It is for precisely this reason that the US legislature does not see fit to prohibit circumvention of TMs that protect a right.[261] Circumvention of access-controlling TMs may be prohibited under other regimes, in particular those concerning the protection of conditional access services, unfair competition law and computer crime. Although these regimes are not specifically aimed at protecting copyright, the rights-holders' interests may nevertheless be adequately protected. Moreover, in view of the ongoing proliferation of intellectual property(-like) rights, the proportionality of adding yet another layer of protection is questionable.[262] Is it really necessary for rights-holders to be (cumulatively)

---

258 See *supra* Section 4.1.
259 See *supra* Section 2.2.
260 See Summary Minutes, *supra* n. 24, No. 527. According to the Singapore delegate "it would be dangerous to conjecture about the future based on a series of assumptions about how the technology would develop and affect copyright owners. It would be preferable to depend on existing laws and remedies to address each specific circumvention technology as it would arise".
261 See *supra* Section 2.2.
262 Hugenholtz 1998, p. 255.

protected by copyright, database protection, contract law, technical protection *and* an additional layer of TM protection? Wand has observed, rather cynically, that "three times stitched holds better".[263] Perhaps, one might add: five times is overdoing it.[264]

Whether legal TM-protection should aim at the act of circumvention or at the preparatory activities to that act is a difficult issue. Arguments against targeting private behaviour are that, until now, copyright-holders and service providers have rarely sued private individual users, partly because it is economically unfeasible[265] and partly because detection of infringement at the level of the individual user is virtually impossible and may interfere with the right to privacy.[266] In the future, metering technologies may make it possible to detect violations of rights at the level of the individual user. However, the right to privacy and the economic unfeasibility of prosecution may keep rights-holders from suing individual users for unlawful circumvention. Even from a rights-holder's or service provider's point of view, it may be preferable to target activities preparatory to circumvention. These will be easier to detect, since detection would not interfere with the right to privacy, and will be more likely to reach the 'deep pockets' that plaintiffs traditionally look for.

On the other hand, one could argue that there may be some inconsistency in prohibiting the production and distribution of devices that enable activities that are perfectly legal. If, however, such preparatory activities are seen as a form of unfair competition law, there is no contradiction in banning merely the supply of devices, while not prohibiting at the same time the use of such devices. After all, a private user of a device does not compete with a service provider. An argument put forward in favour of criminalising the possession and use of devices is that such legislative measures would serve as a deterrence. Another advantage of targeting circumvention, rather than preparatory activities, may be that it is easier to bring the prohibition in line with the limitations of copyright. As was discussed in Section 3.4 above, if the copyright limitations were to affect the scope of a prohibition on circumvention devices, the result might be that only few devices, if any, would in fact be banned. If, on the other hand, all circumvention-enabling devices were covered, the balance embodied in copyright law would be disturbed. As there are no limitations (yet) affecting the protection of conditional access services, the latter dilemma plays no role in respect of the law protecting conditional access services. There are indications, however, that legislators are aware of the negative social impact of total control of access to (certain kinds of) information, and may therefore set limits upon access-prevention to information services as well.

---

263 Wand 1996.

264 See Spoor 1998, p. 30, quoting the Spanish reporter to the ALAI Conference who speaks of 'hyper-protection'.

265 Litman 1997b, text near n. 49. Cf. Landes and Posner 1989, p. 358: "the potential fee (or damages) per user might be so small ... that enforcement proceedings would be unfeasible".

266 See Bygrave and Koelman, elsewhere in this volume, p. 108.

It is often argued, particularly in the copyright context, that it may be too early to draft legislation aimed at protecting TMs.[267] The difficulties law-makers currently experience in drafting comprehensible and conceptually sound legislation, are symptomatic. Perhaps the legislature should let rights-holders experiment with the new technological tools first before adopting legislation.[268] If and when the time is ripe for legislative measures, legislatures should look not only at protecting the interests of rights-holders and service providers, but also consider fundamental users' freedoms and the interests of society at large. The confusing and complicated interrelationship between TM protection, copyright exemptions, protection of conditional access services and the public interest in widely available and accessible information is ample proof that finding an adequate balance will not be an easy task.

References

S. Bechtold (1998), 'Multimedia und Urheberrecht — einige grundsätzliche Anmerkungen', [1998] *GRUR* 18.

T.W. Bell (1998), 'Fair Use vs. Fared Use: The Impact of Automated Rights Management on Copyright's Fair Use Doctrine', [1998] *North Carolina Law Review* 557.

D. Bender (1986), 'The Computer/Trade Secret Interface', [1986] *University of Pittsburgh Law Review* 909.

K. Beucher and S. Engels (1998), 'Harmonisierung des Rechtschutzes verschlüsselter Pay-TV-Dienste gegen Piraterieakte', [1998] *Computer und Recht* 101.

J. Browning (1997), 'Africa 1 — Hollywood 0', (1997) 5 *Wired Magazine* (March 1997), available at <http://www.wired.com/wired/5.03/netizen.html>.

C. Clark (1996), 'The Answer to the Machine is in the Machine', in P.B. Hugenholtz (ed.), *The Future of Copyright in a Digital Environment*, The Hague/London/Boston: Kluwer, 1996, pp. 139–148.

H. Coble (1998), 'The Spring Horace S Manges Lecture — The 105th Congress: Recent Developments in Intellectual Property Law', [1998] *Columbia VLA Journal of Law and the Arts* 269.

---

267 Vinje 1996a, p. 439; Bell 1998, p. 591.

268 Samuelson 1996, p. 27: "Let copyright owners use technology to build 'fences' around their works and explore new markets. If the fences they use are inadequate to protect against market failure, there will be time enough to adopt appropriate legislation at that time".

J. E. Cohen (1996), 'A Right to Read Anonymously: A Closer Look at 'Copyright Management' (1996) 28 *Connecticut Law Review* 981-1039.

J.E. Cohen (1997), 'Some Reflections on Copyright Management Systems and Laws Designed to Protect Them', [1997] *Berkeley Technology Law Journal* 161.

S.J. Davidson and N.A. Engisch (1995), 'A Survey of The Law of Copyright Misuse and Fraud on the Copyright Office: Legitimate Restraints on Copyright Owners or Escape Routes for Copyright Infringers?' (1995), available at <http://stevedavidson.com/html/imprintbodyc-misuse.htm>.

F.G. DePeiza (1997), 'The Frontiers of Fair Use in a Copyright Management World' (1997), available at <http://cobra.law.miami.edu/~fd1883/paper.html>.

A. Dietz (1998), 'Die EU-Richtlinie zum Urheberrecht und den Leistungsschutzrechten in der Informationsgesellschaft', [1998] *ZUM* 438.

G. Dworkin and R.D. Taylor (1989), *Blackstone's Guide to the Copyright, Designs and Patents Act 1988*, London: Blackstone Press Ltd 1989.

N. Elkin-Koren (1997), 'Copyright Policy and the Limits of Freedom of Contract', [1997] *Berkeley Technology Law Journal* 93.

T. Goddard (1998), 'UK National Report', paper presented at the ALAI Study Days, Cambridge, 14-17 September 1998.

S. Greenstein (1996), 'News from WIPO, Day Seven — The AudioVisual Debate, and What's Fair is Fair Use' (10 December 1996), available at <http://www.hrrc.org/wr_12-10.html>.

P. Groves (1991), *Copyright and Designs law: a Question of Balance*, London: Graham and Trotman Limited 1991.

N. Helberger (1999a), 'Hacking BSkyB: The legal protection of conditional access services under European law', [1999] *Entertainment Law Review* 88.

N. Helberger (1999b), 'Hacken von Premiere bald europaweit verboten?', (1999) 4 *Zeitschrift für Urheber- und Medienrecht* 295.

P.B. Hugenholtz (1992), 'Convergence and Divergence in Intellectual Property Law: The Case of the Software Directive', in W.F. Korthals Altes *et al.* (eds.), *Information Law towards the 21st Century*, Deventer/Boston: Kluwer 1992, pp. 319–324.

P.B. Hugenholtz (1996), 'Adapting Copyright to the Information Superhighway', in P.B. Hugenholtz (ed.), *The Future of Copyright in a Digital Environment*, The Hague/London/Boston: Kluwer 1996, pp. 81–102.

P.B. Hugenholtz (1998), 'Het Internet: het auteursrecht voorbij?', [1998] *Handelingen NVJ* 197.

J. Hughes (1988), 'The Philosophy of Intellectual Property', [1988] *The Georgetown Law Journal* 287.

Institute for Information Law (D. Gervais) (1998), *The Law and Practice of Digital Encryption*, Amsterdam: Institute for Information Law 1998.

W.M. Landes and R.A. Posner (1989), 'An Economic Analysis of Copyright Law', [1989] *Journal of Legal Studies* 325.

R.H. Lauwaars and C.W.A. Timmermans (1994), *Europees Gemeenschapsrecht in kort bestek*, Groningen: Wolters Noordhof 1994.

J. Litman (1997a), 'Symposium: Copyright Owners' Rights and Users' Privileges on the Internet: Reforming Information Law in Copyright's Image', [1997] *Dayton Law Review* 587.

J. Litman (1997b), 'New Copyright Paradigms', in L.N. Gassaway (ed.), *Growing Pains: Adapting Copyright for Libraries, Education and Society*, Littleton, Co.: Rothman 1997, available at <http://www.msen.com/~litman/paradigm.htm>.

A. Lucas (1997), 'Le droit d'auteur et protections techniques', in M Dellebeke (ed.), *Copyright in Cyberspace, ALAI Study Days Amsterdam, 4-8 June 1996*, Amsterdam: Cramwinckel 1997, pp. 343–356.

A. Lucas (1998a), 'Intellectual property and global information infrastructure', [1998] *Copyright Bulletin* 3.

A. Lucas (1998b), *Droit d'auteur et numérique*, Paris: Litec 1998.

E. Mackaay (1992), 'An Economic View of Information Law', in W.F. Korthals Altes *et al.* (eds.), *Information Law towards the 21st Century*, Deventer/Boston: Kluwer 1992, pp. 43–66.

E. Mackaay (1996), 'The Economics of Emergent Property Rights on the Internet', in P.B. Hugenholtz (ed.), *The Future of Copyright in a Digital Environment*, The Hague/London/Boston: Kluwer 1996, pp. 13–26.

K. Murray (1998), 'The Draft Directive on the Harmonisation of Certain Aspects of Copyright and Related Rights in the Information Society', [1998] *Entertainment Law Review* 190.

D. Nimmer (1998), 'Time and Space', [1998] *IDEA The Journal of Law and Technology* 501.

M.B. Nimmer and D. Nimmer, *Nimmer on Copyright*, New York/San Francisco: Mathew Bender & Co, looseleaf.

W. Page Keeton (1984), *Prosser and Keeton on the Law of Torts*, St. Paul, Minn.: West Publishing 1984.

T.G. Palmer (1989), 'Intellectual property: A Non-Posnerian Law and Economics Approach', [1989] *Hamline Law Review* 261.

M. Peters (1996), 'Register of Copyrights, Letter to the Chairman of Subcommittee on Courts and Intellectual Property in Response to Questions Concerning the National Information Infrastructure Copyright Protection Act', Answer to Question 4 (15 February 1996), available at <ftp://ftp.loc.gov/pub/copyright/cpypub/niistat.html>.

A.A. Quaedvlieg (1992), 'The Economic Analysis of Intellectual Property Law', in W.F. Korthals Altes *et al.* (eds.), *Information Law towards the 21 Century*, Deventer/Boston: Kluwer 1992, pp. 379–393.

A. Raubenheimer (1996), 'Beseitigung/Umgehung eines technischen Programmschutzes nach UrhG und UWG', [1996] *Computer und Recht* 69.

J.R. Reidenberg (1996), 'Governing Networks and Rule-Making in Cyberspace', (1996) 45 *Emory Law Journal* 911.

J.R. Reidenberg (1998), 'Lex Informatica: The Foundation of Information Policy Rules through Technology', [1998] *Texas Law Review* 553.

J. Reinbothe (1998), 'Der EU-Richtlinienentwurf zum Urheberrecht und zu den Leistungsrechten in der Informationsgeselschaft', [1998] *ZUM* 429.

D.A. Rice (1992), 'Public Goods, Private Contract and Public Policy: Federal Preemption of Software License Prohibitions against Reverse Engineering', [1992] *University of Pittsburgh Law Review* 543.

S. Ricketson (1987), *The Berne Convention for the Protection of Literary and Artistic Works: 1886–1986*, Deventer: Kluwer 1987.

H. Saito (1998), 'Fluid Relationship of Normal Exploitations to Acts Permissible under Exceptions and Limitations', paper presented at the ALAI Study Days, Cambridge, 14-17 September 1998.

P. Samuelson (1996), 'Technological Protection for Copyrighted Works' (draft), available at <http://www.sims.berkeley.edu/~pam/courses/cyberlaw/docs/techpro.html>.

E. Schlachter (1997), 'The Intellectual Property Renaissance in Cyberspace: Why Copyright Law Could Be Unimportant on the Internet', [1997] *Berkeley Technology Law Journal* 15.

H. Schweitzer and B. Hummer (1996), *Europarecht*, Berlin: Luchterhand 1996.

U. Sieber (1998), 'Legal Aspects of Computer-Related Crime in the Information Society (COMCRIME-Study)', Brussels 1998, available at <http://www2.echo.lu/legal/en/comcrime/comcrime.html>.

N.A. Smith (1997), 'United States of America', in: M Dellebeke (ed.), *Copyright in Cyberspace, ALAI Study Days Amsterdam, 4-8 June 1996*, Amsterdam: Cramwinckel 1997, pp. 416–430.

J.H. Spoor (1998), 'General Aspects of Exceptions and Limitations to Copyright', paper presented at the ALAI Study Days, Cambridge, 14-17 September 1998.

I.A. Stamatoudi (1998), 'The Hidden Agenda in *Magill* and its Impact on New Technologies', [1998] *Journal of World Intellectual Property* 150.

M. Stefik (1997), 'Shifting the Possible: How Trusted Systems and Digital Property Rights Challenge Us to Rethink Digital Publishing', [1997] *Berkeley Technology Law Journal* 137.

I. Trotter Hardy (1996), 'The Ancient Doctrine of Trespass to Web Sites', *The Journal of On-Line Law* (1996), available at <http://www.wm.edu/law/publications/jol>.

R.V. Vaidyanatha Ayyar (1998), 'Interest or Right?, The Process and Politics of a Diplomatic Conference on Copyright', [1998] *Journal of World Intellectual Property* 3.

T.C. Vinje (1995), 'The Final Word on Magill', [1995] *EIPR* 297.

T.C. Vinje (1996a), 'A Brave New World of Technical Protection Systems: Will There Still Be Room for Copyright?', [1996] *EIPR* 431.

T.C. Vinje (1996b), 'All's not quiet on the Berne Front', [1996] *EIPR* 585.

S. von Lewinsky (1998), 'A Successful Step towards Copyright and Related Rights in the Information Age: The New E.C. Proposal for a Harmonisation Directive', [1998] *EIPR* 135.

P. Wand (1996), 'Dreifach genäht hält besser! — Technische Identifizierungs- und Schutzsysteme', [1996] *GRUR Int.* 897.

D.L. Zimmerman (1992), 'Information as Speech, Information as Goods: Some Thoughts on Marketplaces and the Bill of Rights', [1992] *William & Mary Law Review* 665.

V. Protection of Copyright Management Information

Annemique M.E. de Kroon

1. Introduction

The information society offers new opportunities to exploit and enjoy copyright protected works. However, in order to ensure that the acquisition of rights for the creation of multimedia works is not obstructed by long and costly procedures and to monitor the use made of (copyrighted) works, the management of rights will have to develop and adjust to the new environment.[1] The digital age and the scope it offers for tracing and monitoring use of a work in general may facilitate rights management in some respects.[2] Rather than having to think in terms of a generalised right to remuneration, a more finely tuned and individualised form of rights management may emerge.[3] Rights management can, apart from traditional collective rights management, take on the form of a 'one-stop-shop' which provides individual management through a central point of request or of a 'clearing house'.[4]

Copyright management information (CMI)[5] comprises all information, be it in electronic form or otherwise, that identifies a copyrighted work (the most obvious example being the ISBN) and anyone who has a particular kind of involvement or interest in the work (author, publisher or other rights-holder, etc.), as well as any other information that would enable or facilitate the management of rights, such as conditions of use. Anything that can be digitised and viewed on a computer screen, be it a representation of a sculptural work, a musical work, a literary work or a movie, can have CMI encoded in it. The importance of CMI lies in the role it can play with regard to online trade in content and the administration of rights, *inter*

1 European Commission, Green Paper on Copyright and Related Rights in the Information Society, COM (95) 382 final. See Gervais 1998.
2 Clark 1996.
3 Lucas 1998a, p. 315.
4 Lucas 1998b.
5 A better term would be 'Rights Management Information' since neighbouring rights may be involved as well. However, in this chapter the most commonly used terminology will be used.

Copyright and Electronic Commerce (ed. P. Bernt Hugenholtz; ISBN 90-411-9785-0; © Kluwer Law International, 2000; printed in Great Britain).

alia by enabling or at least facilitating the creation and exploitation of multimedia works.

The recent WIPO Treaties,[6] the proposed EU Directive on the Harmonisation of Certain Aspects of Copyright and Related Rights in the Information Society ('Copyright Directive') and the Digital Millennium Copyright Act (DMCA) seek to protect CMI through provisions prohibiting the removal or alteration of such information.[7] The provisions protecting CMI are directed at future developments when the introduction of electronic copyright management systems will have made safe and smooth transactions on the Internet possible.

The accuracy of CMI may become crucial to the ability of consumers to make authorised uses of copyrighted works. CMI to a large extent relies on the use of standards that uniquely identify content. This chapter will first provide a closer look at identification standards used for CMI (Section 2). Subsequently, the legal protection of CMI against removal or alteration will be examined. What legal rules existed before the introduction of international regulations (Section 3)? Finally, current and proposed provisions which specifically protect CMI against removal or alteration, will be discussed (Section 4).

2. Identification Standards

2.1 Introduction

Copyright management information is not a new phenomenon. The most prominent example of CMI in the analogue world is the International Standard Book Number (ISBN), which was established in 1967 and which is widely used in the book publishing industry, facilitating business communications between publishers and booksellers and the identification of materials by libraries.[8] Identifiers such as the ISBN indicate that two instances of a work that have been assigned the same identifier are the same, while two instances of a work with different identifiers are distinct.[9] A universal system of identification similar to that of the ISBN will enable or facilitate an effective system of electronic commerce in digital objects.[10]

With regard to numbering systems a distinction can be made between intelligent or compound identifiers on the one hand and unintelligent, dumb or

6 WIPO Copyright Treaty (WCT) and WIPO Performances and Phonograms Treaty (WPPT).
7 Article 12 WCT; Art. 19 WPPT; Art. 7 of the proposed Copyright Directive and s. 1202 DMCA.
8 *Handleiding voor het internationaal standaard boek nummer*, Culemborg: Centraal Boekhuis 1997.
9 See Lynch.
10 See Green and Bide 1996.

simple identifiers on the other.[11] A dumb identifier is a mere random number, a unique label which in and of itself provides no information about the object that is identified by the number. The number can only be interpreted by reference to a central database or a table of data containing relevant further information to which the dumb identifier is linked. An intelligent identifier, on the other hand, in addition to being a reference that uniquely identifies a document, carries explicit information or metadata about the object. Metadata associated with a digital object may contain information regarding usage terms and restrictions, the sources and contributors of the underlying information components, information on how to negotiate special arrangements and so on.[12] When using an intelligent identifier, there is no need for central registries of metadata. For a transaction in an object, a wide array of metadata can be required, such as data regarding the author, copyright owner and copyright fee. Thus, the intelligent identifier will be quite lengthy and diverse.

At present, the concept of simple identifiers seems more suitable for use in digital (multi)media. The different kinds of content that have to be described encompass much more than just the traditional text and pictures, and include for example sound and moving pictures. Furthermore, it is not clear at this point what metadata will need to be added to an object. Moreover, information that is subject to change, such as data concerning a work that has passed out of copyright and into the public domain, can be kept up to date in a repository.[13] Therefore, an unintelligent identifier which is linked to separate metadata information is probably more suitable for use in a digital environment.

Another issue that needs to be addressed with regard to identifiers, is the question of granularity. Currently, there are identifiers which, for instance, identify an entire book, a serial publication or a specific issue of a serial or a specific contribution within an issue. With the help of digital identifiers, it is feasible to identify even the smallest possible item of information and its rights owner, even to the level of components of a document and an individual quotation. To what degree of granularity of identification does content need to be identified for online commerce in content to be effective? This question will be answered by market demand as more granular identifiers are created with the development of the relevant market.[14] Another question that arises is the effect on the existing copyright exemptions, such as the quotation right, when such a fine level of granularity is established and individual 'grains' are subjected to licensing.[15]

---

11 Paskin 1997.

12 CNRI White Paper of Cross-Industry Working Team, 'Managing Access to Digital Information: An Approach Based on Digital Objects and Stated Operations', May 1997.

13 Clark and Koskinen 1997, pp. 227-242.

14 DOI website, <http://www.doi.org>.

15 See Guibault, elsewhere in this volume, p. 140.

2.2 ISBN

ISBN is an identification system for books and other media which allows for order-processing by booksellers, libraries, universities, wholesalers and distributors. The ISBN system was established as a standard for books and other monographic publications. Today, the scope of the system has expanded to include other media such as spoken word audio-cassettes, video-cassettes and electronic media. Virtually every item sold in a bookstore requires an ISBN as increasing numbers of publishing systems base their entire inventory on the ISBN. It is assigned shortly before publication so that it can be printed on the book's title page.

An ISBN is a ten-digit number that uniquely identifies a title or edition of a title and is unique to that title or edition. The ten digits represent four components: the country code or a region in which one specific language is spoken; a code identifying the publisher; some digits that refer to the title and a last digit that is a control or check digit calculated by a special formula to protect against errors in the ISBN. The number of digits comprised by each of the components differs from country to country. An ISBN can be structured in the following manner: ISBN 90-12345-67-9. In this random example 90 indicates that the publication is in Dutch (90 is the number allocated to the Netherlands and Flanders); 12345 represents the publisher; 67 refers to the title (comprising all bibliographic details) and 9 is a check digit. Due to the abundance of publications from countries where English is the prevailing language, both the 0 and the 1 refer to books published in those countries.[16]

2.3 OTHER IDENTIFIERS

All audio-visual and two-dimensional objects capable of copyright protection should be uniquely identified for an electronic copyright management system (ECMS) to be effectively implemented. Various systems have recently been proposed and a number of standards have been or are currently being developed.[17] For (parts of) publications, these standards include the International Standard Serial Numbering (ISSN) which uniquely identifies a serial publication; the Serial Item and Contribution Identifier (SICI) which identifies a specific issue of a serial or a specific contribution within an issue; and the Book Item and Contribution Identifier (BICI), which is being developed to identify contributions for non-serial items. The BICI can be used to identify a component such as a chapter or an introduction within a book or a specific volume within a multi-volume work.[18]

---

16 *Handleiding*, *supra* n. 8.

17 The following enumeration of standards is not claimed to be exhaustive and does not follow a particular order.

18 For identifiers see Green and Bide 1996 and Lynch.

The ISSN is the internationally used eight-digit standardised code for the identification of any serial publication, printed or available in any other medium. The criterion which defines a serial publication is that its component parts are published successively under the same title for a period of time without a predetermined final component. The ISSN is a numeric code used as an identifier which has no signification in and of itself and does not itself contain any information referring to the origin or contents of the publication. The ISSN consists of the acronym ISSN followed by two groups of four digits, separated by a hyphen. The eighth character is a control digit.[19]

With the emergence of the Internet and multimedia, new initiatives have been taken to develop global digital identification standard systems for creative works. The International Confederation of Societies of Authors and Composers (CISAC) has launched the Common Information System plan (CIS) which includes WorksNet, a global system for managing information about works, their creators and owners, embracing both the International Standard Work Code (ISWC) and the International Standard Audiovisual Number (ISAN).

WorksNet promises to provide: accurate information about works and their creators and owners; a global standard for exchanging information about the use of creative works; faster royalty payment; the tracking of the use of works; increased protection for creators and copyright owners and lower costs of rights administration.[20] WorksNet combines an identification code and an international data exchange network and is meant to enhance the efficiency of performance measurement and payment systems for creators and copyright-holders in the digital age.[21]

The ISCW system involves the allocation of a number to a creative work and is intended eventually to encompass all such works. The ISCW has already been introduced for musical works. ISCWs for other works are expected to be introduced in the near future. The ISCW for music will facilitate fully automatic recognition of the use of compositions in any recorded media when the ISCW is stored as an electronic fingerprint or when linked to other standard numbers such as ISRC in a database. An ISWC is a dumb identifier composed of a letter indicating the kind of work, followed by nine digits and a check digit. It can only be assigned when all the authors of the work have an international Compositeur, Auteur, Editeur (CAE) number. The CAE number identifies creators and publishers of text and music with a view to encompassing all CISAC repertoires, at which point it will be renamed the Interested Party (IP) number.[22]

The ISAN is a unique digital code intended to be assigned to each individual audio-visual work, consisting of an animated series of images with or without

19 ISSN web site, <http://www.issn.org>.
20 CISAC Web site, <http://www.cisac.org>.
21 *Ibid.*
22 *Ibid.*

sound, such as a movie or a television programme, a video-clip or a multimedia work. Different versions of a work (for example, full-length or abridged versions or colour versus black and white) will have different ISAN numbers.[23]

Other identifiers include the International Standard Music Number (ISMN), identifying the published edition of printed music, and the EAN/UPC, a cross-industry article number for consumer products which identifies the carrier of the recorded music and can take the form of a bar-code.[24]

The ISRC is the International Standard Recording Code, a code optionally assigned to each music track on a CD which uniquely identifies a track by reference to the country and year of recording, and serial number. ISRC works by providing a unique number for each individual sound recording which can be inaudibly encrypted at the mastering stage and cross-referenced to computer-archived information. Recordings can be identified by an ISRC, while songs and other musical compositions have their own identifier in the ISWC.[25]

With respect to digital copyright management information, the Digital Object Identifier (DOI) is currently being designed and tested with a view to introducing a standard identifier that facilitates the unique identification of digital content. The DOI system aims at solving problems arising from (issues of) granularity and the presence of different manifestations of the same underlying intellectual content and different versions of the same content.[26] As the DOI is one of the most promising endeavours when it comes to digital CMI and at this stage is most likely to become the 'ISBN for the digital world', the DOI will be addressed in detail below. It should be stressed here that this is not a technical paper. Nonetheless, some familiarity with the technology which underpins the use of the DOI is necessary for an understanding of the discussion of legal protection of CMI in Section 3.

2.4 DIGITAL OBJECT IDENTIFIER

The Digital Object Identifier[27] is a standardised tool for identifying source files of electronic data. It is a mechanism which enables the permanent identification of digital content, including a resolution system[28] that accurately directs Internet traffic to the content associated with the DOIs. The DOI system comprises three components: an identifier (the DOI), a directory, and a database.

---

23 *Ibid.*

24 Green and Bide 1996.

25 The International Standard Recording Code, available at <http://www.aprs.co.uk/repro/isrc/isrcExpl.html>.

26 Bide 1998.

27 It should be noted that the DOI is continuously undergoing further development. Therefore, it may be possible that some of the information provided in this paragraph is somewhat outdated.

28 'Resolution' is the act of getting other information in exchange for an identifier, see Caplan 1998.

The Association of American Publishers has entrusted the Corporation for National Research Initiatives (CNRI) with the task of developing an identification system for digital media for the publishing industry. The Digital Object Identifier (DOI) system which was subsequently developed, is currently being tried out as a prototype by several international book and journal publishers[29] in a pilot programme, and is overseen by the International DOI Foundation. The DOI is not a standard identifier in the sense of being an official standard of an (inter)national standards organisation.[30]

The DOI system uses the Handle system to store and manage digital object identifiers.[31] The Handle system as developed by CNRI, is a computer system built to record and resolve names of items on the Internet.[32] It is combined with a centrally administered naming authority registration service and it provides a comprehensive system for managing and assigning persistent identifiers (known as 'handles') for digital objects. A handle — an identifier which at the same time functions as the name for the object — contains information used to locate and access digital items. When the status of the identified content changes, for example when its location changes, this information changes accordingly to reflect the current state, without requiring any changes to the handle. Hence, the handle and consequently the name for the object can endure changes of location and other state information.

The DOI system involves a central directory since digital content may change ownership or location. When a user clicks on a DOI, a message is sent to the central directory with information on the location of the content. A message telling the system to go to that particular Internet address where the item is located is sent back to the user's Internet browser whereupon the user will see a web page response screen on which the publisher offers the reader either the content itself or further information about the object and information on how to obtain it. When the object is moved to a new server or the copyright-holder sells the product line to another company, one change is recorded in the directory and all subsequent users will be sent to the new site. It is claimed that the DOI will remain reliable and accurate because the link to the associated information or source of the content can be readily and efficiently updated.[33]

The flexibility and ease of modification of the DOI system can be said to constitute an important advantage of the DOI over the Uniform Resource Locator

---

29 For an analysis of the DOI from a user perspective, see Bide 1998. Some view the DOI system as publisher-centric. 'Publisher's Digital Object Identifier' is suggested as an alternative name for Digital Object Identifier; see Caplan 1998. The International DOI Foundation itself claims that it is there "to support the needs of the intellectual property community in the digital environment"; see <http://www.doi.org/welcome.html>.

30 Caplan 1998. The DOI may, however, become a NISO standard in the future.

31 Other applications of the Handle system can be found at <http://www.handle.net/apps.html>.

32 DOI website, *supra* n. 14. See <http://www.handle.net> for the technical details of this system.

33 DOI website, *supra* n. 14.

(URL). A URL identifies a location, rather than the digital content to be found at that location. If one moves a document on the Internet, its URL changes. Suppose this URL is embedded in numerous references on web pages, then all these references need to be changed or else the dreaded "(404) File not found" message will appear on the computer screen.[34] URLs do not identify documents and do not specify logical content, but identify specific locations and consist of instructions on how to access an object. URLs offer a convenient means of making references to materials on the Web; they are not intended to serve as enduring names for content.[35] If some other identifier, e.g. a DOI, would be used in all those references and that identifier leads the user to a directory that maps from the identifier to the URL of the digital document, the problem will be greatly reduced. Each time a digital object is moved, only the single directory entry needs to be located and changed and not every reference to it.[36]

In this respect the DOI resembles the Persistent Uniform Resource Locator (PURL). PURLs are persistent URLs which point to an intermediate resolution service which maintains a database linking the PURL to its current URL and returning that URL to the user.[37] The persistence of DOIs, therefore, is not a significant improvement on the PURL. Eventually, a DOI is supposed to do more than just persistently locate to enable the retrieval of an object. In order for the DOI to be capable of facilitating myriad additional services, mechanisms which can implement these services are needed. To this end, services such as those allowing users to purchase objects need to be defined and application mechanisms need to be developed. DOIs are intended to have an application extending beyond managing resource discovery and distribution, to which resource mechanisms such as URL and PURL are limited. The aim of the DOI system is to also supply a sufficient framework for the management of intellectual property.[38]

The DOI system is meant to act as an electronic branding system for tracking digital objects through the Internet for the purpose of commercial transactions. The exact scope of the DOI system has not yet been defined. Initially, a DOI was supposed to consist of a unique, permanent and persistent number applied by a publisher to any digital object created or accessible in cyberspace. However, discussions about the scope of the DOI are still ongoing and guidelines are being developed. The scope of the DOI system is now defined as extending to digital services for both digital and non-digital content.[39] Thus, a DOI may also identify creations contained in physical packages which are traded over the Internet. The

34 Caplan 1998.
35 Lynch.
36 Caplan 1998.
37 Green and Bide 1996.
38 Paskin 1998.
39 Paskin 1998.

metadata to be registered with the DOI will include information on whether the object is electronic or physical.

In short, the DOI routes the user through a central directory that will instantaneously locate the current repository of the document. Clicking on a DOI connection will do one of two things: either instantly download the document itself or present a response screen containing information about how to purchase the content. In addition to an identifier and a directory, the DOI system also involves a database. Information about the object, beyond that displayed on the response screen, is maintained by the publisher. It may include the actual content, information on where and how to obtain the content or other related data.[40]

For a DOI to be assigned, a minimum set of metadata which enables a look-up service is required. It has not yet been decided by the International DOI Foundation what these metadata should be. Most likely they need to include, among other things, information about the assignor, the journal name, volume, issue and page numbers and possibly the name of the first author.[41] For the DOI system to support fully online content transactions it would ideally contain, or include a reference to:[42]

1. content identification;
2. content description;
3. conditions of use;
4. display formats;
5. content protection schemes;
6. financial-transaction information.

This, however, might be too ambitious. To begin with, the DOI is set up for content identification. It is envisaged that in the future, use of the DOI will enable transactions such as licensing and clearing house payments. A DOI in and of itself is not a rights management system; it can, however, be incorporated into such a system. Thus, it could be used for resource discovery, management of copyright and neighbouring rights, trade in digital objects (including public domain works), safeguarding authenticity, and control of the distribution of goods and services.

2.4.1 Structure of the DOI

A DOI consists of a simple set of numbers, letters and other characters that have no intrinsic meaning. Even though the suffix can have meaning to the entity that

40 DOI website, *supra* n. 14.
41 Paskin 1998.
42 Rosenblatt 1997.

chooses to use it, once assigned, the DOI functions as a 'dumb number'.[43] It is composed of a prefix and a suffix which are in turn comprised of different components. As far as granularity is concerned, a DOI can be assigned to a digital object of any size.

The syntax of a DOI is structured as shown below. The entire DOI can be up to 128 characters long. As this limit is not a function of the underlying technology, this number is likely to be increased.[44]

Syntax of a DOI*

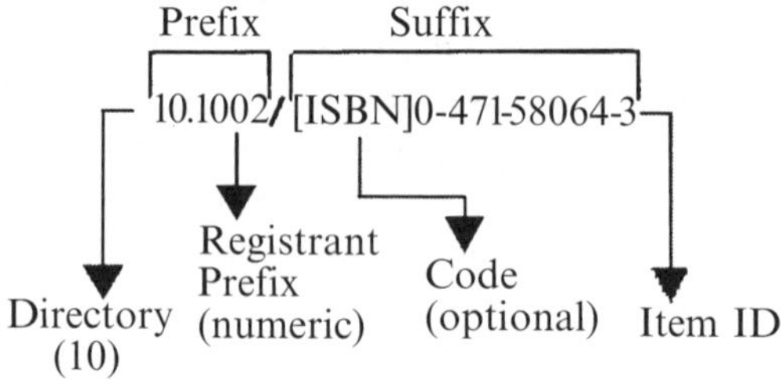

* Source: International DOI Foundation

2.4.2 The prefix

DOIs, together with their associated URLs, are stored in a DOI directory, which is managed by a directory manager. The prefix is secured by the registrant which is the entity that actively deposits the DOI into the system. The prefix consists of two components, connected by a full stop. The first element (the number "10" in Figure 1) identifies the directory or directory manager which maintains the current record for that particular DOI. The second part of the prefix ("1002"), the registrant prefix, is a sequential number assigned to organisations (mostly publishers, but also collecting societies) by the directory manager; "1002" refers to the publisher who assigns the suffix.

The International DOI Foundation and ISBN International have signed a letter of intent to pursue an agreement, stating that the global network of ISBN product numbering agencies will become authorised registration agencies and directory managers for DOIs. Both organisations intend to, as soon as possible, make available to the communities currently served by ISBN International basic DOI registration and directory management facilities through the national ISBN agencies of Germany, the United Kingdom and the United States and over time

43 DOI website, *supra* n. 14.
44 *Ibid.*

through other national ISBN agencies and to encourage the adoption and use of DOIs on a widespread basis.[45]

2.4.3 The suffix

The prefix is followed by a slash, which in turn is followed by a suffix. The registrant chooses a numbering system for the suffix, for example the internationally recognised identifying standard for the object at hand, such as the ISAN for motion pictures, the ISSN for journals, the SICI for a specific issue of a journal or an article/contribution within a journal or the ISBN for books.[46] It is recommended that, if one of these recognised systems is used, the suffix begin with the official code for that particular standard between brackets.

To the user, the DOI will appear on the computer screen as a button, an icon or a hyperlink (see below). When clicked on, a response screen will appear. Response screens may vary depending on the type of objects to be retrieved. When DOIs are used in an internal tracking system, clicking on a DOI might return the actual digital object. In a commercial system a response page may be offered that identifies the object and tells the user how to obtain further information, including purchaser instructions.

DOI on the computer screen*

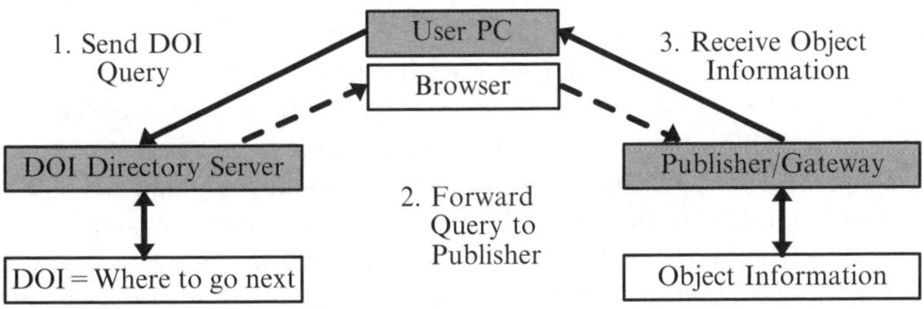

*Source: International DOI Foundation

DOIs might play a role in an ECMS in the following way.[47] A rights owner would apply for a DOI from a 'unique number issuer'. The work along with the DOI would be stored in a database and offered to the public by a 'media distributor' who

45 The text of the agreement is available on the DOI website, *supra* n. 14.

46 The choice of suffix is entirely optional. Other options besides the identification standards include simple sequential numbering, or the re-use of existing catalogue or internal numbering. See DOI website, *supra* n. 14.

47 See Imprimatur Business Model.

would add CMI specifying the terms and conditions of use. A user accessing the database would pay electronically and subsequently download the work. The media distributor would then pay royalties to the rights owner.[48]

Embedding CMI into protected digital objects can be done through watermarking, a method by which an identifier can be permanently attached to a given content. Digital watermarking affixes a coded and usually invisible label containing CMI to a digital object on the Internet. Watermarking is especially useful for the detection of piracy as it is capable of detecting any alteration (or modification) of the original object. This could have the side-effect of deterring potential pirates who will refrain from copying, knowing that their actions could invisibly be embedded in the work.[49] Apart from watermarking, there are other ways to link DOIs to digital objects, such as by embedding the DOI in another object or incorporating the DOI into a secure envelope containing the object.[50]

In spite of the high expectations directed at the implementation of the DOI system, it remains to be seen how the DOI will develop. It is questionable whether the DOI will meet all requirements for unique digital content identification.[51] A number of questions will first need to be answered satisfactorily before a successful incorporation of DOIs can be guaranteed.

As explained above, according to the International DOI Foundation problems with regard to persistency will not occur with the DOI. Nevertheless, scepticism reigns. Many questions have been raised expressing doubt as to the capacity of the DOI system to deliver what it is claimed to be capable of. It is alleged that the DOI remains reliable and accurate because the link to the associated information or source of the content can be readily and efficiently altered. But what if that information is not kept up-to-date, even when it can be done so easily? In most cases it will be up to the publisher to keep the information on the status of the content identified by a DOI up-to-date, but he may for whatever reason cease to do so. Just as nowadays there are publishers who have difficulties in maintaining ISBN records, there will be publishers in the not-so-distant digital future who may not be capable of maintaining the more complex sets of data required by the DOI.[52] And what happens in the event that the publisher's server goes down? Another question which arises is what will happen when copyright in a work expires and the work enters the public domain. And what if multiple vendors sell the same content: do they each assign their own DOI to the same item? And how can those wishing to cite material find the DOI?[53] DOIs cannot be derived from any bibliographic information about

48 Oman 1997, pp. 207-226.
49 Oman 1997.
50 DOI website, *supra* n. 14.
51 Green and Bide 1996.
52 Bide 1998. Bide is not too concerned about this since publishers who are incompetent in this respect will not become players in the network economy.
53 Berinstein 1998.

the object. It seems impossible to find out the DOI of a certain object without approaching the publisher.[54] And lastly, how difficult is it to remove or manipulate a DOI? The International DOI Foundation admits that at this point it cannot guarantee that the DOI cannot be removed. It hopes that third party developers will design authenticity checks and copyright management systems that will block access if a DOI is missing or has been tampered with.[55]

It should be noted that CMI tools such as the DOI may not work as well as rights-holders would hope. For example, CMI may over time become outdated when, for example, copyrights are transferred. These flaws should be resolved — and developers of CMI tools seem to claim that they have done so — for modern-day digital rights management to be effective. It has been said that the development of the DOI has only just begun. The effort "needs now to be extended to ensure that the DOI meets the identification needs of the entire information chain".[56]

3. Protection of Copyright Management Information

3.1 INTRODUCTION

In an environment built on trust in CMI, there is a need for legal protection against removal or manipulation of CMI. What are the existing legal rules that would cover DOIs and other CMI, on the basis of which removing CMI or tampering with it would be considered wrongful? Do these existing provisions provide complete legal protection? What is the relation between existing rules on the one hand and the need to fully protect DOIs, and the question of who can invoke that protection, on the other?

It is conceivable that in civil law countries the author of the work could be protected by moral rights in respect of acts of removal or alteration of information identifying the work. In the United States, section 43(a) of the Lanham Act (the act on unfair competition and trademark law) could possibly offer the required protection.[57] These provisions, however, do not seem to cover the elimination or modification of terms and conditions for use of the work. The relation between CMI and moral rights will be discussed further in Section 3.3 below.

Other areas of law that appear to offer protection against the removal or alteration of CMI and that will be discussed in this part are copyright law, more specifically (contributory) copyright infringement (Section 3.2), unfair competition/misrepresentation (Section 3.4), trademark law (Section 3.5) and criminal law

54 Caplan 1998. To solve this problem a look-up service has to be (and supposedly is being) developed.
55 DOI website, *supra* n. 14.
56 Bide 1998.
57 Cohen 1997.

(Section 3.6). The protection offered by these individual laws, however, varies from country to country and the question is whether this protection suffices or not. If not, then full and harmonised protection on a global scale, which at the same time guarantees the interests of the users, may be desirable.

3.2 CONTRIBUTORY COPYRIGHT INFRINGEMENT

Copyright infringement occurs whenever an act which is reserved exclusively for the copyright owner is carried out without the owner's authorisation. The removal and alteration of CMI in and of themselves do not constitute acts which interfere with the exclusive rights provided for by the Berne Convention. Thus when CMI is being tampered with, it will not constitute a copyright infringement as such. It may, however, facilitate copyright infringement and could therefore be considered unlawful. Different countries will have different ways of dealing with this. In most countries, relief may be offered by the doctrine of contributory infringement which may be considered a tort or a civil injury similar or comparable to a tort. Liability for copyright infringement can be imposed on persons who have not themselves engaged in the infringing activities.[58] Pursuing dispersed infringing users to recover losses suffered as a result of unauthorised exploitation can be quite costly. The rights-holders can secure some of the lost value by obtaining relief from those who facilitate these dispersed uses.

Liability for contributory infringement may arise when a person, with knowledge (or 'reason to know') of the infringing activity, induces, causes or materially contributes to the infringing conduct of another since the activities aid the primary infringer in accomplishing the illegitimate activity.[59] Some examples of acts or activities which have been considered contributory infringement are: the manufacturing and selling of decoders whose sole purpose is decoding pay-TV programmes; knowingly acting as an intermediary for the sale or import of (products which include) unauthorised reproductions; the sale of (video) tape recorders knowing or having reasonable grounds to know that these will be used in the production of a substantial number of copies of protected works,[60] and placing non-infringing advertisements for the sale of infringing records.[61]

It is by no means inconceivable that removing or altering CMI may serve to induce, cause or materially contribute to the infringing conduct of another. When one knowingly removes, for example, the information which identifies the work or the rights-holder, or information about the terms and conditions of use of the work,

---

58 Gorman and Ginsburg 1993, p. 656.

59 See the US case of *Gershwin Publishing Corp. v. Columbia Artists Management Inc.*, 443 F.2d 1159, 1162, 170 U.S.P.Q. 182 (2d Cir. 1971). See generally Koelman, elsewhere in this volume, pp. 17–18.

60 Gerbrandy 1988, pp. 327-331.

61 Nimmer and Nimmer, § 12.04[A][2][b].

and the underlying work can subsequently be accessed without permission or without the relevant management of rights, the removal or alteration could very well amount to contributory infringement. Where, however, tampering with CMI does not enable the work to be accessed, the rights-holder could in effect suffer losses, but not under a contributory infringement regime.

Whether contributory infringement offers a solution or not will most likely depend not only on the effect of the removal or alteration of CMI, but also on the purpose and intention with which it is done. Suppose that, for example, a library removes CMI to enable its members or visitors to access a work and a user then uses the material in a manner that infringes copyright. In that case the removal is less likely to be considered contributory infringement than in the case where it is removed for the sole purpose of committing piracy.

An important aspect of contributory infringement is that not every act that in one way or another furthers copyright infringement is considered objectionable or unlawful. If these acts or activities make substantial non-infringing uses possible, they will not be considered unlawful.[62] Therefore, if (part of) the information accessed after the removal or alteration of CMI is not protected by copyright, because an exemption applies or the work is in the public domain, the removal or alteration of CMI could be considered as done for a non-infringing purpose. In that case, removing or altering CMI would probably not amount to (contributory) infringement.

3.3 MORAL RIGHTS

In nearly all countries of the world, copyright not only protects economic rights, but moral rights as well. Moral rights recognise the personal bond between the author and his work. The following moral rights are to be discerned:

1. the right of disclosure (*droit de publication/divulgation*);
2. the right to withdraw or disavow (*droit de repentir*);
3. the attribution right or the right of paternity (*droit à la paternité*);
4. the right of integrity (*droit au respect*).[63]

3.3.1 Moral rights and the Berne Convention

Article 6bis of the Berne Convention requires recognition of the attribution right and the right of integrity. The moral rights recognised in the Berne Convention are

62 Cf. *Sony Corp. of America v. Universal City Studios, Inc.*, 464 U.S. 417, 104 S.Ct. 774, 78 L.Ed.2d 574, 220 U.S.P.Q. 665 (1984).
63 Goldstein 1993, p. 759.

attributed strictly to authors. Holders of neighbouring rights have only recently found international recognition of their moral rights in Article 5 of the WIPO Performances and Phonograms Treaty (WPPT).

The attribution right has numerous forms, including the right to be known as the author of the work; the right not to have works for which one is not responsible falsely attributed to oneself; the right not to be named as the author of one's work; the right to publish anonymously or pseudonymously, as well as the right to claim authorship under one's own name even after the work was already published under a different name or anonymously. In the context of CMI and its possible removal or alteration the first aspect of the attribution right, viz. the right of an author to be recognised and named as the author of a work, is the most important one.

Even among Berne Union countries, there exist disparities as regards the nature and scope of moral rights. However, regardless of their scope and extent, moral rights are generally not transferable and sometimes may not be waived.[64] Even though Article 6bis of the Berne Convention does not disallow waiver of moral rights, these rights are generally believed to belong exclusively to the author of the work and therefore cannot be assigned to anyone else.[65] In France, for example, moral rights are considered '*perpétuel, inaliénable et imprescriptible*'.[66] In certain countries, upon the author's death the moral rights can be exercised by the heirs, if this is provided for in the author's will. The unwaivability of moral rights may pose difficulties for the enforcement of rights with regard to the removal or alteration of CMI and therefore for the commercialisation of works in the global information infrastructure, for it is unlikely that the creator himself will oppose the removal of the rights management information which includes his name. This will usually be done by the publisher who cannot directly invoke moral rights.

Even where the moral right of attribution is not expressly recognised, in certain industries this right can be based not only on an express contractual provision, but may also arise from the usage and custom of the medium in which the work is or will be exploited, in the absence of a contrary contractual provision.[67] An example of this is that of the motion picture industry, where the author's right to credit — the right to require use of his name in a credit line — may be inferred from commercial practice. In order for such a right to be inferred, custom and usage will have to be steady and continuous. A Dutch court decided against a publisher who claimed that it is customary in scientific publishing that the name of the publisher and not that of the author is mentioned to indicate authorship. The court found that in practice the indication of authorship may consist of the name of the publisher, or the name of the author or rights-holder and in some instances of both.[68] Moreover, in the

64 Ricketson 1987, p. 467.

65 There is no absolute agreement on this. See for example Nimmer and Nimmer, p. 8D: 9.

66 Art. L. 121-1 of the French Act on Intellectual Property.

67 Nimmer and Nimmer, § 8D.03[A][3].

68 *Brouwer v. N.V. Boekhandel en Drukkerij*, District Court The Hague, 9 May 1988, [1988] Informatierecht/AMI 102.

absence of evidence to the contrary, authorship will generally be attributed to the person designated as the author of the work. In the absence of any such designation, authorship will be attributed to the party proclaimed to be the author of the work when it is made available to the public. In this regard removing CMI which contains information on who the author is will be considered unlawful, even when moral rights are not recognised.

3.3.2 How do moral rights relate to CMI and the digital publication of works?

Does the attribution right cover information which identifies the author of the work such as is included in identifiers like a DOI? Could the removal or alteration of CMI which identifies the work and its author be protected by the attribution right? The attribution right gives authors the right to have their work published under their own name. This means that when the work is published, authorship should be stated in the usual way and in the proper, customary place. For a book, for example, this means that the name of the author appears on the cover, the title page and (possibly) the spine of the book.[69] Would the inclusion of the name of the author in a DOI, separate from the work itself, be protected by the moral right to attribution? The usual way of stating authorship in digital publications seems to be by placing the author's name at the top or bottom of the work. When an identifier is attached to the work, permanently and persistently, this could be considered as one indication of authorship of digitally distributed works. The elimination or alteration thereof could then be regarded as contrary to the attribution right and thus as a breach of the moral rights of the author.[70] On the other hand, if upon clicking on a DOI a response screen is displayed with instructions on how to access the work without stating the name of the work or the author, removing that DOI will probably not amount to an infringement of any moral rights.

Furthermore, moral rights do not seem to cover the elimination or modification of information on the rights-holders or of the terms and conditions of use of the work. Moral rights extend only to copyright management information insofar as the authorship of works is concerned. Moreover, since moral rights cannot be assigned, they are of no use to the publisher or any party other than the author. Hence, moral rights are not the appropriate means to provide full legal protection for CMI.

69 Gerbrandy 1988, p. 293.
70 Lucas 1998a, p. 237.

3.4 Unfair competition

Can CMI be protected by unfair competition law? A great number of countries adhere to the Paris Convention which means that they have some form of protection against unfair competition. This does not imply, however, that unfair competition law has been harmonised.

Unfair competition embraces a broad continuum of competitive commercial misconduct. Such conduct includes misrepresentation which involves any manifestation in words or other conduct by one person to another that, under the circumstances, amounts to an assertion not in accordance with the facts.[71] It is conceivable that removal or alteration of CMI will amount to misrepresentation. In case CMI is tampered with in the sense that information on authorship has been deleted or altered, consumers that would not have purchased the book had they known the work had been made by that particular author, would be injured or deceived. Similarly, in a situation where the licensing terms or information on the conditions of use have been changed, it can be argued that consumers might have foregone the purchase had they known the terms of use.

Unfair competition law is likely to be available in all jurisdictions, but it may be embodied in judicial decisions, tort law or specific legislation. This disparity leads to an uncertain situation for competitors in international conflicts who may not know whether the court hearing the matter will apply the same sort or set of rules that are available under their own jurisdiction. Applying unfair competition law as legal protection against the removal or alteration of CMI, therefore, creates legal uncertainty. Furthermore, conflicts about CMI will not arise only between competitors. When a consumer or a library manipulates CMI, unfair competition law may not apply, thus offering only limited protection for CMI.

3.5 Trademark law

Can a DOI be considered a trademark?[72] Generally speaking, a trademark will include any sign or combination thereof used or intended to be used to identify and distinguish particular goods and services from those manufactured and sold by others. Article 2 of the European Trademarks Directive[73] states that "a trademark may consist of any sign capable of being represented graphically, particularly words, including personal names, designs, letters, numerals, the shape of goods or of their packaging, provided that such signs are capable of distinguishing the goods or services of one undertaking from those of other undertakings". Thus, the legal

---

71 *Black's Law Dictionary*, abridged sixth edn, Minnesota: West, 1991, p. 692.

72 Formal requirements such as registration of trademarks will not be discussed here.

73 First Council Directive 89/104/EEC of 21 December 1988 to approximate the laws of the Member States relating to trademarks, OJ L 040.

protection of a trademark protects consumers from confusion and, to a certain extent, trademark owners from losing their market.

The outwardly visible manifestation of a DOI consists of a string of characters such as in the example given in Section 2.4 above. It is a sign that can be represented graphically and it is used as an identifier that distinguishes a particular digital object from another. The requirement of distinctiveness, necessary for protection to be afforded by trademark law, would clearly be fulfilled by a DOI since it is by its very nature distinct and unique. Nevertheless, a DOI or any other type of CMI is not likely to be used or intended to be used to identify and distinguish goods from those manufactured and sold by others. A DOI could possibly be regarded as a guarantee of quality, in that it will mostly be reliable and professional publishers who have DOIs affixed to the works. The DOI itself, however, is not capable of distinguishing the goods of one undertaking from those of others. Moreover, it is highly improbable that the user will actually see the character string itself on the computer screen and perceive it as a mark. An icon with the term "DOI" will appear and clicking on it will display the response screen associated with the digital object.

If a DOI were to be considered a trademark, its alteration could possibly be considered an infringement, but would its removal also amount to trademark infringement? Generally, the removal of a trademark is not considered use of the trademark and therefore not an infringement,[74] but this viewpoint is certainly not unopposed. It has been argued that removal of a trademark by someone other than the trademark owner constitutes use to which the trademark owner should be able to object. Removing the trademark negates the purpose for which the distinctive sign has been applied thus denying the trademark owner the advantages one can expect from the trademark indicating the trademark owner's association with the relevant goods or services.[75]

Suppose the removal of CMI were to be considered use of a trademark, would Article 7 of the European Trademark Directive then come into play? The Article, entitled "Exhaustion of the rights conferred by a trade mark" reads as follows:

> "1. The trade mark shall not entitle the proprietor to prohibit its use in relation to goods which have been put on the market in the Community under that trade mark by the proprietor or with his consent.
> 2. Paragraph 1 shall not apply where there exist legitimate reasons for the proprietor to oppose further commercialization of the goods, especially where the condition of the goods is changed or impaired after they have been put on the market".

74 Wichers Hoeth 1993, p. 144.
75 Gielen and Wichers Hoeth 1992, § 1020, p. 418.

It could be argued that the condition of the goods, i.e. the digital objects with the unique and supposedly permanent DOI attached to them, has been changed or impaired by the removal of the CMI after the goods have been put on the market. After all, the unique code enables the publisher to control what happens to the digital object[76], and that will have been undermined.

It should be noted that according to the European Commission exhaustion is a concept that does not apply online. In the Explanatory Memorandum to the proposed Copyright Directive it is stated that "Article 3(3) reiterates that the on-line transmission of a work or other subject matter with the consent of the rightholder does not exhaust the relevant right which protects this act of exploitation, i.e. the communication to the public right, including its 'making available' form".[77]

It should also be noted that a DOI or other CMI can contain trademarks such as that of the publisher of the work. In the analogue world, erasing copyright management information from a book by removing the page that contains the ISBN, the copyright notice and the name of the rights-holder (which will often consist of the publisher's trademark) after the book has been put on the market by the trademark owner or with his consent, would probably — on the basis of the concept of exhaustion — not be considered unlawful. Since exhaustion may not apply online, the alteration and possibly the removal of CMI containing trademarks may be protected by trademark law. The licensing conditions contained in the CMI, however, do not constitute trademarks. Consequently, trademark law will, at most, provide only partial protection against the removal of CMI.

3.6 Criminal law

Different countries have different criminal procedures and penalties for wilful infringement of intellectual property rights on a commercial scale, such as counterfeit and piracy. Criminal law is primarily an area of national law. Attempts at harmonising criminal law regarding the infringement of intellectual property have been made at the European level, for example in the European Anti-piracy Regulations, but these Regulations cannot be applied for the protection of CMI. Legislation on computer crime offering remedies with regard to the removal or alteration of CMI, if available, will also differ from country to country.

As an example of national penal provisions, the Dutch Penal Code imposes penalties upon persons who deliberately and wrongfully modify, delete or make useless or inaccessible, data which are stored, being processed or transmitted by

76 Cf. *Lancôme v. Kruidvat*, Court of Appeal Amsterdam, 12 September 1996, [1998] IER 36; and District Court Utrecht, 19 November 1997, [1998] IER 126.

77 European Commission, Explanatory Memorandum with the Proposal for a European Parliament and Council Directive on the Harmonisation of Certain Aspects of Copyright and Related Rights in the Information Society, COM (97) 628 final, p. 34, Recital 4.

means of an automated or computerised work, or add other data.[78] Article 350b of the Code imposes penalties on parties responsible for unlawfully changing, deleting or making useless or inaccessible, data which are stored, being processed or transmitted by means of an automated or computerised work, or for adding other data, if serious damage is caused to the data.[79] Electronic CMI would be considered data covered by these articles and the wilful infringer who removes or alters it could be liable to punishment under Article 350a. This could mean that the removal of CMI by a user for privacy considerations, would amount to an offence under the Code. Article 350b implies that even parties who through sheer negligence or carelessness produce changes in data resulting in serious damage, are liable. This has, in effect, introduced an obligation for *bona fide* users of computers to provide the necessary safeguards to prevent any such damage.[80] These provisions, which have been construed very broadly, could offer protection for CMI, but they are not available on an international scale.

Only in severe cases where the public interest is at stake will the public prosecutor act. If the public prosecutor does not act, criminal law does not provide a remedy. Breach of criminal law, however, amounts to an unlawful act which in some countries gives rise to the application of tort law.

3.7 DATABASE DIRECTIVE

Legal protection against copying of CMI, rather than against its removal or alteration, may be offered by the European Database Directive[81] which gives a rather broad definition of 'database'. For the purposes of this Directive, a 'database' is "a collection of independent works, data or other materials arranged in a systematic or methodical way and individually accessible by electronic or other means".[82] A collection of DOIs will probably not be protected by copyright by virtue of its selection or arrangement. The Directive, however, orders the Member States to "provide for a right for the maker of a database which shows that there has been qualitatively and/or quantitatively a substantial investment in either the obtaining, verification or presentation of the contents to prevent extraction and/or re-utilisation of the whole or of a substantial part, evaluated qualitatively and/or quantitatively, of the contents of that database".[83]

Identifiers are valuable to third party abstracting and indexing services. The maker of a database containing a collection of DOIs may find protection in the *sui*

78 Article 350a Dutch Penal Code, translation by the author.
79 Article 350b Dutch Penal Code, translation by the author.
80 Franken 1997, p. 382.
81 Council Directive 96/9/EC of 11 March 1996 on the legal protection of databases, OJ L 077 ('Database Directive').
82 Article 1(2) Database Directive.
83 Article 7(1) Database Directive.

generis right provided for in the Directive. If the maker of the database coincides with the person who wants to invoke protection against unlawful tampering with (in this case, copying) CMI, the provisions of this Directive may offer some protection.

3.8 CONCLUSION

Certain elements of the CMI may be protected by existing laws against removal or alteration. Removal of the name of the author, for example, will interfere with the moral right of attribution. It is more likely, however, that instead of just one component of the CMI, the DOI representing the entire CMI will be removed or tampered with. CMI does not seem fully protected against such acts by existing laws. Moreover, in many cases it is not the rights-holder who can invoke the protection unless, for example, his capacity as rights-holder happens to coincide with that of competitor or trademark owner. Thus, existing legal rules will only partly provide the necessary protection.

Different countries have different legal solutions for the same conduct, a situation that could very well lead to different outcomes in similar cases which could be an unwanted state of affairs in an era where digital technology is "erasing the legal jurisdictions of the physical world".[84] Moreover, at EU level, unharmonised intellectual property rights and unharmonised protection of rights management information can have the effect of preventing the free movement of goods and services within the European Community. Globally harmonised and complete protection which at the same time guarantees the interests of users may need to be introduced. The new laws that have been or are being developed based on WIPO or EU obligations (which will be discussed in the next section) may offer such protection.

4. Legislative Developments

4.1 WIPO TREATIES

In December 1996 two WIPO Treaties were adopted, the WIPO Copyright Treaty (WCT) and the WIPO Performances and Phonograms Treaty (WPPT). These Treaties comprise substantively identical provisions, Article 12 WCT and Article 19 WPPT, requiring contracting parties to protect the integrity of CMI.[85] The two Treaties will enter into force three months after the thirtieth ratification or

84 Barlow 1994.
85 Since these two articles are almost identical, only Art. 12 WCT will be discussed here.

accession.[86] Within the European Union, the proposals were considered somewhat premature. ECMS and CMI have not yet reached maturity and it was thus said to be too early to regulate such systems.[87]

At the WIPO International Forum on the Exercise and Management of Copyright and Neighbouring Rights in the Face of the Challenges of Digital Technologies of May 1997, there was wide consensus on the idea that solutions with regard to rights management information, i.e. solutions for standardisation, should emerge from the marketplace without state intervention.[88] Standardised CMI has to be developed by the private sector while the government or the legislature will provide legal protection.

Article 12 WCT reads as follows:

> "(1) Contracting Parties shall provide adequate and effective legal remedies against any person knowingly performing any of the following acts knowing, or with respect to civil remedies having reasonable grounds to know, that it will induce, enable, facilitate or conceal an infringement of any right covered by this Treaty or the Berne Convention:
> (i) to remove or alter any electronic rights management information without authority;
> (ii) to distribute, import for distribution, broadcast or communicate to the public, without authority, works or copies of works knowing that electronic rights management information has been removed or altered without authority.
> (2) As used in this Article, 'rights management information' means information which identifies the work, the author of the work, the owner of any right in the work, or information about the terms and conditions of use of the work, and any numbers or codes that represent such information, when any of these items of information is attached to a copy of a work or appears in connection with the communication of a work to the public".

The Agreed Statement concerning Article 1(4) of the WCT specifies that the reproduction right provided under Article 9 of the Berne Convention and the exceptions permitted thereunder fully apply in the digital environment, in particular to the use of works in digital form. This should be taken into consideration in the interpretation of the term "without authority" in Article 12. Thus, the removal or alteration of electronic rights management information will only be prohibited when it is not permitted by law or lacks the authorisation of the rights-holder. In other words, existing copyright exemptions will be acknowledged.

86 Art. 20 WCT and Art. 29 WPPT.
87 Arkenbout 1996, p. 181.
88 WIPO International Forum on the Exercise and Management of Copyright and Neighbouring Rights in the Face of the Challenges of Digital Technologies, Seville, Spain, 14-16 May 1997.

Furthermore, the Agreed Statements concerning the WCT and the WPPT state that the Contracting Parties should not rely on Article 12 WCT or Article 19 WPPT to devise or implement rights management systems that would have the effect of imposing formalities which the Berne Convention or the WIPO Treaties themselves do not allow, or which would hamper the free movement of goods or impede the enjoyment of rights available under the WCT or WPPT.[89] The WIPO Basic Proposal underlines that the use of electronic rights management information is entirely voluntary. The Basic Proposal expounds that in implementing their obligations Contracting Parties may limit the scope of their national legal provisions such that no technically unfeasible requirements are imposed on broadcasting organisations and similar entities.

Article 12 WCT prohibits the removal of information relating to the copyright status of a work. The obligations set out in this provision cover rights management information in electronic form only, provided it is attached to a copy of a work or appears in connection with the communication of a work to the public. However, nothing precludes a broader application of the provisions on rights management information in national legislation.[90] According to the Basic Proposal, the wilful removal or alteration of rights management information in order to achieve financial gain is a matter which, in most countries, will already fall within the scope of criminal law.[91]

4.2 EUROPEAN COPYRIGHT DIRECTIVE

The Explanatory Memorandum accompanying the proposal for a European Copyright Directive[92] emphasises that "the proposal does not introduce radical changes to the existing Internal Market regulatory framework in the area of copyright and related rights. It is the environment in which works and other subject matter are being created and exploited which has changed — not the basic copyright concepts".[93] Apparently, the European Commission does not consider the

89 Agreed Statements concerning the WIPO Copyright Treaty adopted by the Diplomatic conference, 20 December 1996.

90 WIPO Basic Proposal for the Substantive Provisions of the Treaty on Certain Questions Concerning the Protection of Literary and Artistic Works to be Considered by the Diplomatic Conference, prepared by the Chairman of the Committees of Experts on a Possible Protocol to the Berne Convention and on a Possible Instrument for the Protection of the Rights of Performers and Producers of Phonograms, WIPO document CRNR/DC/4, 30 August 1996, notes on Art. 14.

91 *Ibid.*

92 European Commission, Proposal for a European Parliament and Council Directive on the harmonisation of certain aspects of copyright and related rights in the Information Society, Brussels, 10 December 1997, COM (97) 628 final; Amended Proposal for a European Parliament and Council Directive on the harmonisation of certain aspects of copyright and related rights in the Information Society, Brussels, 21 May 1999, COM (99) 250 final.

93 Explanatory Memorandum, *supra* n. 77, pp. 9-10.

introduction of legal protection for electronic CMI to be a radical change in European copyright law.

Article 7 of the proposed Copyright Directive (amended proposal) reads as follows:

> "1. Member States shall provide for adequate legal protection against any person performing without authority any of the following acts:
> (a) the removal or alteration of any electronic rights-management information;
> (b) the distribution, importation for distribution, broadcasting, communication or making available to the public, of copies of works or other subject matter protected under this Directive or under Chapter III of Directive 96/9/EC from which electronic rights-management information has been removed or altered without authority, if such person knows, or has reasonable grounds to know, that by so doing he is inducing, enabling or facilitating an infringement of any copyright or any rights related to copyright as provided by law, or of the *sui generis* right provided for in Chapter III of Directive 96/9/EC.
> 2. The expression 'rights-management information', as used in this Article, means any information provided by rightholders which identifies the work or other subject matter referred to in this Directive or covered by the *sui generis* right provided for in Chapter III of Directive 96/9/EC, the author or any other rightholder, or information about the terms and conditions of use of the work or other subject matter, and any numbers or codes that represent such information.
>
> The first subparagraph shall apply when any of these items of information are associated with a copy of, or appear in connection with the communication to the public of, a work or other subject matter referred to in this Directive or covered by the *sui generis* right provided for in Chapter III of Directive 96/9/EC".

Article 7 of the Proposal follows the structure of Articles 12 WCT and 19 WPPT and is construed narrowly, leaving Member States appropriate leeway for its implementation. For example, the provision does not mandate that the protection of CMI be regulated under copyright law. Similar to Article 12 WCT, Article 7 is explicitly restricted to the protection of electronic CMI; other kinds of information that could be attached to copyrighted material are not covered.[94]

The alteration or removal of CMI in and of itself is not made unlawful. Only those acts that have been executed by someone who knew or had reasonable

94 *Ibid.*, p. 41.

grounds to know that in so acting a copyright infringement would be enabled or facilitated are considered unlawful.

The acts covered by Article 7 must be done "without authority". The Explanatory Memorandum specifies that removal or alteration of CMI with the authorisation of the rights-holder or permitted or required by law (e.g. for data protection purposes) is permitted. For protection to apply, the prohibited act should (potentially) lead to infringement of an intellectual property right.[95] When is removing or altering CMI permitted or required by law? Is it permitted to remove CMI in order to access a work for one of the copyright exempted purposes such as news reporting or private copying? Or does the legal protection offered by Article 7 overrule the copyright exemptions? According to the European Commission, the objective of the words "without authority" is to allow the removal or alteration of CMI when these acts are permitted either by law, e.g. when the work is in the public domain, or by the rights-holder.[96]

The Explanatory Memorandum underlines that since protection schemes such as CMI may allow for the tracing of online behaviour, the right to privacy has to be guaranteed. In the Proposal no reference is made to the 'intelligence' of the CMI; 'intelligent' CMI within an ECMS would enable monitoring of individual usage of information. Individual users should be adequately protected against unauthorised commercialisation or abuse of individual information use profiles.[97] Thus the Proposal does not explicitly deal with issues of data protection and privacy, but the 'without authority' clause as mentioned above will probably allow CMI removal when done for privacy purposes.

The proposed Directive was not only inspired by considerations of protection of copyright and related rights. According to the European Commission, a national approach would also have a negative impact on the proper functioning of the internal market. Discrepancies in levels of protection may hinder the development of new services at the European level and may entail serious distortions of competition.[98]

An interesting question that needs to be addressed is what kind of right is conferred here. Is it a right to collect damages, which would be transferable only after the unlawful act has been committed? Or would it be an exclusive right, such as copyright, that can be assigned to a third party at any time?

---

95 *Ibid.*, p. 41.

96 European Commission, Conclusions of the hearing of 8 and 9 January 1996 on technical systems of identification and protection and acquisition and management of rights, Brussels, 27 February 1996.

97 Legal Advisory Board.

98 Explanatory Memorandum, *supra* n. 77, p. 24.

4.3 US DIGITAL MILLENNIUM COPYRIGHT ACT

The Digital Millennium Copyright Act (DMCA) was signed into law on 28 October 1998. Section 1202 of Title I, which constitutes one of the five sections of Chapter 12 that will be added to Title 17 of the US Code, implements the obligations contained in Article 12 WCT and Article 19 WPPT and reads as follows:

> "**1202. Integrity of copyright management information**
> (a) FALSE COPYRIGHT MANAGEMENT INFORMATION – No person shall knowingly and with the intent to induce, enable, facilitate, or conceal infringement –
> (1) provide copyright management information that is false, or
> (2) distribute or import for distribution copyright management information that is false.
> (b) REMOVAL OR ALTERATION OF COPYRIGHT MANAGEMENT INFORMATION – No person shall, without the authority of the copyright owner or the law –
> (1) intentionally remove or alter any copyright management information,
> (2) distribute or import for distribution copyright management information knowing that the copyright management information has been removed or altered without authority of the copyright owner or the law, or
> (3) distribute, import for distribution, or publicly perform works, copies of works, or phonorecords, knowing that copyright management information has been removed or altered without authority of the copyright owner or the law, knowing, or, with respect to civil remedies under section 1203, having reasonable grounds to know, that it will induce, enable, facilitate, or conceal an infringement of any right under this title.
> (c) DEFINITION – As used in this section, the term 'copyright management information' means any of the following information conveyed in connection with copies or phonorecords of a work or performances or displays of a work, including in digital form, except that such term does not include any personally identifying information about a user of a work or of a copy, phonorecord, performance, or display of a work:
> (1) The title and other information identifying the work, including the information set forth on a notice of copyright.
> (2) The name of, and other identifying information about, the author of a work.
> (3) The name of, and other identifying information about, the copyright owner of the work, including the information set forth in a notice of copyright.
> (4) With the exception of public performances of works by radio and television broadcast stations, the name of, and other identifying

information about, a performer whose performance is fixed in a work other than an audiovisual work.

(5) With the exception of public performances of works by radio and television broadcast stations, in the case of an audiovisual work, the name of, and other identifying information about, a writer, performer, or director who is credited in the audiovisual work.

(6) Terms and conditions for use of the work.

(7) Identifying numbers or symbols referring to such information or links to such information.

(8) Such other information as the Register of Copyrights may prescribe by regulation, except that the Register of Copyrights may not require the provision of any information concerning the user of a copyrighted work.

(d) LAW ENFORCEMENT AND INTELLIGENCE ACTIVITIES – This section does not prohibit any lawfully authorized investigative, protective, or intelligence activity of an officer, agent, or employee of the United States, a State, or a political subdivision of a State, or a person acting pursuant to a contract with the United States, a State, or a political subdivision of a State.

(e) LIMITATIONS ON LIABILITY –

(1) ANALOG TRANSMISSIONS – In the case of an analog transmission, a person who is making transmissions in its capacity as a broadcast station, or as a cable system, or someone who provides programming to such station or system, shall not be liable for a violation of subsection (b) if –

(A) avoiding the activity that constitutes such violation is not technically feasible or would create an undue financial hardship on such person; and

(B) such person did not intend, by engaging in such activity, to induce, enable, facilitate, or conceal infringement of a right under this title.

(2) DIGITAL TRANSMISSIONS –

(A) If a digital transmission standard for the placement of copyright management information for a category of works is set in a voluntary, consensus standard-setting process involving a representative cross-section of broadcast stations or cable systems and copyright owners of a category of works that are intended for public performance by such stations or systems, a person identified in paragraph (1) shall not be liable for a violation of subsection (b) with respect to the particular copyright management information addressed by such standard if –

(i) the placement of such information by someone other than such person is not in accordance with such standard; and

(ii) the activity that constitutes such violation is not intended to induce, enable, facilitate, or conceal infringement of a right under this title.

(B) Until a digital transmission standard has been set pursuant to subparagraph (A) with respect to the placement of copyright management information for a category or works, a person identified in paragraph (1) shall not be liable for a violation of subsection (b) with respect to such copyright management information, if the activity that constitutes such violation is not intended to induce, enable, facilitate, or conceal infringement of a right under this title, and if –

(i) the transmission of such information by such person would result in a perceptible visual or aural degradation of the digital signal; or

(ii) the transmission of such information by such person would conflict with –

(I) an applicable government regulation relating to transmission of information in a digital signal;

(II) an applicable industry-wide standard relating to the transmission of information in a digital signal that was adopted by a voluntary consensus standards body prior to the effective date of this chapter; or

(III) an applicable industry-wide standard relating to the transmission of information in a digital signal that was adopted in a voluntary, consensus standards-setting process open to participation by a representative cross-section of broadcast stations or cable systems and copyright owners of a category of works that are intended for public performance by such stations or systems.

(3) DEFINITIONS – As used in this subsection –

(A) the term 'broadcast station' has the meaning given that term in section 3 of the Communications Act of 1934 (47 U.S.C. 153)); and

(B) the term 'cable system' has the meaning given that term in section 602 of the Communications Act of 1934 (47 U.S.C. 522))".

Section 1202 DMCA does not prescribe the use of CMI. It merely seeks to protect the integrity of CMI by prohibiting the use of false CMI as well as the deliberate alteration or removal of the information. It could be, however, that in the future a court will decide that one has acted carelessly by failing to attach CMI to a digital object. Furthermore, under section 1202, CMI need not be in digital form. Falsification, removal and alteration of information which falls outside the scope of this section, will not be prohibited. Additionally, the section does not address the question of liability for manufacturing devices or providing services which enable the removal of CMI. Rather, it imposes liability for specified acts.

The provision contains a knowledge requirement; accidental or unintentional falsification, removal or alteration of CMI is not a violation. Tracking and usage information regarding the identity of the user is not included in the definition of

CMI. The House Report states that the inclusion of such information within the scope of CMI would be inconsistent with the purpose of the Bill and contrary to the protection of privacy.[99] This seems to be aimed at countering criticism, such as that voiced by Professor Samuelson, that including CMI in digital works will help documents in spying on the user.[100]

The definition of CMI includes a threshold requirement that the information be conveyed in connection with copies or phonorecords, performances or displays of a copyrighted work. The term 'conveyed' is meant to indicate nothing more than that the information be accessible in conjunction, or appear with, the work being accessed.[101] Information identifying the copyrighted work is defined in the first paragraph of subsection (c). Information set forth on a copyright notice is included in the definition of CMI. In the definition reference is made to (hyper)links to a CMI, because deleting or changing a link to the information will have the same detrimental effect as deleting or changing the CMI itself. The definition is flexible in that it can be supplemented by the Register of Copyrights, allowing adequate flexibility for the future when other kinds of information may become important.

Subsection (d) creates an exception for officers, agents or employees of the United States when the removal or alteration of CMI is necessary to carry out lawfully authorised investigative, protective or intelligence activities. Subsection (e) recognises special problems that certain broadcasting entities may have with the transmission of CMI. If avoiding a breach of subsection (b) with regard to an analogue transmission is not technically feasible or would create an undue financial hardship, an eligible person will not be held liable, provided that this person did not intend, by engaging in such activity, to induce, enable, facilitate, or conceal infringement. Averting a violation of subsection (b) with respect to, for example, the transmission of credits that are of an excessive duration considering standard practice in the relevant industry (such as the motion picture and television broadcast industries) may create undue financial hardship under subsection 1202(e)(1).[102]

With respect to digital transmissions, subsection 1202(e)(2) provides a limitation on liability. This provision deals with voluntary digital transmission standards for the placement of CMI. Different categories of works will have separate standards for the location of CMI. According to paragraph (A) of the subsection, an eligible person is not liable for violating subsection (b) if the relevant CMI was not placed in a location specified by the standard for that particular information, provided that the digital transmission standard for the category of works is set in a voluntary, consensus standard-setting process involving a

99 US House of Representatives, WIPO Copyright Treaties Implementation and On-line Copyright Infringement Liability Limitation, 22 May 1998, Report 105-551, Part 1, p. 22.

100 Samuelson 1996a.

101 US Senate, The Digital Millennium Copyright Act of 1998, 11 May 1998, Report 105-190, p. 35.

102 Compare WIPO Basic Proposal, *supra* n. 90, section 4.1.

representative cross-section of the relevant copyright owners and relevant transmitting industry.[103] The eligible person cannot, however, escape liability if he is responsible for placing the CMI on a location not in accordance with standard placement. If a voluntary digital standard has not been set yet, an eligible person will not be held liable for a violation of subsection (b) if, would he transmit the CMI, a perceptible visual or aural deterioration of the digital signal would result or, if it would conflict with an applicable government regulation or industry standard relating to transmission of information in a digital signal, provided that the applicable standard complies with standards specified in subparagraphs (II) and (III).

4.4 COMPARISON

4.4.1 Definition

In comparing the definitions of CMI in the three separate provisions discussed above many similarities and some differences become apparent. The WIPO Treaties and the proposed EU Copyright Directive both protect 'rights management information' whereas the DMCA defines the subject matter as 'copyright management information'. In all, (copy)rights management information is defined to encompass information that identifies the work, the author and the owner of any right in the work, information about the terms and conditions of use and numbers or codes that represent any of the aforementioned information. All three provisions state that the information has to be attached to, or be associated with, a copy of the work or appear in some way connected with the communication of the work or its copies to the public.

The scope of the WIPO definition is limited to the above-mentioned elements. The proposed Copyright Directive contains two extra provisions. First, rights management information is expressly restricted to information provided by rights-holders. Secondly, the information included is that which identifies and appears in connection with a work or subject matter referred to in the Directive or covered by the *sui generis* right of the Database Directive.

The DMCA is more detailed and flexible. Information about the user is explicitly excluded from the scope of the provisions. That is also the only explicit limit for the Register of Copyrights who may supplement the definition of CMI by regulation. Explicit mention of both links and the copyright notice is made; hyperlinks to relevant CMI as well as information set forth in the notice itself are

103 US House of Representatives, Digital Millennium Copyright Act of 1998, 22 July 1998, Report 105-551, Part 2, p. 47.

included in the definition. Both the proposed Directive and the DMCA include information identifying neighbouring rights-holders.

4.4.2 Electronic or analogue CMI

The acts prohibited by the WCT and the proposed Directive are related to electronic rights management information. In the DMCA no distinction is made between electronic or analogue forms of CMI for the purpose of the application of the provisions.

4.4.3 Acts

Liability is imposed for specific acts of interference with CMI only, rather than for manufacturing devices or providing services. The acts prohibited are:

1. to remove or alter CMI;
2. to distribute or import for distribution copies of works from which CMI has been removed or altered;
3. to broadcast or communicate to the public (WCT and Copyright Directive) or publicly perform (DMCA) copies of works knowing that CMI has been removed or altered;
4. to broadcast, communicate or make available to the public (WCT) copies of works from which CMI has been removed or altered.

4.4.4 Intent

All three provisions impose some sort of knowledge requirement for liability to arise. In the WIPO Treaties it is required that the person who performs these acts does so knowingly. The acts are prohibited only when performed with knowledge, or reasonable grounds to know, that they would contribute in some way to an infringement. The word used in the DMCA is 'intentionally' rather than 'knowing(ly)'. Thus, the knowledge requirement is stricter in the DMCA; one is liable, not when knowing or having grounds to know that the act would lead to infringement, but only when acting with the intention of causing (or concealing) an infringement.

4.4.5 Without authority

The words 'without authority' are used in all three provisions. According to the Basic Proposal for the WCT, the Contracting Parties are free in designing the exact field of application of the provisions on condition that the implementing legislation does not impede lawful practices.[104] In general, the objective for the inclusion of the words 'without authority' is to allow the removal or alteration of CMI when those acts are permitted or required by law, e.g. when the work is in the public domain, or where the relevant acts are permitted by the rights-holder.

4.4.6 Contributory infringement

For protection to apply, the prohibited act should in some way be related to infringement of an intellectual property right. The WIPO Treaties and DMCA provisions encompass 'inducing, enabling, facilitating and concealing' an infringement whereas the proposed Directive is restricted to 'enabling and facilitating' only. 'Inducing' seems to be covered by 'enabling and facilitating', but 'concealing' is not covered by the Directive.

The WCT and WPPT refer to infringements of any right covered by the WCT or WPPT respectively or the Berne Convention. The proposed Directive applies to infringements of copyright or any rights related to copyright as provided by law including the *sui generis* right of the Database Directive. The DMCA, finally, prohibits the specific acts when they lead to an infringement of any right 'under this title', i.e. the US Copyright Act of 1976.

4.4.7 False CMI

In addition to prohibiting the removal or alteration of CMI as provided for by Article 12 WCT and Article 7 of the proposed Directive, the DMCA also forbids 'providing, distributing or importing for distribution' CMI that is false.[105] Concern has been expressed that if one has a lawfully acquired copy of a work bearing false information, it would be illegal both to distribute the copy with the false information and to change the copyright information to correct the error.[106] This problem will not arise under the DMCA. It expressly states that the acts have to be performed knowingly and with the intent of contributing to an infringement.

---

104 WIPO Basic Proposal, *supra* n. 90, notes on Art. 14.
105 See s. 1202, subsection (a).
106 Samuelson 1996b.

5. Conclusions

The new opportunities offered by the Information Society to exploit and enjoy protected works and other material call for a re-assessment and possibly an adjustment of the manner in which copyrights have until now been managed. To ensure that the acquisition of rights for the creation of multimedia works is a smooth and cost-effective process and to monitor the use made of (copyrighted) works and other protected materials, the management of rights will have to develop and to adjust to the requirements of the digital age. A much more individualised form of rights management may emerge.

Many expect copyright management information to play an increasingly important role in the future online trade in content and in the administration of rights. Therefore, the accuracy of CMI will become essential to the ability of consumers to make authorised uses of copyrighted works. Arguably, if CMI is to fulfil this role, it may need adequate legal protection. As was concluded in Section 3 above, certain elements of CMI, such as the name of the author, may already enjoy protection against removal or alteration under existing laws. However, this protection will not always suffice, since in all probability it will not be just one component of the CMI that will be removed or tampered with, but the DOI representing the entire CMI. CMI does not seem fully protected against such acts by existing laws. Moreover, in many cases it is not the rights-holder who can invoke protection under existing laws. Thus, existing legal rules seem only partly to provide the necessary protection.

In the world of digital technology, national borders lose their significance. Legal solutions for certain conduct detrimental to copyright owners in the digital environment may, however, differ from one country to another. This could very well lead to different outcomes in similar cases, which would be undesirable. Moreover, especially at the European level, the lack of protection of rights management information can prevent or hamper the free movement of goods and services within the European Community. In conclusion, harmonised protection against the alteration or removal of CMI, which at the same time guarantees the interests of the users and ensures access to information and knowledge for all, would be desirable. To what extent this aim is achieved in the WIPO Treaties and the proposal for a Copyright Directive was discussed in Section 4 above.

Finally, one important question remains to be addressed. Why is legislation being introduced while it is still uncertain and undecided where current technological developments will lead to? The answer to this question depends on one's view of what the legislation seeks to achieve. Is legislation protecting CMI merely aimed at facilitating electronic commerce by establishing a minimum level of protection or should the legislature be more ambitious and seek to enhance the public's faith in the electronic highway? Of course, legislation can steer instead of follow developments. Protection is then introduced so that public confidence in

CMI is strengthened. Consumers want to be certain that the CMI is reliable and that when they pay, their money goes to the rights-holder. The legal protection could thus be seen to be vouching for the authenticity of the material to which CMI is attached. The introduction of legal rules protecting CMI will provide the necessary climate for market development.

Supposing there is a true need for the legal protection of CMI, it could nevertheless be wise to first wait and see how the digital information market develops. ECMSs are still in an experimental stage and it is as yet uncertain exactly how they will operate. Standardisation with regard to CMI tools such as the DOI has not yet come about. And how can we be sure that CMI will not, in time, become outdated? The existing legal rules do not provide complete legal protection for CMI. When eventually implementing the WIPO Treaties or the European Copyright Directive, countries will probably have to adapt their national laws. However, it will be difficult for national legislatures to enact new rules before it has become evident where interventions are necessary to avoid or combat market failures or other undesirable effects.

References

E. J. Arkenbout (1996), 'Nieuwe internationale regels over auteursrecht en naburige rechten', (1996) 5 *IER* 176.

J. P. Barlow (1994), 'The Economy of Ideas. A Framework for Rethinking Patents and Copyrights in the Digital Age (Everything you know about intellectual property is wrong)', (1994) *Wired* 2.03

P. Berinstein (1998), 'DOI: A New Identifier for Digital Content', available at <http://www.infotoday.com/searcher/jan/story4.htm>.

M. Bide (1998), 'In Search of the Unicorn — The Digital Object Identifier from a User Perspective', BNBRF Report 89 (British Library Research and Innovation Report 84), revised February 1998, available at <http://www.bic.org.uk/rights.html>.

P. Caplan (1998), 'DOI or Don't We?', (1998) *The Public-Access Computer Systems Review* 9(1)

C. Clark (1996), 'The Answer to the Machine is in the Machine', in P. B. Hugenholtz (ed.), *The Future of Copyright in a Digital Environment*, The Hague: Kluwer Law International 1996, p. 139.

C. Clark and T. Koskinen (1997), 'New Alternatives for Centralized Management: One-Stop-Shops', in *WIPO International Forum on the Exercise and Management of*

Copyright and Neighbouring Rights in the Face of the Challenges of Digital Technologies, Seville, Spain, 14-16 May 1997, p. 227.

J.E. Cohen (1997), 'Some Reflections on Copyright Management Systems and Laws Designed to Protect Them', [1997] *Berkeley Technology Law Journal* 161.

H. Franken (1997), 'Misbruik van informatie en van middelen van informatie- en communicatie-techniek', in H. Franken et. al., *Recht en Computer*, Deventer: Kluwer 1997.

S. Gerbrandy (1988), *Kort commentaar op de Auteurswet 1912. Commentaire de la loi néerlandaise sur le droit d'auteur*, Arnhem: Gouda Quint 1988

D. J. Gervais (1998), 'Electronic Rights Management and Digital Identifier Systems', study prepared for the first session of the Advisory Committee on Management of Copyright and Related Rights in Global Information Networks, held in Geneva, 14 and 15 December 1998, WIPO ACMC/1/1, 23 November 1998, *Journal of Electronic Publishing* available at <http://www.press.umich.edu/jep/04-03/gervais.html>.

C. Gielen and L. Wichers Hoeth (1992), *Merkenrecht*, Zwolle: Tjeenk Willink 1992.

P. Goldstein (1993), *Copyright, Patent, Trademark and Related State Doctrines. Cases and Materials on the Law of Intellectual Property*, New York: The Foundation Press 1993.

R. A. Gorman and J. C. Ginsburg (1993), *Copyright for the Nineties*, Charlottesville, VA: The Michie Company 1993.

B. Green and M. Bide (1996), 'Unique Identifiers: a brief introduction', available at <http://www.bic.org.uk/uniquid.html>.

Imprimatur Business Model, Version 2.1, 6 January 1999, IMP/4039B, available at <http://www.imprimatur.net/model.html>.

International DOI Foundation, 'A Guide to Using Digital Object Identifiers. For Creators, Publishers, and Information Providers', available at <http://www.doi.org/guidebook/guidebook.html>.

Legal Advisory Board, Reply to the Green Paper on Copyright and Related Rights in the Information Society, Brussels 1995, available at <http://www2.echo.lu/legal/en/ipr/reply/reply.html>.

A. Lucas (1998a), *Droit d'auteur et numérique*, Paris: Litec 1998.

A. Lucas (1998b), 'Intellectual property and global information infrastructure', (1998) 32 *Copyright Bulletin* 3.

C. Lynch, 'Identifiers and Their Role In Networked Information Applications', available at <www.arl.org/newsltr/194/identifier.html>.

M. D. Nimmer and D. Nimmer, *Nimmer on Copyright,* New York/San Francisco: Mathew Bender & Co., looseleaf.

R. Oman (1997), 'From Scourge to Savior: How Digital Technology will save Authorship in the Age of the Internet', in *WIPO International Forum on the Exercise and Management of Copyright and Neighbouring Rights in the Face of the Challenges of Digital Technologies*, Seville, Spain, 14-16 May 1997, p. 207.

N. Paskin (1997), 'Information identifiers', (1997) 10 *Learned Publishing* 135

N. Paskin (1998), 'The Digital Object Identifier Initiative: current position and view forward', DOI discussion paper, August 1998, available at <http://www.doi.org/policy.html>.

S. Ricketson (1987), *The Berne Convention for the Protection of Literary and Artistic Works: 1886-1986*, London: Eastern Press 1987.

B. Rosenblatt (1997), 'The Digital Object Identifier. Solving the Dilemma of Copyright Protection Online', (1997) 3 (2) *Journal of Electronic Publishing*, available at <http://www.press.umich.edu/jep/03-02/doi.html>.

P. Samuelson (1996a), 'The Copyright Grab', (1996) *Wired* 4.01

P. Samuelson (1996b), 'A Prohibition Law glides over Internet', available at <http://negocios.com/tendencias/artic11.htm>.

L. Wichers Hoeth (1993), *Kort begrip van het intellectuele eigendomsrecht*, Zwolle: Tjeenk Willink 1993.

VI. Legal Support for Online Contracts

Bernardine W.M. Trompenaars

1. Introduction

A growing number of transactions are being completed over the Internet. The use of online or mouse-click contracts is increasing. However, much uncertainty still exists about the validity of such contracts. In this chapter we shall examine whether under current national laws a special type of online contract, i.e. the online mass market licence, is enforceable. Online mass market licences contain the terms and conditions under which consumers are allowed to use a product which is protected by intellectual property rights; the enforceability of these licences will be the focus of the first part of this chapter (Section 2).

The second aim of this chapter is to discuss the international and European rules that have been or are being developed in order to promote electronic commerce. In particular, we shall investigate to what extent these international legal instruments support the formation and validity of online contracts. In this context we shall discuss (in Section 3) the UNCITRAL Model Law on Electronic Commerce and (in Section 4) European Council Directive 97/7/EC, the so-called Distance Contracts Directive. Finally, we shall briefly review the Proposal for a European Parliament and Council Directive on certain legal aspects of electronic commerce in the internal market (Electronic Commerce Directive).

2. Enforceability of Online Licences

2.1 End-user licences on information products in the electronic era

An owner of intellectual property rights relating to an information product (e.g., a book, newspaper, CD-ROM or computer software) may choose to commercialise his product by way of licensing. Licensing means that in return for payment (a

Copyright and Electronic Commerce (ed. P. Bernt Hugenholtz; ISBN 90-411-9785-0; © Kluwer Law International, 2000; printed in Great Britain).

licence fee) the end-user will acquire the right to use the product. The end-user's right to use is, however, not unlimited. In a licence agreement a rights owner (usually the creator or publisher) will set the terms and conditions under which the end-user is allowed to use the protected product. The licensor may, for example, restrict the copying or modification of the information product, limit the duration of the licence and the territory of use, or limit liabilities.

Generally, an end-user will buy an information product from a retailer. This means there will be no direct contact between the rights owner and the end-user. The terms and conditions that the rights owner sets to the use of his product will thus be presented to the end-user through the retailer.[1] The question is whether it is possible to conclude a valid licence agreement between a rights owner and an end-user in such a setting. In the software industry this is the common setting; producers sell their software products to end-users through retailers. Since software producers want to set terms and conditions to the use of their products by consumers, a special type of end-user licence has been developed, known as a 'shrink-wrap licence'.[2] This type of mass market licence is based on the assumption that an end-user will be bound by the terms and conditions set by the software publisher from the moment the end-user opens the shrink-wrap in which the software is packed. If the end-user does not agree with the terms, he has the opportunity promptly to return the software to the retailer for a refund. The shrink-wrap licence will be discussed in greater detail below (Section 2.2). In particular, the question of its enforceability in a number of national jurisdictions (United States, United Kingdom and The Netherlands) will be addressed. The issue of the validity of a shrink-wrap licence is significant due to the growing prevalence of a new type of licence in electronic commerce — the *online licence* (also known as 'mouse-click', 'click-through', 'click-wrap' or 'web-wrap' licence).[3] The online licence is somewhat similar to the shrink-wrap licence. It is based on the assumption that an end-user will be bound by the licence terms and conditions set by the information provider from the moment he has clicked on the 'I agree' or 'I accept' button . We shall further compare the online licence with the shrink-wrap licence and discuss its enforceability in Section 2.3. In addition, the role of online licences in online trading of information products will be examined in the context of the Imprimatur Business Model (Section 2.4). This is followed by a discussion of the enforceability of online mass market licences under Draft Article 2B of the Uniform Commercial Code (UCC). In April 1999 the US National Conference of Commissioners on Uniform States Laws and the American Law Institute announced that the rules laid down in this draft will not become part of the UCC, but will be promulgated for adoption by US states as the Uniform Computer Information Transactions Act (Section 2.5).

---

1 See *infra* Section 2.4 for a discussion of three-party transactions in online trading of information products .
2 Also known as: 'box-top', 'tear-me-open' and 'blister-pack' licence. See Einhorn 1992.
3 Hugenholtz 1998, p. 237.

2.2 ENFORCEABILITY OF SHRINK-WRAP LICENCES

2.2.1 A variety of shrink-wrap licences

As explained above, a shrink-wrap licence is based on the assumption that an end-user will be bound by the licence terms and conditions set by the publisher from the moment the end-user opens the shrink-wrap in which the software is packed. In the software mass market industry various types of shrink-wrap licences occur. These types differ from each other in the way the licence terms and conditions are presented. One common type of shrink-wrap licence is a licence where a reference to the terms and conditions appears on the outside of the package, the full text of which can be found in the user guide inside the box. This means the shrink-wrap has to be removed first. Generally a written notice to the user is displayed on the outside of the package to read the licence carefully before using the software and to return the software promptly to the vendor for a refund in case the user does not agree to the terms of the licence. There are also shrink-wrap licences that set out the complete text of the terms on the outside of the package. These terms can thus be read through the transparent packing. Another type of shrink-wrap licence presents only a small selection of the terms under the shrink-wrap and refers for the remaining terms to the user guide inside the package.

2.2.2 Enforceability of shrink-wrap licences in national law

United States

Under current US law the enforceability of shrink-wrap licences is uncertain.[4]

Case law. For many years courts have held that shrink-wrap licences are not enforceable. In *Vault v. Quaid*[5] the court held that shrink-wrap licences were unconscionable for the user, and therefore unenforceable. In both *Step-Saver v. Wyse*[6] and *Arizona Retail Systems v. Software Link*[7] the courts decided the shrink-wrap licences were unenforceable because the sales contract between the producer and the user had already been concluded before the user learned of the producer's licence terms. According to the courts, these terms could not change the conditions of the existing sale of goods contract.[8]

---

4 See Kochinke and Günther 1997; Levi and Sporn 1997; Farrell 1996; Raysman and Brown 1996; DAmico and Oliver 1996; Davies 1996, pp. 52-53; Lemley 1995; Einhorn 1992; Scott 1990, pp. 620-624.

5 847 F. 2d 255, 270 (5th Cir. 1988). See Kochinke and Günther 1997, p. 134; Einhorn 1992, pp. 411-414; Scott 1990, pp. 620-624.

6 939 F. 2d 91 (3rd Cir. 1991).

7 831 F. Supp. 759 (D. Ariz. 1993).

8 These decisions were based on Article 2-207 UCC (additional terms in acceptance or confirmation). See Kochinke and Günther 1997, p. 133.

In June 1996, in the case of *ProCD, Inc. v. Zeidenberg*, a federal appeals court for the first time explicitly validated a shrink-wrap licence.[9] The facts of the case were as follows. Zeidenberg, a consumer,[10] bought a copy of SelectPhone, a CD-ROM database produced by ProCD. The CD-ROM was delivered to him in a package. The text on the package referred to the licence terms in the user guide inside the package. The licence stated that by using the disks, the user would agree to be bound by the terms of the licence; if the user could not agree to these terms, he should promptly return the disks and the user guide to the place from which he had obtained it. Once the CD-ROM was activated, the PC-screen again displayed a text referring to the licence terms (to be found in the user guide or the help menu). Zeidenberg then distributed the CD-ROM data on the Internet in spite of the explicit prohibition in the terms of the licence to commercialise the data. Consequently, ProCD commenced legal action against Zeidenberg for breach of the licence. Zeidenberg argued that the shrink-wrap licence was unenforceable since he did not know its contents at the time of the sale.

The District Court decided the licence was unenforceable. The court held that the licence was not part of the contract of sale because the purchaser could not know its contents before the sale was concluded. The US Court of Appeals for the Seventh Circuit, however, found the shrink-wrap licence enforceable. The court admitted that Zeidenberg was unable to know the contents of the licence at the time of purchase. But at the moment he concluded the contract he had been aware that the licence terms would be part of the contract. He had not rejected the goods after inspecting the package, learning of the licence (in the user guide and on screen) and trying out the software. By this conduct Zeidenberg was said to have accepted the terms. In his opinion Judge Easterbrook refers to Article 2-204 UCC (1):

> "A contract for sale of goods may be made in any manner sufficient to show agreement, including conduct by both parties which recognizes the existence of such a contract".[11]

Judge Easterbrook explains:

> "A vendor, as master of the offer, may invite acceptance by conduct, and may propose limitations on the kind of conduct that constitutes acceptance. A buyer may accept by performing the acts the vendor proposes to treat as acceptance.

---

9 86 F. 3d 1447 (7th Cir. 1996). See Raysman and Brown 1996, and Guibault, elsewhere in this volume, p. 157.

10 Unlike the three cases mentioned above the licensee/user in the *ProCD* case was a consumer, not a commercial user. See Raysman and Brown 1996 (suggesting that the *ProCD* holding may extend beyond consumer software transactions).

11 Cf. Kochinke and Günther 1997, pp. 131-132 (arguing that the decision is primarily based on pragmatic economic grounds and not on sophisticated legal reasoning).

> And that is what happened. ProCD proposed a contract that a buyer would accept by using the software after having an opportunity to read the licence at leisure. This Zeidenberg did".

The Court of Appeals held that "shrinkwrap licences are enforceable unless their terms are objectionable on grounds applicable to contracts in general (for example if they violate a rule of positive law, or if they are unconscionable)".[12]

It seems the trend against the enforceability of shrink-wrap licences is stopped by the decision in *ProCD v. Zeidenberg.* In 1997, in *Hill v. Gateway 2000 Inc.*,[13] the US Court of Appeals for the Seventh Circuit again held a 'pay-now-terms-later' software transaction valid. The Seventh Circuit found that an order-taker does not need to gain the purchaser's assent to the licence terms at the moment the order is placed for the agreement to be binding once the purchaser starts using the software. On 1 February 1999 in *M.A. Mortenson v. Timberline Software Corp.*,[14] the Washington Court of Appeals held that Mortenson's conduct in installing and using the Timberline software was enough to manifest assent to the software licensing terms, binding him to the terms to the extent that they were legal and conscionable.

Efforts of individual US States to codify the enforcement of shrink-wrap licences have not been successful. Louisiana's Software Licence Enforcement Act (1987) was invalidated because one of its provisions was held to be pre-empted by the US Copyright Act.[15] The Software Licence Enforcement Act of Illinois was repealed.[16] At the federal level a new effort is now being undertaken. The National Conference of Commissioners on Uniform State Laws has designed a model law dealing with computer information transactions: the Uniform Computer Information Transactions Act (UCITA) (formally known as 'Article 2B UCC'). The UCITA provisions dealing with mass market licences will be discussed in Section 2.5.

United Kingdom

Under British law the legal qualification of a shrink-wrap licence is rather complex. First there is the doctrine of privity of contract. This doctrine prescribes a direct contractual connection between parties. In the software business there is no such direct relationship between producer and user; software is usually sold through retailers. Secondly, one has to reckon with the doctrine of consideration whereby in order for a licence between a producer and a user to be binding, consideration has

---

12 86 F.3d 1449.

13 105 F.3d 1147 (1997) (2 ECLR 84 (1/17/97)). Similar decisions, by an Illinois district court in *Filias v. Gateway 2000 Inc.* (No. 97 C 2523 (N.D. III. 1/15/98), reported in (1998) 3(6) Electronic Commerce & Law Report, and by the New York Supreme Court, Appellate Division, in *Brower v. Gateway 2000 Inc.* (N.Y. App. Div., No. 750, 8/13/98), reported in (1998) 3(35) Electronic Commerce & Law Report.

14 Wash. Ct. App., No. 41304-0-1, 1 February 1999, reported in (1999) 4(12) Electronic Commerce & Law Report, available at <http://www.bna.com/e-law/>.

15 *Vault v. Quaid* (1988), *supra* n. 5.

16 See Einhorn 1992, p. 412.

to be given. It is doubtful whether merely breaking a cellophane seal can be said to amount to consideration.[17] Courts confronted with a shrink-wrap case will have to apply these doctrines, but may also want to give effect to a shrink-wrap licence. The two may be difficult to reconcile under British law.

In December 1995 the first British judgment on the enforceability of shrink-wrap licences was handed down in the case of *Beta v. Adobe*[18]. In this case Adobe placed an order with retailer Beta for the supply of software produced by Informix. Beta delivered the software package to the user, Adobe. Adobe ultimately did not want the software, and relying on the producer's shrink-wrap provisions, which included a right to return the software, attempted to return the package. But Beta refused and later sued Adobe for the invoiced price. Beta contended that the purchaser had made an unconditional order. The delivery had been made, so the price was due. Adobe's position was that the shrink-wrap terms were incorporated in the contract at the point of sale. The court gave judgment for Adobe. It gave effect to the shrink-wrap licence by applying the Scottish doctrine of *ius quaesitum tertio*. This doctrine allows a party to a bilateral contract (i.e. Beta) to create contractual rights for the benefit of a third party (i.e. the producer). This implies the third party is able to enforce these rights directly against the end-user.[19] In 1997 another shrink-wrap case was decided, the case of *Microsoft v. Electrowide*. Again the court gave legal effect to a shrink-wrap licence.[20]

The Netherlands

Two decisions dealing with the enforceability of a shrink-wrap licence have been reported. The first one is a judgment by the Amsterdam District Court in the case of *Coss Holland B.V. v. TM Data Nederland B.V.*[21] A distributor, TM Data, supplied software produced by Raima, to user Coss. TM Data asserted that the text of Raima's shrink-wrap licence terms were enclosed in the packaging of the software, while this was denied by Coss. When the computer program failed to function properly and attempts to repair it were unsuccessful, Coss sought to claim damages from TM Data. TM Data refused to pay damages contending that TM Data was not a party to the shrink-wrap licence, the licence being concluded between Raima and Coss. The court rejected this argument. It held that a licence agreement cannot be concluded by simply opening the packaging, unless the user is aware that by opening the packaging he becomes party to the licence agreement. Moreover, the contents of the licence terms will have to be clear to the user beforehand.

17 See Goodger 1996.

18 [1996] FSR 367. See Goodger 1996; Lea 1996; Grosheide 1997; Griffiths 1997, p. 4; MacQueen, Hogg and Hood 1998, pp. 201-203.

19 This judgment has been criticised for being only a solution under Scottish law. See Lea 1996, p. 241 (advocating statutory intervention to ensure a clear legal relationship between producer and user); Goodger 1996, p. 638.

20 [1997] FSR 580. See Griffiths 1997, p. 4.

21 Amsterdam District Court (*Rechtbank*), 24 May 1995, Computerrecht 1997/2, p. 63; see also Grosheide 1997.

The second case, *Vermande v. Bojkovski*[22], was heard by the Hague District Court. In this case Bojkovski, a law student, placed parts of a CD-ROM containing Dutch legislation, published by Vermande, on his website. Vermande applied for injunctive relief. One of the legal arguments raised by the publisher was that the student had breached the contract by not complying with Vermande's standard licence terms. A general condition stating that unauthorised downloading or other kinds of copying were prohibited was visible on the product's packaging at the time of purchase. According to the Court, the student had not violated this general condition. The Court interpreted the clause as concerning only limitations of use provided by the Dutch Copyright Act, rather than broader limitations following from contract.

From both these decisions it can be concluded that under Dutch civil law shrink-wrap licences may be enforceable provided that users are aware of the use of such licences and have been offered the opportunity to read the licence terms before the agreement is concluded.[23]

Conclusion

From the case law of the countries discussed one can conclude that the enforceability of shrink-wrap licences is not yet clearly established. Courts do, however, seem to recognise the interests of the software industry in the efficient management of transactions, and for that reason are willing to give legal effect to the terms of a shrink-wrap licence whenever possible.[24] It should be noted that some cases discussed in this section deal with licences between producers and commercial users. One might expect that in a transaction between a producer and a consumer greater value will be attached to the fact that, and the way in which, a consumer is instructed about the applicability of a licence and the contents of its terms. From case law it becomes clear that the enforceability of shrink-wrap licences will be determined by the following factors:

1. The awareness of the user of the existence of a shrink-wrap licence: is a user aware that the product he ordered is subject to a shrink-wrap licence and if so, is he aware that by opening the product's packaging he is taken to have agreed to the licence terms?
2. the user's familiarity with the contents of the licence terms; the licence terms must be available, and
3. the point in time at which the user was informed about the terms.[25]

---

22 The Hague District Court (*Rechtbank*), 20 March 1998, IER 1998/3, p.111.
23 See Grosheide 1998, p. 301; Grosheide 1997, p. 154; Koelman 1998, pp. 117-118.
24 See opinion of Judge Easterbrook, in *ProCD v. Zeidenberg, supra* n. 9; Goodger 1996, p. 638.
25 Compare with harmonisation in European Union of rules relating to unfair terms in consumer contracts: Council Directive 93/13/EEC of 5 April 1993 on Unfair Terms in Consumer Contracts, OJ L 95/29.

2.3 ONLINE LICENCES

2.3.1 Examples of online licences

An online licence sets the conditions for use of a copyright-protected product that is to be delivered to a user online. This chapter focuses on end-user licences. A reference to an online licence thus relates to an end-user licence presented and applied online, unless otherwise indicated. By way of illustration, consider the following examples of how online licences may be presented to end-users.

Example I

In this scenario, the terms of the licence are first presented, together with 'accept button', e.g. as follows:

> "Carefully read all of the terms and conditions of this licence agreement before using this product. By pressing the 'accept button', you indicate your acceptance of the following terms and conditions".

Example II

"Warning: This product is protected by copyright law and international treaties. This copy was installed in accordance with a right to use licence and can only be run under these terms. If you agree to the terms of the licence then you may use the product now. If you do not agree then you may not use the product. If you want to read the licence agreement then click the button marked 'Read Licence'".

[buttons:] *Agree* *Disagree* *Read Licence*

2.3.2 Online licences compared to shrink-wrap licences

An online licence is the online variant of a shrink-wrap licence. There is however an important difference. In an online transaction between a distributor and a user it is technically possible to ensure that:

1. the user knows the transaction is subject to a licence (by way of a notice);
2. the licence terms are presented to the user before he orders the licenced product and executes any download commands[26];

26 It is doubtful whether a consumer can be expected to read the terms. In order to ensure that a user in fact reads the terms and not only 'browses' through them, licence terms should be as short and as simple as possible. See also Farrell 1996; decision by a German court (*Landgericht Freiburg)* of 7 April 1992 ('Bildschirmtext – AGB III'), 9 S 139/90, NJW-RR 1992, 1018.

3. the user takes affirmative steps to signify agreement, e.g., by hitting certain keys or clicking on certain icons, if recorded, which could later be used as evidence of agreement.[27]

Only one reported court decision dealing with the enforceability of an 'on-screen licence' was found.[28]

Legal writers are positive about the enforceability of online licences because of the technical advantages of online licences.[29]A disadvantage compared to shrink-wrap licences is, however, the difficulty of checking the identity and (legal) capacity of the user.[30] These are problems of online contracting in general. Technical solutions may also be found to tackle these problems, such as digital signatures, icons to confirm legal capacity of user, etc. Another question to be resolved is whether a consumer can be bound to the terms of a licence when these are agreed upon by an 'electronic agent'[31], i.e. a computer program used to initiate or respond to electronic messages or performances without review by an individual.[32]

2.3.3 Recommendations

1. From the point of view of consumer protection, in an online situation the best moment to inform an end-user about the terms seems to be before ordering.
2. The 'accept button' should preferably follow the text of the licence, as in example I above. In the interest of both consumer and producer a 'Read licence' button, as in example II, is not to be preferred. A user should be inevitably confronted with the terms of a licence rather than having the choice whether or not to review them, as in example II.[33]

---

27 Farrell 1996 lists seven basic features that any system implementing online licences should include. Noteworthy are also the instructions for drafters of shrink-wrap licences formulated by Raysman and Brown 1996.

28 *Storm Impact, Inc. v. Software of the Month Club*, 44 U.S.P.Q.2d 1441 (N.D. Ill. 1997), referred to in Reporter's Notes, no. 3, to section 2B-208 UCC (draft 1 February 1999; *infra* n. 43). Judge Easterbrook referred to the phenomenon of online licences in his opinion in *ProCD v. Zeidenberg*, *supra* n. 9.

29 See Kochinke and Günther 1997, p. 137; Goodger 1996, p. 639; Raysman and Brown 1996; DAmico and Oliver 1996; Farrell 1996.

30 Griffiths 1997, p. 4.

31 See Levi and Sporn 1997; Griffiths 1997, p. 4.

32 See Draft Sections 2B-204 and 2B-119 UCC.

33 See also *supra* n. 26.

2.4 ONLINE LICENSING ACCORDING TO THE IMPRIMATUR BUSINESS MODEL

In the so-called IMPRIMATUR Business Model[34] current business practices for trading and licensing multimedia documents are reflected. The Business Model identifies the main active parties, their relationships and corresponding transactions in the context of an electronic copyright management system. The main actors are the creator, the creation provider, the rights-holder, the intellectual property rights database producer, the unique number issuer, the media distributor and the purchaser. In this section we focus on the relationship between the two last-named actors: the media distributor and purchaser. Various types of media distributors can be distinguished: technical service providers, multimedia contents archives (libraries, museums) and multimedia content providers (publishers). Within the IMPRIMATUR Business Model the multimedia content provider is the most probable type of media distributor.[35] The purchaser can be an intermediate user or a final end-user. Retailers, database producers, publishers, libraries etc. can be intermediate users. A consumer is a final end-user. The legal approach to each of these categories (professionals and consumers) may differ. National and international legal instruments may contain different regimes for professionals on the one hand and for consumers on the other. Consumers often receive extra legal protection.

A media distributor may acquire digital works protected by copyright from a creation provider. This transaction will be subject to licence terms and conditions set by the rights-holder. The relationship between a media distributor and a user[36] is somewhat more complex. In fact this constitutes a three-party transaction. On the one hand there is a direct transaction between the media distributor and the user, on the other hand the use of the information product by the purchaser is subject to licence terms and conditions which are set by the rights-holder but are presented to the purchaser by the media distributor. One could argue that the transaction between media distributor and purchaser is a sale of goods transaction; the purchaser orders goods from the seller, the seller delivers the goods to the purchaser and the seller receives payment in exchange. However there are essential differences between the sale of goods and a transaction involving digital information.[37] In the first place, goods are tangible property whereas information is intangible. Secondly, the purpose of a sale of goods is to pass title in tangible property; a transaction involving intellectual property entails a licence. Unlike the average sale of goods the

---

34 Version 2, IMP/4039-A, 21 November 1997, see also The Business Model Synthesis, January 1999; both documents are available at: <http://www.imprimatur.net/download.htm>

35 See Business Model, *supra* n. 34, para. 4.6.1.1.

36 The more neutral term 'user' is to be preferred over 'purchaser'. See e.g., definition of 'user' in s. 1(2) of the German Multimedia Act (*Gesetz zur Regelung der Rahmenbedingungen für Informations- und Kommunikationsdienste*), available at <http://www.iid.de/rahmen>.

37 See e.g., notion of 'teleservices' in s. 1 of the German Multimedia Act, *supra* n. 36. See also Hugenholtz 1998, p. 240; Sander and Bartels 1998, pp. 411-412; Sander 1997a, pp. 261-264.

purpose of a transaction in digital information is not to pass title but to grant rights and privileges in the use of the information to the licensee.[38] Therefore we prefer to qualify the transaction between media distributor and user as a combination of a 'service'and a licence. It is the media distributor who renders a service to the user by allowing him to download a digital work. The use of the work is, however, subject to licence terms and conditions set by the rights-holder. These terms are presented to the user by the media distributor. The conceptual differences between a sale of goods and a transaction involving digital information have been the main motive for the US National Conference of Commissioners on Uniform State Laws to draft a uniform law dealing specifically with transactions in information,[39] Article 2B of the UCC (later renamed Uniform Computer Information Transactions Act), as distinct from Article 2 UCC which deals with the sale of goods.[40]

A media distributor will store the information products he acquires in databases on a server. He may want to sell the products via public networks such as the Internet. For that purpose he may advertise these digital works in a catalogue which is accessible on the network. Net-users, whether professionals or consumers, may browse the catalogue, and purchase digital works online. After payment of the price requested for the copy, the media distributor will generate a personalised copy of the work and will allow the purchaser to download it.

A purchaser will be subject to a licence containing the terms and conditions under which the purchased digital product may be used. The terms will restrict the user from making further copies for distribution and exploitation. They may also limit the duration of the licence and the territory of use; they may also limit liabilities and disclaim warranties. These licence terms are set by the rights-holder. They will be presented to the user by the media distributor. In electronic commerce these terms will be presented to the user online, most probably before payment can be made and before the product can be downloaded.

2.5 ENFORCEABILITY OF ONLINE LICENCES UNDER THE UNIFORM COMPUTER INFORMATION TRANSACTIONS ACT

2.5.1 Special regime for mass market licences in the Uniform Computer Information Transactions Act

Some years ago committees of the National Conference of Commissioners on Uniform State Laws (Conference), the American Bar Association and other interest

38 See Uniform Commercial Code Revised Article 2B, Preface (1 December 1995), I-II, available at <http://www.law.penn.edu/library/ulc/>.

39 The initial draft of Article 2B UCC (1 December 1995) was restricted to transactions in digital information. Later drafts covered all kinds of transactions in information regardless of technology.

40 See *infra* Section 2.5.

groups concluded that information transactions differ substantially from transactions involving the sale of goods and represent an important commercial interest in today's economy. Therefore it was decided to develop uniform law treatment of information transactions, and to do this by drafting a separate statute on information transactions in the Uniform Commercial Code, a new Article 2B UCC.[41] The first draft dates from December 1995; several amended drafts have followed. The law has been finally adopted not as Article 2B UCC but as the Uniform Computer Information Transactions Act (UCITA), at the annual meeting of the Conference in the summer of 1999. It was targeted by the Conference for immediate introduction and enactment in the 50 US States, the Columbia District, Puerto Rico and the US Virgin Islands.[42]

In this chapter, we shall refer to the law by its original name (Draft Article 2B UCC), since the final text of the UCITA was not yet available at the time of writing. Draft Article 2B UCC consists of approximately 100 sections. In our discussion we shall focus on Draft Section 2B-208 UCC, which deals with mass market licences.

2.5.2 Draft Section 2B-208 UCC: mass market licences

A mass-market licence is defined as 'a standard form that is prepared for and used in a mass-market transaction' (Draft Section 2B-102 UCC). In its version of 1 February 1999[43] Draft Section 2B-208 UCC reads as follows:

> "(a) A party adopts the terms of a mass-market licence for purposes of Section 2B-207 only if the party agrees to the licence, by manifesting assent or otherwise, before or during the party's initial performance or use of or access to the information. A term is not part of the licence if:
> (1) if it is unconscionable under Section 2B-110 or is unenforceable under Section 2B-105(a) or (b); or;
> (2) subject to Section 2B-301, the term conflicts with terms to which the parties to the licence expressly agreed.
> (b) If a licencee does not have an opportunity to review a mass-market licence or a copy of it before becoming obligated to pay and does not agree, by manifesting assent or otherwise, to the licence after having that opportunity, the licencee is entitled to a return and to:
> (1) reimbursement of any reasonable expenses incurred in complying with the licensor's instructions for return or destruction of the licenced subject

41 For background to Art. 2B, see Samuelson and Opsahl 1998, pp. 166-168.
42 Announcement by American Law Institute and NCCUSL, 7 April 1999, available at <http://www.ali.org/ali/pr040799.htm>
43 Article 2B UCC, draft 1 February 1999, available at <http://www.law.upenn.edu/library/ulc/ucc2/2b299.htm>.

matter and documentation or, in the absence of instructions, incurred for return postage or similar reasonable expense in returning them; and

(2) compensation for any reasonable and foreseeable costs of restoring an information processing system to reverse changes in the system caused by the installation, if:

(A) the installation occurs because information must be installed to enable review of the licence; and

(B) the installation alters the system or information in it but does not return the system or information upon removal of the installed information because of rejection of the licence.

(c) In a mass-market transaction, if a licensor does not have an opportunity to review a record proposing terms before the licensor delivers or becomes obligated to deliver the information, and if the licensor does not agree, by manifesting assent or otherwise, to those terms after having that opportunity, the licensor is entitled to a return".

2.5.3 UCC Draft Reporter's Notes[44]

Draft Section 2B-208 UCC deals with mass market licences, including consumer transactions. Online mass market licences are not explicitly mentioned as a category of licences covered by Draft Section 2B-208 UCC (nor are shrink-wrap licences). But it must be concluded from the text of Draft Section 2B-208 UCC[45] and the Reporter's Notes that this section will surely apply to online licences.

What are the rules laid down in Draft Section 2B-208 UCC?

Draft subsection (a) sets out the conditions under which the terms of a mass market licence become the terms of the contract. These rules apply to records of terms irrespective of when they are presented to the user (before or during the user's initial performance or use of or access to the information). Briefly these rules are:

1. A party adopts the terms of a mass-market licence only if the party agrees to the licence by manifesting assent or otherwise. A party cannot manifest assent unless it has had an opportunity to review the terms before giving assent. This means the terms must be available for review and called to the person's attention in a manner such that a reasonable person ought to have noticed them.[46]

44 The following explanation is based upon the Draft 'Reporter's Notes' to Draft Section 2B-208 UCC (1 February 1999).

45 See e.g., Draft subsection (b)(2).

46 See Draft Reporter's Notes to Draft Section 2B-208, no. 2a.

2. A term does not, however, become part of the contract if it is unconscionable under Section 2B-110 [47] or unenforceable under Section 2B-105(a) or (b), or if it conflicts with terms to which the parties to the licence have expressly agreed.

Depending on the moment of presentation of the licence terms, a licensee will have additional rights, alongside the general protection created for all mass market licences. In this context a distinction is made between so-called 'pre-payment licences' and 'post-payment licences'. Pre-payment licences are licences whereby the licence terms are presented to the user for review before he becomes obliged to pay, whereas the terms of a post-payment licence are presented to the user after the obligation to pay arises. In practice shrink-wrap licences are typically post-payment licences. By creating additional rights for the licensee the drafters of this section wished to prevent abuse.[48] They also sought to encourage licensors to, wherever practicable, present the terms of the licence before payment.[49] For online licences it may be technically possible to present the terms before payment.

The rules laid down in Draft subsection (b) deal with 'post-payment licences'. In case of a post-payment licence the licensee has the following additional rights: a right to return, right to reimbursement and a right to compensation. The objective of this provision is to guarantee the licensee a real opportunity to review and an effective choice to accept or reject a licence. Thus the licensee has a (cost-free) right to reject the proposed licence.

In case of online presentation of licences a licensor may not only be confronted with reimbursement claims but also with a special claim for compensation. This is because Draft subsection (b)(2) creates a right to compensation for any reasonable and foreseeable costs for restoring an information processing system caused by the installation of information which enables review of the licence terms. It is clear that this right to compensation applies only to licences presented digitally and not to licences presented on paper (such as shrink-wrap licences).

It should be emphasised that one consequence of the difference in treatment of 'pre-payment' and 'post-payment' licences under Draft Section 2B-208 UCC, is that a user will not have any right to a refund, reimbursement or compensation if a licence is presented before payment, whether online or on paper. It will thus be a strong incentive for a licensor to present his licence terms before payment by the licensee. For instance, remote publishers who want to prevent reimbursement and compensation claims from end-users may develop their online commerce system technically in such a way that licence terms will always be presented before payment.

New in this Draft is subsection (c) which creates a return right for licensors as well. Here the drafters seem to anticipate future changes in contracting practices:

47 The unconscionability doctrine invalidates terms that are bizarre and oppressive and hidden in boilerplate language. See *ibid.*, no. 2b.

48 See *ibid.*, no. 4.

49 See *ibid.*, no. 1.

"it recognizes that in the mass market, under developing technologies, the concept of requiring this right [to return] may apply to either the licensee or the licensor, whichever is asked to assent to a record presented after the initial agreement".[50]

2.5.4 *Conclusions*

Our conclusions with respect to online mass market licences under Draft Section 2B-208 UCC are:

1. Online licences are enforceable under Draft Section 2B-208 UCC.
2. Online licence terms can be presented both before or after payment by the licensee.
3. If an online licence is first presented to a licensee after payment, however, a licensee has additional rights, i.e. a return right, a right to reimbursement and/or a right to special compensation. If an online licence is presented before payment a licensee has no such rights.
4. Because of the additional rights of the licensee in case of a post-payment licence, licensors may be motivated to present their licence terms before payment.

3. The UNCITRAL Model Law on Electronic Commerce

3.1 INTRODUCTION

In June 1996 the United Nations Commission on International Trade Law (UNCITRAL) adopted the Model Law on Electronic Commerce.[51] In this section the character, purpose and principles of the Model Law will be discussed (Section 3.3-3.8). First we shall briefly describe the work of UNCITRAL (Section 3.2). The acceptance of the Model Law and its significance for the formation and validity of online contracts are subsequently examined (Sections 3.9-3.10). Finally, we shall describe the state of preparation of the Draft Uniform Rules on Electronic Signatures by the UNCITRAL Working Group on Electronic Commerce (Section 3.11).

---

50 See *ibid.*, no. 4, under c.

51 Publications on (draft) Model Law: see Caprioli and Sorieul 1997; Heinrich 1994; Heinrich 1995; Hill and Walden 1996; Howland 1997; Mitrakas 1997, pp. 156-163, 268-272.

3.2 UNCITRAL

The Model Law on Electronic Commerce ('the Model Law') was drafted under the auspices of UNCITRAL.[52] This is a specialised commission of the United Nations, established in 1966. The UNCITRAL mandate can be summarised as "the promotion of the progressive harmonization and unification of the law of international trade law".[53] The main tasks of UNCITRAL are to co-ordinate the work of organisations active in the field of international trade law, to promote existing international trade law and to prepare and promote new international trade law. Other fields of activity are the promotion of uniform interpretation of international trade law, and the collection and dissemination of information on national legislation in the field of international trade.

Representatives of 36 UN Member States (usually experts in the field of international trade law) participate in UNCITRAL. These are nominated by the UN General Assembly for a period of six years. UNCITRAL has a permanent secretariat, directed by a Secretary-General, based in Vienna. This Secretariat contributes substantially to all projects initiated by UNCITRAL (e.g., by preparing studies and drafting texts). The preparation of trade law projects usually takes place in working groups, in which UNCITRAL members and staff-members of the secretariat participate. These working groups meet whenever necessary. A plenary session of UNCITRAL takes place each Spring.

Though primarily established to fulfil a coordinating role, UNCITRAL itself has made a substantial contribution to the creation of international trade law. The subjects dealt with have been, *inter alia*, transport, sale of goods, arbitration, finances, construction, public procurement, counter-trade, electronic commerce and insolvency. UNCITRAL has formulated five international conventions,[54] five model laws[55] and various legal standards facilitating international trade.

3.3 Model laws and their non-binding character

A model law itself is not legally binding. National legislators are free to decide whether or not they will issue legislation based upon a model law. Only through national legislation can the principles laid down in a model law become legally

52 About UNCITRAL see *UNCITRAL Yearbooks,* Volumes I — XXVI, United Nations (ed.); <http://www.un.or.at/uncitral>; Trompenaars 1989, pp. 31-53.

53 See UN General Assembly Resolution 2205 (XXI), in *UNCITRAL Yearbook* Vol. I (1968-1970), pp. 65-66.

54 See e.g., Convention on Carriage of Goods by Sea (1978) and Convention on International Sale of Goods (1980).

55 Model laws on International Commercial Arbitration (1985), International Credit Transfer (1992), Procurement of Goods, Construction and Services (1994), Electronic Commerce (1996) and Cross-Border Insolvency (1997). See current status of enactments, <http://www.un.or.at/uncitral>.

binding. A model law should be regarded as a balanced set of rules and as such would best be enacted as a single statute. However, depending on the situation in an enacting state, it can also be implemented in several pieces of legislation. If, or as long as, a model law has not been enacted by a state, its principles can nevertheless be applied by private parties. Parties may decide to formulate their contracts in accordance with principles derived from a model law.

In enacting a model law, national legislators may take into account particular national circumstances. They may supplement or limit the content of a model law. The Model Law on Electronic Commerce explicitly permits a degree of flexibility to national legislators to limit the model law provisions. For instance, various articles of this Model Law end with the following *optional* clause (which an enacting state can make use of):

> "The provisions of this article do not apply to the following: [specific subjects]".[56]

It should be noted that the optional clause was included with a view to enhancing the acceptability of the Model Law. It is clear however that frequent use of this clause will not further uniformity of the law. It may instead raise new obstacles to modern means of communication.[57] It would be in the interest of a uniform international legal regime for electronic commerce that states which decide to enact the Model Law, implement it as a single statute and try, as far as possible, to avoid national variations.

The Model Law also contains a special provision dealing with 'variation by agreement' (Article 4). This provision refers to the possibilities the Model Law offers to parties to vary by agreement the rules on communication of data messages laid down in Chapter III of the Model Law (Articles 11-15).[58]

3.4 PURPOSE OF THE MODEL LAW

The Model Law seeks to facilitate the use of modern techniques for recording and communicating information in various types of circumstances by providing principles and procedures.[59] It does not intend to cover every aspect of the use of electronic commerce. Its purpose is to offer national legislators a set of internationally acceptable rules in order to remove legal obstacles to the use of

56 Articles 6-8, 11, 12, 15, 17. See nos 9, 29 and 51 of *Guide to Enactment of the UNCITRAL Model Law on Electronic Commerce* ('Guide'), at <http://www.un.or.at/uncitral/english/texts/electcom/ml-ec.htm>.

57 Guide, nos 1, 13, 52.

58 See *infra* Section 3.8; Guide, nos 44-45; 'Draft uniform rules on electronic signature: note by the Secretariat' (December 1997), no. 14.

59 Guide, nos 2-6, 13.

information presented in a form other than a traditional paper document. Many national laws contain requirements with respect to the form of specific legal acts, for example, a requirement that a legal act be in writing or signed by hand[60]. If these form requirements are not fulfilled, the legal act will be invalid or void. The Model Law aims to remove these barriers to electronic commerce. The Model Law also deals with the uncertainty as to the legal effect or validity of information spread by or stored in electronic means. It seeks to achieve the same degree of legal certainty for both paper-based and electronic communications (see Section 3.8 below).

3.5 The Guide to Enactment of the Model Law

The Model Law is accompanied by an explanatory guide. The *Guide to Enactment of the UNCITRAL Model Law on Electronic Commerce* ('Guide')[61] is intended to give guidance to states that wish to enact the Model Law. It is also intended as a source of help for users of electronic means of communication who, in the absence of national legislation on electronic commerce, may want to formulate their contracts in accordance with the principles expressed in the Model Law. The Guide is also an important source for scholars.[62]

Most of the text of the Guide is drawn from the discussions on the Model Law on Electronic Commerce held in the Working Group on Electronic Data Interchange (renamed in 1996 as the Working Group on Electronic Commerce)[63] and during the annual sessions of UNCITRAL. A number of issues that were discussed were finally not included in the Model Law itself, but were nonetheless addressed in the Guide. These 'extra' issues discussed in the Guide may also inspire national legislators.

3.6 Structure of the Model Law

The Model Law consists of two parts. Part 1 is devoted to electronic commerce in general. Part 2 deals with specific areas of electronic commerce.[64] Chapter I (of Part 1) contains a number of general provisions, i.e. provisions on the sphere of

---

60 For examples of these form requirements in national laws, see Hill and Walden 1996, p. 18, nn. 5-10, 15, 18; Mitrakas 1997, pp. 41-43, 111.

61 See *supra,* n. 56.

62 See Guide, no. 1.

63 See 'Report of the Working Group on Electronic Commerce on the work of its thirty-first session' (February 1997), no. 9.

64 At present only transport has been dealt with, but in the future other specific areas may be added. See Guide, no. 108. It has been suggested to add special rules on electronic contracts to Part 2. See 'Report of the Working Group on Electronic Commerce on the work of its thirty-first session' (February 1997), no. 6.

application (Article 1), definitions (Article 2), interpretation (Article 3) and variation by agreement (Article 4). Chapters II and III (of Part 1) are the core of the Model Law. Chapter II deals with the application of form requirements to data messages, like those of 'writing' and 'signature'. According to the Guide:

> "[t]he provisions contained in chapter II may, to some extent, be regarded as a collection of exceptions to well-established rules regarding the form of legal transactions. Such well-established rules are normally of a mandatory nature since they generally reflect decisions of public policy. The provisions contained in chapter II should be regarded as stating the minimum acceptable form requirement and are, for that reason, of a mandatory nature, unless expressly stated otherwise in those provisions".[65]

Chapter III deals with the legal effects of communication of data messages between originator and addressee. 'Originator' of a data message is a person[66] by whom, or on whose behalf, the data message purports to have been sent or generated prior to storage. 'Addressee' refers to a person who is intended by the originator to receive the data message.[67]

According to the Guide, the rules contained in Chapter III "may be used by parties as a basis for concluding agreements. They may also be used to supplement the terms of agreements in cases of gaps or omissions in contractual stipulations. In addition, they may be regarded as setting a basic standard for situations where data messages are exchanged without a previous agreement being entered into by the communicating parties, e.g., in the context of open-networks communications".[68]

3.7 SPHERE OF APPLICATION OF THE MODEL LAW

3.7.1 Data message

The central notion of the Model Law is not 'electronic commerce' but 'data message'.[69] It is defined as:

---

65 Guide, no. 21. See, however, *supra* Section 3.3. about the non-binding character of a model law.

66 Natural person or corporate body or other legal entity; Guide, no. 35.

67 Both originator and addressee do not include a person acting as an intermediary with respect to that data message. See Article 2, under c-e, Model Law.

68 Guide, no. 20.

69 In earlier drafts the notion 'data record' was used. See the discussion about the final choice for 'data message' in 'Report of the Working Group on EDI on the work of its twenty-eighth session' (1994), no. 133.

> "information generated, sent, received or stored by electronic, optical or similar means including, but not limited to, electronic data interchange (EDI), electronic mail, telegram, telex or telecopy".[70]

The Model Law applies "to any kind of information in the form of a data message used in the context of commercial activities".[71] This includes information transmitted over the Internet.[72]

3.7.2 National and international data messages

The Model Law applies to both national and international data messages. The drafters indicate that a national legislator may decide to limit the applicability to international data messages but make clear that such a restriction is not the preferred approach.[73]

3.7.3 Commercial activities

The Model Law applies to data messages in the context of all relationships of a commercial nature, whether contractual or not. The drafters give a non-exhaustive list of such relationships. This list includes *inter alia*:

1. licensing;
2. transactions for the supply or exchange of goods or services;
3. distribution agreements;
4. commercial representation or agency.[74]

States can extend the scope of the Model Law to uses of electronic commerce outside the commercial sphere, e.g., its use between public authorities and users.[75]

It should be noted that the rules of the Model Law do not, in principle, apply to the substance of the information, i.e. the commercial transaction, as such but merely to the exchange and storing of data messages in the context of commercial activities and the rights and obligations that result therefrom.[76]

---

70 Article 2(a) Model Law.
71 Article 1 Model Law. As a matter of principle no communication technique (including future techniques) is excluded from its scope. The Model Law is 'media-neutral'; see Guide, nos. 6, 8.
72 See Guide, nos. 7, 8.
73 See explanatory footnote * to Article 1; Guide, nos 28, 29. About the use of footnotes, see Guide, no. 25.
74 See explanatory footnote **** to Article 1; Guide, no. 25.
75 See Guide, no. 26.
76 See Heinrich 1995.

3.7.4 *Consumers*

In principle, situations involving consumers are not excluded from the scope of the Model Law. But the Model Law does not override any rule of law in an enacting state intended for the protection of consumers. So national consumer protection law may prevail over the Model Law provisions.[77]

3.8 PRINCIPLES EXPRESSED IN THE MODEL LAW

The Model Law contains the following principles:

1. *Legal recognition of data messages* (Article 5). Information shall not be denied legal effect, validity or enforceability solely on the ground that it is in the form of a data message. It should be noted that this rule indicates that the form in which information is presented or retained cannot be used as the sole basis for denying legal effectiveness, validity or enforceability of that information[78], it *does not* establish the legal validity of any given data message or of any information contained therein.

2. *Incorporation by reference* (Article 5bis). At its thirty-first session in June 1998, UNCITRAL decided to add this provision to the 1996 Model Law. This provision deals with incorporation by reference in electronic commerce.[79] So-called 'incorporation by reference' is recognised in respect of traditional contracts under the laws of many states. It means that a mere reference to standard terms and conditions is sufficient to consider these terms as part of the contract as if the terms were fully set out therein. Using this technique makes the setting out of lengthy standard terms and conditions unnecessary when negotiating or concluding contracts. According to Article 5bis:

> "Information shall not be denied legal effect, validity or enforceability solely on the grounds that it is not contained in the data message purporting to give rise to such legal effect, but is merely referred to in that message".

This provision seeks to confirm that incorporation by reference in electronic commerce is equally effective as incorporation by reference in a traditional paper-based environment.[80] Another aim of the provision, although not expressed in the

---

77 See explanatory footnote ** to Article 1; Guide, no. 27; 'Draft uniform rules on electronic signature: note by the Secretariat' (December 1997), no. 13.

78 See Guide, no. 46.

79 See Guide, nos 46-1/46-7, and list of references to, *inter alia*, 'Possible addition to the UNCITRAL Model Law on Electronic Commerce: draft provision on incorporation by reference, note by the Secretariat' (April 1998); 'UNCITRAL Report on the work of its thirty-first session' (1998), Ch. III, B.

80 'UNCITRAL Report on the work of its thirty-first session' (1998), no. 221.

text, is to recognise that consumer protection law or other national or international law of a mandatory nature should not be interfered with. For example, in a number of jurisdictions, existing rules of mandatory law only validate incorporation by reference if the following three conditions are met:

1. the reference clause is inserted in the data message;
2. the document being referred to, e.g., general terms and conditions, is in fact known to the party against whom the reference document might be relied upon; and
3. the reference document is accepted by that party.[81]

3. *Legal recognition of a functional equivalent of information in writing* (Article 6). Where the law requires information to be in writing, that requirement is met by a data message if the information contained therein is accessible so as to be usable for subsequent reference. National laws may specify exceptions.

4. *Legal recognition of a functional equivalent of a hand-written signature* (Article 7). Where the law requires a signature of a person, that requirement is met in relation to a data message if a reliable method is used to identify that person and to indicate that person's approval of the information contained in the data message, and that method is as reliable as is appropriate for the purpose for which the data message was generated or communicated, in light of all the circumstances, including any relevant agreement. National laws may specify exceptions.

According to the Guide, "this rule does not imply that the mere signing of a data message by means of a functional equivalent of a hand-written signature is not intended, in and of itself, to confer legal validity on the data message. Whether a data message that fulfilled the requirement of a signature has legal validity, is to be settled under the law applicable outside the Model Law".[82]

5. *Legal recognition of a data message as an original document* (Article 8). Where the law requires information to be presented or retained in its original form, that requirement is met by a data message if there exists a reliable assurance as to the integrity of the information from the time when it was first generated in its final form, as a data message or otherwise, and that the information can be displayed if required. National laws may specify exceptions.

6. *Legal recognition of admissibility and evidential weight of data messages* (Article 9). In legal proceedings nothing in the application of the rules of evidence shall apply so as to deny the admissibility of a data message in evidence on the sole ground that it is a data message, or, in case it is the best evidence obtained, on the grounds that it is not in its original form. Information in the form of a data message

---

81 'Possible addition to the UNCITRAL Model Law on Electronic Commerce: draft provision on incorporation by reference, note by the Secretariat' (April 1998), Annex II; 'Planning of future work on electronic commerce: note by the Secretariat' (December 1996), no. 79.

82 Guide, no. 61.

shall be given due evidential weight.

7. *Legal recognition of retention of data messages* (Article 10). Where the law requires that certain documents, records or information be retained, that requirement is met by retaining data messages, provided that the prescribed conditions are satisfied.

8. *Formation and validity of electronic contracts* (Article 11(1)). In the context of contract formation, unless otherwise agreed by the parties, an offer and the acceptance of an offer may be expressed by means of data messages. Where a data message is used in the formation of a contract, that contract shall not be denied validity or enforceability on the sole ground that a data message was used for that purpose. National laws may specify exceptions.[83]

9. *Recognition by parties of data messages related to the performance of contractual obligations* (Article 12).[84] Between originator and addressee, a declaration of will or other statement shall not be denied legal effect, validity or enforceability solely on the grounds that it is in the form of a data message. National laws may specify exceptions.

10. *The attribution of data message* (Article 13). Basic rule is that a data message is that of the originator if it was sent by the originator itself. Under specific circumstances prescribed by the Model Law, it may be assumed that the data message is that of the originator.

11. *Acknowledgement of receipt* (Article 14). The Model Law provides rules for the situation in which, on or before sending a data message, or by means of that data message, the originator has requested or has agreed with the addressee that the receipt of that message is to be acknowledged.

12. *Time and place of dispatch and receipt of data messages* (Article 15). The Model Law contains rules on when and wherefrom a data message has been or is deemed to have been dispatched or received. National laws may specify exceptions.

3.9 ACCEPTANCE OF THE MODEL LAW

The acceptance of the Model Law will depend on how close its provisions are to commercial reality.[85] According to Hill and Walden the approach adopted by the Model Law is pragmatic and corresponds both to current practices and to the thinking of leading scholars.[86]

---

83 The time and place of formation of contracts is not covered by the Model Law. Here the national law applicable to contract formation is decisive. See Guide, no. 78.

84 Article 11 is limited to messages geared to the conclusion of a contract, whereas Art. 12 applies to messages related to the performance of contractual obligations (e.g., offer to pay, notice of place of performance). See Guide, no. 81.

85 Heinrich 1995.

86 Hill and Walden 1996, p. 22; see also Mitrakas 1997, p. 162.

In his speech "A Framework for Global Electronic Commerce" of 1 July 1997, US President Clinton advocated the adoption by all nations of principles in accordance with those expressed in the Model Law "as a start to defining an international set of uniform commercial principles for electronic commerce".[87]

At this stage it seems too early to judge the success of the Model Law which was adopted in June 1996. According to the UNCITRAL status of enactments of 1 February 1999[88] so far only two states have adopted legislation based on the Model Law, i.e., Illinois (the Electronic Commerce Security Act of 1997)[89] and Singapore (the Electronic Transactions Act of 1998).[90]

Most countries, faced with the growing role of the Internet in electronic commerce, are still investigating the legal obstacles to (international) electronic commerce existing in their national laws. A consideration of possible remedies to remove these obstacles is the next step. Enacting the Model Law may offer such a remedy.

Though it is premature to pass a final judgement on the success of the Model Law, there are indications that national legislators do consider enacting the Model Law. The Report of the Working Group on Electronic Commerce on the work of its thirty-fourth session (February 1999) reads:

> "It was reported that several countries had introduced recently, or were about to introduce legislation either adopting the Model Law or addressing related electronic commerce facilitation issues. A number of these legislative proposals also dealt with electronic (or some cases, specifically digital) signature issues. Other countries had established policy working groups, a number in close association with private sector interests, which were working on the need for legislative changes to facilitate electronic commerce, actively considering adoption of the Model Law and preparing necessary legislation, working on electronic signature issues including the establishment of public key infrastructures or other projects on closely related matters".[91]

As indicated above, according to UNCITRAL's latest status of enactments the Model Law has been enacted in Illinois and Singapore. The Report of the Working Group does not specify the names of the countries which are considering adoption of the Model Law at this moment. Elsewhere we found indications that other countries were considering the enactment of the Model Law.

---

87 See Ch. II, no. 3, of this speech, available at <http:www.iitf.nist.gov/eleccomm/ecomm.htm>.

88 See for latest update of 'status of enactments' of the Model Law, <http//:www.un.or.at/uncitral>.

89 Enacted on 14 August 1998; text available at <http://www.mbc.com/iecsa.html>.

90 The Singapore Act is inspired not only by the UNCITRAL Model Law, but also by the Illinois Electronic Commerce Security Act (*supra* n. 89), the German Multimedia Act and the Utah/ Malaysian Digital Signatures Act; see reference to Singapore at <http://www.cwis.kub.nl/~frw/people/hof/DS-lawsu.htm>.

91 Report, no. 16.

In the United States, a Uniform Electronic Transactions Act is being prepared by the US National Conference of Commissioners on Uniform State Laws.[92] The UNCITRAL Model Law is one of its main sources.[93] In Australia the Electronic Commerce Expert Group has recommended the adoption of legislation based on the Model Law.[94] In The Netherlands the Ministry of Justice has published a memorandum entitled 'Legislation for the Electronic Highway' in February 1998. The memorandum concludes that under current Dutch civil law there are no substantial barriers to the performance of legal acts (e.g., concluding contracts) by electronic means. Even so, it is proposed that special provisions be added to the Dutch Civil Code to encourage electronic transactions. The memorandum indicates the UNCITRAL Model Law on Electronic Commerce could serve as a model for such provisions.[95]

In seeking to create uniform law on electronic commerce among the Member States of the European Union, the incorporation of the provisions of the UNCITRAL Model Law into a European Directive would seem somewhat idealistic.[96] On various occasions the European Commission has expressed its willingness to build on the work already initiated by international organisations in the field of electronic commerce, such as the Model Law adopted by UNCITRAL.[97] However, it remains to be seen whether Community rules in the field of electronic commerce will be influenced by rules formulated by (other) international organisations, like UNCITRAL, the WTO and the OECD. From the Proposal for a European Parliament and Council Directive on certain legal aspects of electronic commerce in the internal market[98] ('Proposal for an Electronic Commerce Directive') presented in November 1998, one can conclude that whereas the European Commission wants Community rules in the field of electronic commerce to be consistent with international rules formulated by international organisations, it does not seek directly to transpose these international rules into Community law. The preamble to the proposed Electronic Commerce Directive reads as follows:

> "Whereas this Directive should not apply to services supplied by service providers established in a third country; whereas, in view of the global

---

92 Draft available at <http://www.law.upenn.edu>.

93 See 'Reporter's Memorandum to Electronic Transactions Act Drafting Committee and Observers', 10 April 1997, and 'Reporter's Memorandum of August 15, 1997', available at <http://www.law.upenn.edu>.

94 Australian Report of Electronic Commerce Expert Group (ECEG), 'Electronic commerce: building the legal framework' (31 March 1998), available at <http://law.gov.au/aghome/advisory/eceg>.

95 *Nota Wetgeving voor de Electronische Snelweg*, II, C, 1.2.4; *Kamerstukken II* 1997-1998, 25 880.

96 This approach has been advocated by Mitrakas 1997, pp. 162-163, 268-272.

97 COM (1997) 157 final, no. 60; COM (1997) 503, IV, 1.2, iii. See *infra* Section 4.1.

98 COM (1998) 568 final, (1999) OJ C 30/4, available at <http://www.ispo.cec.be/commerce>. About this proposal, see *infra* Section 4.8.

dimension of electronic commerce, it is, however, appropriate to ensure that the Community rules are consistent with international rules; whereas this Directive is without prejudice to the results of discussions within international organisations (WTO, OECD, UNCITRAL) on legal issues".[99]

The Explanatory Memorandum reads:

"It is clear that the Internal Market approach followed in this Directive, and in particular the application of the country of origin rule, cannot be taken, at this stage, as a model for possible future international negotiations, in view of the fact that this approach can only be followed when a sufficient degree of legal integration exists".[100]

In its Proposal for an Electronic Commerce Directive the Commission has formulated a European legal regime which applies only to services supplied by providers established in the European Union. It seems the Commission is of the opinion that international rules, such as those formulated by UNCITRAL, may be appropriate to deal with international transactions in which services are supplied by service providers not established in the European Union.

The International Chamber of Commerce (ICC) has also contributed to the promotion of the Model Law. In November 1997 the ICC adopted a new instrument to facilitate electronic commerce: GUIDEC (General Usage for International Digitally Ensured Commerce). According to the drafters this legal instrument builds upon and extends the Model Law principle of recognition of electronic signatures.[101]

3.10 SIGNIFICANCE OF THE MODEL LAW FOR THE FORMATION AND VALIDITY OF ONLINE CONTRACTS

The non-binding character of a model law implies that the content of such a law will only acquire legal effect after it has been enacted by a state. This means, for example, that an online transaction between a media distributor and a user will only be affected by the Model Law on Electronic Commerce if the national law applicable to this transaction[102] is based upon the Model Law. In principle the rules laid down in the Model Law are only relevant for online contracts if these rules are

99 See Recital 20 of Proposal for an Electronic Commerce Directive (*supra* n. 98), executive summary and Explanatory Memorandum, COM (1998) 568 final, section IV, no. 4.

100 Explanatory Memorandum, COM (1998) 568 final, section IV, no. 4.

101 See section I.2, V, of GUIDEC, available at <http://www.iccwbo.org/guidec2.htm>.

102 If it concerns an international transaction, private international law will decide which national law is applicable. See about private international law and electronic networks, *inter alia:* S. Eiselen, 'Implications of Private International Law for EDI', [1995] *EDI Law Review* 9; M.V. Polak,

implemented into the national law which is applicable to the contract.[103] An online contract between, for example, a media distributor and a professional user concerning the purchase of a media work will fall under the scope of the Model Law, because it is a commercial relationship. If the user is not a professional but a consumer, the Model Law may be applicable as well, unless a national legislator enacting the Model Law chooses to exclude transactions with consumers.[104]

On the whole the Model Law is favourable to online commercial transactions. It lowers the barriers of conventional form requirements (such as that of a written document, a hand-written signature and an original document), and it recognises the formation and validity of electronic contracts.

The recognition of incorporation by reference in electronic messages (Article 5*bis*) is important for the development of electronic commerce, for it enables sellers of goods and providers of services to incorporate their general terms and conditions into their online offers to potential buyers, without having to include the terms in their entirety (provided the applicable law recognises incorporation by reference as such).

According to Article 6(1) of the Model Law, online equivalents of paper-based information should be recognised provided they are accessible for subsequent reference. An enacting state may exclude specific categories from this general rule. For instance, in some states licence agreements have to be in writing.[105] If such a state enacts Article 6 of the Model Law, a licence agreement will not have to be in writing (paper-based) but may be presented online instead, unless the enacting state chooses to exclude licences from this general rule.

In many jurisdictions it is not yet obvious that contracts can be concluded by electronic means. National laws explicitly recognising the formation and validity of online contracts therefore appear necessary.[106] Article 11(1) of the Model Law provides that a valid contract can be concluded by exchanging offer and acceptance in the form of electronic messages.[107] However, an enacting state is allowed to make exceptions to this rule in certain instances to be specified in the legislation enacting the Model Law.

(Cont.)
'Internationaal privaatrecht: vangnet voor het Internet', in 'Recht en Internet', *Handelingen Nederlandse Juristen-Vereniging*, Vol. 128, 1998-I, pp. 59-118.

103 Model Law principles may also affect an online contract even though they are not implemented into national law, i.e. if the parties themselves include these Model Law principles in their contract (provided they are not contrary to the applicable national law).

104 See *supra* Section 3.7.

105 For example in Belgium and France.

106 'Report Working Group on EDI on the work of its twenty-eighth session' (1994), no. 37.

107 Article 11 also covers situations in which only the offer or the acceptance is communicated electronically. See Guide, no. 78.

3.11 CURRENT UNCITRAL PROJECT ON ELECTRONIC SIGNATURES

In 1996 UNCITRAL decided to place the issues of digital signatures and certification authorities on its agenda. Following a report by the Working Group on Electronic Commerce examining the desirability and feasibility of preparing uniform rules on digital signatures, UNCITRAL entrusted the Working Group with the drafting of such rules.[108] These rules should be consistent with the provisions of the Model Law on Electronic Commerce, especially with the principles expressed in Article 7 of the Model Law (i.e., recognition of functional equivalents of a hand-written signature).[109]

The draft Uniform Rules primarily focus on digital signatures (techniques involving the use of public-key cryptography), but other electronic signatures are dealt with as well.[110] The draft rules further contain provisions on certification authorities, certificates, liabilities and recognition of foreign electronic signatures. The latest drafts considered here date from November 1998 (WP.79)[111] and December 1998 (WP.80)[112]. During its session in February 1999 the Working Group expressed preference for the WP.80 draft as a basis for further discussion.[113]

An interesting question is what this UNCITRAL project will add to the legislative work that has already been undertaken or is currently being done with respect to the legal recognition of electronic signatures in various countries. Of course UNCITRAL is aware of these developments. Thus it makes reference to the special objective of the Uniform Rules, viz., the prevention of disharmony among national laws applicable to electronic commerce.[114]

The Uniform Rules on Electronic Signatures may be too late for countries that have already adopted legislation dealing with digital signatures (in Europe:

---

108 See 'Report of the Working Group on Electronic Commerce on the work of its thirty-first session' (1997), nos 25-150; 'Planning of future work on electronic commerce: digital signatures, certification authorities and related legal issues: note by the Secretariat' (December 1996). Other issues mentioned for future work by UNCITRAL are: alternatives to public-key cryptography, functions performed by third-party service providers, electronic contracting, jurisdiction, applicable law and dispute settlement on the Internet. See 'Draft uniform rules on electronic signatures: note by the Secretariat' (December 1997), nos 2, 5.

109 The working assumption is that the Uniform Rules should be consistent with the Model Law provisions and include provisions along the lines of Arts 1, 2, 3 and 7 of the Model Law. See 'Report Working Group on Electronic Commerce on the work of its thirty-second session' (February 1998), no. 25.

110 'Draft uniform rules on electronic signatures, note by the Secretariat' (December 1997), no. 4; 'Report Working Group on Electronic Commerce on the work of its thirty-first session' (1997), nos 20, 22.

111 'Draft uniform rules on electronic signatures, note by the Secretariat' (November 1998), referred to as 'WP.79'.

112 'Electronic signatures, note by the Secretariat' (December 1998), referred to as 'WP.80'.

113 'Report of the Working Group on Electronic Commerce on the work of its thirty-fourth session' (February 1999), no. 21.

114 'Draft uniform rules on electronic signatures, note by the Secretariat' (November 1998), no. 12.

Germany and Italy)[115] or intend to adopt legislation in this field (e.g., Denmark).[116] These countries may not be eager to adapt their modern laws to the UNCITRAL Uniform Rules. At least they will not be obliged to adapt their laws if the uniform rules are given the form of a *model* law.

In July 1998 a decision on the final form of the Uniform Rules on Electronic Signatures was postponed. The working assumption was that the Uniform Rules are prepared as 'draft legislative provisions'. A proposal by the US delegation to prepare a convention based on both the provisions of the Model Law on Electronic Commerce and the draft Uniform Rules (May 1998) did not receive sufficient support.[117] The Working Group was suggested to make proposals during its session in February 1999 as to whether the Uniform Rules should constitute a separate legal instrument or whether they should be incorporated in an extended version of the Model Law on Electronic Commerce, for example as a new Part III of the Model Law.[118] However, in February 1999 the Working Group again did not make a final decision with respect to the form of the Uniform Rules. It did express an overall preference for dealing with the Uniform Rules as a separate instrument.[119]

In the meantime, for EU Member States the Proposal for a European Parliament and Council Directive establishing a common legal framework for the use of electronic signatures ('Proposal for an Electronic Signatures Directive'), submitted on 16 June 1998,[120] has become the more important legal instrument. If an Electronic Signatures Directive were adopted,[121] Member States will be obliged to implement the directive into their national legislation. This implies that Member States which have already adopted legislation on electronic signatures which is not in conformity with the Directive, will need to amend their legislation.

4. A Community Legal Framework for Electronic Commerce

4.1 TOWARDS A COMMUNITY LEGAL FRAMEWORK FOR ELECTRONIC COMMERCE

In its communication on 'A European initiative in the field of electronic commerce' of April 1997, the European Commission announced its intention to create a

---

115 For Germany see s. 3 of the German Multimedia Act (*Gesetz zur Regelung der Rahmenbedingungen für Informations- und Kommunikationsdienste*, available at <http://www.iid.de/rahmen>); For Italy see references at <http://www.cwis.kub.nl/~frw/people/hof/DS-lawsu.htm>.

116 See references at <http://www.cwis.kub.nl/~frw/people/hof/DS-lawsu.htm>.

117 'Report of the Working Group on Electronic Commerce on the work of its thirty-third session' (July 1998), nos 9, 10; 'Proposal by the United States of America, note by the Secretariat' (May 1998).

118 'Draft uniform rules on electronic signatures, note by the Secretariat' (November 1998), nos 15, 16.

119 'Report of the Working Group on Electronic Commerce on the work of its thirty-fourth session' (February 1999), no. 19.

120 COM (1998) 297 final, OJ C 325/5, available at <http://www.ispo.cec.be/commerce>.

121 The proposal was due for approval by the EU Council in November 1998, but it was not adopted. Adoption in the near future remains doubtful; see Dumortier and Van Eecke 1999, at pp. 3, 9.

Community legal framework in the field of electronic commerce,[122] to be realised by the year 2000. In this legal framework both the needs of business and consumers are to be met. The Commission intends to draft European rules on, *inter alia*, digital signatures, financial services contracts concluded at a distance, and electronic payments.[123] Concrete measures to remove legal barriers to the enforceability of online contracts, like form requirements and evidence rules, were also put on the agenda.[124] Following the Communication the European Parliament and Council have adopted a directive amending Directive 98/34/EC laying down a procedure for the provision of information in the field of technical standards and regulations[125] and another on the legal protection of conditional access services.[126] In addition, the Commission has submitted the following proposals for directives:

1. Proposal for a European Parliament and Council Directive establishing a common legal framework for the use of electronic signatures ('Proposal for an Electronic Signatures Directive');[127]
2. Proposal for a European Parliament and Council Directive concerning the distance marketing of consumer financial services ('Proposal for a Financial Distance Contracts Directive');[128]
3. Proposal for a European Parliament and Council Directive on certain legal aspects of electronic commerce in the internal market ('Proposal for an Electronic Commerce Directive').[129]

A forerunner of the Community legal framework on electronic commerce, and in particular its contractual aspects, is the Directive on the Protection of Consumers in respect of Distance Contracts of 20 May 1997 ('Distance Contracts Directive').[130] In the following paragraphs (Section 4.2 to 4.7) we shall discuss this Directive with a view to ascertaining whether it applies to contracts negotiated and concluded over the Internet (or any other network) between consumers and suppliers, and what rights and obligations derive from the Directive for consumers and suppliers. In Section 4.8 we shall briefly discuss the Proposal for a European Parliament and Council Directive on certain legal aspects of electronic commerce in the internal market ('Electronic Commerce Directive') submitted by the Commission in November 1998, especially the rules regarding the online conclusion of contracts.

---

122 16 April 1997, COM (1997) 157 final.
123 See *supra* n. 122, pp. 29-31.
124 See *supra* n. 122, no. 45; COM (1997) 503 final, Ch. II, para. 3.3.
125 Directive 98/48/EC of 20 July 1998, OJ L 217/18.
126 Directive 98/84/EC of 20 November 1998, OJ L 320/54.
127 See *supra* n. 120.
128 COM (1998) 468 final, 14 October 1998, available at <http://europa.eu.int/comm/dg15/en/finances/consumer>.
129 COM (1998) 568 final, OJ 1999 C 30/4.
130 Directive 97/7/EC of 20 May 1997, OJ L 144/19.

4.2 DISTANCE CONTRACTS DIRECTIVE: ITS ADOPTION, ENTRY INTO FORCE AND IMPLEMENTATION

The Distance Contracts Directive was adopted on 20 May 1997, and entered into force on 4 June 1997. It is to be transposed into the national laws of the Member States by 4 June 2000.[131]

In The Netherlands the Directive will be implemented into Book 7.1 (on sale) of the Civil Code. In January 1999 a proposal to this effect has been submitted to the Dutch Council of Ministers.[132] As regards Germany, it is suggested to implement the Directive into the 1986 German Colportage Act (*Gesetz über den Widerruf von Haustürgeschäften und ähnlichen Geschäften*).[133]

4.3 OBJECTIVE OF THE DISTANCE CONTRACTS DIRECTIVE

The Distance Contracts Directive aims to harmonise the Member States' laws on the protection of consumers in respect of distance contracts. This will enable consumers to profit from the free movement of goods and services in the internal market. The Commission launched its first Proposal for a Distance Contracts Directive as early as May 1992.[134] With this initiative the Commission reacted to the growing use of new technologies both for offering products or services and for obtaining consumers' orders. The new interactive technologies applied to distance selling at that time were telephone, teletext, home computers (e.g., Minitel in France, Bildschirmtext in Germany, Viditel in The Netherlands) and audiotext.

A Member State by Member State analysis made in 1992 shows that until 1987 there were hardly any laws on the protection of consumers in respect of distance selling. In 1987 Denmark, France and Portugal adopted specific legislation on distance selling. Other Member States (except the Netherlands, Ireland and the United Kingdom) followed in the years thereafter.[135] The legislation on distance selling turned out to be different among the Member States which had, according to the Commission, "a detrimental effect on competition between businesses in the internal market".[136] It therefore concluded it was necessary to introduce "a minimum set of common rules"[137] on the protection of consumers in respect of distance contracts at Community level.

131 Articles 15(1) and 18 Distance Contracts Directive.

132 *See* 'Antwoord op Kamervraag', [1999] *Nederlands Juristenblad,* p. 420; Kersemakers 1999, at pp. 21-22; Van der Beek 1999, p. 29.

133 Sander 1997b, pp. 196-197.

134 20 May 1992, COM (92) 11 final.

135 See COM (92) 11 final, pp. 10-11 (pp. 7-9 and Annex 2 contain the results of this state-by-state analysis).

136 Recital 4 of the Directive.

137 Recital 4 of the Directive.

4.4 SCOPE OF DISTANCE CONTRACTS DIRECTIVE

The Distance Contracts Directive is applicable to distance contracts between consumers and suppliers. A 'distance contract' is defined as:

> "any contract concerning goods or services concluded between a supplier and a consumer under an organized distance sales or service-provision scheme run by the supplier, who, for the purpose of the contract, makes exclusive use of one or more means of distance communication up to and including the moment at which the contract is concluded".[138]

The Directive does not apply to contracts relating to financial services,[139] concluded by means of automatic vending machines or automated commercial premises, concluded with telecommunications operators through the use of public payphones, concluded for the construction and sale of immovable property or relating to other immovable property rights (with the exception of rental), and those concluded at an auction.[140]

Under the Directive a 'consumer' is any natural person acting for purposes which are outside his trade, business or profession; a 'supplier' is defined as any natural or legal person who is acting in his commercial or professional capacity.[141] 'Means of distance communication' are any means which without the simultaneous physical presence of the supplier and the consumer, may be used for the conclusion of a contract between those parties. Annex I to the Directive provides an indicative list of such means of distance communication. This list includes printed matter, catalogues, telephone, radio, videotex, electronic mail, fax and TV.

Interestingly, electronic mail is on the list of means of distance communication, whereas the Internet (or any other open network) is not. Though the list is non-exhaustive, it is remarkable that the Internet is not explicitly mentioned. The Internet is more embracing than electronic mail. In the context of electronic commerce the Internet is a crucial medium. A supplier will give information about his products or services on his website. After consultation of the site, the interested consumer will place orders for these products and/or services, for example by e-mail.[142] The ninth recital of the Directive states that:

> "the constant development of means of distance communication does not allow an exhaustive list to be compiled but does require principles to be defined

138 Article 2(1).

139 See recent Proposal for a Financial Distance Contracts Directive, *supra* n. 128. This proposed Directive is meant to complement Directive 97/7/EC.

140 Article 3(1).

141 Article 2(2) and (3).

142 See also Sprey 1997, p. 1049.

which are valid even for those which are not as yet in widespread use".[143]

It is safe to conclude that the Directive is indeed applicable to communication over the Internet (or any other open network).[144]

The subject of a distance contract can be either goods or services. These notions, however, are not defined in the Directive. Under the Directive the same regime applies to goods and services except for the right of withdrawal (see Section 4.5 below). A 'distance contract' is defined as a contract concluded between a supplier and a consumer under 'an organised distance sales or service-provision scheme' (Article 2(1)). The Directive does not explain what 'an organised scheme' is meant to be. Does it mean that only regular delivery of goods or services by a supplier falls under the regime of the Directive? If so, it would mean that an occasional sale by a supplier by means of a distance contract is excluded from the scope of the Directive. According to the Explanatory Memorandum to the Proposal for a Financial Distance Contracts Directive this is indeed the correct interpretation. This proposal contains a similar definition of the notion of distance contracts and its Explanatory Memorandum reads as follows:

> "The Directive applies only to structured and organised schemes concerning the offer, negotiation and conclusion of distance contracts put in place by suppliers. Hence the Directive does not cover contracts negotiated and concluded at a distance on a purely occasional basis by a supplier and a consumer".[145]

4.5 CONSUMERS' RIGHTS AND SUPPLIERS' OBLIGATIONS

The following rights are guaranteed to a consumer negotiating and concluding a contract at a distance with a supplier of goods or services.

4.5.1 The right to receive information

In a reasonable period of time before concluding a distance contract the consumer must receive from the supplier certain specific information about the supplier and the content of the contract. This information is specified in Article 4(1) of the

---

143 See earlier drafts of the Directive: COM (1996) 36 final; COM (1992) 11 final, p. 10; Recital 12 of the Proposal for a Financial Distance Contracts Directive, *supra* n. 128.

144 See Recital 14 of Proposal for an Electronic Commerce Directive, *supra* n. 98; Explanatory Memorandum to Article 2 of Proposal for a Financial Distance Contracts Directive, *supra* n. 128; Sander 1997b, p. 193.

145 Explanatory Memorandum to Article 2 of Proposal for a Financial Distance Contracts Directive, *supra* n. 128.

Directive and includes the identity of the supplier, the main characteristics and price of goods or services, the arrangements for payment, delivery or performance and the period for which the offer or the price remains valid. The commercial purpose of the information must be made clear.

The information has to be provided in a clear and comprehensible manner in any way appropriate to the means of distance communication used, with due regard in particular to the principles of good faith in commercial transactions and the principles governing the protection of those who are unable to give their consent (such as minors).[146] The Directive leaves the matter of languages used for distance contracts to the Member States.[147]

4.5.2 The right to receive the information confirmed in a durable medium available and accessible to the consumer

The information[148] has to be confirmed to the consumer in writing or 'in another durable medium that is available and accessible to him'. The notion of 'durable medium' is not defined in the Directive. Recital 13 of the Directive reads:

> "Whereas information disseminated by certain electronic technologies is often ephemeral in nature insofar as it is not received on a permanent medium; whereas the consumer must therefore receive written notice in good time of the information necessary for proper performance of the contract".

The Commission has clarified the meaning of 'durable medium' in the Proposal for a Financial Distance Contracts Directive.[149] It is defined in Article 2(f) as:

> "any instrument enabling the consumer to store information, without himself having to record this information, and in particular floppy disks, CD-ROMs, and the hard drive of the consumer's computer on which electronic mail is stored".

According to the Explanatory Memorandum to Article 2(f) the consumer must be able to get the information without any particular action being required on his part. More specifically, the consumer must not be required to store the data at his own initiative. The supplier should send the information on floppy disks, CD-ROMs or by e-mail to the consumer. An acceptable method of confirmation should also be

146 Article 4(2).

147 Recital 8 of the Directive. The May 1992 Proposal stipulated that the information should be in the language used in the contract solicitation; COM (1992) 11 final, Art. 10(1) and commentary to this article.

148 This is the information referred to in Art. 4(1)(a) to (f), and in the second sentence of Art. 5(1).

149 *Supra* n. 128.

that upon the conclusion of an online contract (e.g., after the consumer has pressed the 'I accept' button), the information is automatically downloaded on the hard drive of the consumer's computer. The definition however seems to exclude the most practical method whereby a consumer withdraws or downloads the information, i.e. via a hyperlink.[150]

The confirmation has to be done during the performance of the contract, and at the latest at the time of delivery where goods other than those for delivery to third parties are concerned.[151] If the prescribed information is not sent in time the consumer is free to withdraw from the contract within a three month-period without a penalty and without giving any reason.[152]

4.5.3 The right of withdrawal

A consumer has the right to withdraw from the contract without any penalty and without giving a reason. If a consumer exercises this right, no charge may be made to the consumer except for the direct costs of returning the goods. The supplier has to reimburse the sums paid by the consumer free of charge ('money back guarantee'). The period for exercising this right is at least seven working days. Where the supplier has not fulfilled the obligation to confirm the prescribed information in a durable medium, this period is three months. The beginning of the right to withdraw period depends on whether the contract involves goods or services. In the case of goods, it commences on the day of receipt of the goods by the consumer, while in the case of services, it starts from the day of conclusion of the contract. If the performance of the service has begun with consent of the consumer within seven days from the moment of conclusion of the contract, the consumer may no longer exercise his right of withdrawal.[153] The grounds for this distinction between goods and services are not explained in the Directive or in earlier drafts.[154]

This distinction seems more favourable to consumers ordering goods than to consumers ordering services. The withdrawal period begins upon the reception of goods. In this period he can try out the product and if he is not content he may send it back and receive a refund. At the moment a service is being performed the right of withdrawal (which commenced on the day of conclusion of the contract) may have already expired.

The right of withdrawal may not be exercised with respect to a number of categories of contracts specified in Article 6(3) of the Directive, unless the parties

150 Sander and Bartels 1998, pp. 408-410; Sander 1997a, p. 262.

151 See Art. 5(1): confirmation should be received in good time during the performance of the contract, unless the information has already been confirmed prior to the conclusion of the contract.

152 Article 6(1).

153 See Art. 6(1) and (3).

154 May 1992 Proposal already made this distinction: COM (92) 11 final, Art. 11(1).

have agreed otherwise. One of these categories is 'contracts for the supply of audio or video recordings or computer software which were unsealed by the consumer'. This exception seems to be written with tangible goods in mind (video tapes, CD-ROMs and software on diskettes), products that have to be unsealed. The exception should also apply to the online supply of audio or video recordings or computer software; once a consumer has downloaded the recordings or software onto his computer, he can no longer exercise the right of withdrawal.

The right of withdrawal is without prejudice to the consumers' rights under national laws (e.g., in the case of damaged products or products or services not corresponding to the description in the offer). It is for the Member States to determine 'the other conditions and arrangements following exercise of the right of withdrawal'.[155]

4.5.4 The right to performance

Unless the parties have agreed otherwise, the supplier must execute the order within 30 days from the day following the day of the consumer's order. If a supplier cannot perform because the goods or services are unavailable, the consumer should be informed about this situation and should obtain a refund of any sum paid.[156]

4.6 MINIMUM STANDARD OF CONSUMER PROTECTION

The level of consumer protection prescribed by the Directive is but a minimum standard. The Directive explicitly allows Member States to introduce or maintain more stringent provisions ensuring a higher level of consumer protection. This includes, where appropriate and in the interest of the national community, a prohibition on the marketing of certain goods or products within the territory of a Member State.[157]

It should be noted that if some Member States decide to introduce more stringent provisions whereas other Member States apply the minimum standard of the Directive, this will again lead to disharmony of national laws and distortion of competition in the internal market.

155 Recital 14 of the Directive.
156 Article 7.
157 Article 14. The Directive explicitly mentions medicinal products as a category of goods which Member States may decide are not to be supplied in their territory by means of distance contracts.

4.7 NATIONAL MEASURES TO ENSURE COMPLIANCE WITH THE DIRECTIVE

Member States must take measures to ensure compliance with the Directive. In their national legislation they may stipulate that the burden of proof concerning the existence of prior information, written confirmation, compliance with time-limits or consumer consent can be placed on the supplier. Member States may also provide for voluntary supervision of compliance with the Directive by self-regulatory bodies.[158]

In a 1992 recommendation, the Commission already anticipated the forthcoming Distance Contracts Directive. Organisations of suppliers were recommended to supplement the basic rules laid down in the Directive with a code of conduct for their specific branches.[159]

4.8 PROPOSAL FOR AN ELECTRONIC COMMERCE DIRECTIVE

In November 1998 the Commission presented a Proposal for a European Parliament and Council Directive on certain legal aspects of electronic commerce in the internal market ('Proposal for an Electronic Commerce Directive').[160] The objective of the proposed Directive is to ensure the proper functioning of the internal market, particularly the free movement of Information Society services between Member States. The Directive is based upon the principle of the country of origin (Article 3(1)). This means that Information Society services are only subject to the national (and of course EU) law of the Member State in which the service provider is established. To the provisions regarding electronic contracts (Articles 9-11), the country of origin principle is only applicable in so far as the law of the Member States applies by virtue of its rules on private international law (Article 3(3)).

The proposed Directive contains rules on five specific issues, i.e.:

1. requirements regarding establishment of Information Society providers (Articles 4-5);
2. rules relating to commercial communications, which are an essential part of most electronic commerce services (Articles 6-8);
3. provisions regarding electronic contracts (Articles 9-11);
4. a liability regime for intermediaries (Articles 12-15);

---

158 Article 11(1), (3a) and (4).

159 Recommendation 92/295/EEC of 7 April 1992, OJ L 156/21.

160 COM (1998) 568 final, (1999) OJ C 30/4. Following discussion in the European Parliament, an amended proposal has been put forward by the European Commission on 1 September 1999, COM (1999) 427 final, available at <http://europa.eu.int/comm/dg15/en/media/eleccomm/eleccomm.htm>. Commentary in this chapter refers to the original proposal.

5. mechanisms to ensure that the Directive can be properly enforced (e.g., codes of conduct, out-of-court dispute settlement, sanctions etc.) (Articles 16-21).

The Directive contains a number of exclusions and derogations (Article 22 and Annexes I-II).

The provisions regarding electronic contracts are as follows. According to Article 9 Member States are obliged to ensure that their legislation allows contracts to be concluded electronically. They are, in particular, to ensure that 'the legal requirements applicable to the contractual process neither prevent the effective use of electronic contracts nor result in such contracts being deprived of legal effect and validity on account of their having been made electronically'. Member States may, however, indicate categories of contracts to which this rule shall not apply (e.g., contracts requiring the involvement of a notary). According to the Explanatory Memorandum with Article 9, this provision requires Member States to carry out a systematic review of those rules which might prevent, limit or deter the use of electronic contracts. This review has to cover all stages of the contractual process, from the contract offer to the archiving of the contract. According to Article 10, a service provider has the obligation to inform the recipient of a service about the manner of formation of an electronic contract. The information (*inter alia,* on the different steps to be followed for concluding a contract electronically) must be clear and unequivocal and has to be provided prior to the conclusion of the contract. This aspect, which is unique to the formation of electronic contracts, is not dealt with by the information obligation in the Distant Contracts Directive.[161] Finally, Article 11 seeks to clearly determine the time at which a contract is concluded. The provision addresses only a specific situation, i.e. when a recipient, in accepting a service provider's offer, is required to give his consent by technological means, such as clicking on a 'Yes' or 'No' icon. In such a situation the contract is concluded when the recipient of the service has received and confirmed the service provider's electronic acknowledgement of the recipient's acceptance.

References

H.L. van der Beek (1999), 'De Europese richtlijn voor "overeenkomsten op afstand"', in Kersemakers *et al.* (eds.), *Privaatrecht in de 21 eeuw. De electronische snelweg*, Deventer: Kluwer 1999, pp. 23-29.

E.A. Caprioli and R. Sorieul (1997), 'Le commerce international électronique: vers l'émergence de règles juridiques transnationales', [1997] *Journal du droit international* 323.

161 See Explanatory Memorandum of Article 10, *supra* n. 129.

Thomas DAmico and Eric Oliver (1996), 'Online contracts and software licences', in *US IP Law and the Internet*, 1996, available at <http://www.dsmo.com/usipltoc.htm>.

Clive Davies (1996), 'Internet Contracts', [1996] *Tolley's Communications Law* 50.

Jos Dumortier and Patrick van Eecke (1999), 'De Europese ontwerprichtlijn over de digitale handtekening: waarom is het misgelopen', [1999/1] *Computerrecht* 3.

David A. Einhorn (1992), 'Box-top licences and the battle-of-the-forms', (1992) 5 *Software Law Journal* 401.

Rob E. van Esch and Corien Prins (eds.) (1993), *Recht en EDI*, Deventer: Kluwer 1993.

Frank S. Farrell (1996), 'From Shrinkwrap to Cyberspace', available at <http://www.weblocator.com>.

Franken, Kaspersen and de Wild (eds.) (1997), *Recht en computer*, 3rd edn., Deventer: Kluwer 1997.

Ben Goodger (1996), 'Beta Plus for Effort: Beta Miners for Clarity?', (1996) 11 *EIPR* 636.

D. Griffiths (1997), 'Contracting on the Internet', (1997) 13 *EIPR* 4.

F.W. Grosheide (1997), 'Shrink-wrap licence', *WPNR* 1997/6260, 153-154.

F.W. Grosheide (1998), 'Mass-market exploitation of digital information by the use of shrink-wrap and click-wrap licences. A Dutch perspective on article 2B UCC', in F.W. Grosheide and K. Boele-Woelki (eds), *Europees privaatrecht*, 1998 *Molengrafica*, Lelystad: Vermande 1998, pp. 263–319.

Gregor Heinrich (1994), 'UNCITRAL und EDI-Einheitsrecht, Aktuelle Entwicklungen', [1994/2] *Computer und Recht* 118.

Gregor Heinrich (1995), 'Harmonised global interchange? UNCITRAL's Draft Model Law for Electronic Data Interchange', (1995) 3 *WEB JCLI,* available at <http://webjcli.ncl.ac.uk/articles3/hein3.html>.

Richard Hill and Ian Walden (1996), 'The Draft UNCITRAL Model Law for Electronic Commerce: issues and solutions', (1996) 13 *The Computer Lawyer* 18.

R.I.L. Howland (1997), 'UNCITRAL Model Law on Electronic Commerce', [1997] *European Transport Law* 703.

P. Bernt Hugenholtz (1998), 'Het Internet: het auteursrecht voorbij?', in 'Recht en Internet', *Handelingen Nederlandse Juristen-Vereniging*, Vol. 128, 1998-I, 199-260.

Michel Jaccard (1996), *La conclusion de contrats par ordinateur*, Bern: Staempfli 1996.

Simon Jones (1996), 'Multimedia and the superhighway: exploring the rights minefield', (1996) 1 *Tolley's Communications Law* 28.

S.J.M.G. Kersemakers (1999), 'De Europese richtlijn inzake overeenkomsten op afstand: de consument afdoende beschermd?', in Kersemakers *et al* (eds.), *Privaatrecht in de 21e eeuw. De electronische snelweg*, Deventer: Kluwer 1999, 9-22.

Clemens Kochinke and Andreas Günther (1997), 'Shrinkwrap-Lizenzen und Datenbank-schutz in den USA', [1997] *Computer und Recht* 129.

Kamiel Koelman (1998), 'Multimedialicenties', in *ITeR-reeks* no. 10, Alphen aan de Rijn 1998, 85-159.

Gary Lea (1996), 'The impossible intangible: shrinkwrap software revisited', (1996) 1 *Tolley's Communications Law* 238.

Mark A. Lemley (1995), 'Shrinkwraps in cyberspace', (1995) 35 *Jurimetrics Journal of Law, Science and Technology* 311.

Stuart D. Levi and Robert Sporn (1997), 'Can programs bind humans to contract?', *The National Law Journal Extra*, 13 January 1997, available at <http://www.ljx.com/internet/0113shrink.html>

Hector L. MacQueen, Martin A. Hogg and Parker Hood (1998), 'Muddling through? Legal responses to E-commerce from the perspective of a mixed system', in F.W. Grosheide and K. Boele-Woelki (eds), *Europees privaatrecht*, 1998 *Molengrafica*, Lelystad: Vermande 1998, pp. 195-224.

Andreas Mitrakas (1997), *Open EDI and law in Europe. A regulatory framework*, The Hague: Kluwer 1997.

Richard Raysman and Peter Brown (1996), 'Shrinkwrap Licences Revisited', *The New York Law Journal*, 13 August 1996, available at <http://www.ljx.com/practice/intellectualproperty/081396.html>

Pamela Samuelson and Kurt Opsahl (1998), 'The Tensions between Intellectual Property and Contracts in the Information Age: an American Perspective', in F.W. Grosheide and K. Boele-Woelki (eds), *Europees privaatrecht*, 1998 *Molengrafica*, Lelystad: Vermande 1998, pp. 163-193.

C.J. Sander (1997a), 'Beschermd kopen op afstand: binnen handbereik?', (1997) 3 *Nederlands Tijdschrift voor Europees Recht* 261.

C.J. Sander (1997b), 'De consument op de electronische snelweg: een inleiding naar Nederlands en Duits recht', [1997] *Tijdschrift voor Consumentenrecht* 191.

C.J. Sander and S.E. Bartels (1998), 'Vraagpunten bij de implementatie van de Europese richtlijn op afstand gesloten overeenkomsten', [1998] *Tijdschrift voor Consumentenrecht* 407.

Michael D. Scott (1990), 'Contemporary issues in domestic transactions for computer goods and services', (1990) 3 *Software Law Journal* 615.

Jetse Sprey (1997), 'Internet; een transactie ontleed', [1997] *Advocatenblad* 1049.

Cees Stuurman (1997), 'Computercontracten', in Franken, Kaspersen and de Wild (eds), *Recht en computer*, 3d edn., Deventer: Kluwer 1997, pp. 74-102.

Bernardine W.M. Trompenaars (1989), *Pluriforme unificatie en uniforme interpretatie. In het bijzonder de bijdrage van UNCITRAL aan de internationale unificatie van het privaatrecht*, Deventer: Kluwer 1989.

Reinoud Westerdijk and Franke van der Klaauw (1991), 'De shrink-wrap licentie', [1991] *Computerrecht* 18.

Information Law Series

1. *Protecting Works of Fact: Copyright, Freedom of Expression and Information Law*, Egbert J. Dommering and P. Bernt Hugenholtz (eds)
   ISBN 90-6544-5676

2. *Information Law Towards the 21st Century*, Willem F. Korthals Altes, Egbert J. Dommering, P. Bernt Hugenholtz and Jan J.C. Kabel (eds)
   ISBN 90-6544-6273

3. *Challenges to the Creator Doctrine*, Jacqueline Seignette
   ISBN 90-6544-8764

4. *The Future of Copyright in a Digital Environment*, P. Bernt Hugenholtz (ed)
   ISBN 90-411-0267-1

5. *From Privacy Toward a New Intellectual Property Right in Persona*, Julius C.S. Pinckaers
   ISBN 90-411-0355-4

6. *Intellectual Property and Information Law: Essays in Honour of Herman Cohen Jehoram*, Jan J.C. Kabel and Gerard J.H.M. Mom (eds)
   ISBN 90-411-9702-8

7. *Copyright and Photographs: An International Survey*, Ysolde Gendreau, Axel Nordemann and Rainer Oesch (eds)
   ISBN 90-411-9722-2